PRAISE FOR *PUTIN'S WORLD*

"Informed by its author's distinguished career in government and academia, this account of Russian president Vladimir Putin's worldview provides an important window into one of the key geopolitical challenges of our time. Casual observers and seasoned experts will benefit from Dr. Stent's brilliant exploration of Putin's strategy and its disturbing implications for the West."

—Madeleine K. Albright, former secretary of state

"Like the judo player he once was, Vladimir Putin has figured out ways to assert Russian power despite his nation's weakness. Understanding how he does it is crucial to America, and Angela Stent's deeply knowledgeable and readable book provides brilliant insights."

—Walter Isaacson, #1 *New York Times* bestselling author of *Leonardo Da Vinci* and *Einstein*

"PUTIN'S WORLD offers a timely twenty-first-century update on George Kennan's 'long telegram.' Russians understand their country through history, geography, empire—and stories of 'great men.' Angela Stent deftly explains how Putin's version of Russian exceptionalism has been redrawing maps of power in Eurasia and beyond. In an era of strongmen who are seeking a new concert of power, Stent offers the wise perspective that we should consider Russia as it is, not as we might wish it to be."

—Robert B. Zoellick, former president of the World Bank, US trade representative, and US deputy secretary of state

"From one of the leading experts on Russian foreign policy, PUTIN'S WORLD is a highly engaging, comprehensive overview of Moscow's international relations. Angela Stent deftly explains Russia's complex role at a fraught moment in history, drawing deeply on the country's history, culture, and other key factors determining Russians' conceptions of themselves and the world."

—Gregory Feifer, author of *Russians: The People Behind the Power*

"PUTIN'S WORLD is the definitive guide to understanding the tangled history of post–Cold War Russia and its place in the world. Angela Stent offers a thoughtful, sober, and elegantly-written perspective that could not be more timely." —William J. Burns, US ambassador

"Stent expertly walks readers through Moscow's relations with every region in the world, avoiding the hysteria that warps discussion of the country. Aware that too many books about Russian foreign policy arrive instantly obsolete because they lack a foundation in history or political culture, Stent opens with those subjects...and the book culminates in a clear-eyed portrayal of the inescapably troubled US-Russia relationship."

—*Washington Post*

"[Stent] counsels strategic patience and preparedness—and suggests that it would be wise to expect the unexpected." —*Foreign Affairs*

"An incisive exploration of 'how and why Russia has returned to the world stage'... [Stent] offers a deeply informed look at why Russia, directed by President Vladimir Putin, persists in behaving in what the West regards as an exceedingly maddening, paranoid, and often aggressive manner...A compelling historico-psychological work delineating how the West should respond to Russia going forward." —*Kirkus* (Starred Review)

PUTIN'S WORLD

PUTIN'S WORLD

RUSSIA AGAINST THE WEST AND WITH THE REST

ANGELA E. STENT

NEW YORK BOSTON

Twelve
Hachette Book Group
1290 Avenue of the Americas, New York, NY 10104
twelvebooks.com
twitter.com/twelvebooks

Originally published in hardcover and ebook by Twelve in February 2019.

First Trade Edition: July 2020

Twelve is an imprint of Grand Central Publishing. The Twelve name and logo are trademarks of Hachette Book Group, Inc.

The publisher is not responsible for websites (or their content) that are not owned by the publisher.

The Hachette Speakers Bureau provides a wide range of authors for speaking events. To find out more, go to www.hachettespeakersbureau.com or call (866) 376- 6591.

Library of Congress Cataloging-in-Publication Data
Names: Stent, Angela, author.
Title: Putin's world : Russia against the West / Angela Stent.
Description: New York : Twelve, [2019] | Includes bibliographical references and index.
Identifiers: LCCN 2018039540| ISBN 9781455533022 (hardcover) | ISBN 9781549194832 (audio download) | ISBN 9781455533015 (ebook)
Subjects: LCSH: Russia (Federation)—Foreign relations—1991– | Russia (Federation)—Politics and government—1991– | Russia (Federation)—Foreign relations—Western countries. | Western countries—Foreign relations—Russia (Federation) | Russia (Federation)—Foreign relations—United States. | United States—Foreign relations—Russia (Federation) | Ideology—Russia (Federation)
Classification: LCC DK510.764 .S75 2019 | DDC 327.470182/1—dc23
LC record available at https://lccn.loc.gov/2018039540

ISBNs: 978-1-4555-3300-8 (trade pbk.), 978-1-4555-3301-5 (ebook)

Printed in the United States of America

LSC-C

Printing 2, 2021

To Danny, Alex, Rebecca, and Jessica.

CONTENTS

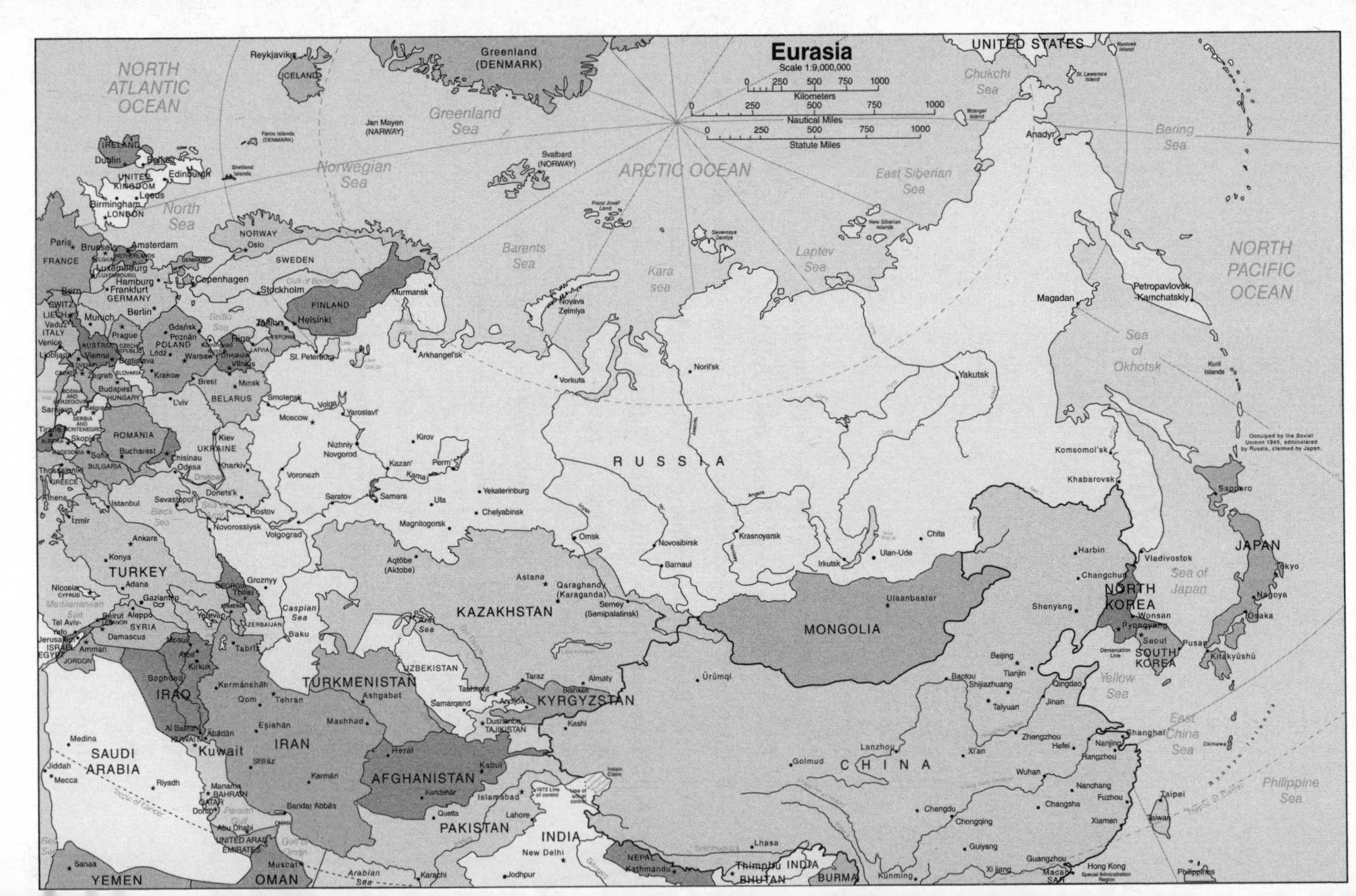

Eurasia
Scale 1:9,000,000
0 250 500 750 1000
Kilometers
0 250 500 750 1000
Nautical Miles
0 250 500 750 1000
Statute Miles
NORTH ATLANTIC OCEAN
ARCTIC OCEAN
NORTH PACIFIC OCEAN
Greenland (DENMARK)
Greenland Sea
Norwegian Sea
North Sea
Barents Sea
Kara sea
Laptev Sea
East Siberian Sea
Chukchi Sea
Bering Sea
Sea of Okhotsk
Sea of Japan
Yellow Sea
East China Sea
Philippine Sea
Caspian Sea
Black Sea
Arabian Sea
UNITED STATES
Jan Mayen (NARWAY)
Svalbard (NORWAY)
Reykjavik
ICELAND
IRELAND
Dublin
UNITED KINGDOM
Edinburgh
Leeds
Birmingham
LONDON
Paris
FRANCE
Amsterdam
Brussels
Luxembourg
Hamburg
Frankfurt
GERMANY
Bern
Berlin
Munich
Copenhagen
NORWAY
Oslo
SWEDEN
Stockholm
FINLAND
Helsinki
Murmansk
Tallinn
Riga
St. Petersburg
Arkhangel'sk
Prague
Vienna
Gdańsk
Poznań
POLAND
Łódź
Warsaw
Krakow
Vilnius
Minsk
BELARUS
Brest
Budapest
HUNGARY
Zagreb
Sarajevo
Belgrade
Skopje
Tirana
Sofia
BULGARIA
ROMANIA
Bucharest
Chisinau
Odesa
L'viv
Kiev
UKRAINE
Kharkiv
Donets'k
Sevastopol
Rostov
Novorossiysk
GREECE
Athens
Istanbul
Izmir
Ankara
Konya
TURKEY
Adana
Gaziantep
Nicosia
CYPRUS
Beirut
Aleppo
SYRIA
Damascus
Tel Aviv-Yafo
Jerusalem
ISRAEL
Amman
JORDON
EGYPT
Smolensk
Moscow
Volga
Yaroslavl'
Nizhniy Novgorod
Kirov
Kazan'
Perm'
Kama
Voronezh
Saratov
Samara
Ufa
Yekaterinburg
Chelyabinsk
Magnitogorsk
Volgograd
Vorkuta
Noyava Zemlya
RUSSIA
Noril'sk
Yakutsk
Magadan
Anadyr
Petropavlovsk-Kamchatskiy
Kuril Islands
Komsomol'sk
Khabarovsk
Vladivostok
Omsk
Novosibirsk
Barnaul
Krasnoyarsk
Irkutsk
Ulan-Ude
Chita
Grozny
Tbilisi
GEORGIA
Yerevan
Baku
Tabriz
Aqtöbe (Aktobe)
Astana
Qaraghandy (Karaganda)
Semey (Semipalatinsk)
KAZAKHSTAN
Almaty
Bishkek
KYRGYZSTAN
Taraz
Tashkent
UZBEKISTAN
Samarqand
Dushanbe
TAJIKISTAN
TURKMENISTAN
Ashgabat
Mashhad
Tehran
Qom
Kermānshāh
Eşfahān
IRAN
Shīrāz
Kermān
Bandar Abbās
Mosul
Kirkuk
Baghdad
IRAQ
Al Başrah
Ābādān
Kuwait
SAUDI ARABIA
Medina
Jiddah
Mecca
Riyadh
Manama
BAHRAIN
QATAR
Doha
Abu Dhabi
UNITED ARAB EMIRATES
Muscat
OMAN
Sanaa
YEMEN
Herat
Kabul
AFGHANISTAN
Kandahār
Quetta
Islamabad
Lahore
PAKISTAN
Karachi
INDIA
New Delhi
Jodhpur
NEPAL
Kathmandu
Thimphu
BHUTAN
BURMA
MONGOLIA
Ulaanbaatar
Ürümqi
Kashi
Golmud
Lhasa
Lanzhou
CHINA
Chengdu
Chongqing
Guiyang
Kunming
Xi'an
Baotou
Beijing
Tianjin
Shijiazhuang
Taiyuan
Zhengzhou
Jinan
Qingdao
Harbin
Changchun
Shenyang
Wuhan
Hefei
Nanjing
Shanghai
Hangzhou
Nanchang
Changsha
Fuzhou
Xiamen
Guangzhou
Hong Kong
Macau
Taipei
Taiwan
Philippines
NORTH KOREA
Pyongyang
Wonsan
Seoul
SOUTH KOREA
Pusan
JAPAN
Sapporo
Tokyo
Nagoya
Osaka
Kitakyūshū
Occupied by the Soviet Unionn 1945, administered by Russia, claimed by Japan.

PUTIN'S WORLD

INTRODUCTION

In July 2018, Russia showed its best face to the world as it hosted the World Cup. The spirited opening ceremony featured bears, dragons, and picturesque onion domes. The Russian team—ranked at the bottom of all those competing—defeated Saudi Arabia in the first game and went on all the way to the quarterfinals, when Croatia defeated it. But even that loss did not diminish the pervasive—and unexpected—atmosphere of good feeling. For a month, Russia welcomed fans from around the world with enthusiasm and camaraderie. Russians and foreign fans partied all night in cities from Kaliningrad in the west to Ekaterinburg, 1,500 miles away in Siberia. Even the normally dour Russian policemen had only smiles for those celebrating. As Russian president Vladimir Putin put it, "People have seen that Russia is a hospitable country, a friendly one for those who come here." He added, "I'm sure that an overwhelming majority of people who came will leave with the best feelings and memories of our country and will come again many times."[1]

The World Cup represented a major success for President Putin. Before the games opened, there were questions about whether Russia would be able to build the facilities in time for the games, about corruption involved in the bidding for the construction, and about how international visitors would be received. Moreover, the games were held in a politically charged atmosphere, when Russia's relations with the West were the worst they had been since post-communist Russia emerged in 1992. Russia's annexation of Crimea and launch of a war in Southeastern Ukraine, its cyber interference in the US and European elections, its support for Bashar al-Assad in the brutal Syrian Civil War, and its domestic crackdowns on opponents of the regime—and the US and EU responses—all this had intensified the already adversarial relationship between Putin's Russia and the West.

The World Cup left foreign fans with positive views of their hosts. Many had arrived in Russia with stereotypes about unfriendly Russians living in a backward country. But they reported being surprised by how "normal" Russia and its people seemed. The US sent the largest number of spectators, even though the American team did not qualify to compete. Western journalists emphasized that it was important to differentiate between the Russian government, which they criticized, and its people, who were hospitable. For their part, the Russians seemed surprised by how approachable the foreign fans were. Russians were used to seeing westerners constantly vilified in their state-run media, but a poll conducted after the games ended showed that Russians' view of Americans and Europeans had significantly improved.[2] The games left an afterglow of positive feelings, even though the Russians realized that, once the foreigners departed, they would no longer be able to celebrate all night in the streets. The Russia team may have lost, but the World Cup was clearly a victory for Vladimir Putin.

The World Cup represented a culmination of Putin's project, which had been nearly two decades in the making: the return of Russia to the world stage as a great power to be respected, feared, and—as the World Cup showed—liked and even admired. Russia's reemergence as a major player capable of projecting power well beyond its immediate neighborhood was unexpected and quite remarkable, given its limited economic resources: a GDP smaller than Italy's, demographic decline, decaying infrastructure, and the negative impact of successive waves of Western sanctions in response to its actions. A few years before, President Obama had described Russia as a "regional power."[3] But Putin proved otherwise. Russia's reach is now clearly global.

This is the new Russian reality that has developed since Putin entered the Kremlin in 2000. At that point Russia was emerging from a decade of political chaos and an economic meltdown. Some went as far as to opine, "Russia is finished."[4] When an ailing Boris Yeltsin handed over the reins of power to a virtually unknown former KGB case officer, it was unclear how the fledgling post-communist Russia could move forward. In retrospect, it is clear that Putin was from the start determined not only to restore firm state control over the Russian polity but also to resurrect Russia as a great power. Remarkably, he has been able to accomplish both of these goals, despite Russia's economic and military constraints.

It is important to understand how and why Russia has returned to the world stage. It is now active in areas from which it withdrew after the USSR collapsed, and its reappearance has affected the ability of the United States and its allies to conduct their own foreign policy effectively. The new reality of Putin's world necessitates a rethinking of how to deal with Russia going forward.

Putin's world is one in which relations with the United States and much of Europe are adversarial. It is also a world in which Russia has a deepening partnership with China, an increasingly influential role in the Middle East, and has returned to areas of the world from which Russia was forced to withdraw after the Soviet collapse. Moreover, Russia's seat and veto on the United Nations Security Council have enabled Moscow to exercise influence well beyond what its current capabilities would suggest. Russia's ability to thwart Western interests has also enabled it to advance its own interests internationally. Western attempts to isolate Russia after the seizure of Crimea have failed. Moreover, the increasing disarray in the transatlantic alliance since Donald Trump came to power, plus Brexit (Britain's decision to leave the European Union) and a European Union beset by new challenges, all these have provided Putin with unanticipated opportunities to advance Russia's interests, which he has skillfully utilized.

This book explains how Putin's Russia has managed to return as a global player and what that new role means. It examines why Moscow's relations with the US and much—although not all—of Europe have deteriorated, and why so many other countries have a positive view of Russia and are working with Moscow productively in a variety of fora. The book also traces the origins and development of the Russian national idea that has been consolidated in the nearly two decades Putin has been in power and that drives policy today, highlighting how important it is to understand how and why Russia has reemerged and how best to approach Moscow in this turbulent new global reality.

It is customary to describe Russians as talented chess players with a grand strategy, but Putin's sport is judo—and that has given him a unique perspective on dealing with competitors and adversaries. Growing up poor in postwar Leningrad, martial arts transformed his life because it was a way of defending himself against larger, tougher boys who tried to beat him up. "It was a tool to assert myself in the pack." The Leningrad evening paper in May 1976 introduced the 24-year-old master "judoist" to the city as "not well known so far amongst specialists or fans" but predicted that that would soon change.[5] In judo, a seemingly weaker practitioner can rely on inner strength and force of will to defeat a larger, more aggressive foe. Putting an opponent off-balance and taking advantage of their temporary disorientation to strike a winning blow is a basic technique. Putin has proven to be adept at seizing opportunities presented to him by the disarray in the West and the indecisiveness of some of its leaders.

Putin's world also has been facilitated by the fraying of the transatlantic alliance. The initial euphoria over the collapse of communism and the end of the Cold War has given way to a sober realization that the consolidation of a Europe "whole and free," the mantra of the 1990s, has been elusive. Democratic backsliding in Central Europe, a renewed challenge from Russia to its neighbors, the persistence of a "post-Soviet syndrome" in all of the former Soviet states, and waves of migrants landing on Europe's shores have led to a rise in populism and a questioning of the European project—the creation of a European Union that would ensure that Europe would eschew conflict going forward—that was such a postwar success. The election of Donald Trump and the pursuit of "America first" economic and political goals have called into question the durability of the seventy-year-old NATO alliance and of the US commitment to Europe. This has played into the hands of a Russian leader who, like most of his predecessors, has sought to profit from transatlantic tensions and prefers dealing with a disunited West.

But Putin's world is also a product of deliberate Russian policies. Russia has focused on building up its military since the 2008 war with Georgia and on using a variety of means to project power. It has also exploited vulnerabilities in open Western societies and seized opportunities presented by the rise of social media. Russian interference in Western elections and support for anti-EU and separatist movements in Europe, and for groups on both extremes of the US political divide, have caught the West off guard. So far there has been no adequate response to the deployment of these "hybrid" tactics in what has become an unending information war.

In exploring the making of Putin's world, this book focuses on the areas that are priorities for Russian foreign policy: the United States, Europe, the post-Soviet states, China, the Middle East, and Japan. Russia is also returning to Latin America and Africa, but until now these areas have represented a lower priority for the Kremlin.

Foreign policy in Russia, as in any country, is driven by domestic considerations. For the current occupants of the Kremlin and their close associates, foreign policy serves their overriding goal to remain in power. As Putin enters what is constitutionally his last term in office amid increasing speculation about a possible succession in 2024, foreign policy could play a key role either in helping to consolidate the system he has created or in what could become a future struggle for power among the different groups of contenders.

How should the West respond to the new Russia—which in many ways still resembles the old Soviet Union? In 1961, George Kennan—the twentieth century's most gifted and knowledgeable American diplomat-scholar and Russia hand—published *Russia and the West Under Lenin and Stalin.* As he surveyed the troubled legacy of the interwar years, he criticized the West for failing to understand both what drove the Kremlin's foreign policy and the militant, universalist Soviet ideology that threatened Western security. He concluded that "the relationship we have with the Soviet Union has to be compared, if we are to determine its real value, not with some nonexistent state of total harmony of interests but with what we might call the normal level of recalcitrance, of sheer orneriness and unreasonableness, which we encounter in the behavior of states anywhere and which I am sure we often manifest in our own."[6]

Today one can argue that the West has been slow to understand the mindset of the Kremlin's occupants determined to restore Russia to what they believe is its rightful place in the world. For Russians, the economic and social dislocation of the 1990s is closely associated with what they view as a misguided Western agenda designed to reshape post-communist Russia. The assumption made in the 1990s—that post-communist Russia was eager to join the West—turned out to have been erroneous. Putin's Russia seeks to offer a different model. Unlike in the Soviet era, the Kremlin no longer promotes a universalist ideology designed to convert other states to its cause. Rather, Putin has cultivated the idea of Russian exceptionalism, of Russia's unique Eurasian destiny, a country bestriding both Europe and Asia, the center of a new, multipolar world in which Moscow deals with governments of all political persuasions.

Russia and the West view each other as competitors, adversaries, and occasional partners. So far they have been unable to achieve a durable post–Cold War modus vivendi. The West remains torn between seeking engagement with Russia in the hopes this will moderate its behavior and trying to contain it. Neither strategy has worked so far. This is the unique challenge of Putin's world for the United States and its allies.

As far as the rest of the world is concerned, Russia is a large authoritarian state ruled by a leader with whom one can do business. Other countries may be wary of the methods Moscow employs to achieve its goals, but they are unconcerned about its domestic situation, recognize that it seeks a sphere of influence in its neighborhood, and are content to pursue engagement without containment.

The first two chapters of the book examine the historical legacies that have shaped contemporary Russia's understanding of itself and its role in the world. Putin's Russia has increasingly focused on a reinterpretation of history that justifies how and why Russia has returned to the world stage as it reclaims what it views as its rightful status as a great power resisting Western attempts to weaken it.

The book then focuses on Russia's relations with major players, beginning with Russia's long and ambivalent relationship with Europe, to which it remains deeply connected, both politically and economically. Yet ties have become increasingly strained since the onset of the crisis in Ukraine. Europe is sharply divided over how to deal with Russia and Moscow has done all it can to derive benefits from these divisions. Nowhere are these tensions more evident than in Russian-German ties, a long and complex relationship that has traditionally fluctuated between amity and enmity. The combination of the Ukraine crisis and the advent of the Trump administration have caused Germany to rethink its policies toward both Russia and the United States. For the first time, Germany is struggling to develop an "America strategy"—something it has never needed to do before—as it reconfigures its ties to Russia. Meanwhile, Putin's insistence that NATO is the "main opponent" continues to shape his relations with Europe and toward the transatlantic alliance. The West and Russia tried and failed to create a Euro-Atlantic security architecture in the 1990s in which Russia had a stake. This led to mounting uncertainty about Russia's relations with NATO and, more recently, stimulated a new Western military buildup in Europe in response to Russian actions.

The next two chapters deal with the complex mosaic of Russia's relations with the former Soviet states. The Kremlin does not regard these nations as distinctly foreign countries, but as part of its "near abroad" which, in its view, should only enjoy limited sovereignty. There is a separate chapter on Russia's fraught ties with Ukraine. The war in the Donbas region in southeastern Ukraine highlights the roots of the Russian-Ukrainian dueling narratives over history, identity, and territory, and is the battlefield for a new type of conflict, hybrid warfare.

Russia's increasingly close ties to China represent a major success of the Putin era and a remarkable development considering that the two countries have a long history of enmity. This section discusses the changing nature of a relationship that is not an alliance but an increasingly robust instrumental partnership that has enabled Russia to avoid the isolation the West sought to impose after 2014. Indeed, in 2018, Chinese troops participated in the largest Russian military exercises held since 1981. By contrast, Russia's ties to its other major East Asian neighbor Japan remain constrained by the two countries' inability to resolve their territorial dispute over four unprepossessing islands, dating back to the end of World War Two. The book examines why it has been so challenging to move relations forward.

The next chapter covers the Middle East, highlighting the other foreign policy success story of the Putin era. Russia has returned to the Middle East as the only major power that can talk to the protagonists and antagonists in all of the major regional conflicts—Iran, the Sunni states, Israel, the Palestinians, and the Kurds.

The final two chapters come to the great conundrum—the increasingly adversarial US-Russia relationship, which resembles a new Cold War that some fear could even deteriorate into a hot war. Why has it been so difficult to create a durable framework for productive ties between the two countries? Unrealistic expectations about the relationship on both sides and fundamentally different views of what drives international politics have created a downward spiral. Moreover, in the aftermath of the 2016 election, Russia has become a toxic domestic issue as never before.

What is the future for Putin's world? The book concludes by discussing Putin's seven pillars for restoring Russia as a great power, and the domestic constraints that will shape Russia going forward. It calls for a combination of realism, push-back, and strategic patience in the West's response to Putin's world.

—1—

THE WEIGHT OF THE PAST

Time and time again attempts were made to deprive Russians of their historical memory, even of their language and to subject them to forced assimilation.... In short, we have every reason to assume that the infamous policy of containment, led in the eighteenth, nineteenth, and twentieth centuries, continues today. [Western countries] are constantly trying to sweep us into a corner because we have an independent position, because we maintain it and because we call things like they are and do not engage in hypocrisy.

—*Vladimir Putin, announcing the annexation of Crimea, March 14, 2014*[1]

We must start working to become self-sufficient, all the more so since Russia is one of the few countries to which God, nature, ancestors, and history have guaranteed this self-sufficiency.

—*Sergei Lavrov, speaking to a youth forum, August 24, 2015*[2]

On February 7, 2014, a beaming, self-confident Vladimir Putin strode out onto the stage and welcomed thousands of athletes and spectators to the first Winter Olympics in Sochi. It had been a tough and controversial competition for Russia to win the games for this picturesque Black Sea resort with a subtropical climate. Rumors abounded about everything from how Russia had won the Olympics to their price tag to shoddy workmanship on the facilities and new hotels. Following a terrorist bombing at a regional railway station, and threats of more attacks, security precautions were extraordinarily tight. No Western leaders were in attendance at the games because of Russia's domestic clampdown, but the Chinese and Japanese leaders were there. The head of the United States delegation was a former cabinet secretary, now chancellor of the University of California. Nevertheless, on this first night the athletes were excited, and television viewers around the world eagerly anticipated the opening ceremony and Russia's chance to present its unique history. This was the Kremlin's opportunity to showcase its view of the world.

Expertly produced, the opening ceremony was a riveting ride through Russian history, notable both for what it included and for what it omitted. The narrator was a young girl, Liuba, who flew through time and space and presented the highlights of Russia's past through the alphabet, each letter representing a major figure in Russia's one-thousand-year history. The heroes she met included Tsar Peter the Great, who built the capital Saint Petersburg on a swampland; Catherine the Great, the German princess during whose rule Russia greatly expanded its borders; the composer Peter Tchaikovsky; the poet Alexander Pushkin; the exiled artist Marc Chagall, who painted fiddlers on the roofs of his native Vitebsk; the film director Sergei Eisenstein; the literary titans Leo Tolstoy and Fyodor Dostoyevsky; and the cosmonaut Yuri Gagarin. Russia's vast spaces, its beautiful snowy landscapes, and its hardworking peasants and scenic villages featured prominently, as did music by Russia's great composers. The Bolshevik Revolution and the Soviet Young Pioneers with their distinctive red scarves and motto "Always prepared" made appearances. There was Soviet-era nostalgia in the form of the great exploits in space and curious 1960s-era Hipsters. But what was missing was also notable. The Gorbachev era with its perestroika and the eventual Soviet collapse were entirely absent, as were the difficult 1990s under Boris Yeltsin. The opening ceremonies for the Sochi Olympics were extravagant, a paean to Russian history, to its triumphs and tragedies. This was Russia at its grandiose best, overcoming difficulties and always returning to its great natural endowments and hardy citizens, who endure and triumph over all adversity with no help from the outside world. This was the Russia Vladimir Putin presented both to his own people and to the outside world.

But even while the games were taking place, and far away from the enthusiasm and sportsmanship, the Kremlin was making plans that would soon drastically undermine the Olympics goodwill. Three days after the main games ended, "little green men"—unidentified military personnel from Russia—began to appear in Sevastopol and other cities on the Crimean Peninsula. Only 315 miles northwest of Sochi and also on the Black Sea, Crimea had belonged to Russia since Catherine the Great wrested it from the Ottoman Empire and the indigenous Crimean Tatars in 1783.

Crimea had occupied a unique place in the Russian imagination for more than two hundred years. It was a popular vacation destination for Russians, immortalized in Anton Chekhov's short stories. For many outside the Soviet Union, its most famous city was Yalta, where Joseph Stalin met Franklin Roosevelt and Winston Churchill just before the end of World War Two in the Livadia Palace to negotiate over the postwar world. Sevastopol was a major warm-water port for the Soviet navy. Crimea had been part of the Russian Empire and, after the establishment of the USSR, part of the Russian republic within the Soviet Union. In 1954, to commemorate the 300th anniversary of Ukraine's union with Russia, Soviet leader Nikita Khrushchev decided to "give" Crimea to the Ukrainian Soviet Socialist Republic. As Putin said in October 2014, "In 1954, Khrushchev, who liked to bang his shoe at the UN, decided for some reason to transfer Crimea to Ukraine."[3] At that point the gesture had limited meaning, since both republics were part of the USSR. But this administrative maneuver had major repercussions once the Soviet Union fell apart at the end of 1991. By an accident of history, Crimea became part of an independent Ukraine. But Russians and their leaders had resented what they considered a historical travesty. Moreover, the Black Sea Fleet was still housed there, but only on a leasing arrangement. By 2014, the Kremlin was determined to right this wrong. A few weeks after the little green men began to appear, Russia organized a referendum in which the majority of

Crimea's citizens voted to leave Ukraine and join Russia.[4] A little more than a month after the opening festivities in Sochi, Russia had officially annexed Crimea, violating agreements signed in 1994 and 1997 to respect the sovereignty and territorial integrity of the new Ukraine. Russia's relations with the West began their descent into their worst phase since the communist red hammer-and-sickle flag was lowered from over the Kremlin on Christmas Day in 1991 and replaced by the red, white, and blue flag of the new Russian Federation.

Misplaced Expectations

The year 2014 was in many ways a watershed for the West in its relations with Russia. The annexation of Crimea and subsequent launch of a war in Southeastern Ukraine led the United States and its allies to question the basic premises of their assessments and expectations of Vladimir Putin's Russia. The Obama administration had realized that the "reset" policy it had pursued with Russia after 2009 ended once Putin returned to the Kremlin in 2012, after the four-year interlude during which he had traded places with Dmitry Medvedev. But Russia's other major Western partner, Germany, reacted differently. After all, Germany had extensive business ties to Russia and imported significant amounts of Russian gas. Moreover, Berlin felt a strong historical responsibility to maintain close ties to the Kremlin both because of the twenty-seven million Soviet casualties inflicted by Germany during World War Two and out of gratitude for Mikhail Gorbachev allowing East and West Germany to reunite peacefully. But the Ukraine crisis changed all that for Chancellor Angela Merkel. She grew up in East Germany, conversed with Putin in both Russian and German, and was his chief Western interlocutor. She concluded that he frequently misled her about what was happening in Ukraine. This was especially true after the shooting down of a Malaysia Airlines plane over the Donbas region of Ukraine in July 2014, in which the Kremlin denied any involvement. Russia's actions in Ukraine caused Germany to rethink its Ostpolitik—the policy of engaging Russia—and produced much greater solidarity between the United States and many of its key European allies. This surely was not the outcome Putin had sought when he sent his troops into Crimea and Southeastern Ukraine.

Most Western leaders had to admit that the expectations they had harbored after the Soviet collapse had been misplaced. They had hoped a post-communist Russia would eagerly cast off the shackles of a dysfunctional twentieth-century ideology—communism—and would embrace joining the democratic, capitalist modern world. That would also mean they would eschew an assertive foreign policy directed against Western interests. President Bill Clinton and his administration believed that democracies did not go to war with each other, and they focused on promoting democratic change inside Russia to help it become a less aggressive state that would work with the West.

But Americans, and to some extent Europeans, failed to understand the humiliation that millions of Russians felt at suddenly losing their "inner" and "outer" empire—the post-Soviet states and Eastern Europe. It was difficult for Russians to accept that they no longer had a natural right to dominate their neighborhood and exercise influence beyond their borders. Certainly the Germans understood this better than the Americans, given their dark twentieth-century history, and they warned the United States that it would take many decades for Russia to accept the loss of empire and status. From the Russian point of view, there was a double humiliation: the loss of the post-Soviet states and the fact that the United States and its allies had created a global order to which they expected Russia to conform. It was indeed a unique unipolar movement with a dominant United States and a Russia that had lost its ability to project power globally. No wonder it sought to recoup its power and influence as soon as it could.

But not everyone had the same expectations as the United States or Europe. China, India, and other countries in the Middle East, Latin America, and Africa viewed Russia through a different lens. They were less concerned about Russia becoming a democracy than about the United

States—which they viewed with different degrees of wariness—becoming an even more dominant global power after the Soviet collapse. This was clear when the United Nations General Assembly in March 2014 voted to condemn Russia's annexation of Crimea. While Western countries voted in favor and only a handful of countries, including Venezuela, Zimbabwe, Syria, and North Korea, voted with Russia against the resolution, many countries abstained, including China, India, Brazil, and South Africa. These countries believe Russia has historically dominated its neighborhood and will inevitably seek to do so in the future. And they believe it is not their or anyone else's business to foist Western democracy on a Russia that does not appear to desire it.

In grappling to understand why Russia has evolved so differently from what the West sought and expected, it has been tempting to personalize the answer: it is all due to Vladimir Putin and his small group of Kremlin insiders. Putin is indeed a striking leader, voted most powerful man in the world by prominent Western publications for several years. Whether he is riding a horse bare chested, salvaging an ancient amphora from a lake, descending to the bottom of the Black Sea in a submarine, or riding a Harley-Davidson motorcycle with the Night Wolves, a Russian biker gang, he cuts an imposing figure. In an opaque system where only one man appears to make decisions, it is tempting to attribute everything to the agency of the president. But that oversimplifies how Russia is ruled. Behind the new tsar stands a thousand-year-old state with traditions and self-understanding that precede Putin and will surely outlast him. He views himself as the defender of Russia's historical legacy and is determined to restore Russia to its rightful place in the world, whether or not other countries like it.

To understand Putin's world, one has to start with the history and geography—and, yes, culture—that shaped it. These factors explain how Russia has been able to bind its diverse population together through the development and propagation of a compelling historical narrative that largely depicts the West as its enemy. And, indeed, how it relies on that depiction for its own legitimacy.

Lost and Restored Empires

A month after introducing that epic tour of Russian history at the Sochi Olympics, Vladimir Putin addressed an admiring audience in the ornate Kremlin Hall in March 2014 to proclaim triumphantly that Russia had annexed Crimea. His speech was replete with historical references to Russia's greatness and its long ties to Crimea, bolstered by accusations that the West was trying to weaken Russia and that it repeatedly failed to respect Moscow's interests. The combination of resentment, criticism of the West, and declarations of Russia's greatness was vintage Putin, and it highlighted an uncomfortable truth for Russia's Western partners. Contrary to what the United States and its allies had hoped and expected, Russia had not accepted its loss of empire. After seventy years of an experiment in building Soviet-style socialism, Moscow was interested in working with the West—but only on its own terms, not ones imposed by Washington or Brussels.

But perhaps the West should have reflected more on Russia's historical legacy before assuming that Russians and their leaders would begin the long and painful journey away from an imperial mindset and would happily accept a new position as a junior partner to a dominant West. What were the closest analogies for the situation in which Russia found itself? Was the year 1918 relevant? World War One had destroyed three empires: the Ottoman, the German, and the Austro-Hungarian. A fourth, the Russian, had collapsed in revolution, but after a three-year bloody civil war, a new Soviet empire had emerged. Like the Russian and Soviet empires, the Ottoman and Austro-Hungarian were multiethnic, landed empires ruled by the dominant ethnic group. But unlike the USSR, they were defeated in war. Their empires were broken up during and after the 1919 Versailles peace settlement. They had little choice but to accept the settlement because of their military defeat. Even then, it took many years for their political elites to accept the loss of empire.

Another possible analogy were the overseas British and French empires that began to wither away after World War Two. In this case, neither country was defeated in war, but the economic burden of empire and the drive of colonial subjects to be free—and their own loss of confidence and conviction in an imperial mission—gradually caused the two empires to disintegrate, beginning with India's independence from Britain in 1947. Moreover, the United States, which emerged as the strongest country after 1945, actively promoted the idea of independence for former colonies. Nevertheless, it took decades for both Britain and France to accept their loss of imperial status.

Russia was a completely different case. The Soviet Union was not defeated in a war. It collapsed as a result of its own internal weakness and inability to confront the desire of its ethnic minorities for greater autonomy and independence. After a year of continuous tension between the Kremlin—under Mikhail Gorbachev, the last Soviet leader—and the fifteen Soviet republics, Russian republic leader Boris Yeltsin met with his Ukrainian and Belarusian counterparts in a hunting lodge in the Belavezha Forest outside Minsk on December 8, 1991. They signed what became known as the Belavezha Accords to create a loose association of post-Soviet states that rendered the Soviet Union defunct and Gorbachev redundant. The ambiguity surrounding what actually happened during this long night has provoked a variety of extravagant theories about how the USSR imploded. It has created a post-Soviet generation more inclined to believe that the USSR collapsed because of sinister outside pressures—in other words, a plot by the United States and what they call its "special services"—and that it was stabbed in the back. It might have been easier to "accept" the Soviet collapse had there been a military defeat. But the fundamental puzzle of 1991 remains: how could a nuclear superpower bestriding one-ninth of the world's landmass simply disintegrate? Because there was no single event to point to, conspiracy theories abounded, making it easy to reject the idea that Russia should accept the loss of the "near abroad," which is the term Russians use for the post-Soviet states, as opposed to foreign countries, the "far abroad."

Of course, the USSR called itself a socialist state, not an empire. But it was in reality the Soviet version of centuries of Russian territorial expansion in all directions. The idea of permanently giving up lands Russia once controlled has been anathema to tsars, general secretaries, and post-Soviet presidents. Almost immediately after the USSR collapsed, some in the new Russian leadership—although not Boris Yeltsin himself—began thinking about how to regain their lost territories. There is no precedent in Russian history for accepting the loss of territory, only for the expansion of it. What is it that propels this Russian drive for expansion?

One person who understood Russia's dilemma was Catherine the Great, the German princess who became Russia's eighteenth-century imperial ruler. She was the one who conquered the territories that today are the scene of the Ukraine-Russia standoff in Eastern Ukraine. At fifteen, the young Lutheran German princess traveled to Russia and married her cousin Tsar Peter III, whom, by all accounts, she disliked greatly. Rumor had it that the marriage was never consummated. But Catherine soon developed great political acumen, understanding how to navigate the labyrinths of court intrigues. Peter was assassinated, and Catherine then ascended to the throne. By this time, she had converted to Russian Orthodoxy, and despite her fondness for French Enlightenment philosophers, she adopted the traditional view of tsars and tsarinas who ruled their subjects with an iron hand. She was also a shrewd foreign policy player, and her armies successfully fought the Ottoman and Persian empires, wresting large swaths of territory in the southeast, taking over today's Crimean Peninsula and an area now referred to as New Russia, or Novorossiya. She came to believe there was only one way for Russia to defend its fluid borders. "That which stops growing begins to rot," she once said, adding, "I have to expand my borders in order to keep my country secure."

Since the fifteenth century, when Russia finally threw off the three-century Mongol yoke, it has constantly alternated between territorial expansion and retreat.[5] With no natural borders and vulnerable to invasion from the south, east, and west, Russia could only be safe if it conquered its neighboring territories. Security for Russia meant defensive expansion. Periodically, Russia would shrink—the result of foreign invasions or domestic upheavals—but it would always recover and "gather in the lands" around it once again. Putin does not see himself as the twenty-first-century "gatherer" of Russian lands after Gorbachev "lost" large swaths of what had been the tsarist and Soviet empires. Nevertheless, he would like to restore Russian influence over these territories. How does he understand Russian history and Russia's relations with its near and far abroad? What are the narratives and founding myths that have molded Russians' understanding of their place in the world?

One of the conundrums that perpetually confront anyone who studies Russia is the temptation to attribute anything the Kremlin does to the overwhelming weight of the past. In this view, continuity is the most important factor explaining why the Kremlin acts the way it does. The seven decades of Soviet communism were just one interlude in a thousand years of repressive autocracy, secretive government, a lack of individual and property rights, and expansionist foreign policy. The Gorbachev and Yeltsin years represented a brief period of reformist respite before Russia once again returned to authoritarianism under Putin. The more things change, the more they remain the same, and it is an illusion to believe that Russia will markedly change in the twenty-first century. As a result of this view, other countries have no choice but to radically readjust how they deal with Russia and change their expectations about what is possible.

Certainly, Vladimir Putin constantly invokes Russia's unique history to justify his worldview. Although he has criticized American exceptionalism, he frequently praises what amounts to Russian exceptionalism.[6] How does Russia see its own history? One old Soviet adage is that the past is hard to predict. In Soviet times—and again under Vladimir Putin—facts about what happened and the interpretation of those facts have changed, depending on the regime's current political agenda. Controversies over how to commemorate the seventieth anniversary of the end of World War Two in 2015 graphically illustrated this. In Soviet times, the 1939 Nazi-Soviet Pact—whose secret protocols carved up Poland between the USSR and Germany, enabling the Soviets to occupy the Baltic states and what is currently Moldova, and kept the USSR out of the war for two years—was justified as a response to Western rejection of Moscow's feelers for an anti-Nazi military alliance.[7] The existence of the secret protocols was vigorously denied. Under Gorbachev, the Kremlin admitted that the protocols of the Hitler-Stalin pact existed and criticized Stalin for signing the agreement. In 2015, Putin once again defended the Nazi-Soviet Pact and prevaricated about the existence of the protocols.[8]

Indeed, in the quarter century since the Soviet collapse, the view of Joseph Stalin has undergone several revisions. During the Soviet dictator's twenty-five-year rule, the NKVD had at least sixteen million Soviet citizens killed during the purges of the 1930s and 1940s, by some estimates.[9] Others claim a total of twenty million deaths as a result of collectivization, famine, and the purges.[10] Stalin led the country to victory in World War Two, in which at least twenty-seven million citizens perished, and industrialized the country from above at a catastrophic human cost.

In the immediate aftermath of the Soviet collapse, there was a broad effort to bring to light Stalin's crimes and to confront that period of Soviet history. Memorial, a human rights NGO dedicated to exposing the truth about Stalin's victims, and to promoting human rights in Russia, did impressive work, including finding many previously hidden graves of his victims. But after Putin became president, the official view of Stalin began to change yet again. Despite his crimes, he was an "efficient manager" and a "patriot."[11] In 2015, Memorial's status as an NGO was challenged, and it has faced continuous harassment. Stalin has gradually been rehabilitated in school textbooks as a great leader who made the world respect and fear the USSR.

Vladimir Putin's version of the past—designed to bolster Russian patriotism and support for him—has been quite effective. History informs any country's leader and population of their role in the world. But in Russia the past haunts the present more vividly than in many other countries, perhaps because Russia has yet to develop a national narrative to which its population can fully subscribe. For centuries, a disparity between Russia's self-concept as a great power and the reality of its capabilities—both natural and man-made—has limited its ability to play the world role it believes it is destined to play. These capabilities have determined Russia's interactions with the outside world.

The Persistent Factors in Russian Foreign Policy

Size and Climate

Russia's understanding of its role in the world begins with a basic geographical reality. Since the sixteenth century it has been the largest country in the world occupying a strategic swath of territory in the heartland of Eurasia, astride two continents and spanning eleven of the world's twenty-four time zones. It has only one natural border, the Arctic sea to the north. Otherwise it has constantly had to redefine its borders. Russia's size as a single consolidated state that has survived for centuries and resisted conquest makes it unique in world history. Invaders have come from the east, south, and west and have eventually been pushed back. And there are few aspects of Russian life on which the country's enormous size has not had an impact.[12] Russia's size certainly helped it resist conquest by outside powers, but it also retarded its ability to modernize. The vast distances made communication difficult.

Added to Russia's size is the enormous diversity in its extreme climate. Large parts of the country were virtually inaccessible in the winter, the growing season was short, and there were few warm-water ports. Although Russia and Canada are on the same latitude, most Canadians live along its southern border. But Russian leaders uniquely settled large numbers of their population in the inhospitable far north, where many of its natural resources were. The fact that roads and rivers were frozen for much of the year further impeded economic development. Moreover, Russia has always been a relatively sparsely populated country. It is rich in natural resources: oil, gas, precious metals, and timber. But most Russians live far away from where these abundant resources are, and it has always been a challenge to fully exploit them.

Soviet leaders moved large numbers of people to Siberia to work with Russia's natural riches, but at a very high human and material cost. The town of Norilsk, founded in the 1930s, is an extreme example of this trend. It is above the Arctic Circle, the northernmost city in the world, has 175,000 permanent inhabitants, and was initially founded as part of Stalin's GULAG, or labor camp, system. It is snowed under for 250 days a year, has temperatures ranging from minus 64 degrees Fahrenheit in the winter to 77 degrees in the summer. It produces valuable nickel and other commodities, but living conditions can be very difficult.[13]

Economic Backwardness

Russia's size, difficult climate, and relatively sparse population have for centuries challenged its leaders as they sought to develop the country economically. But Russia's persistent relative economic backwardness compared to Europe was also the product of its leaders' choices. The tsars feared the creation of a middle class that might challenge the absolute monarchy and delayed encouraging the development of a capitalist economy. Stalin imposed industrialization and forced agricultural collectivization of the Soviet population from above, to drag the USSR out of its backward state. He abolished whatever remained of private property. He herded unwilling peasants onto collective farms, forced others to move into the industrial cities, and presided over the deaths of many others. But ultimately the dysfunctional Soviet economic system proved unable to keep up with the West as the era of modern technology dawned.

The Imperative of Centralized Rule and Russification

But perhaps the most important impact of Russia's size has been the way tsars and general secretaries have ruled their people. Whether the capital was in Saint Petersburg or Moscow, the issue has been how to govern such a vast, ethnically diverse country, which is 6,000 miles wide (the United States, for instance, is 2,600 miles wide). As the Russian state expanded from the sixteenth century on, it conquered wide-ranging groups of people. By the time Russia's expansion was over, at the end of the nineteenth century, the empire was home to more than one hundred ethnic groups at very different stages of social and economic development. Some of them—notably the Poles and Chechens—resisted Russian rule and openly rebelled against it. Successive attempts to solidify St. Petersburg's rule by imposing a policy of Russification on potentially rebellious non-Russian groups succeeded only partially. No wonder Lenin called the Russian Empire at the turn of the century a "prison house of nationalities."

The Chechens have actively resisted Russian rule since the early nineteenth century. Leo Tolstoy's late-nineteenth-century novella *Hadji Murad,* a story of Russia's wars with Chechnya, is a testament to the ongoing struggle with the North Caucasus's Islamic groups. Others—such as the various nomadic tribes in Central Asia—were more accommodating to the Russian Empire. But the tsars and later the Soviets realized that Russia would always face an internal security problem. The solution was to govern with an iron hand from the capital, dispatching bureaucrats far and wide to collect taxes and impose the laws. And the rulers were always wary of sedition and treason. Tough penalties for criticizing the tsar and centralized autocratic rule have characterized Russia for centuries. The 1649 law code provided for the death penalty if someone in word and deed (*slovo i delo*) criticized the tsar, meaning that a peasant drinking too much in a tavern had to be careful about what he said about his ruler lest someone overhear and report him.

The Improbable "Start-Up"

Russia was in many ways an improbable country. Its natural endowments—its size, extreme climate, often impassable roads, and huge distance from centers of world trade and civilization (both the ancient trade routes in Persia and China and the more modern Atlantic routes)—all contributed to retard its progress toward modernity. "Russia was remote in time and space . . . a 'start-up' founded hundreds of miles from the rest of civilization in a vast forest."[14] Its location helped it survive. Russia was not accessible by sea, and it managed to fend off several waves of European would-be invaders. And then there was the climate. The adage that General Winter defeated both Napoleon and Hitler when they sought to conquer Russia is the ultimate testimony to the country's ability to persevere and resist until the enemy succumbed to the cold and ice. These enemies of Russia, as Putin is fond of reminding the world, underestimated the ability of Russians to endure and overcome adversity.

Russia in many ways remained out of the mainstream of European civilization. It largely missed the Renaissance, the Reformation, and the Enlightenment. Its history has contributed to a collective memory of exceptionalism, endurance, resistance to conquest, but also vulnerability. The lack of natural borders and repeated threat of invasion reinforced a determination not to lose territory and to steel the country against future attempts to encroach on its sovereignty. When Putin accuses the West of trying to "break up" Russia and impose an agenda that is inimical to the country's real interests, he appeals to the dual legacies of superiority and inferiority complexes that for centuries have shaped Russia's view of its role in the world.[15] They have enabled a series of authoritarian rulers to justify their harsh rule by warning of enemies within and without and have made Russia a military foe to be feared. Putin insists Russia is what he calls an absolutely sovereign country with no limits on its ability to determine its own fate. This powerfully resonates with many Russians who believe their right to self-determination is constantly challenged by the West. What ties them all together is the "Russian Idea."

—2—

THE RUSSIAN IDEA

> There can be no alliance between Russia and the West, either for the sake of interests or for the sake of principles. There is not a single interest, not a single trend in the West, which does not conspire against Russia, especially her future, and does not try to harm her. Therefore Russia's only natural policy towards the West must be to seek not an alliance with the Western powers but their disunion and division. Only then will they not be hostile to us, not of course out of conviction, but out of impotence. —*Fyodr Tyutchev, Poet and Slavophile, 1864*[1]

What ideas drive the Kremlin elite? What binds Russia together? During the Soviet times, what held together the population was a mixture of ideology and nationalism. In the beginning of the communist era, people may have believed in Marxism-Leninism, but over time they became cynical as they understood the difference between communist slogans about equality and the dictatorship of the proletariat and the reality of a society in which the Communist Party elite (about 8 percent of the population) lived substantially better than those not in the party. By the time the USSR collapsed, Soviet official national identity was a mixture of patriotism and a belief in the superiority of the socialist system. But it had been increasingly challenged by Mikhail Gorbachev, the provincial Communist Party ideology secretary who rose to become leader of the USSR in 1985. He understood that he had to reform the atrophied Soviet system:

> Imagine a country that flies into space, launches Sputniks, creates such a defense system, and it can't resolve the problem of women's

> pantyhose. There's no toothpaste, no soap powder, not the basic necessities of life. It was incredible and humiliating to work in such a government.[2]

Since the Soviet collapse, Russians have been searching for a new identity. But after twenty-five years, there is still no consensus, and the potential ethnic minefields are evident. What does it mean to be Russian? This question for centuries has provoked controversy and never has been fully answered. Is being Russian an ethnically exclusive concept? In Soviet times, the "fifth point" in every internal Soviet passport was nationality. At age sixteen, every citizen had to state his or her nationality, and this largely determined their career trajectory. Being Russian was the most desirable category and most career enhancing. Then came Ukrainian and other Slavic ethnicities. Being Jewish—defined as a non-Russian nationality—often meant exclusion from the most prestigious academic institutions or Communist Party positions. Being Kazakh, Uzbek, Chechen, or Azeri could also be problematic. This, then, is the exclusive definition of what it means to be Russian: the privileged nationality in a multinational state. Since the Soviet collapse, there have been attempts to define "Russianness" in a more inclusive, civic-based way—as a citizen of Russia, irrespective of ethnicity. The government attempted in the 1990s to introduce the inclusive term "*Rossianin*" (citizen of Russia) for Russian, as opposed to the ethnically exclusive "*Russky*." It never caught on, and during the Putin era, the ethnically exclusive expression has become mainstream. Indeed, in 2017, Putin stated that the Russian language is the "spiritual framework" of the country, "our state language" that "cannot be replaced with anything."[3]

After seventy-four years of communist rule, and the loss of the non-Russian Soviet republics, it was not clear what Russia's new national identity should be nor who was a Russian. So in a rather unusual move, in 1996, Boris Yeltsin created a commission with a unique charter: to come up with a new Russian Idea. He appointed an advisory committee headed by the Kremlin's assistant for political affairs, Georgii Satarov, and the government newspaper offered the equivalent of $2,000 to the person who produced the best essay on the topic in seven pages or less. But from the outset the project was doomed. Satarov admitted that a national idea could not be imposed from above but had to come from the bottom up. No one was able to come up with an appropriate national idea, even though one contestant won a prize for his essay on the "principles of Russianness." In 1997, the project was terminated.[4] Trying to have a commission create a new national identity on the spot in a fluid political transition was almost certain to fail. But a new identity is indeed gradually emerging.

In 2007, the Kremlin backed the creation of an international organization: Russky Mir (Russian World). Its head is Vyacheslav Nikonov, grandson of Stalin's long-serving foreign minister Vyacheslav Molotov, whose dour demeanor and his equally dour negotiating style were legendary. Nikonov, an outspoken defender of the Kremlin and critic of the United States, has served in the Duma and has held academic positions. His foundation is designed to promote Russian culture and language worldwide and also to appeal to people who have emigrated from Russia over the past century to return to their roots. It usually defines as "Russian" inclusively anyone who speaks Russian (Russko-Yazichny) and identifies with Russian culture irrespective of their ethnicity.

The seeming confusion about what it means to be Russian has its roots in the origins of the Russian state. Muscovy became a consolidated state at the same time as it began to expand and conquer adjacent territories in the fourteenth century. For the next five hundred years it expanded (and sometimes contracted) as the state grew stronger. Along the way, it fought wars with Tatars, Livonian knights, Poles, Swedes, Turks, and Persians—and its population constantly became more ethnically diverse. Many "Russians" were in fact the product of mixed marriages, with a variety of roots. Indeed, one-third of the prerevolutionary Russian imperial foreign ministry was staffed by Baltic Germans, ethnic Germans who lived in the Baltic states when the Russian Empire acquired them. For instance, the Russian foreign minister in the early twentieth century was Count

Vladimir Lamsdorf. One of his descendants later became West Germany's economics minister. Russians' sense of their own identity was also increasingly bound up with their sense of imperial destiny, of paternalistically ruling those around them, including Ukrainians, who were known as their "little brothers."

Perhaps because of this ambiguity about what it meant to be Russian, the elite grappled with the issue by focusing not so much on ethnicity but on the uniqueness of Russian civilization. Over the years, the Russian Idea became a powerful cornerstone of the country's evolving identity. Its core was "the conviction that Russia had its own independent, self-sufficient, and eminently worthy cultural and historical tradition that both sets it apart from the West and guarantees its future flourishing."[5] Russian rulers early on defined themselves by how they differed from Europe, stressing their Eurasian vocation. That, rather than comparing themselves, say, to Asia, was their starting point. In the nineteenth century, deputy minister of education and classical scholar Count Sergei Uvarov summed up the essence of the Russian Idea in the famous triad "Orthodoxy, Autocracy, and Nationality." This is what defined the Russian state. Its three basic institutional pillars were the Orthodox Church, the monarchy, and the peasant commune.

Inherent in this nineteenth-century definition of what it meant to be Russian was the belief in the superiority of a communal, collective way of life, as opposed to the competitive individualism of the more developed European countries. Tolstoy's *Anna Karenina,* for instance, vividly portrays the contrast between the artificial, mannered lives of the Saint Petersburg courtiers who spoke only French to each other and the pure, simple, moral life Levin leads on his country estate. The organic ties between the monarch, the peasants, and the Church had little room for an emerging middle class, which might eventually challenge the power of the absolute monarch. The peasant commune, or *mir* (which also means both "world" and "peace"), formed the basis not only of the Russian Idea but also of an incipient political system that still influences the way Russians view relations between rulers and the ruled.

Harvard historian Edward Keenan elaborated on the distinctive aspects of the Russian system, which began in medieval times and arguably persists today. He described it in a pioneering article published just before the Soviet collapse. The political culture of both the Russian peasant commune and the Russian court, he argued, emphasized the importance of the group over that of the individual and discouraged risk-taking. At the court, it was important for the boyars (nobles) to act as though they supported a strong tsar, even if the reality was otherwise and the tsar was weak. Informal mechanisms were far more important than formal institutions of governance, and it was important to obscure the rules of the game from all but a small group of power brokers who were privy to these rules. Moreover, foreign emissaries in Russia were largely kept ignorant of what was really happening at court. Over centuries, the persistence of opaque rules of the game within the Kremlin walls has always made it difficult for outsiders and foreigners to understand how Russia is ruled and what motivates its foreign policy.[6]

The traditional tendency to emphasize Russia's uniqueness also focused on the moral and spiritual qualities of the Russian Idea. The nineteenth-century poet Fyodr Tyutchev famously wrote:

> With the mind alone Russia cannot be understood,
> No ordinary yardstick spans her greatness:
> She stands alone, unique—
> In Russia one can only believe.[7]

The notion that Russia was somehow beyond a rational understanding became part of the image of a country that could not adhere to norms constructed in the West.

Indeed, Russians have long been divided over whether they should look to the West or the East. Although the Russian Idea had a significant number of adherents in the nineteenth century, it also had its opponents. Dissent and opposition have as long a tradition in Russia as has autocracy. After Russia's humiliating defeat by Britain, France, and the Ottoman Empire in the Crimean War in 1856, there was growing pressure at home for reform. The serfs were emancipated in 1861, and Tsar Alexander II created local legislative councils, reformed the judiciary, and introduced other measures designed to give a small portion of the population a voice in the political system. But it was not enough for those who wanted Russia to adopt European institutions. Indeed, Alexander was assassinated in 1881 by members of a revolutionary group seeking radical change.

As the nineteenth century wore on, those who believed in Russia's unique and superior destiny—the Slavophiles—were challenged by the Westernizers, those who wanted Russia to adopt European values and institutions, the rule of law, and greater democracy. More radical elements turned to socialism or anarchism, but they all looked west to construct the socioeconomic model they wanted Russia to adopt. Although successive Russian tsars, beginning with Peter the Great, had looked to Europe as a technological and economic model they wanted to emulate, they resolutely rejected the idea of emulating Europe's political model, because that would have spelled the end of Russian absolutism.[8] In today's Russia, those committed to perpetuating Russia's unique system and protecting their own vested interests continue to battle the minority who would like Russia to become a fully modern state with the rule of law and institutions that serve the population.

Just as Russians have been ambivalent about the West, the West has been ambivalent about—if not downright hostile toward—Russia. The scathing—and ultimately incorrect—criticism in the Twittersphere of the shoddy state of Russian hotels in Sochi in 2014 on the eve of the Olympics had echoes of many past criticisms of Russia's backwardness. Indeed, for centuries the outside world was generally suspicious of Russia. A series of Western travelers to Russia in the nineteenth century described a Russia that shocked many of their readers: backward, even barbaric, and the antithesis of what an enlightened society should be. The French

Marquis de Custine published *La Russie en 1839* after a trip to Russia, in which he wrote:

> He must have sojourned in that solitude without repose, that prison without leisure that is called Russia to feel all the liberty enjoyed in other European countries, whatever form of government they may have adopted. If ever your sons should be discontented with France, try my recipe: tell them to go to Russia. It is a useful journey for every foreigner; whoever has well examined that country will be content to live anywhere else. It is always good to know that a society exists where no happiness is possible because, by law of nature, man cannot be happy unless he is free.[9]

Another renowned traveler was the American George Kennan, a cousin of the grandfather of the famous diplomat and historian George Frost Kennan. George Kennan the elder traveled extensively in Russia in the nineteenth and early twentieth centuries, producing the two-volume *Siberia and the Exile System,* for which he interviewed political exiles sent to Siberia by tsarist bureaucrats. He became a fierce critic of the repressive tsarist system but soon became disillusioned with the Bolsheviks, writing, "The Russian leopard has not changed its spots.... The new Bolshevik constitution... leaves all power just where it has been for the last five years—in the hands of a small group of self-appointed bureaucrats which the people can neither remove nor control."[10]

Soviet Ideology

How have ideas influenced Russian foreign policy? And does Russia need an ideology to guide its foreign policy? Or is nostalgia for the nineteenth-century days when Russia was a great power enough to inspire today's Kremlin? Certainly the current occupants of the Kremlin are fond of invoking the 1815 Congress of Vienna, when the great powers divided

Europe, as a model to be admired. Tsarist Russia's ideological trilogy of Orthodoxy, Autocracy, and Nationality was directed mainly toward Russia's internal evolution. There was no official foreign policy ideology in an era when Russia became a major player in the nineteenth-century Concert of Europe. When the Bolsheviks took power, however, that changed. Marxism-Leninism became the official ideology with an explicit foreign policy component. Of course, the Bolshevik leader Vladimir Lenin took the writings of the German Karl Marx—and adapted them to the Russian environment. Marx had been dubious that the largely peasant Russia was ripe for revolution, and Lenin had to explain why it was. Nevertheless, what appeared revolutionary at the beginning increasingly began to resemble the imperial era as time went on. "Soviet socialism turned out to bear a remarkable resemblance to the Russian tradition it pretended to transform."[11] This was equally true in foreign as in domestic policy. Soviet ideology blended the rhetorical aspects of Leninism with a heavy dose of Russian nationalism. And whatever the formal ideology, the predominant feature of the Soviet attitude toward the international arena was a dialectical view of the world. It was the USSR against the West, which was out to defeat the Soviet Union. Agreement with the West might be possible on a case-by-case basis, but in the long run, the interests of Russia and the *glavnyi protivnik* (main enemy) were opposed. This dialectical view and suspicion of the outside world has been remarkably durable throughout the reign of tsars, communist general secretaries, and post-Soviet presidents.

What was the international component of Marxism-Leninism? Ironically, Karl Marx believed that international relations would be irrelevant once the revolution took place. "The worker has no country," he wrote.[12] Foreign policy was the preserve of the bourgeoisie. Once the proletariat was in power, there would be no more national states. Of course, in Marx's thousands of pages of writing, he said very little about the future, only about the past and present. It was left to his Russian disciple Vladimir Lenin to explain how Marx's ideas pertained to relations between states. Lenin's major contribution was his treatise *Imperialism, The Highest Stage of Capitalism,* written in 1916, in which he sought to explain why World War One had broken out and why it would bring about the end of the capitalist system and the beginning of the socialist era. Without delving into the minutiae of Lenin's arguments, *Imperialism* explained that capitalist countries would inevitably come to blows over competition for colonies, and the proletariat in both the metropolises and the colonies would rise up to defeat their oppressors. Long after Soviet citizens had become cynical about their ideology, this theory retained its appeal in third world countries—and one can hear echoes of these theories in contemporary Cuba, Zimbabwe, and Venezuela. Lenin remained a committed internationalist until his early death in 1924, as did his would-be successor Leon Trotsky. But Trotsky was no match for his rival, the one-time Georgian seminarian Joseph Stalin, who defeated him in the succession struggle in the late 1920s and eventually had him murdered with an ice pick in Mexico City in 1940.

Unlike the other Bolshevik leaders, Stalin had spent very little time abroad, spoke no European languages, and was suspicious and resentful of his more cosmopolitan comrades. But precisely because his rivals did not take him as seriously as they should have, he was able to outmaneuver them and amass power. Once he was securely in the Kremlin, Stalin realized the international revolution predicted by Marx and Lenin would not happen any time soon—if ever. So he redefined internationalism in 1928: "An internationalist is one who unreservedly supports the Soviet Union." From then until the end of the USSR, Soviet ideology, under the guise of internationalism, became increasingly nationalistic. Behind the rhetoric was an understanding that Russian national interests should be paramount and that the Soviet Union's Eastern European allies after 1945 should define their interests in terms of Moscow's needs. During the height of Sino-Soviet hostility, when the USSR and China engaged in a brief border war in 1969, the struggle was explained in ideological terms, while the real reason was a classical struggle for territory, power, and influence. Therefore, by the end of the Soviet era, very few in the Soviet elite believed in the tenets of Marxism-Leninism. It was only when Gorbachev came to power that the USSR officially eschewed the doctrine of the inevitable clash between communism and capitalism and began to promote the idea of mutual interdependence. Nevertheless, the dialectical view of the world continued to influence many officials—including a mid-level KGB officer working in Dresden in the late 1980s.

The Eurasianists

While Soviet leaders espoused the official doctrine of internationalism and world revolution, another Russian view of the world was emerging, one developed by anti-communist exiles and one from which Vladimir Putin has increasingly drawn. Both of these ideologies grapple with issues that also engaged the nineteenth-century Slavophiles and Westernizers, namely why Russia had not followed a political and economic path similar to that taken by Europe and what it should aspire to be going forward. Eurasianism was a worldview developed in the 1920s by exiled Russians who despised communism and dreamed of a conservative utopia. But it also had its dissident adherents within the USSR, the most prominent of whom was Lev Gumilev, who spent much of his life in and out of labor camps. A rejection of Western values, Eurasianism stressed Russia's unique civilization, which incorporated both European and Asian elements, including the coexistence of Christianity and Islam, celebrating Russia's Asian heritage.[13] The early Eurasianists argued that Russia had an inalienable right to rule over its imperial territories and urged Russia not to try to emulate the West.[14] One conservative exiled Russian philosopher whose writings have influenced Putin is Ivan Ilyin, who accused the Bolsheviks of knowing nothing about Russia, failing to understand its unique national traditions, and deciding to "rape it politically."[15] Ironically, although they passionately disagreed, the Stalinists and their exiled opponents both believed that Russia had a unique destiny that set it apart from the West and legitimized its right to rule over large swaths of adjacent territory.

The New Russian Idea

When the Soviet Union collapsed, the official ideology abruptly disappeared, with nothing to replace it. The country had imploded and with it the justification for an expansionist foreign policy. Indeed, territories that had for two centuries or more been part of imperial Russia and the USSR suddenly emerged as fifteen independent states. How were the new—and old—elites to deal with this? Amid the chaos of the Soviet collapse almost immediately came the search for a new Russian Idea.

A small group of pro-Western liberals around the new president, Boris Yeltsin, initially sought to redefine Russia's interests in a revolutionary way: Russia should join the West. Chief among them was a young diplomat, Andrei Kozyrev, who had worked in the Soviet Foreign Ministry and had decided to throw his lot in with Yeltsin in 1990, acting as an important liaison with the United States during the abortive August 1991 coup against Gorbachev. Yeltsin appointed him foreign minister in 1992, much to the consternation of the old Soviet diplomatic corps. Kozyrev's position was clear: "Our choice is . . . to progress according to generally accepted rules. They were invented by the West, and I am a Westernizer in this respect. . . . The West is rich, we need to be friends with it. . . . It's the club of first-rate states Russia must rightfully belong to."[16] Note the acknowledgment that the West had set the global rules and Russia had to accept them—a sentiment Putin later came to reject vigorously.[17]

The idea that Russia could find greatness again by renouncing its uniqueness and otherness went against centuries of Russian traditions. Russia's American and European interlocutors welcomed the apparent desire of Yeltsin's reformers to become part of the West. But in their enthusiasm to reform and reimagine Russia, they misjudged the extent to which these desires were shared by the majority of the political class. Kozyrev's own views of the West became more skeptical and ambivalent as the decade wore on. Boris Yeltsin replaced Kozyrev in 1996 with the veteran Soviet diplomat Yevgeny Primakov, who repudiated a pro-Western stance. Instead, he proposed an alliance among Russia, China, and India.[18] Today Kozyrev lives in the United States, and his ideas have been uniformly rejected by his successors.

After the USSR's collapse, the debate between post-Soviet Westernizers and Slavophiles reprised. This time the Westernizers called themselves Atlanticists, and the Slavophiles, Eurasianists, harking back to the 1920s. The immediate focus was on how Russia's relations with the former Soviet states—the "near abroad," as they preferred to call them—should evolve. Andrei Kokoshin was a prominent writer and member of the Duma, the newly elected parliament, which had taken its name from the prerevolutionary days. He advocated that Russia create, on the territory of the former Russian Empire and USSR, a new Eurasian state political structure. The Russian Federation would be the nucleus around which all other states would unite on a mutually beneficial basis. The Russian language would be an important factor in this reintegration.[19]

Sergei Karaganov, another influential intellectual, argued that Russian speakers living in newly independent countries, such as Ukraine, Belarus, and the Baltic states, would become the prime guarantors of Moscow's political and economic influence over its neighbors, predicting that Moscow might one day feel compelled to use force to protect them, and thus its interests in the former USSR. "We must be enterprising and take them under our control, in this way establishing a powerful political enclave that will be the foundation for our political influence," he wrote.[20] Right from the start, therefore, there was a general consensus that Russia had the right to proclaim its own Monroe Doctrine in the post-Soviet space. This Monroe Doctrine would ensure that no post-Soviet state would join Western structures. The Russian Monroe Doctrine differed from the American original in that it was really an "anti-doctrine with no discernible strategic programme, encompassing disjointed responses to growing Western interest in the FSU."[21] The consensus among most of the Russian elite was that some form of reintegration with the post-Soviet space was inevitable because, without the former Soviet space, Russia could not become a great power again. The Western assumption that Russia would gradually accept the loss of empire and its new, diminished role in the global order turned out to be a product of wishful thinking.

Under the presidency of Vladimir Putin, these ideas have become more structured and elaborate. It is customary to say that, in contrast to the Cold War years, there is no ideological antagonism between Russia and the West. But this ignores the fact that Putin's Russia has defined its role in the world as the leader of "conservative international" supporting states that espouse "traditional values" and as a protector of leaders who face challenges from "color" revolutions—popular uprisings against authoritarian governments, which Putin believes are orchestrated by the West. The image of Russia as the defender of the status quo—against what is depicted as a revisionist, decadent West trying to promote regime change against established leaders, be they in the Middle East or in the post-Soviet space—is an integral part of this new Russian Idea. Russia today argues that its values and policies are different from and superior to those of the United States. Putin has said that Western Christianity is decadent because it supports LGBTQ rights and multiculturalism. In 2013, he said:

> We can see how many of the Euro-Atlantic countries are actually rejecting their roots, including the Christian values that constitute the basis of Western civilization. They are denying moral principles and all traditional identities: national, cultural, religious, and even sexual. They are implementing policies that equate large families with same-sex partnerships, belief in God with the belief in Satan.[22]

Russia is depicted as the bastion of forces that oppose revolution, chaos, and liberal ideas. A new element in Putin's worldview has been his explicit commitment to the idea that a Russian world (*Russky mir*) exists, one that transcends Russia's state borders, and that Russian civilization differs from Western civilization. Since the annexation of Crimea, Putin has invoked the concepts of a "divided people" and "protecting compatriots abroad." The central argument is that, since the Soviet collapse, there is a mismatch between Russia's state borders and its national or ethnic borders, and that this is both a historical injustice and a threat to Russia's security. After the Soviet collapse, twenty-two million Russians found themselves outside Russia, living in other post-Soviet states. Russia, in Putin's view, has a right to come to the defense of Russians under threat in the post-Soviet space.

Putin's eighteen years in power have created a new Russian Idea that resembles the old Russian Idea: Russia is a unique civilization, in many ways superior to that of the West, and is both European and Eurasian. Western concepts of individualism, competition, and untrammeled free expression are alien to the more holistic, organic, communal Russian values. Russia has a right to a sphere of influence in the lands that were part of both the Russian Empire and the USSR, and Moscow has a duty to defend the interests of compatriot Russians living outside the motherland. The West represents a threat to both Russian values and interests. And its agents inside Russia are poised to do its bidding.

Authoritarian Foreign Policy?

Throughout the Soviet era, outsiders debated the relationship between the USSR's political system and its foreign policy. Did the Soviet Union behave internationally just as other great powers did or was there something unique about its domestic system that made it more difficult to deal with? Communist ideology committed the USSR to pursuing world revolution, but in practice, the Kremlin had to interact with other states.

In the interwar years, there were two Soviet foreign policies. One was the policy of a normal state with diplomats and government officials interacting with their foreign counterparts. Georgii Chicherin, Soviet commissar of foreign affairs from 1922 to 1930, was the scion of a distinguished tsarist diplomatic family who had defected to the Bolshevik cause. He attended international meetings—such as the Genoa conference where the USSR and Germany signed the infamous Treaty of Rapallo, which eventually enabled Weimar Germany to rearm—in full morning dress. The other foreign policy was that of a revolutionary state. Moscow created the Communist International—known as the Comintern—an organization of foreign communist parties led by the Kremlin that sought to overthrow the very governments with which the Soviet commissar of foreign affairs was dealing. Chicherin's counterpart in the Comintern would attend international meetings in proletarian garb, plotting how to overthrow the bourgeois governments with whom Chicherin was negotiating. With the exception of the popular-front strategy from 1934 to 1939, when communists in Europe were encouraged to collaborate with socialists and other anti-fascist groups against the rise of Hitler, this schizophrenic view of the world lasted until Stalin, at the height of World War Two's grand alliance with the US and the UK, who saw no reason to keep it going, dissolved the Comintern in 1943.

During World War Two, those in the West who dealt with Russia were divided into two camps. The first camp, of whom Franklin Roosevelt was the most prominent member, believed there was no option but to deal with the Soviet Union as one would with any great power. "I have a hunch," Roosevelt said, "that if I give Joseph Stalin what he wants, and ask nothing in return, noblesse oblige, he will work for the good of his people." This view—that one could make deals with Moscow—was paramount during the Yalta Conference in February 1945, when the victorious powers divided Europe in two, with the Soviet Union occupying and controlling the eastern half.

In September 2015, during a speech to the United Nations General Assembly, Putin praised the Yalta Conference: "The Yalta system—helped the humanity through turbulent, at times dramatic events of the last seven decades. It saved the world from large-scale upheavals."[23] For the next half century, some Western leaders sought to make pragmatic deals with Moscow on the basis of mutual interests, the détente era from 1972 to 1980 being the most prominent example. Richard Nixon and Henry Kissinger believed that one could do business with the Soviet leaders and succeeded in signing a number of arms control and trade agreements. Pursuing classical balance-of-power policies, they took advantage of the hostile relations between the USSR and China to woo the Soviets. West German chancellor Willy Brandt's new Ostpolitik was another example of striking successful deals with the Kremlin, and it eventually led to German reunification.[24]

Arrayed against the proponents of pragmatic cooperation with Russia were those who viewed the USSR and its leaders through a much darker lens and were convinced that the communist ideology made it impossible to deal with the Kremlin as if it were just another great power. George F. Kennan, father of the theory of containment, expressed these sentiments in his seminal Mr. X article in the journal *Foreign Affairs* in 1947. Soviet behavior, he argued, was a product of the traditional suspicious tsarist view of the world reinforced by the Soviet adaptation of Marxism-Leninism implacably opposed to the capitalist West. The USSR was inherently expansionist, and the only way to counter it was to pursue a "long-term, patient but firm and vigilant containment of Russia's expansive tendencies."[25] But Kennan was also convinced that, contained, the Soviet Union would eventually collapse from its own internal rot.

Of course, during the Cold War numerous countries outside the Western alliance were willing to do business with the USSR irrespective of its domestic system. Many developing countries viewed Moscow through an anti-colonialist lens, believing the Kremlin would support their interests against the West, until some began to experience Soviet heavy-handedness and the competition for influence between China and the USSR. African delegates at international conferences would complain about Soviet officials trying to persuade them over lunch to support their cause, followed by Chinese officials insisting over dinner that theirs was the correct path forward. China itself felt subordinated to the USSR and emerged as an ideological rival as well as a claimant on the Soviet Far East. After Stalin died, Mao Tse-tung believed that he should lead the international communist movement, and he looked down on the uncouth (in his view) Nikita Khrushchev, who refused to cede that role to him.

Between the initial Sino-Soviet split in 1958 and Gorbachev's ascent to power in 1985, Beijing was arguably seen to be as great a threat to Moscow as was Washington.

When the USSR collapsed and Boris Yeltsin wrested the Kremlin from Gorbachev to become the first president of the Russian Federation, the Chinese were horrified, and the West was cautiously optimistic although wary of Yeltsin's unpredictability. When Bill Clinton came into office, he and his closest aides were convinced of the crucial link between a country's domestic political system and its foreign policy. The liberal internationalist ideas in which they believed, as already noted, held that democracies do not go to war with each other and that it was imperative for the United States to do all it could to help Russia become a democracy.

When Vladimir Putin took over from Yeltsin, he was determined to restore Russia's greatness, and he understood the connection between domestic and foreign policies differently from those in power during the brief Yeltsin interlude. Foreign policy was increasingly driven by domestic considerations. During his first term, from 2000 to 2004, Putin appeared to seek greater integration into the global economy and introduced a number of modernizing reforms. This was also a time of cooperation with the West—the post-9/11 partnership with the United States in Afghanistan and a rapprochement with Germany—until events in Russia's neighborhood and beyond caused a domestic crackdown. Putin had initially favored closer ties to the West. But when he realized that the West expected Russia to become more democratic and to encourage the development of competing political parties, he began to view closer ties with the West with suspicion because of their implications for his hold on power. The George W. Bush administration's Freedom Agenda involved regime change—be it in Iraq, Georgia, or Ukraine. At least that is how Putin saw it. And that represented a direct challenge to Russian interests.

During Putin's second presidential term, domestic freedoms were curtailed in the name of security. Putin had blamed the West for a 2004 terrorist attack in Beslan in the North Caucasus, when hundreds of children were killed. "Some would like to cut a juicy piece of our pie. Others help them."[26] After the shock of the color revolutions that deposed rulers in Ukraine and Georgia, Putin appointed Vladislav Surkov, his half-Chechen "grey cardinal" to direct the transition to what has become known as "managed democracy." A former public relations man, Surkov describes himself as the author of the current "Russian system." The system which he calls "sovereign democracy" combines "democratic rhetoric and undemocratic intent."[27] Surkov stresses sovereignty over democracy, meaning that no outside power should interfere in Russia's domestic affairs. He created a pro-Putin youth group, Nashi (Ours), to battle liberal youth and created a series of patriotic summer camps that resemble the Soviet-era Young Pioneer and Young Communist conclaves. Independent media were slowly closed down as the state took over virtually all broadcast media.

Putin attempted to introduce pension reforms in 2005, but the pensioners took to the streets in protest, and the government was forced to back down. After that, economic reform ceased. The rise in oil prices and strong GDP growth from 2000 to 2008 bolstered Putin's self-confidence and determination not to be subordinate to the West.

During his second term, Putin increasingly turned against the West, and in his third presidential term, which began in 2012, foreign policy was largely used to bolster his domestic ratings. In 2011, he had been shocked by demonstrations protesting falsified parliamentary elections and his announced return to the Kremlin. A change in US ambassadors further convinced Putin that Washington was out to undermine him. Career diplomat John Beyrle, whose father had fought with both the US and Soviet armies in World War Two, after escaping German captivity, was replaced by Michael McFaul, a Stanford professor and adviser to Barack Obama who had worked on democracy promotion in Russia in the 1990s and who was hounded by the Russian media from the day of his arrival in Moscow.[28]

Once the Ukraine crisis began in late 2013, Russia portrayed itself as being at war with the West, accusing its "fifth columnists" inside Russia of trying to destroy the country. With his approval rating hovering around

90 percent and an increasingly assertive and unpredictable policy, Putin had managed to persuade many in the West that dealing with Russia was not like dealing with another great power and that the more authoritarian the government, the more aggressive the foreign policy. Nevertheless, many non-Western countries view Russia as a partner that does not interfere with their domestic policies or their internal political system and that seeks to create new international rules and organizations not dominated by the West.

Vladimir Putin has skillfully appealed to tsarist and Soviet nostalgia to emphasize Russia's unique place in the world and his own part in restoring Russia's rightful role as a great power. The tsarist two-headed eagle—symbolizing that Russia looks both East and West—has replaced the hammer and sickle on the Russian flag. The rousing tune of the Soviet national anthem has been brought back after Yeltsin's experiment with a new tune failed miserably. But the anthem now has new words. While extolling Russian exceptionalism, Putin has re-created the enemy image of the West and its purported agents in Russia. He portrays himself as the protector of Russians living in the near abroad, because of the perceived historical injustice that followed the Soviet collapse. He defends Russia's right to restore the global role it lost after 1992.

Russia is unlikely to become a truly modern state if it looks too much to its past glories and grievances. The problem with the appeal to the past as the harbinger of Russia's future is that it idealizes the nineteenth century, when Russia was a major player in the Concert of Europe, and the Red Army's victory in World War Two under Stalin's leadership. But that is no model for the twenty-first-century global disorder in which Russia finds itself today. Trying to re-create the Congress of Vienna with nuclear weapons and many international players will inevitably lead to rifts with countries that have a different stake in the emerging global order. If the new Russian Idea is the old Russian Idea popularized with twenty-first-century technology, it threatens to render Russia a continuing prisoner of its past.

Putin's fourth inaugural ceremony in May 2018 showcased the new

Russian Idea, emphasizing tradition and patriotism. He was filmed leaving his office and walking briskly to a shiny new Russian-made armored limousine—the first time the vehicle had been used. He emerged from the limousine at the Great Kremlin Palace and swore his oath on a copy of the Russian Constitution. In his brief speech, he evoked Russia's glorious past, with an appeal to the future.

> We all are the inheritors of Russia and its thousand years of history, the inheritors of this land that has given birth to exceptional sons and daughters, workers, warriors, and creators. They have passed down to us this huge, great state. There is no doubt that we can draw strength from our past. But even the most glorious history is not enough to ensure us a better life. Today's generations of Russians must reinforce this grandeur through their own acts.[29]

This is the vision that animates Putin's world.

—3—

AMBIVALENT EUROPEANS

Whatever is dividing us, we live on the same planet and Europe is our common home, a home, not a theater of military operation.

—*Mikhail Gorbachev, 1984*[1]

We have never viewed Europe as a mistress. I am quite serious now. We have always proposed a serious relationship.

—*Vladimir Putin, 2015*[2]

Every Russian ruler since Peter the Great has looked to Europe with both fascination and suspicion, and Putin is no exception. In the interview with Italian journalists in which he denied seeing Europe as a mistress, he claimed to want a "serious relationship" with it. But he also complained about the European Union's discrimination against Russia. Indeed, geography and history have ensured that Europe plays a crucial role in Vladimir Putin's evolving view of Russian national interests, as it did for tsars and Soviet Party leaders before him. Russia lies in the strategic heartland of Eurasia and, since Peter the Great, has looked to Europe as an economic partner. Today Europe is the largest market for Russian energy, and its investments and exports have fueled Russian economic growth. But Europe since the 1940s has also been the United States' key ally in containing Russia. So the USSR and post-Soviet Russia sought to minimize the impact of transatlantic cooperation on Russia's freedom of maneuver. Europe's current and future development remain a major influence on Russia's foreign policy.

Where does Russia belong? In Europe or Asia? The maps illustrate the reason for this ambiguity. Over the centuries, Russian leaders have offered different answers, but for at least the past two centuries two things have been clear. Russia belongs to both Europe and Asia, but it is neither fully European nor fully Asian. This unique Eurasian identity has meant that Russia can adopt from both civilizations. But it has also meant that neither Europe nor Asia has accepted Russia as an integral part of its own orbit. Historically, the Russian state has interacted far more with Europe than with Asia. Indeed, Russia became a great power by virtue of its role in the nineteenth-century Concert of Europe. But its leaders have often eyed Europe warily, and European leaders certainly questioned whether Russia was a European country.

Russians have at best been reluctant Europeans, and this ambivalence continues today. So far, Europe has not succeeded in integrating Russia since 1991 largely because Russia has been neither willing nor able to accept the conditions for integration that are on offer and Europe has rejected what Russia insists are prerequisites for greater integration. The Ukraine crisis dramatically exacerbated tensions between Russia and Europe and brought that relationship to its lowest level since the fall of the USSR, a process of "escalated alienation." But the inherent tensions and contradictions of Russia's relations with Europe have been there since the end of the Soviet era. Russia has so far not decided where it belongs, and neither has Europe.

This chapter will examine how Europe and Russia have dealt with each other since the Soviet collapse, and ask whether Putin, in many ways the most "European" of Russian leaders in the past century, can reconcile his vision of Russian exceptionalism with the reality of a Europe facing unprecedented challenges to its own future. Where does Europe fit into Putin's world?

Europe: The Idea, the Model, and the Geopolitical Reality

Europe has historically been important for Russia in three distinct but interrelated ways: as a political idea, an economic model, and a geopolitical reality that enabled Russia to become and remain a great power. The idea of "Europe" involves concepts associated with the legacy of the Enlightenment: the importance of the individual, representative government, religious tolerance, limits on the power of rulers, the development of a *Rechtsstaat*—in which the rule of law prevails—and, later, the development of capitalism and democracy. For hundreds of years, until 1991, Russia was ruled first by tsars, who were absolute monarchs, and then by commissars and general secretaries, who faced few limits on their powers. Thus, the idea of Europe appealed to only the few progressive, intelligentsia, the Westernizers who wanted Russia to become truly European.

The question of why a Westernized Russian intelligentsia who looked to Europe in the nineteenth century was unable to prevail politically—and is still unable to gain much traction even today—was addressed by the British historian E. H. Carr sixty years ago:

> From the Russian political equation, as from the economic equation, the middle class was absent. The Russian intelligentsia was no substitute for the Western middle class. Institutions and social groups, deriving directly from imitation of Western models, were quickly transformed in Russian conditions into something alien to the West and distinctively national.[3]

It proved impossible to transplant Western normative practices such as freedom of speech, freedom of assembly, and due process to Russia because Russia's rulers were determined not to let them take root. The idea of Europe has repelled those who supported authoritarian rule, from the tsarist autocracy to the communist *nomenklatura*.[4]

The current Kremlin also regards these freedoms as a threat. Putin views the European Union's attempts to draw Russia into its "community of values" as a challenge to his system of "managed" or "sovereign" democracy.

Europe as an economic model has always had a different and broader resonance for Russians. From Peter the Great to Putin, Russian rulers have admired Europe as a collection of technologically advanced societies whose economic achievements were to be emulated even if their political systems were considered inappropriate for Russia's unique conditions. Russian leaders have for centuries tried to import European economic practices and technology that could make Russia a more prosperous, stronger country. Peter the Great traveled incognito to Western Europe to learn its ways, especially its shipbuilding techniques. In 1697, he set off as "Peter Mikhailov" with a large entourage to Sweden, Germany, Holland, and England. "Wherever he went, Peter was dazzled by the technical sophistication of the West, while the West was horrified by his uncouth ebullience and barbaric rages: few royal trips have had so many diplomatic incidents."[5]

Three centuries later, Dmitry Medvedev, after a trip to Silicon Valley, was determined that Russia should build its own "innovation city." He chose Skolkovo, a business complex in the suburbs of Moscow, as his project. Declaring that the complex would have its own laws protecting intellectual and other property rights, he partnered with businesses and universities in the US and Europe. He hoped to import Western scientists and their innovation culture by creating a small city where innovation would be directed from the top down. But, although Skolkovo has a respected business school and some successful businesses, it has not become a hub for start-ups, simply because innovation happens usually from the bottom up, not the top down. Although Russian attempts to import European modernization techniques have historically had some impact, their success always has been limited by the fact that Russia's authoritarian political system discourages both political and technological innovation. Russia has for centuries been a borrower and importer of European technology. Today Russia still faces the challenge of becoming a twenty-first-century technological innovator, even though Putin has promised that it will become a leader in artificial intelligence.

Europe as a geopolitical reality has been Russia's gateway to the achievement of great power status. Russia rose to prominence internationally through the European interstate system, whose rules, by and large, it had to accept and whose development it was able to influence. Russia projected power internationally as a player in the complex and shifting alliances of nineteenth-century Europe. Russia's engagement with Europe continued during periods of domestic reform and domestic repression. Today Russian officials praise the Concert of Europe, which largely dominated the continent between 1815 and 1914 and in which Russia played an important role. An assassin's bullet in Sarajevo in June 1914 and the Battle of Tannenberg two months later, when Germany trounced Russia, ended imperial Russia's European century. The model of great powers dividing the continent, ruling over smaller powers and determining their fate, appeals to Putin. He has explicitly praised the Yalta system, which, of course, remains controversial. For Eastern Europeans, it symbolizes a cynical division of labor in which they lost their independence and came under Soviet domination.

In the nineteenth century, Europe validated Russia's role as a great power player on the continent. In the twentieth century, the United States was arguably more important in conferring legitimacy on the USSR as the other nuclear superpower. Nevertheless, it was through the Soviet Union's domination of the eastern half of Europe and its nuclear arsenal that it became a military superpower—though never an economic one. When the Soviet Union lost its Eastern European empire in 1991, its great power status was challenged. Could twenty-first-century Russia remain a great power without dominating half of Europe?

The Soviet Legacy

After the Bolshevik Revolution, the Soviet Union largely retreated from Europe. In the interwar years, it remained on the sidelines of European developments. The USSR's ties with most European governments were largely strained. The August 1939 Nazi-Soviet Pact, which kept Russia out of the war for two years, enabled Germany and the USSR to march into Poland in September. But it ultimately facilitated the launch of Operation Barbarossa, the German invasion of the Soviet Union, to the shock of Stalin, who had expected the alliance with Germany to last.

At the end of the war, the USSR again became a great power by the division of Europe into two halves and its domination of Eastern Europe, which the Red Army had occupied. Geographically, postwar USSR was the most "European" of any Russian state, reaching as far west as the Elbe River with the Baltic states, Kaliningrad, Moldova, and Eastern Poland part of the newly expanded USSR. But as the USSR became more European territorially, it imposed the Soviet system on Eastern Europe, making that part of Europe less European internally.

Russia's unprecedented military power and its ability to control Eastern Europe's fate became the new European reality. While the idea of Europe lived on among the Soviet dissident community, post-1964 Brezhnev-era officials, realizing that the USSR was falling behind technologically, returned to Europe as a model, seeking to import Western technology to substitute for their own lack of innovation. Like previous Russian rulers' attempts to transplant the European model, this one also failed because the communist leadership's obsession with political control stifled the free exchange of ideas necessary for true innovation. The need to catch up economically with the West also motivated the Kremlin to seek a political rapprochement with Western Europe and respond to the détente initiatives promoted by West Germany and France. Thus, for the last twenty years of the USSR's existence, Moscow pursued a two-pronged strategy in Europe: trying to maintain control over an increasingly restive Eastern Europe while pursuing closer ties with Western Europe, hoping to loosen the bonds of the transatlantic alliance.

In 1985, Russia's attitude toward Europe began to change radically. In the more than three centuries since Russia became a player in the European state system, only one leader has actively engaged all three dimensions of Europe. That was Mikhail Gorbachev. His six years in power saw the resurgence of the idea of Europe inasmuch as his support for glasnost (greater openness) was an appeal to European values. Perestroika—the restructuring and modernization of the economy—reflected the attraction of Europe as a model. And in calling for a "common European home," Gorbachev pursued a rapprochement with Western Europe, seeking to mitigate the Cold War geopolitical reality of a divided Europe.[6] He wanted the Soviet Union to play a different role in Europe and increasingly realized that the ailing Soviet system had much to learn from Western Europe. In his first major speech to the British parliament in December 1984 before he became general secretary, the young, smiling, energetic Politburo member with his stylish wife impressed his audience with his refreshingly conciliatory ideas, so different from those of the grim-faced gerontocracy that had ruled the USSR for the previous decade. The striking refrain of "our common European home" had major and unforeseeable consequences.[7]

Gorbachev reversed four decades of Soviet policy toward Europe by loosening control over Eastern Europe and eventually renouncing the Soviet empire there, allowing communism to collapse peacefully. But it remains difficult for many Russians to accept that the Kremlin could willingly have abdicated its great power role in Europe. While the Soviet renunciation of the Eastern European Empire was an unintended consequence of Gorbachev's policies, the rapprochement with Western Europe that followed was both deliberate and initially successful. A major legacy of the Gorbachev era was Western European gratitude toward Russia for allowing a common European home to rise from the ashes of the moribund communist system. The nations of Eastern Europe were far more ambivalent: relieved that they had finally regained their sovereignty but resentful of four decades of Soviet rule. With the end of the Warsaw Pact military alliance, Moscow's presence in and influence over the European continent was sharply reduced. Russia's geographic European reach shrunk to that of the seventeenth century. At the very time when Russians appeared to be most open to European ideas and models of government, Russia had the least influence over Europe than it had had for two centuries. This set the stage for a new Russia-Europe reality.

From Yeltsin to Putin: Rediscovering Europe

During the first years of the Yeltsin presidency, Foreign Minister Andrei Kozyrev was determined that Russia should seek to emulate Europe and its institutions. He and other Yeltsin supporters initially embraced both the idea and model of Europe, wishing to join the major Western clubs, such as the G-7, the World Trade Organization, and the Council of Europe. Meanwhile, relations with Central and Eastern Europe atrophied, as the countries in these regions, plus the Baltic states, also sought to join European institutions as quickly as possible to put more distance between them and Russia. The Kremlin viewed the European Union (EU) and its key members, such as Germany and France, as sources of political and economic support during difficult post-1991 years, and Western Europe was generally eager to participate in the post-communist transition and increase its economic ties with Russia.

Russia's trade with Europe grew in the 1990s, and Brussels and Moscow signed a Partnership and Cooperation Agreement in 1994, which came into force in 1997. In those days, many believed that increased economic ties would promote better political relations. The agreement with the EU was designed to encourage economic and scientific ties and to facilitate Russia's integration into European structures. But as the 1990s wore on, Russia's relations with Europe became increasingly strained by NATO's campaign to end the wars in Yugoslavia. Whereas Russia cooperated reluctantly with NATO during the Bosnian campaign, the Kosovo campaign and NATO's bombing of Serbia caused major problems with Europe. Yeltsin's deteriorating health and erratic behavior, the replacement of pro-European Kozyrev with the more hard-line Yevgeny Primakov, Russia's economic problems culminating in the ruble crash in 1998, and the increasingly opaque nature of Russian politics and business led to greater European questioning of the direction Russia was taking and whether its evolution was at odds with their original expectations.

But while the Russian state and the EU were experiencing mutual alienation and disappointment, the new middle class and wealthy Russians were becoming more European. They established businesses, bank accounts, and residences in London, Paris, and Berlin; they sent their children to British boarding schools; and they vacationed in Courchevel, Cannes, and Crete. The rise of capitalism in Russia and the end of Soviet-era travel restrictions created a new class of wealthy and middle class, peripatetic European Russians. They became personally integrated with Western society. And they began to influence Europe. Western Europe inevitably began to change with the influx of Russian money and ways of doing business.

Vladimir Putin: The Wary European

Vladimir Putin's personal experience in Europe was—distinctively—his five years as a KGB case officer in Dresden. The Europe in which he lived was the artificial, repressive East German state that viewed West Germany as its main enemy and a threat to its very existence. But it was also a country that, although it had largely replicated the Soviet economic system, managed to provide its population with a significantly higher standard of living than that in the Soviet Union, largely due to West German economic support. Putin came to admire German and European economic achievements. Europe's primary attraction for him—as for Peter the Great—is the economic model of successful modernization. But he has never viewed the idea of Europe as a model to be emulated, nor does he appear to understand that Europe's successful modernization was a product of both a free market economy and a democratic political system based on the rule of law. Putin has rather looked to China's model of successful authoritarian modernization. Under Putin's leadership, the Russian economy recovered and the state became stronger. Europe's dependence on Russian energy grew, and Russia was able to reassert influence in Europe for two reasons: its rise as an energy superpower and the modernization of its military.

The Russians, and the Soviets before them, have always had difficulty understanding how the EU operates, both because of its complex bureaucracy and because of its self-perception as a community of values. Putin's relationship with Europe began before the EU enlargement. It was easier for the Kremlin to deal with a Europe in which there were fifteen member states, in 2000, than with the twenty-eight member states after the 2004, 2007, and 2013 enlargements to include Central Europe and the Baltic states. "Old" Europe, to quote Donald Rumsfeld, was less wary of Russia than "new" Europe, and after 2004, ties with the EU became more complicated.[8] Putin, like his predecessors, has always favored focusing on bilateral ties with the most important European states. His attitude toward the EU echoes that of Henry Kissinger, who famously once asked, "What telephone number do I call if I want to call Europe?" He has questioned how effective an institution can be if it rotates presidents every six months and if member states have to give up sovereignty voluntarily. For Putin, the whole system is implausible. He believes absolute sovereignty is one of the most important attributes of statehood and *derzhavnost'* (great-power strength). It is hard for him to comprehend why Germany, France, or the UK would have ceded their sovereignty to Brussels-based bureaucrats, and it was gratifying to him when Euroskeptical movements began to grow and when Britain voted to leave the EU—Brexit. For Moscow, it is infinitely preferable to deal with nation-states and cultivate bilateral relations than to deal with the EU.

The Council of Europe

Russia's difficult relations with the Council of Europe (COE) highlight the ambivalence with which Russia and Europe deal with each other. The COE, which dates back to 1949, is an organization that promotes democracy, human rights, and the rule of law in Europe. It is not part of the European Union. It sees itself as the "democratic conscience of Europe."[9]

It has an executive branch, a Parliamentary Assembly (PACE), and the Strasbourg-based European Court of Human Rights (ECHR), which hears cases brought by individuals in any member state. Before the fall of communism, the COE's membership was limited to Western Europe, but after 1991 the former communist states began to join, as they sought to move closer to Europe. Today the COE has 47 member states, and the PACE has 324 parliamentarians representing the major political parties in the member states.[10]

Russia became a member of COE in 1996. A main motivation for joining was the search for recognition and international respectability, which began in the Yeltsin era. The council agreed to admit Russia and its neighbors not because they were democracies that respected the rule of law and human rights but because it hoped to encourage them in that direction. Russia joined as a means of legitimizing its new status as an emerging democracy. From the beginning, there were doubts about whether Russia belonged in the COE, in view of Yeltsin's 1993 firing on the Russian parliament when it opposed his policies, the war in Chechnya, the growth of nationalist and neo-communist parties, and the hardening of Russian foreign policy after Primakov replaced Kozyrev. But many members believed that it would be unwise to isolate Russia and affirmed that Russia belonged in Europe.

Russia signed on to the European Convention on Human Rights (ECHR) and also agreed to abolish the death penalty, two necessary conditions for joining. The Russian legal system incorporated elements of the COE's human rights code, and the Russian Constitutional Court acknowledged legal precedents set in the Strasbourg-based ECHR and sometimes refers to them in its own legal decisions.

In the more than twenty years since it joined, Russia has several times had its voting rights suspended because of the war in Chechnya and the war in Ukraine. Its parliamentarians have engaged in acrimonious debates with their European counterparts. But despite these problems, Russia insists on remaining in the organization because it values the international recognition it brings and the public forum it provides for Russian officials to present their point of view. As the largest member state, it sends one of the biggest parliamentary delegations, including such harsh critics of the COE as the ultranationalist Vladimir Zhirinovsky and the former communist leader Gennady Zyuganov.

Perhaps the most unexpected aspect of Russia's membership in the COE has been the role of the ECHR. The largest number of cases brought before the court come from Russia, and these cases form 25 percent of the court's total caseload. Russian citizens who believe they cannot receive justice from their own legal system present their cases in Strasbourg, and frequently the judgment goes in their favor. Most surprisingly, the Russian courts often honor the decisions made in Strasbourg, including paying financial compensation to plaintiffs. The ECHR complains that its agenda is dominated by Russian cases and has repeatedly suggested that the Russian court system needs to improve and redress its citizens' grievances at home, not in Strasbourg. But so far the European consensus is that it is preferable to have Russia in the ECHR—"integration is better than isolation: cooperation is better than confrontation."[11] As the head of Human Rights Watch in Russia said, "The European court...has been the most successful international protection mechanism" for rights in Russia. It is the "court of last resort in a situation when they cannot find justice in domestic courts."[12]

In July 2018, the court ruled to award €37,000 in damages to the members of the anti-Kremlin Pussy Riot rock group. They were jailed for two years on charges of hooliganism for a 2012 unsanctioned performance in Moscow's Cathedral of Christ the Saviour of a song titled "Punk Prayer: Mother of God Drive Putin Away." The ECHR ruled that Russia had violated the group's rights to liberty, a fair trial, and freedom of expression.[13]

The European Union and Russia

The legal framework that governs Russia's relations with the EU is the 1994 Partnership and Cooperation Agreement, which has been renewed annually since its initial ten-year mandate expired. It was further refined in 2005 by the addition of a road map for four Common Spaces, projects on which Russia and the EU are supposed to work together: the Common Economic Space; the Common Space of Freedom, Security, and Justice; the Common Space of External Security; and the Common Space in Research, Education, and Culture. Initially intended to give new momentum to the relationship, this road map has never been implemented.[14] The problem with the EU-Russia relationship is one of incompatible structures and misunderstanding of the relationship. The EU is all about detailed formal rules. Russia operates largely on the basis of informal arrangements, in which formal institutions are far less important. It has always, therefore, been a challenge for the EU and Russia to make progress on complex issues because of these fundamentally different—and often diametrically opposed—political and legal cultures.

During Putin's first term in office, Russia was officially committed to improving ties to the EU. Annual summits were held, and Brussels maintained its promise to seek to integrate Russia into Europe and nudge it toward accepting EU standards. They had important mutual interests. After all, Europe was importing 30 percent of its gas from Russia after the 2004 enlargement, Russia was one of the EU's most important trading partners, and Russia is the EU's largest neighbor. However difficult a neighbor, it was imperative to maintain and seek to improve relations. But after the 2004 enlargement it became more challenging to move the relationship forward. The new members from Central Europe and the Baltic states, despite their overwhelming dependence on Russian energy, were far more suspicious of Russian intentions and policies, and the new common neighborhood between the EU and Russia became increasingly contentious.

This was evident after the EU introduced its Eastern Partnership initiative in 2009, a joint program between Brussels and six of Russia's neighbors—the three South Caucasus states (Armenia, Azerbaijan, and Georgia) plus Ukraine, Moldova, and Belarus—designed to bring them closer to European standards. Its most visible and controversial—from Russia's point of view—achievement has been the signing of Association

Agreements with Ukraine, Georgia, and Moldova.[15] From the EU's perspective, these agreements are intended as a substitute for EU membership, but Russia has chosen to interpret them as a prelude to membership and to bringing the EU to Russia's borders.

The Kremlin has always objected to the EU's attempts to bring Russia's western neighbors into its orbit. After all, this threatens Russia's ability to secure a "sphere of privileged interests" in the post-Soviet space. Moreover, Putin's major project for his third term was the creation of the Eurasian Economic Union (EEU), a union of post-Soviet states that is intended to strengthen Russia's influence in its neighborhood. The Association Agreements are incompatible with the EEU, as the Ukraine crisis has demonstrated.

EU-Russia Relations After Crimea

The origins of the 2013 Ukraine crisis go back to Brussels's negotiations with Kyiv for an Association Agreement, which began in 2008 and were completed in 2013. Ukrainian president Viktor Yanukovych himself was ambivalent about whether Ukraine should sign on with the EU, but many of Ukraine's influential oligarchs favored closer economic ties to Europe. The Kremlin viewed Brussels's negotiations with Kyiv with suspicion but did not pay undue attention to them until the summer of 2013. Until then, Russia had always depicted NATO as a much greater threat to Russia's interests than the EU. Meanwhile, EU negotiators focused on a myriad of technical issues. With hindsight, people have criticized Brussels for not understanding the broader geopolitical implications of its negotiations with Kyiv. EU officials argue that they offered to talk to Russia, but Moscow showed no interest. Whatever the truth, Ukraine was a core interest for Moscow, and in mid-2013 the Kremlin woke up to the fact that the thousands of pages of EU legal documents essentially meant that Ukraine—an important trade partner for Russia—would not be able to join the Eurasian Economic Union and that it would eventually orient its trade more West. So Russia belatedly began to pressure Yanukovych not to sign the deal, with Putin eventually offering him a $15 billion loan if he turned down the Association Agreement.

Since the annexation of Crimea, EU-Russia relations have dramatically deteriorated, although there are considerable differences between the ways individual members view the relationship. Following the Crimean annexation, Brussels imposed sanctions on individual Russians said to be involved in the seizure, but these were modest. The July 2014 downing of MH-17, the Malaysia Airlines flight shot down in the fields of the Donbas that was transporting many Europeans to an AIDS conference, convinced the EU—led by Germany—to impose much tougher financial sanctions. Russia retaliated by imposing counter-sanctions on European foodstuff imports, which initially had a negative impact on some European economies. So far, the EU has reaffirmed its sanctions every six months since July 2014, despite considerable opposition from Italy, Greece, Hungary, Slovakia, the Czech Republic, Cyprus, and business groups in many countries. The EU has accepted that Russia does not desire to be integrated into Europe on Europe's terms, and it remains conflicted over how to deal with Moscow.

The EU's foreign policy chief Federica Mogherini has led several efforts to redefine Brussels's relations with Moscow, the latest being the declaration of five principles that will govern the relationship: full implementation of the Minsk II cease-fire agreement designed to end the war in the Donbas as a precondition for any change in EU policy; an increase in ties with Russia's neighbors; a strengthening of the EU's resilience, "and that of our neighbors, to future Russian pressure, intimidation, and manipulation, including energy security, cyber security, security of civilian aviation, a response to Russia's financing of radical parties in Europe, and the countering of Russian propaganda"; selective engagement with Russia on foreign policy issues vital to the EU; and a boosting of people-to-people contact and support of Russian civil society. Moscow has pushed back, accusing the EU of "making the future of EU-Russia relations hostage to the Ukrainian authorities."

The Ukraine crisis has unfolded during a time when the EU itself has come under increasing strain, both as a result of problems with the EU's and Greece's near default and as waves of migrants from Syria, other countries in the Middle East, Afghanistan, and Africa have provoked opposition in European societies and led to the rise of populist, anti-EU parties. Germany alone has taken in more than one million migrants since the intensification of the Syrian Civil War in 2015. Russia's actions in Syria have exacerbated the refugee crisis since it began its bombing campaign in September 2015. Tensions over migrants have manifested between countries such as Germany, which has pursued a generous policy toward admitting refugees, and Poland, Hungary, and other former communist countries, which have insisted on accepting only Christian migrants and have claimed that their societies are not equipped to integrate these migrants. Tensions have also flared up within most countries, notably Germany, where the anti-migrant party AfD (Alternative for Germany) gained 13 percent of the vote in the September 2017 elections, making it the largest opposition party in the Bundestag. Russia has sought to take advantage of these EU tensions and has given support to groups and countries that oppose accepting migrants. Moreover, the 2016 British vote to leave the EU has further weakened it.

Despite all of these tensions, the EU has remained united over the imposition of sanctions on Russia. In 2014, the EU was Russia's largest trading partner, constituting 48 percent of Russia's foreign trade. EU exports are mainly of machinery, electronic goods, and food. Russia, on the other hand, accounted for 8 percent of total EU trade, and 82 percent of its exports are fossil fuels. Germany was Russia's largest trade partner within the EU, followed by the Netherlands. The EU is by far the largest investor in Russia.[16] After Russia's invasion of Crimea, the EU introduced a number of diplomatic measures, pushing Russia out of the G-8 (making the group once again the G-7), suspending its negotiations to join the Organization for Economic Co-operation and Development and the International Energy Agency, and cancelling its regular summits. It issued visa bans and asset freezes to a total of 151 people and prohibited most imports originating in Crimea and investments in Crimea.

Following the downing of MH-17, when the EU joined US financial sanctions against Russia, it forbade loans to five major Russian state-owned banks and the export of dual-use technology. It also joined the US ban on export of energy-related technology to be used in Arctic oil exploration and production. The Russians' counter-sanctions banned what amounted to 43 percent of EU agri-food exports to Russia and 4.2 percent of worldwide EU agri-food exports. Although the overall percentage numbers are small, the impact on individual sectors and countries has been disproportionately large. Whereas EU's financial sanctions have had a significant impact on the Russian economy, the counter-sanctions have stimulated domestic Russian agricultural production while they have adversely impacted Poland and the Baltic states.[17] China has now replaced the EU as Russia's largest trading partner.

As time wore on, EU unity in support of sanctions began to wane. The economies of member countries experienced different degrees of economic challenges, and the business communities in many EU countries began to lobby their governments to rethink the utility of sanctions. After all, Russia remained entrenched in Crimea and continued to support the separatists in the Donbas region. Despite the economic difficulties caused by the sanctions, not only has the Kremlin not modified its policy in Ukraine; it has also scapegoated the West for the Russian population's economic hardships while rallying them to the patriotic flag of resisting pressure and beating the sanctions. Putin clearly hoped that Western support for sanctions would wane and that the EU would eventually want to get back to business with Russia, and would blame the United States—for whom economic ties to Russia were far less important—for forcing it to suffer economically. Criticism from a number of EU members has raised serious doubt about how long the sanctions regime will last, but so far it has, partly due to inertia and the continuing support of the EU's major players, Germany and France.

The Kremlin and the Euroskeptics

Because EU unity on sanctions has increasingly irked Moscow, it is not surprising that Russia has supported any movement that might weaken that unity. Moreover, Putin has elevated the EU as a potential threat to Russia's ability to preserve its sphere of influence in their shared neighborhood. The growing number of groups in Europe on the Right and the Left that dislike the European Union and would like their countries to leave it have generally met with Kremlin approval.

Criticisms of the EU are wide-ranging. There is anger at what people see as unfair subsidization of poorer countries by richer ones. There is opposition to "faceless Brussels bureaucrats" imposing excessive regulation on them, including forcing them to take in migrants from the Middle East and Africa. What unites these groups is anger at the loss of national sovereignty and self-determination to a supranational bureaucracy—as well as thinly disguised racism. They also share characteristics with the identity politics of those Americans who elected Donald Trump, yearning for an imagined past when their country was more ethnically homogeneous and independent. The cry "Take our country back again" resonates with all of these groups.

Since sovereignty is such a key part of Putin's ideology, there is a natural affinity between the Kremlin and these groups. They formed their own voting bloc in the European parliament in June 2015: Europe of Nations and Freedom (ENF). The irony of Euroskeptical parties banding together in the most symbolic of EU institutions—the European Parliament in Strasbourg—was apparently not lost on Moscow. The major parties in this bloc are the French National Front, led by Marine Le Pen; Geert Wilders's Dutch Party for Freedom; and the British UK Independence Party (UKIP). They account for about 5 percent of members of the European Parliament (MEPs), but because of the way votes are apportioned, as many as 20 percent of MEPs can vote in favor of Kremlin-friendly positions. This group—sometimes supported by Far Left pro-Russia parties—has voted against sanctions on Russia and against assistance for Ukraine.[18]

Russian support for Far Right European parties is difficult to document in full, but it is known that the French National Front has received loans from Russian banks. In 2014, it confirmed receiving a $10 million loan from Russia.[19] In February 2016, its leader, Marine Le Pen, asked Russia for a €28 million loan.[20] There are rumors of Russian support of other groups, including UKIP, which led the successful move to have Britain leave the EU. One prominent Brexit supporter met multiple times with the Russian ambassador to the UK.[21] Putin repeatedly denied that he was in favor of Brexit, but Russian comments after the vote would suggest the opposite.[22] Shortly after her election as the new UKIP head, Diane James said that Vladimir Putin was a great leader, "up there with Winston Churchill and Margaret Thatcher."[23] It sounds like a mutual admiration society.

Beyond support for Euroskeptical movements, Russia has organized conferences for nationalist groups and for a motley collection of separatists. In 2015, it hosted the first International Russian Conservative Forum in Saint Petersburg, attended by Far Right nationalist, neo-Nazi, and anti-Semitic groups, who regard themselves as marginalized by the European mainstream. For them the "fascist" enemy is in Ukraine.[24] Later that year, the Russian government helped fund a conference in Moscow that brought together separatists from Eastern Ukraine, Europe, and even the United States.[25] The "Dialogue of nations: the right to self-determination and the construction of a multipolar world" included representatives of a collection of fringe groups who denounced the US and Europe for the Ukrainian and refugee crises but had not a word to say about Russia's role in these events.[26] Ironically, the Kremlin is encouraging these groups even though Russia itself fought two bloody wars with Chechnya and defeated a separatist movement on its own territory.

"New" Europe's Changing View of Russia

One of the more notable surprises of the past few years—at least for those in the West—is the extent to which some countries in Central Europe have become much more favorably inclined toward the Kremlin. After all, when Germany united and communism fell in Central and Eastern Europe, the former members of the Warsaw Pact could not wait to join the West. Forty years of Soviet domination had left them deeply suspicious of Russia's intentions even after the USSR collapsed. They hastened to embrace the West to preclude a renewed embrace by Moscow. Their first order of business was to develop ties with NATO. Poland, the Czech Republic, and Hungary eventually joined the organization in 1999, and Bulgaria, Romania, Slovakia, Slovenia, and the Baltic states joined in 2004. Most also joined the EU in 2004, with Bulgaria and Romania following in 2007.

However, even as political relations were strained, economic ties between Central Europe and Russia grew, especially in the energy field. Bilateral intergovernmental commissions for economic cooperation were reestablished between Russia and these countries after their accession to the EU, and trade expanded by a factor of four. Energy supplies continued to dominate Russian exports to Eastern Europe, and these countries developed a trade deficit with Russia. This "economization" of relations led to a slow improvement of ties before the annexation of Crimea.[27]

Of course, informal ties between Russia and East-Central Europe had continued after the collapse of communism through networks that outlasted the USSR. Ties between different business groups continued, as did ties between former members of the intelligence services.[28]

Even before the annexation of Crimea, there were signs that some governments—particularly that of Hungary's Victor Orban—were growing more pro-Moscow as they became more authoritarian domestically. Orban, to the dismay of the EU, began to limit press and judicial freedom and to criticize EU "imperialism" when Brussels censured him. Vaclav Klaus, Czech president from 2003 to 2013, called the EU a greater threat to freedom than the Soviet Union had been and praised Vladimir Putin as a strong leader. Sitting next to Putin in 2015, he warned of the dangers of "political correctness" and "multiculturalism" eroding Western freedoms, echoing what Putin himself had said.[29] His successor, Milos Zeman, was the only Western leader to attend the 2015 Red Square commemoration of the seventieth anniversary of the end of World War Two. Indeed, after the poisoning of the Skripals on British soil in 2018, Zeman was the only EU leader to question whether Russia was responsible. But on the other side is another illiberal democracy: Poland. Since the PiS (Law and Justice) government guided by Jaroslaw Kaczynski came to power, Poland remains decidedly anti-Russian and has accused the Kremlin of culpability in the 2010 plane crash over Smolensk that killed former Polish president Lech Kaczynski, Jaroslaw's twin brother. PiS's domestic crackdown—including limiting judicial independence, seeking to muzzle the press, and criminalizing the interpretation of history that would suggest any Polish culpability in the Holocaust—has been criticized by fellow EU members.

Why have Central European countries seemingly changed their attitude toward Russia and sought to have Western sanctions lifted? Their behavior can be explained less by their fading memories of the communist period than by their experiences since 1990 and their newly discovered sense of national identity.[30] They are much more closely tied economically to Russia than are other EU members, and therefore they have paid far higher costs for the sanctions than has Western Europe. They also believe the EU has not accepted them as fully equal partners, and they resent the loss of sovereignty to Brussels. For instance, Bulgaria's post-communist experience has been more difficult than that of other countries, and it sees Turkish hegemony and religious fundamentalism among its Turkish population (the largest minority group in Bulgaria) as more of a threat than potential Russian aggression. Bulgarians also share much of Russia's resentment against the West and feel that the EU has treated them as second-class citizens. Moreover, given what has happened in Ukraine, the newer members of NATO question how committed the West would be to defending them from Russian aggression.

Recently, Russia has begun to pursue a more active and destabilizing policy in the Western Balkans, hoping to preempt these countries from moving closer toward Euro-Atlantic structures.[31] There was evidence in 2016 that a group of local nationalists and Russians tied to the GRU attempted a coup in Montenegro as it was poised to join NATO, going as far as to seek to assassinate the prime minister the day before an election.[32] The coup failed and Montenegro joined NATO. Russian-Serbian relations have grown closer, and the Serbian leadership believes it should not have to choose between the EU and Russia. And as the fragile federal state of Bosnia-Herzegovina struggles to hold together, Russia is supporting the Republika Srpska—one of its two constituent republics—as it seeks to leave the federation.[33] The EU and the US have paid far less attention to the Western Balkans in the past decade, and Russia has moved in to fill the vacuum, citing its historic, cultural, and religious ties with the region. For Southeastern Europe, closer ties to Russia are a useful means of balancing ties with the European Union and the United States, and they bring the added benefit of Russian money and oil and gas.

This complex mosaic means that Rumsfeld's famous differentiation between good "new" Europe and bad "old" Europe no longer holds, if it indeed ever did. Moscow can count on a divided EU finding it increasingly difficult to agree on how to approach Russia, with Germany now pursuing a far tougher stance than Hungary or Slovakia. This reinforces the Kremlin's belief in the importance of pursuing bilateral ties with key European states, seeking to benefit from intra-EU tensions.

Key Bilateral Relations

France

Although Germany has become Russia's most important European partner in the post-Soviet era, Franco-Russian ties also play an important role for Moscow. Unlike the complex German-Russian history of both cooperation and enmity, France's relations with Russia have, since the signing of the 1892 Franco-Russian Alliance, been more cooperative, with the exception of the early Bolshevik period. And the mutual cultural attraction has been enduring. Franco-Russian relations have always had a pragmatic, instrumental, and sometimes cynical quality to them. After all, the last time France invaded Russia was in 1812, and since Napoleon's defeat, France and Russia have been on the same side in most European wars, with the exception of the 1853–1856 Crimean War. Moscow's modern courtship of France goes back to the days of General Charles de Gaulle. He called for Europe "from the Atlantic to the Urals," signaling that he believed the Western part of Russia was indeed part of Europe. He sought improved ties with Moscow as he distanced France from the United States, withdrew from the integrated military part of NATO, and offered the Kremlin "détente, entente, and cooperation." His 1966 visit to the USSR was the first official trip by a Western head of state to the USSR, and it marked the end of Western isolation of the Soviet Union, increasing its international prestige.[34] The Kremlin's relations with his successors fluctuated, but France's fundamental commitment to Gaullist principles—irrespective of which party was in power—sustained close ties.

Under Vladimir Putin, Russia has continued to cultivate relations with France to play Berlin against Paris as well as Paris against Washington. In 2003, both French president Jacques Chirac and German chancellor Gerhard Schroeder wooed Putin to join their "coalition of the unwilling" against George Bush's invasion of Iraq. Chirac literally rolled out the red carpet for Putin when he arrived in Paris just before the war began and went to the airport to meet him. This was the high point of Franco-Russian cooperation, but the trio of opponents was unwilling or unable to parlay their anti-US stance into a more permanent partnership once the war was over, and their cooperation soon fell apart.

When Nicolas Sarkozy became president in 2007, he waxed enthusiastic about the United States—in contrast to his predecessor—and was known as "Sarko, *l'Americain*" (Sarko, the American). But as his presidency wore on, he developed a relationship and fascination with Vladimir

Putin. During the 2008 Russia-Georgia War, it fell to him as the head of the EU's rotating presidency to negotiate an end to the hostilities. When he arrived in Moscow, his interlocutor was the new Russian president Dmitry Medvedev, but it soon became clear that there was only one negotiator: the then prime minister Putin. Sarkozy's negotiations have been criticized, including assertions that the French team arrived in Moscow without an appropriate map of the area whose future they were negotiating. However, as a result of these talks, a cease-fire was put in place and the war ended.[35]

After he left office in 2012, Sarkozy visited Putin several times and praised him. In his book *France for Life,* he wrote of Putin, "I am not one of his intimates, but I confess to appreciating his frankness, his calm, his authority. And he is so Russian!" adding that he could detect in Mr. Putin the same "Russian soul" shared by Tolstoy, Gogol, and Dostoyevsky.[36] Socialist president Francois Hollande came into office determined to maintain the cordial ties with the Kremlin that his predecessor had established. He inherited from Sarkozy a €1.3 billion deal involving the sale of two Mistral-class amphibious assault ships to Russia, which Sarkozy termed a "gesture of trust."[37] At the time, the deal was controversial. The ships can carry up to sixteen helicopters, four landing crafts, thirteen tanks, and more than four hundred soldiers.[38] Opponents in the West pointed out that had Russia had these ships during the Russia-Georgia War, it could have deployed them in the Black Sea and imposed a crushing defeat on Georgia in a matter of hours. Opponents inside Russia—especially in the military—objected to having these ships built in France, arguing that Russia should develop the capacity to build this military hardware itself.

After the Crimean annexation and the imposition of EU sanctions, France came under increasing pressure to cancel the deal. Hollande prevaricated. He was under pressure from the trade unions and business groups not to cancel a project that promised employment and revenue. But, finally, he did cancel the contract. To loud criticism from Moscow, France repaid Russia the money it had been advanced and sold the two ships instead to Egypt. Hollande became increasingly critical of Moscow as the Syrian war unfolded. Putin was supposed to visit Paris in October 2016 to inaugurate a Russian cultural center, but Hollande refused to meet him, and so the trip was cancelled.

During the French presidential election campaign in 2017, Putin met with Marine Le Pen, leader of France's Far Right National Front party. In his formal remarks, Putin insisted that he was not trying to influence the election's outcome, and both he and Le Pen stressed their joint commitment to fighting terrorism.[39] During the election campaign, the young upstart outside candidate Emmanuel Macron became the subject of an increasingly aggressive smear campaign. His party, En Marche, said that its website was targeted by thousands of hacking attempts and that Kremlin-controlled outlets spread defamatory information about his personal life. However, shortly after his surprise election in May 2017, Macron invited Putin to Paris to celebrate three hundred years since Peter the Great first visited France. Putin accepted. Macron treated Putin with respect as they toured an exhibition about Tsar Peter at Versailles and inaugurated a Russian Orthodox cathedral.[40] But during their joint press conference, Macron did not mince words. He had accused Kremlin-sponsored media outlets RT and Sputnik of purveying "lying propaganda," and he raised the issue of Russia's election interference as he stood next to Putin. He described his discussion with Putin as "an extremely frank, direct conversation." Putin, needless to say, denied any knowledge of hacking or election interference.

Macron has continued this dual-track policy. He has pushed back against Russian interference and joined the US and UK in the bombing raids following the Syrian chemical attacks in 2018. France expelled diplomats in response to the poisoning of Sergei Skripal and his daughter in the UK. But Macron has also called for dialogue with Moscow on Syria and a range of other issues. In May 2018, he sat on stage with Putin at the Saint Petersburg International Economic Forum. Praising Russian history and culture, addressing Putin as "*cher* Vladimir" (dear Vladimir), he expressed the desire to improve ties with Russia but also urged Russia to resolve the Ukrainian crisis.[41] He brought a delegation of one hundred seventy businessmen with him, and twenty new contracts were signed.[42] Business and other groups in France favor better relations with Russia and argue that France and Russia share a common interest in fighting Islamic terrorism—especially after the attacks in Nice and Paris—which should outweigh the desire to punish Russia with sanctions for its actions in Ukraine.

The United Kingdom

Russia's relations with the United Kingdom are the most contradictory of its ties with any European country. Historically, imperial England and imperial Russia were competitors in the nineteenth-century Great Game, the struggle for domination over Afghanistan, Central Asia, and India. The British feared that Russia had designs on India, the jewel in the crown of the empire, and on the trade routes connecting India with Central Asia and Afghanistan. Russia and England also fought each other during the Crimean War. On the other hand, the British and Russian royal families intermarried, and the last Russian Tsar, Nicholas II, bore a striking resemblance to his cousin King George V. Stalin mistakenly viewed Britain as the USSR's major global competitor after their World War Two alliance ended. It took some time for him to understand fully the British Empire's decline after India's independence in 1947. During the Cold War, Moscow viewed London as Washington's closest ally and a key adversary—and a top target for espionage.

Since the Soviet collapse, wealthy Russians have flocked to London, creating a virtual "Londongrad," depositing their fortunes in British banks, buying soccer clubs, and even British media outlets, such as *The Independent* and *Evening Standard,* purchasing the most expensive real estate, arranging IPOs of their companies on the London Stock Exchange, and suing each other in British courts of law.[43] They have even managed to secure coveted places for their sons at Eton College, where the British elite, since 1440, have been educated and groomed for public office. Indeed, in September 2016, Vladimir Putin invited a group of eleven Eton pupils for an hour's audience in the Kremlin. The young men commented approvingly after the meeting on Putin's "human face."[44] For wealthy Russians, the UK has been the preferred European destination. But the British have recently introduced legislation to tighten banking laws and crack down on money laundering.[45]

While more than 300,000 Russians—including many from the middle class—have made their homes in the UK and integrated into British society, relations between the two governments have become increasingly strained during Putin's time in the Kremlin. Britain has granted political asylum to several prominent Putin critics, including Chechen leader Akhmed Zakayev; billionaire Boris Berezovksy, who helped engineer Putin's rise to power but ultimately fell out with him and was expelled by him; and Alexander Litvinenko, a former KGB agent who defected and accused Putin of complicity in a wide range of criminal activities. In November 2006, Litvinenko fell ill and died a few weeks later. Just before his death, British doctors established that he had been poisoned with radioactive polonium, a substance only available in specialized laboratories in Russia. But Russia refused to extradite the two men accused of poisoning him. After a long investigation, an official British inquiry in January 2016 issued its findings, stating that the murder had been ordered at the highest levels, possibly that of the president himself, because top officials believed Litvinenko had betrayed his country and was working for British intelligence.[46] The Litvinenko case created considerable stress between London and Moscow and affected most other aspects of the relationship.

Economic ties between the UK and Russia have been adversely affected by the Ukraine crisis and Britain's adherence to the EU sanctions. But even before the Crimean annexation, UK-Russia economic relations were modest. In 2013, trade with the UK formed 4 percent of Russian exports and 3 percent of its imports. Russian investment formed 0.53 percent of total foreign investment in Britain, and Russian firms constituted 1.4 percent of all the firms listed on the London Stock Exchange.[47] The most visible joint UK-Russia business deal was the agreement between British

Petroleum (BP) and the Russian oil company TNK to form a joint venture. In 2003, Lord John Browne, chief executive of BP, signed an agreement with Mikhail Fridman of TNK with Vladimir Putin and Prime Minister Tony Blair looking on. The two firms agreed to combine their oil assets with fifty-fifty ownership of the new firm. BP had asked for 51 percent, but TNK would not agree. At the time, Putin warned Browne that "an equal split never works." Although the deal was profitable for BP, it indeed proved very difficult to run the joint company with the Russian partners, and battles erupted over governance and over exactly what fifty-fifty control meant.[48] Eventually, Robert Dudley, then head of TNK-BP and subsequently chief executive of BP, left Russia under pressure, and the initial arrangement fell apart. BP and its partners then crafted a new agreement. Rosneft bought the company in 2013, and BP was given a 19.5 percent stake in the new company.[49]

Given the strained political relationship between Moscow and London, Russian officials welcomed the British vote to leave the European Union in June 2016. It weakened the EU and divided Britain. Prime Minister David Cameron accused Putin personally of backing the no vote: "It is worth asking the question: who would be happy if we left? Putin might be happy. I suspect [ISIS leader] al-Baghdadi would be happy." To which Putin replied: "This is nothing more than a demonstration of the low level of political culture."[50] Brexit was viewed positively in Russia for several reasons. The UK leaving the EU could lead to other countries following suit in the longer run. Moreover, there was the hope that a Britain weakened by leaving the EU might be more amenable to improving economic and political ties with Russia. On the other hand, there was also an acknowledgment that the European and global economic fallout from Brexit could adversely affect the Russian economy. Theresa May, who succeeded Cameron as prime minister, and her foreign minister, Boris Johnson, had initially committed themselves to improving ties with Putin's Russia.

And then came the poisonings in the medieval cathedral city of Salisbury in southern England. Sergei Skripal is a former GRU double agent who had spied for the British, was arrested in Russia in 2004, and then became part of the 2010 spy exchange involving ten sleeper agents in the United States. Normally, when spies are exchanged, the countries involved in the swap agree to leave the former agents alone. But a few days before the 2018 Russian presidential election, Skripal and his daughter—who was visiting him from Moscow—were found slumped over on a park bench. It subsequently emerged that they had been poisoned with the military-grade highly toxic nerve agent Novichok, which was developed in the Soviet Union. The Skripals survived, as did the policeman who discovered them and was also contaminated. The British government accused the Russian state of poisoning the Skripals. "It is clear that Russia is, I am afraid, in many respects now a malign and disruptive force," said Foreign Minister Boris Johnson. Adding that Russia was launching cyberattacks against British infrastructure, he concluded, "I increasingly think that we have to categorize [these] as acts of war."[51] Britain expelled twenty-three Russian diplomatic personnel, and the United States followed suit, as did most EU countries. Whatever message was sent to future double agents by this poisoning failed to take into account its cost to Russia through new rounds of sanctions.

Russia vigorously denied that it had anything to do with the poisonings. State-run media outlets came up with a series of increasingly more fanciful alternative explanations at a frenzied pace. But they all stressed one theme: the UK and their allies—especially the United States—poisoned the Skripals to make Russia look bad and to disrupt the presidential election and discourage people from attending the World Cup in Russia.[52] The Organisation for the Prohibition of Chemical Weapons sent inspectors to analyze the nerve agent, and they confirmed that it was Novichok but were unable to pinpoint in which laboratory it had been produced. The Russian media's response—echoed by skeptical Western journalists—was to challenge the premise that the nerve agent had come from Russia. Then there was the question of motivation and timing, about which there was considerable speculation. The consensus among those who saw a Russian hand in the assassination attempt was that Moscow was sending the same message that it had with the Litvinenko poisoning: traitors are never safe, wherever they are. And from the Kremlin's point of view, there were many more of them in the West.

But that was not the last Novichok poisoning. Halfway through the World Cup games, two British citizens from Amesbury, eight miles from Salisbury, collapsed from poisoning with a more concentrated dose of Novichok. One of them died. The British defense secretary was clear about who was responsible. "The simple reality," he said, "is that Russia has committed an attack on British soil which has seen the death of a British citizen."[53] Apparently whoever poisoned the Skripals had not disposed properly of the vial containing the poison, and the victim believed that she was in possession of a bottle of perfume plucked from a trash can.[54] The UK subsequently identified the two GRU agents who, using false names, had entered Britain and carried out the poisonings, releasing detailed film footage of their movements.[55] Needless to say, Putin claimed that the men were "civilians" and in a subsequent interview on RT they claimed that they had just wanted to see Salisbury Cathedral.[56]

Russian-British relations are unlikely to recover from the Skripal poisonings for some time as the UK reappraises its relationship with Putin's Russia.

Europe à la Carte

Germany, France, and the UK are Russia's most important European interlocutors, but Putin has cultivated ties with a variety of European leaders since he came to power. Probably one of his favorite leaders was Italy's Silvio Berlusconi, with whom he enjoyed a close personal relationship. Indeed, when Berlusconi was forced to resign after a series of financial and sexual scandals, Putin praised him and publicly regretted that he had to leave office.[57] He also developed good ties with former Italian prime minister Matteo Renzi, who was the only European leader to appear on a platform with Putin at the 2016 Saint Petersburg International Economic

Forum, saying, "We need Europe and Russia to become wonderful neighbors again."[58] Renzi also called for sanctions to be lifted, as did his populist successor Giuseppe Conte, who has praised Putin and called for closer ties. Similar sentiments have come from Greek prime minister Alexis Tsipras. Putin has courted Greece since its difficult relations with Brussels and Berlin over its economic bailout began, highlighting the two countries' common Orthodox heritage. Add to this the newly improved ties with Hungary, Slovakia, and other Central European countries, and the outlook for the Kremlin looks quite promising. In a Europe sharply divided over how to respond to the migrant crisis, economic problems, and the specter of terrorism, the possibilities for increasing Russian influence are certainly there. But Russia's ability to benefit from the shifting European landscape is limited by its own economic difficulties. Until 2008, Russia's role as an energy superpower gave it considerable leverage over the EU. How real is that today?

The Energy Card

In 2006, when Vladimir Putin was asked whether Russia was an energy superpower, he replied: "I have never referred to Russia as an energy superpower. But we do have greater possibilities than almost any country in the world. This is an obvious fact. Everyone should understand that, above all, these are our national resources, and should not start looking at them as their own."[59]

For the first eight years of Putin's time in the Kremlin, as oil prices rose from $12 a barrel to $147, Russia did indeed act as an energy superpower in Europe, using its gas and (to a lesser extent) oil supplies both to fill its state coffers and to solidify its influence in Europe. Russia is the most important external supplier of energy to the EU, and the energy trade has created strong interdependencies between Russia and Europe. Of Europe's imported gas, 37 percent comes from Russia, but some countries receive nearly all their gas from Russia. Finland, Slovakia, Bulgaria, Estonia, and Latvia import 100 percent of their gas from Russia. Lithuania has built its own liquefied natural gas (LNG) terminal to reduce its dependence on Russia and now imports only half of its gas from Russia. Germany imports 40 percent of its gas from Russia; Italy, 20 percent; and France, 18 percent. Ironically, Russian gas exports to Europe were a key element promoting détente with Western Europe during the Cold War. In fact, during the Cold War, the USSR was a reliable supplier of gas to Western Europe, and the fluctuations in supply that occurred were attributed to climate conditions. Moscow did sometimes manipulate oil and gas supplies to pressure its "fraternal" Eastern European allies, but it scrupulously adhered to its agreements with Western Europe.

In 1970, the USSR and the Federal Republic of Germany signed their first natural gas contract promoting their bilateral détente and the Ostpolitik of Chancellor Willy Brandt.[60] Gas exports to other Western European countries quickly followed. The United States was originally concerned that if its allies became dependent on Soviet gas, Moscow might use gas supplies for political purposes, and it warned its allies not to go ahead with the contracts. Indeed, in 1982, the Reagan administration tried unsuccessfully to stop the construction of the Yamal gas pipeline by imposing sanctions on its allies who were exporting pipeline components to the USSR. British prime minister Margaret Thatcher, normally a great supporter of Ronald Reagan, was so incensed by this move that she personally traveled to the shipyards in Scotland from which the firm John Brown and Company was exporting pipeline components. Compliance with the sanctions would have cost many British jobs.[61]

After the Soviet collapse, and with questions about the reliability of Middle Eastern energy supplies and the stability of that region, it appeared that Russia was a promising alternative. It has the world's largest oil and gas reserves and was eager to increase sales to Europe to boost its earnings. But by 2006 there were growing concerns about the reliability of Russian gas exports. At that point 80 percent of the exports to Europe went through Ukraine, and Ukraine paid heavily subsidized prices for gas. But a year earlier Russia and Ukraine had been unable to agree on the price for gas—Ukraine sought a bigger discount—and negotiations dragged on for months. Eventually, Gazprom, the Russian gas behemoth, announced that it was cutting off the gas to Ukraine on a bitterly cold New Year's Eve. Although it warned Ukraine not to siphon off gas that should have gone to Europe, Ukraine did precisely that. As a result, Austria, Germany, Slovakia, and Germany faced a shortfall of 33 percent of their gas supplies, and other countries were also adversely affected. The EU energy commissioner responded by calling for "a clear and more collective policy on the security of our energy supply." The Austrians called explicitly for reducing dependence on Russia. To which the CEO of Gazprom responded, "Get over your fear of Russia or run out of gas."[62] Gazprom, although not technically a state-owned company, has very close links to the Kremlin. The question in 2006 was whether it was really Gazprom or the Kremlin that cut off the gas, since Putin had plenty of reasons to punish the Ukrainians after the Orange Revolution, which had ousted the Kremlin's preferred presidential candidate Viktor Yanukovych. It was probably a mixture of commercial and political reasons, but it left the Europeans wary of possible future threats to their energy security from Russia.

As a result of these concerns, the EU has taken steps to improve its energy security and better coordinate the individual members' energy relations with Russia. But external factors have also combined to lessen Europe's energy dependence on Russia. The financial crisis of 2008 reduced gas demand in Europe. At the same time, the United States' success in developing shale oil and gas freed up LNG exports for Europe. LNG from other exporters, such as Qatar, also became available. Europe focused on developing its own alternatives to Russian gas as well. Then came the annexation of Crimea, the outbreak of the war in the Donbas, and Western sanctions. As the conflicts and sanctions unfolded that year, there was a growing concern in Brussels about how the sanctions would affect security of supply. The EU published its European Energy Security

Strategy in May 2014, designed to diversify suppliers and moderate energy demand. Russia responded by trying to diversify its own energy markets, particularly to China.[63]

Despite EU concerns, the reality is that Europe will be a major consumer of Russian gas for the foreseeable future. The Dutch Groningen field, which has been the backbone of European gas supplies, is being progressively shut down. The interconnection of the Russian and European gas pipeline systems provides flexibility. Geographical proximity and the interest of European energy companies in doing business with Russia will guarantee continued Russian gas imports. But Europe is also wary of becoming too dependent on Russia and is determined to find alternative supplies. Europe is now equipped with a large number of LNG-receiving terminals. But they are underutilized. For now, at least, Russian gas will be far more economical than, say, imports of US LNG.

Beginning with the détente era, there was an assumption that economic and energy interdependence with Russia would promote better political relations. But the past quarter century since the Soviet collapse has shown that Russia is quite capable of decoupling its economic from its political relations. After all, it annexed Crimea and launched a war in the Donbas fully realizing that this might jeopardize its economic ties to Europe. Russia continues to pursue energy deals—particularly the Nord Stream II pipeline—at the same time as it confronts the EU politically.[64] The fall in oil prices in 2013 and 2014 reduced Russia's energy leverage in Europe, but rising oil prices in 2018 have restored some of that leverage. The energy superpower may have been weakened. But Russia remains a key energy player in Europe.

Putin's European Future

Putin's first foreign visit after his inauguration in May 2018 was to Vienna to celebrate fifty years since Austria first agreed to import Soviet gas.[65] In contrast to his tense relations with other European leaders, he received an impressive welcome, complete with full military honors. Austria's thirty-two-year-old conservative chancellor Sebastian Kurz, in coalition with the Far Right Freedom Party, greeted a beaming Putin with warmth. Kurz had declined to expel any Russian diplomats after the Skripal poisonings and called for the EU to begin to lift the post-Ukraine sanctions. He said he was eager to resume Austria's Cold War–era role as a bridge between East and West. And in a move that drew a great deal of attention, Putin attended the Austrian Foreign Minister's wedding, waltzing with her around the estate in which the nuptials took place.

After his talks with Putin, Kurz spoke in deferential terms that no other European leader had used since 2014: "Today we had the opportunity to talk about international issues, that Russia as a superpower has a great significance in Syria and eastern Ukraine, and that Russia has a great responsibility. We hope Russia will contribute to people finally seeing what they are longing for: peace."[66]

In view of Russia's deteriorating relations with the West and Europe's increasing brittleness, the Kremlin is likely to continue to focus on its bilateral ties with those countries it considers key to its own interests, while seeking to have EU sanctions removed and pursuing new energy deals like Nord Stream II and TurkStream, both of which would reduce Ukraine's role as an energy transit country. Criticism of Europe's policies toward Russia will not diminish attempts to conclude new energy deals with it.

Vladimir Putin began his tenure in office as the most "European" of recent Russian leaders. But he has become increasingly wary of Europe and more enamored of the idea of Russia's Eurasian destiny. He has answered the question of where Russia belongs by stressing Russia's exceptionalism, its unique civilization and embodiment of conservative values. Russia's place in Gorbachev's vision of a common European home is today that of an ambivalent neighbor who keeps his distance from those who live next door. The Kremlin will continue to watch as the European Union deals with its internal political and economic battles and with Brexit, hoping that the European project ultimately fails and that there will be a return to a Europe where individual countries seek their own separate deals with Russia. As the idea of Europe is increasingly questioned in a Russia that rejects the EU concept of a community of values, Russia will move further away from its European roots. In no European country are Russia's ties more complicated and important than with Germany.

—4—

RUSSIA AND GERMANY

The Fateful Relationship

Russia has always had special sentiments for Germany, and regarded your country as one of the major centers of European and world culture (-) Between Russia and America lie oceans,- while between Russia and Germany lies a great history (-) Today's Germany is Russia's leading economic partner, our most important creditor one of the principal investors and a key interlocutor in discussing international politics.

—Vladimir Putin at the Reichstag, 2001[1]

If Russia continues its course of the last weeks, this would not just be a catastrophe for Ukraine. We would then sense that—as a threat. This would then change not only the relationship of the EU as a whole with Russia—I cannot say it often enough or with enough emphasis—the clock cannot be turned back. Conflicts of interest in the middle of Europe in the 21st century can only be successfully overcome when we do not resort to the example of the 19th or 20th centuries. They can only be overcome when we act with the principles and means of our time, the 21st century.

—Angela Merkel, 2014[2]

On a wintry January day in 2001, Vladimir Putin, German chancellor Gerhard Schroeder, and their wives climbed into a red troika, the traditional Russian sled, driven by a man in elegant livery and pulled by three horses wearing bells that jingled as they rode through the snow. They toured the sixteenth-century royal Kolomenskoye estate in Moscow with its red wooden houses and onion-domed churches. Without hats or fur coats, they bundled up in blankets, obviously enjoying the ride. They admired a portrait of Peter the Great in the estate house.[3] The Schroeders had arrived in Russia to celebrate Russian Orthodox Christmas with the Putins, and together they visited the fourteenth-century Sergiev Posad monastery, which is regarded as the spiritual center of Russian Orthodoxy, and were greeted by women in traditional folk dresses and a choir chanting solemn Russian liturgy. There they met with Patriarch Alexy II, the head of the Russian Orthodox Church.[4] The sleigh ride not only captured the spirit of Christmas but also carried the spirit of the new relationship between Russia and Germany.

Putin was new on the job. He had been in power for barely a year. Schroeder had come into office in 1998 vowing to eschew the "sauna diplomacy" of his political opponent Helmut Kohl. In his opinion, Kohl had developed too cozy a relationship with the erratic Russian president Boris Yeltsin—including sharing a sauna with him—and Schroeder vowed to take a more critical stance toward Russia.[5] But things were moving in a decidedly different direction. For Schroeder was fast developing a close relationship with the new German-speaking young Russian president. Three years later, he and his then wife adopted a Russian child from a Saint Petersburg orphanage, and later another one from the same place.

German-Russian business ties flourished, and the two countries agreed to build the Nord Stream gas pipeline, which would carry Russian gas directly to Germany under the Baltic Sea, bypassing Ukraine, through which 80 percent of Gazprom's exports to Europe had flowed until then. Shortly before his defeat in the 2005 election by Angela Merkel, Schroeder had proposed extending a government-backed $1.1 billion loan to finance the pipeline. Soon after he left office, Schroeder would be named chairman of the shareholders' committee of the Nord Stream pipeline, making him a business partner of Russian magnates close to Putin.[6] Nord Stream's managing director is Matthias Warnig, a former East German intelligence official and a close associate of Putin.[7] Schroeder's appointment created considerable controversy, but it also symbolized how close political and business ties between the two countries had grown since Putin entered the

Kremlin.[8] In 2004, when asked whether Putin was a *Lupenreiner Demokrat* (crystal-clear democrat), Schroeder said, "Yes, he is."[9] At Putin's inauguration for his fourth term in May 2018, Schroeder stood in the front row, next to Prime Minister Medvedev and Patriarch Kirill, and was one of the first VIP guests to shake Putin's hand and congratulate him.

Fast-forward to the 2014 G-20 summit in Brisbane, Australia, seven months after Russia's annexation of Crimea and subsequent launch of a war in Southeastern Ukraine, and after Russia's expulsion from the G-8. Chancellor Angela Merkel, the pastor's daughter from East Germany who speaks fluent Russian and had been instrumental in leading the EU's imposition of sanctions on Russia, met a tense Putin for a one-on-one meeting. It dragged on into the early morning hours. They failed to agree on how to resolve the Ukraine crisis and talked past each other. The next day, none of the G-20 leaders would sit with Putin at lunch. Resenting the isolation, he abruptly left the summit early, but not before exchanging sharp words with the Australian prime minister and accusing the Europeans of "switching their brains off" when they imposed sanctions. He also said he needed to get some sleep.[10]

After the summit ended, Merkel gave an unusually blunt speech in Sydney, eschewing her normally cautious style. Putin, she said, had apparently lied to her about Russia's intentions in Crimea just before Russian troops moved in there.[11] Warning that there were forces in Europe "which refuse to accept the concept of mutual respect," she accused Russia of flouting international law:

> Russia is violating the territorial integrity and the sovereignty of Ukraine. It regards one of its neighbors, Ukraine, as part of a sphere of influence. After the horrors of two world wars and the end of the Cold War, this calls the entire European peaceful order into question.[12]

The close Germany-Russia partnership that had been the cornerstone of post–Cold War Europe was shattered. Sanctions disrupted the economic relationship, and political ties dramatically deteriorated. Merkel felt that whatever trust had existed between her and Putin had been eroded by his prevarication and repeated failure to carry through on promises he made.

Since the Crimean annexation, Germany has divided into two camps on Russia. Major segments of the German population no longer trust Russia and criticize both its policies in Ukraine and its domestic clampdown on freedoms. Public opinion data show that 64 percent of Germans believe that Putin is not a credible partner, and the same percentage believe that relations with Russia are "rather bad." However, 33 percent favor closer cooperation with Russia.[13] The latter are the *Putin-Versteher.* The verb *verstehen* in German means literally "to understand" but more specifically "to have understanding for." Thus, the *Putin-Versteher* interpret Russia's arguments and actions from the Kremlin's point of view, often blaming the West for the Ukraine crisis because it threatened Moscow's vital interests by carelessly offering Kyiv an EU Association Agreement. The story of how German-Russian relations deteriorated from the Schroeder-Putin sleigh ride to the Merkel-Putin standoff epitomizes Russia's gradual estrangement from Europe under Putin. Yet this remains a complex and close relationship. Putin has the distinction of being the first Russian leader who has lived and worked in Germany, and his experiences there had a profound influence on how he views the world.

Vladimir Putin: *Der Deutsche im Kreml* (The German in the Kremlin)

Putin was dubbed "the German in the Kremlin" by Alexander Rahr, one of his early, admiring biographers.[14] Indeed, the German language was in many ways Putin's ticket out of poverty and into the KGB. He had a hardscrabble childhood growing up in a postwar Leningrad *kommunalka* (communal apartment) with parents who had lost two sons, one of whom died in the nine-hundred-day Nazi siege of the city, during which one million civilians perished. An indifferent student who often got into brawls and into trouble, he eventually began to concentrate on his studies, focusing on German. His first German teacher, Vera Gurevich, was interviewed for the official biography that came out as he ascended to the presidency in 2000, and she praised his language skills and hard work: "He had a very good memory, a quick mind."[15]

Once he joined the Leningrad KGB after graduating with a law degree from Leningrad State University, he continued his German studies in preparation for being sent to Germany. But to which Germany? Putin claims that in order to go to West Germany, he would have had to spend another couple of years in the USSR for extra training, so he opted for East Germany, which did not require more training, because he wanted to leave "right away."[16] So the thirty-three-year-old KGB agent set out for Dresden, which at that time was considered a provincial backwater in the GDR, although its party chief, Hans Modrow, was a leading reform-minded politician. A more prestigious posting would have been in the capital, East Berlin. But Putin apparently relished being in East Germany, which compared to the Soviet Union was a consumer paradise. His two-and-a-half-room apartment in a drab building on the Angelikastrasse was a decided improvement on his childhood *kommunalka,* and he was able to buy a car. Putin's former wife, Ludmilla, later recalled that life in the GDR was very different from life in the USSR. "The streets were clean. They would wash their windows once a week."[17]

What did Vladimir Putin do in Dresden during his five-year stay? There is no agreement on this question, largely because information about his years there is very scant. Putin's own account of what he did is minimalist. He says he was engaged in "the usual" textbook political intelligence activities: "recruiting sources of information, analyzing it, and sending it to Moscow—recruitment of sources, procurement of information, and assessment and analysis were big parts of the job. It was very routine work."[18] He was a senior case officer. In 2001, he elaborated on his training by saying that the key attributes of a good case officer are the ability to work with people and with large amounts of information.[19] Putin has downplayed the extent of his activities in the GDR. Soviet and

East German senior intelligence officials have confirmed that he was not on their radar screens, as have Western intelligence officials.[20]

Others have suggested that Putin's KGB activities in the GDR may have been more extensive. Rahr claims that a "thick fog of silence" surrounds Putin's Dresden years, and anyway it would not be in the interest of the German government to reveal what it knows.[21] Some have claimed that Putin was part of Operation Luch ("ray," or "beam"). This was a KGB project to steal Western technological secrets. Others argue that Luch involved recruiting top party and Stasi officials in the GDR with the aim of using them to replace the anti-reform die-hard Honecker regime.[22] Indeed, Luch became the subject of an investigation by the German authorities after Putin came to power because they were concerned he might have recruited a network in East Germany that survived the fall of the wall.[23] Apparently he did begin to recruit people, only to have them exposed after the Stasi (secret police) files were opened following unification.[24]

Whatever the extent of his activities in the GDR, Putin may have seen Dresden as the first stepping-stone in an international career. But his time there ended very differently than he had expected. On November 9, 1989, the Berlin Wall fell, largely because, in the face of mass, peaceful street protests, Gorbachev made a principled decision not to use force to keep in power unpopular communist governments and because the East German police state had run out of steam.[25] When an angry mob showed up at the Dresden Stasi headquarters—where the KGB was co-located in December 1989—demanding access to its voluminous files, Putin had to defend the building and burn the documents, "saving the lives of the people whose files were lying on my desk."[26] Indeed, the furnace exploded because it could not burn all the files fast enough.[27] In his autobiography, Putin complains bitterly that there were no instructions from Moscow. "Moscow was silent.... Nobody lifted a finger to protect us" from the crowd outside. At this moment, he feared for his own safety.[28]

One month later, a dejected Putin left Dresden. As a parting gift, his German friends gave his family a twenty-year-old washing machine, with which they drove back to Leningrad. The GDR would disappear nine months later, and the USSR would follow suit two years later. Putin's 2000 epitaph on German unification was critical but unsentimental: "Actually, I thought the whole thing was inevitable. To be honest, I only regretted that the Soviet Union had lost its position in Europe, although intellectually I understood that a position built on walls and dividers cannot last. But I wanted something different to rise in its place. And nothing different was proposed," he concluded. "They just dropped everything and went away."[29]

Putin emerged from five years in the GDR not only with a deep understanding of East German society but also with a foundation that would prove important to him in his post-Soviet career. One East German who later became an important member of his inner circle was Matthias Warnig. After the fall of the wall, Warnig became head of the Dresdner Bank office in Saint Petersburg in 1991, and by 2002 he ran all their operations in Russia.[30] He subsequently became the managing director of Nord Stream.

The five years in Dresden influenced Putin in other ways. He lived through the sudden collapse of a rigid, repressive system that was unable to deal with dissent. The experience of fending off the mob at the Stasi headquarters apparently gave him a lifelong aversion to dealing with hostile crowds. It also reinforced for him the need for control, particularly over opposition groups. Nothing like that should ever happen again, especially in Russia. He left the GDR humiliated by Moscow's unwillingness and inability to support him during his most difficult hour, and not knowing what would await him when he returned to the USSR, which had dramatically changed during his five years abroad.

Angela Merkel and Russia

Angela Merkel's experience growing up in the GDR has given her a complex view of Russia. According to her Stasi file, to which she had access after unification, "Although Angela tends to see the leading role of the Soviet Union as something of a dictatorship to which all socialist countries are subordinated, she is enthusiastic about the Russian language and the culture of the Soviet Union."[31] This description would be equally true today. Just as Putin knows more about Germany than any of his predecessors, Merkel knows more about Russia than any previous chancellor. In her office hangs a silver-framed portrait of Princess Sophie von Anhalt-Zerbst—better known by her Russian name of Catherine the Great. Merkel admires Catherine as a strong ruler and a reformer.

Merkel was born in Hamburg, the daughter of a pastor, but the family moved to East Berlin shortly after her birth. There is some debate about why her father chose to go to East Germany to minister to East German Lutherans, whose activities were closely watched by the Stasi. It could have been ideological or a shrewd career move. Relatively little is known about her early life and about the extent to which her father worked with the East German authorities. She has said, "I never felt that the GDR was my natural home."[32] She excelled at mathematics and Russian in high school, initially placing third in the Russian language Olympiad for all GDR students and winning a trip to the USSR. Two years later she placed first in the Olympiad. Merkel often speaks Russian with Putin and understands Russia partly through the lens of its rich culture. She has a deeper understanding of Russia than most of her European counterparts.

But Merkel's attitude toward Russia has also been shaped by her experiences in the GDR, beginning with the construction of the Berlin Wall in 1961 and the pain it imposed on so many divided families. The repression she experienced firsthand and the pervasiveness of Stasi informers instilled in her a strong commitment to human rights and personal freedoms. She is also undoubtedly more attuned to the modus operandi of former communist intelligence officials than many other Western leaders, having lived in a police state for the first part of her life. A chemist by training, she entered politics in the last days of the GDR in 1989. Merkel and Putin are more familiar with each other's background and culture than is the case for many other world leaders. They understand each other in a unique way. They epitomize the centuries-old symbiotic relationship between Russia and Germany.

Partners and Rivals—the Historical Legacy

The interaction between Russia and Germany has been one of the defining—and sometimes fateful—influences on the security and prosperity of Europe. In the twentieth century, Germany played a major role in the birth and death of the Soviet Union. After imperial Germany's defeat in World War One and the Bolshevik Revolution, both "new" countries decided to forge a new relationship. The 1922 Treaty of Rapallo established diplomatic relations between Weimar Germany and Bolshevik Russia and was signed when both countries were outcasts in the international system. It was the midwife to the infant Soviet state's birth as a European power and to its entry into the world of international diplomacy. At the end of World War Two, Germany was divided and Stalin helped himself liberally to economic reparations from the German Democratic Republic in order to help rebuild the Soviet Union's shattered economy. Forty years later, in 1990, German unification was the final act in the decline and fall of the Soviet Union's imperial project. It sounded the death knell for Soviet power in Eastern Europe and ultimately for the USSR itself. The Soviet–West German–East German triangle was the defining relationship of the European Cold War. Control over East Germany—and East Berlin—was the sine qua non of Moscow's relationship with the West. The central nightmare for Soviet leaders was a revived and militarized united Germany looking—and marching—east, as it had in 1941. Hence Germany's continuing gratitude toward Russia for having allowed unification to happen peacefully.

Historically, Germans played an important role in imperial Russia's development—much more so than Russia played in Germany's development. Russians have always admired Germany's technological and organizational prowess. Peter the Great first brought Germans to Russia to help in developing the economy. Catherine the Great was even more convinced than Peter that Russia needed Germans to modernize its economy. She created a large German immigrant colony on the Volga River with the promise of no taxation so they could help develop Russia's agricultural sector. There were also a significant number of aristocratic Germans who played an important role in the life of the imperial court. The house of Romanov often intermarried with the German nobility.

Germans also had a major impact on the development of nineteenth- and twentieth-century Russian political movements of the Right and the Left. Karl Marx inspired Russian radicals as they sought to overthrow the tsarist system. He himself was skeptical about whether imperial Russia was ready for a socialist revolution—since it had barely developed a capitalist system. But in one of history's great ironies, Bolshevik Russia was the first country to put his ideas into practice, and Lenin certainly considered himself a Marxist. On the Right, Georg Wilhelm Friedrich Hegel's philosophy influenced the rise of the Slavophile movement and Russian nationalism.

There were also less edifying meetings of minds between the Russian and German rulers. Both Kaiser Wilhelm II and Tsar Nicholas II were admirers of the notorious anti-Semitic forgery *The Protocols of the Elders of Zion,* which purported to prove there was a nefarious international Jewish conspiracy to take over the world. (The pamphlet was in fact penned by the Russian secret police.) Both rulers attributed their forced abdications to a Jewish plot. Indeed, Nicholas took a copy of the pamphlet with him into his exile in Ekaterinburg, where the Bolsheviks ultimately killed him and his family.[33]

The tangled history of German-Russian relations has left three main legacies whose echoes continue to resonate in the twenty-first century. The first is a powerful one and as relevant in the nuclear age as it was in the nineteenth century. It is the legacy of geography and resources and their impact on both countries' national identities and national interests. The lack of natural frontiers between the two countries and the compatibility of their economies—Russian raw materials in exchange for German manufacturing—inevitably produced both cooperation and confrontation. Russians have traditionally depicted Germans as a major potential threat to their security, focusing on Germany's invasion of the

USSR during the Great Patriotic War. Germans likewise focused on the Russian threat during the Cold War. The heavily fortified Fulda Gap separated the two German states during the Cold War and would have been the route through which the USSR could have invaded West Germany. On either side were heavily armed East and West German soldiers eyeing each other warily.

The second legacy is that of two kinds of cooperation between Russia and Germany. The benign partnership—often in economic, scientific, and cultural fields—has had a positive impact on Russia and Germany and on their common neighbors in Central Europe. But there is also a malign cooperation between the two countries at the expense of their neighbors and wider Europe. The 1939 Molotov-Ribbentrop Pact enabled the USSR to stay out of World War Two for two years, and its secret protocols divided territories in Poland, Romania, and the Baltic states between the two occupying countries. Soviet–East German collaboration in repressing their own populations and those in other countries reinforced a historical pattern of Russo-German cooperation to the detriment of the security and independence of the countries that lie between them.

The third legacy is of Russo-German enmity, which produced two world wars and made the divided city of Berlin the tensest outpost of the Cold War. Soviet–West German relations for the first two decades of the Cold War were largely confrontational. Then Willy Brandt became chancellor in 1969. An exile in Norway during World War Two, he came to power determined to mitigate the division of Germany by pursuing a more conciliatory policy toward the USSR. His Ostpolitik was based on the premise of "Change Through Rapprochement," believing that Moscow would modify its policies on the two Germanys if Bonn were to offer incentives.[34] He signed treaties normalizing relations with Moscow, Warsaw, Prague, and East Berlin, ushering in an era of détente that began to erode the Iron Curtain. All subsequent German leaders have been determined never to repeat the pattern of Russo-German enmity.

Although Gorbachev came to power intending to strengthen both the Soviet Union and its ties to its "fraternal" Eastern European allies, he eventually had to accept that he could no longer keep the Soviet empire intact by force. He allowed Germany to reunify without a shot being fired, and agreed that a united Germany could be a member of NATO. Germany remains grateful to him and his successors for permitting the Berlin Wall to fall, and remains committed to pursuing peaceful engagement. This gratitude is always mixed with a deep sense of historical responsibility for what the Nazis did to the Russians during a war in which twenty-six million Soviet citizens perished.

The Yeltsin Era, 1992–1999

In 1994, Berlin hosted a formal send-off to bid farewell to the last Soviet troops leaving Germany. Boris Yeltsin was the guest of honor. The ceremony began at the Soviet War Memorial in Treptower Park. But later Yeltsin went off script. To the consternation of his German hosts (and his own retinue) an obviously inebriated Yeltsin seized the baton from the conductor of the military band. He then proceeded to conduct the band himself and sing along. His German hosts were dumbfounded.[35] Later he admitted that he had drunk to ease the stress, explaining, "I snapped."[36]

It was a major challenge to arrive at this point. In 1990, Germany emerged from unification geographically larger but economically weakened by the staggering costs of unification (eventually costing $1.7 trillion) and unsure where its future lay. The USSR was still intact but ailing. In August 1991, while Gorbachev was on vacation on Crimea, a group of disgruntled hard-line Soviet officials unsuccessfully tried to oust him. He was held captive in his summer home, but the coup plotters were so inept that they failed to arrest Boris Yeltsin, then head of the Russian republic, who led the resistance to the coup. During the tense three-day coup, Germany worried whether the commitments Gorbachev had made—primarily the withdrawal of Soviet troops from Eastern Germany—would be kept. After the coup collapsed, Gorbachev returned to the Kremlin for another four months until he was ousted by Yeltsin in December 1991.

Yeltsin's ascension to the Kremlin also caused great concern in Germany because the emerging Russian state looked quite weak and unpredictable. The Germans were worried too by the prospect of an independent Ukraine, the military-industrial heartland of the USSR, which at that point was the third largest nuclear state in the world. But Chancellor Helmut Kohl, who in 1987 had said that he did not believe German unification would happen in his lifetime, was determined to develop a good relationship with the new occupant in the Kremlin and offered German assistance in rebuilding Russia.

In the aftermath of the Soviet collapse, Germany was a major source of economic support as Russia embarked on its difficult post-communist transition. Moscow realized that German gratitude for unification and concern that Russia's weakness had the potential to disrupt European security were two key sources of Russian leverage. Moreover, Germany believed that it understood Russia's situation better than other countries, drawing on its own experiences after its defeat in 1945. Unlike the United States, which initially hoped Russia's transformation from a socialist to a democratic, free-market state would happen fairly quickly, the Germans realized it would take many decades. During Yeltsin's tenure as president, Germany—despite having to deal with the daunting economic and social challenges of its own unification—was the stronger partner, supporting the Yeltsin administration politically and economically, and acting as Russia's advocate in European structures. It was an asymmetrical interdependence that Russian leaders recognized and sometimes resented. Four major bilateral issues dominated their relationship in the 1990s: troop withdrawals, ethnic Germans, economic ties, and Germany's support for Russia's domestic evolution.

In 1990, there were 546,000 Soviet troops and their dependents in the GDR. As a result of the negotiations that ended Germany's division, Russia had agreed to withdraw its troops within four years, but the process was not only a logistical challenge for both Russia and Germany but enormously confusing. To which country would these "Soviet" soldiers return? Once the USSR split into fifteen independent countries, how would these military personnel determine where they belonged (for instance, 30 percent of the officer corps was ethnically Ukrainian)? Who would provide housing for them? Withdrawing such a huge military machine held many potential pitfalls. As they withdrew from their military bases, the soldiers took with them anything that was not chained to the floor. Yet despite these challenges, all the soldiers had left by 1994. Given the obstacles, it is remarkable that the operation proceeded as smoothly as it did.[37]

The situation of ethnic Germans in post-Soviet Russia also caused consternation after 1990. Many of these descendants of settlers—brought over by Catherine the Great and deported to Kazakhstan and Siberia from the Volga region after the German invasion of the USSR in 1941—had sought to emigrate to the Federal Republic during the Soviet period. At that point they sought to leave an oppressive political system and pursue better economic opportunities in Germany. After unification, with all the economic burdens it faced, Germany tried to encourage ethnic Germans to remain in post-communist Russia but was largely unsuccessful. These people wanted to escape the chaos in Russia and no longer faced the same barriers to emigration as they had in Soviet times. Altogether, 1.2 million ethnic Germans have emigrated from the former Soviet states to Germany since unification, and ironically, many of them now form a reliably pro-Putin bloc.

Germany became Russia's most important economic partner after unification. Russia anticipated that Germany would be a major source of economic assistance, trade, and investment for its emerging market economy. The complementary character of the economic relationship continued, with Russia exporting oil, gas, and other raw materials to Germany and importing German finished goods. The German private sector remained involved in the Russian economy but was cautious about investing during the Yeltsin era, given the absence of the rule of law and the paucity of an enforceable legal structure to protect investments. Indeed, the most dynamic period of Russia-German economic ties began only after the Russian financial crash of 1998, when the economy had begun to recover. In the 1990s, Germany also contributed to and supplemented

American programs designed to help secure and dismantle Russian nuclear weapons and materials and reduce the dangers of proliferation by providing safeguards for nuclear facilities. Germany offered training to unemployed nuclear scientists in the Russian Federation so they could find alternative jobs instead of selling their skills to countries or terrorist groups seeking to acquire nuclear weapons.

While Germany supported US security programs, German policy toward Russia during this time—and since then—has differed from US policy in one major area: democracy promotion. Promoting democracy abroad often has been part of US foreign policy—albeit selectively applied—but it never has been a central element in the German foreign policy tool kit. During the Clinton administration (1993–2001), a variety of NGOs—some allied with the two main American political parties—participated actively in democracy promotion in Russia after the Soviet collapse. All the German political parties had their foundations open offices in Moscow and work with different political groups, but they eschewed overt democracy promotion and direct interference in the way groups were organized.

As one representative of a German political foundation put it, "We see the Russians as partners with whom we must work and take a long-term approach, which features continuous dialogues and bringing younger Russians to Germany."[38] Chancellor Schroeder was quite explicit about the inadvisability of overt democracy promotion: "The Russian reality of a multinational state demands different rules than Holland does." He told George W. Bush, "In Russian history (including the most recent) no real foundation for democracy has been laid." But, he added, he was convinced that Putin really wanted to democratize. So two decades later, when Putin closed down all the US NGOs actively working in democracy promotion, the German political foundations were able to remain in Russia.[39]

From 1998 to 1999, the German-Russian relationship experienced strains. The Russian economic crisis, the succession of five prime ministers in Moscow between March 1998 and August 1999, and Yeltsin's failing health and erratic behavior adversely affected ties. Moreover, other

European developments caused further strains in bilateral relations, most notably the 1999 enlargement of NATO to include Poland, Hungary, and the Czech Republic, as well as the Kosovo War—both of which Germany supported and Russia opposed. By the end of 1999, therefore, with Yeltsin on his way out, a fragile economy, and growing Russian alienation from the West, the Germany-Russia relationship appeared to be on a downward path.

The Putin-Schroeder Years, 2000–2005

In his essay "Russia at the Turn of the Millennium," published on December 30, 1999, meant to introduce him to Russians and to the world as he entered the Kremlin, Putin laid out his vision for his time in office. He acknowledged the myriad of economic, social, and political problems Russia faced—a year after the ruble collapsed—and promised to rebuild the state and make Russia a great power again. Although he acknowledged Russia's European roots, he also highlighted the exceptionalism of the Russian Idea—based on people's desire for a strong state and patriotism. Putin's definition of what that meant in 1999 is notable: "A strong state power in Russia is a democratic, law-based, workable federative state."[40]

Putin was largely unknown outside the small circle of foreigners who had met him in Saint Petersburg in the early 1990s; after spending a year looking for work when he returned from the GDR, Putin's former law professor and the mayor of the city, Anatoly Sobchak, had hired him. At the beginning of Putin's presidency, Chancellor Schroeder, like his other European counterparts, was cautious about him, with his dual biographies of KGB officer in East Germany and assistant to the reformist mayor of Saint Petersburg. Although Putin had committed himself to pursuing economic reforms and further modernization of Russia, he had also launched the Second Chechen War in 1999. Nevertheless, his initial commitment to greater economic integration with the West, to more effective governance, and to battling corruption found a sympathetic ear in most of Europe.

Early on in his tenure, Putin concentrated on cultivating ties with Germany as the first step to restoring Russia's position as a great power.

Schroeder and Putin had much in common. They both were outsiders from poor backgrounds and both had climbed their way up the political ladder with ambition and intelligence. They both had studied law, developed a healthy skepticism about those in power, and appreciated the good life and wealth—having been deprived of it when they were young.[41]

The German government soon responded to Russian overtures, and the relationship recovered from the difficulties of 1999. Both sides spoke of their "strategic partnership," designed to integrate Russia into Europe and strengthen the rule of law. Indeed, Germany put a great deal of effort into crafting structures that would encourage Russia's integration. These ranged from official bilateral commissions to encouragement of the private sector to enter Russia. But Berlin also focused on creating a group of civil society stakeholders. Putin and Schroeder founded the Petersburg Dialogue, whose regular meetings aimed to bring together a wide range of Germans and Russians from politics, the private sector, and academia. Although Schroeder had criticized Kohl for the over-personalized nature of the Germany-Russia relationship during Yeltsin's tenure, he now admitted that "without President Putin little gets done in Russia."[42]

The terrorist attacks on the World Trade Center in New York on September 11, 2001, gave an additional impetus to German-Russian relations. Putin's support for the United States reflected what appeared to be a strategic choice in siding firmly with the West against international terrorism. Shortly after the attacks, he traveled to Germany and made a historic speech in the newly restored glass-domed Berlin Reichstag, which is full of historical symbolism—including the graffiti on the walls left by triumphant Soviet soldiers as they completed their conquest of Berlin in 1945. Speaking in German, he regretted that he had not warned the West more directly about the possibility of such a catastrophic attack, made a direct connection between Al-Qaeda and Chechen separatists, and pledged support in the international fight against terrorism.

The Schroeder government reciprocated this view. Germany developed a strong stake in its bilateral economic and political relationship with Russia and viewed itself as Russia's major advocate within the European Union. Schroeder believed that Putin was a modernizer who deserved personal support. The initial US-Russia rapprochement had soured by the end of 2002, as Putin came to believe that the Bush administration had not given Russia what it deserved after it supported the US in its war in Afghanistan. As the White House moved closer to attacking Iraq, Putin turned to Schroeder, both leaders wary of US military plans. Russian and German criticism of US plans eventually crystallized into a joint front (with France) against the war. Reacting to the anti-war troika, a US official complained that "Chirac and Schroeder turned against us and they recruited Putin."[43] This "coalition of the unwilling" did not develop into the alliance Putin might have wished for, but it ensured that Russia was not isolated in its opposition to the war.

Thereafter, until the end of Schroeder's tenure in office, the bilateral relationship flourished. Roughly 200,000 Russians had come to live and work in Germany since 1992, moving between the two countries and building a network of personal and business ties. Venues for civil society interaction grew, as did the number of stakeholders in the relationship. Despite criticism in the German media of Putin's moves toward a more centralized and less competitive political system and his muzzling of independent broadcast media, the chancellor continued to defend him.

Both Mikhail Gorbachev and Boris Yeltsin had the misfortune to be in power when oil prices were very low. This exacerbated Russia's economic problems. Putin, however, was more fortunate. Oil prices rose steadily from 2000 to 2008, the Russian economy grew at a robust 7 percent per year, and Russian-German economic relations flourished. Energy became a key factor in the Russia-Germany relationship. The most significant aspect of Putin's first two terms as president was the rise of Russia as an energy superpower.

During Schroeder's tenure, Germany imported about 36 percent of its natural gas supplies through pipelines from Russia, although the figure was proportionately much higher in some parts of the country, especially

Bavaria. After the 2004 Orange Revolution, when relations between Moscow and Kyiv were tense, Gazprom intensified its discussions with German companies about building a pipeline under the Baltic Sea to bypass Ukraine. The Nord Stream deal was signed in 2005, and the pipeline opened in 2011. From Gazprom's point of view, it would solidify and possibly increase European—and especially German—reliance on Russian gas at a time of high energy prices as well as bypass Ukraine. It is the most visible—and controversial—legacy of the close ties between Schroeder and Putin. Today, in addition to his role in Nord Stream, Schroeder is the chairman of the board of Rosneft, Russia's largest oil company, run by Igor Sechin, rumored to be one of the most powerful men in Russia.

Merkel and Putin

At one of Angela Merkel's early meetings with Putin, she came to understand with whom she was dealing. On a visit to Sochi in 2007 to discuss energy issues, she was sitting with him in his elegantly furnished residence overlooking the Black Sea. Suddenly his black Labrador Koni bounded into the room and jumped up on her. Merkel had previously been bitten by a dog and was known to fear dogs, a fact that surely had not been lost on her ex-KGB host. As she looked on uncomfortably, Putin smiled. Merkel was furious. She later commented to the press on this incident: "I understood why he has to do this to prove he is a man. He's afraid of his own weakness. Russia has nothing, no successful politics or economy. All they have is this."[44]

Angela Merkel became Germany's first woman chancellor in 2005. But she had won a narrow victory over Gerhard Schroeder and went into coalition with his Social Democratic Party (SPD), choosing Frank-Walther Steinmeier as her foreign minister. Her initial instinct was to toughen German policy toward Russia and move away from the Schroeder-Putin "bromance," but she also understood the realities of Germany's international situation. Germany relies heavily on exports—with a population of eighty million, its exports rank third in the world after the United States and China. As a geo-economic power, where trade is seen as a vital aspect of national security, Germany traditionally has defined its interests largely in terms of commercial realpolitik, viewing the pursuit of its economic interests as the ultimate test of the success of its foreign policy.[45] Shortly after assuming office, Merkel met with representatives of German industry, who made it clear they expected her to continue to pursue close ties with Russia and support their business interests there.

Indeed, the new German government sought to further improve ties with Russia. During Merkel's first term in office, Steinmeier was determined to continue the SPD's policy of engagement with Russia and to create programs that would integrate Russia more closely into Europe. His ministry proposed a new policy of *Annaeherung durch Verflechtung* (Rapprochement Through Integration), an updated version of Willy Brandt's original formulation of Change Through Rapprochement some four decades earlier. The premise was still that Russia would eventually change for the better if Germany engaged in a constant dialogue with it and took its interests seriously.

Germany encouraged Russia's fuller participation in the G-8, postponing its own chairmanship by a year to give Russia the chair in 2006. Putin appreciated the gesture. The G-8 summit in Saint Petersburg that year was a major milestone for Russia, demonstrating that it had recovered from the economic collapse and political weakness of the 1990s and was once again a player. Moreover, Putin relished the attention being paid to his home city.

The Medvedev Interlude

Given Merkel's complicated relationship with Putin, she, like many other Western leaders, welcomed the election of forty-two-year-old Dmitry Medvedev, Putin's chosen successor, as president in 2008. Putin appointed himself prime minister, and no one was sure how the arrangement might work. Merkel hoped that a younger post-Soviet leader not connected to the intelligence services might eventually liberalize domestically and pursue a less assertive foreign policy. She wanted to believe his rhetorical commitment to modernizing Russia and hoped he would be able to break free of Putin's control. Although Medvedev, unlike Putin, had no German background, he too singled out Germany as a key partner for Russia. But Merkel was astute enough to hedge her bets. Unlike the Obama administration, which focused solely on Medvedev as its interlocutor as it pursued its reset policy, the German government maintained contacts with Putin while he was prime minister from 2008 to 2012.

Medvedev's first trip to a Western country was to Germany, in May 2008. He used the occasion both to court German business and to make a speech in Berlin proposing a new security architecture, based on a legally binding treaty covering "the whole Euro-Atlantic area from Vancouver to Vladivostok," adding that "Atlanticism as a sole historical principle has already had its day."[46] Arguing that the West had reneged on its promise to include Russia in a post–Cold War European security structure, he made a case that resonated across much of the German political class. Russia looked to Germany to play a leading role in the design of this new architecture. It is unclear how serious this proposal was. It was short on specifics but represented Medvedev's attempt to answer the question of where Russia belonged. Despite the German government's attempts to promote this plan, it withered away because of lack of support from other countries and the vagueness of the proposal itself. Later, some Germans would question whether his was a missed opportunity to bind Russia to Euro-Atlantic structures.

The 2009 German elections had produced a new coalition government. Guido Westerwelle from the Free Democratic Party became foreign minister but largely continued his predecessor's policy. Germany was the prime mover behind the EU's 2010 Partnership for Modernization plan with Russia, a technical program aimed at promoting rule-of-law and modern governance, fighting corruption, and encouraging a more diverse economy—policies Medvedev himself repeatedly promoted.[47] Merkel also met with Medvedev to seek a solution to the conflict in Transnistria.[48] There was a flurry of activity from Berlin to encourage Russia to modernize its economy and pursue more cooperative ties with the West, mirroring the Obama administration's reset effort. In the end, however, Medvedev was unable to implement most of his ambitious plans, stymied by the officials and magnates around Putin whose vested interests would have been threatened by real reforms. By the time Putin announced his return to the Kremlin, triggering mass protests a few months later at election time, German hopes for a better relationship with Russia had faded. Indeed, when Putin announced in September 2011 that he and Medvedev had agreed from the beginning that they would switch jobs in 2012, she felt duped by this "castling" move.[49]

Putin, Merkel, and Frostpolitik

Russia's annexation of Crimea and launch of a war in Southeastern Ukraine had a major impact on its relations with all of its Western partners, but the rift with Germany was greater and more unanticipated in both Moscow and Berlin than with any other country. From 1992 to 2014, German policy toward Russia had been premised on a series of fundamental principles. Involvement with Russia was essential, however challenging the process was. Russia was viewed as a large, important, but difficult neighbor with whom Germany—and indeed all of Europe—was fated to engage. Moreover, Germany's gratitude toward Russia for facilitating the peaceful unification of the country meant that Berlin had a unique role and responsibility in Europe in assisting Moscow in its difficult post-communist transition. It was assumed that Russia wanted to be integrated into the West, that closer economic ties would promote a better investment climate, and that Russia and Germany shared similar views about European security. But the fivefold increase in German exports to Russia between 2000 and 2011 had promoted neither the rule of law nor a better investment climate. And Russia's aggression against Ukraine threatened to tear down the peaceful post-unification European edifice Merkel had worked so hard to construct and maintain. "Putin surprised everyone," said one of her senior aides. "The swiftness, the brutality, the coldheartedness. It's just so twentieth century—the tanks, the propaganda, the agents provocateurs."[50] Ostpolitik had become Frostpolitik.[51]

Within the span of six weeks in 2014, the post–Cold War peaceful European order stretching back to German unification in 1990 and in which Chancellor Merkel had invested so much effort to nurture and sustain was shattered.

Yet initially the German response was cautious. Given the considerable German economic stake in relations with Russia, Berlin was reluctant to impose robust sanctions on Russian individuals and companies. However, the downing of Malaysia Airlines flight MH-17 changed all that. The catastrophic loss of Dutch lives and the callous way in which the separatists hindered access to the crash site had a profound effect on European public opinion. Chancellor Merkel took the lead in securing EU backing for far-reaching financial sanctions that have made it difficult for Russia to access global capital markets and, along with the halving of oil prices, initially imposed considerable economic pain. The sanctions come up for review every six months, and so far, Germany has persuaded its partners to renew them until Russia complies with the provisions of the February 2015 Minsk II agreement. This most recent agreement lays out what Russia and Ukraine have to do in order to end the conflict and includes Russia returning control of the border to Ukraine.

Given the German business community's stake in trade with Russia—underwriting up to 200,000 German jobs at the height of the economic relationship—there was considerable pushback against the adoption of sanctions. Eventually, however, the head of the Federation of German Industries gave his support to the chancellor, acknowledging that security considerations had to come before economic interests: "As painful as further economic sanctions will be for European business development, for German exports, and for individual companies, they cannot and must not be ruled out as a way to apply pressure on the Russian government."[52]

The Ost-Ausschuss der Deutschen Wirtschaft, the main business lobbying group for Russia, however, demurred and has repeatedly criticized the sanctions, saying they hurt German industry and have not changed Russian policy. They have allies in both the Social Democratic Party and in Merkel's own Christian Democratic Union and its sister party the Christian Social Union of Bavaria. The Kremlin understands these internal German divisions very well, and Putin has done his best to encourage them by welcoming an array of German officials from different political parties in Moscow to discuss new trade and investment opportunities.

Angela Merkel has a complex double role as both chief enforcer and chief negotiator in this complicated relationship. Even as German-Russian relations have deteriorated, she has taken the lead in negotiating with President Putin and seeking to de-escalate the conflict in Eastern Ukraine. Indeed, during the Obama administration the White House delegated much of the diplomacy of the Ukraine crisis to Germany and took a back seat in trying to resolve the crisis. The US is not involved in the quadrilateral Normandy format—Germany, France, Russia, and Ukraine—that negotiated the Minsk II agreement. In what was apparently an understanding between Obama and Merkel, the chancellor agreed to maintain a tough sanctions regime if the White House vetoed Congress's attempts to supply lethal defensive weapons to Ukraine. Merkel believes there is no military solution to the conflict and is adamantly against doing anything that could provoke Russia further. Merkel is the Western leader who has had the most intense contact with Putin, speaking with him repeatedly by phone. She has also been the lead negotiator in the two Minsk ceasefire agreements. Her frequent and frustrating conversations with Putin led her apparently to remark to President Obama that the Russian president "lives in another world" to that of his Western counterparts. German officials say that Merkel's experience of having Putin often say one thing and do another has hardened her view of the Russian leader.

Russia's 2015 commemoration of the end of World War Two illustrates Merkel's careful approach. Putin invited Schroeder in 2005 to attend the sixtieth anniversary Victory Day Parade in Moscow's Red Square, the first time a German leader had been invited to these celebrations of the defeat of Nazi Germany. It was an emotional moment for Schroeder, whose father died on the Eastern Front in 1944 six months after he was born.[53] But in 2015, with a war raging in Ukraine, no Western leader attended the seventieth anniversary Victory Day Parade. Instead, the Chancellery announced that although Angela Merkel would not attend the May 9 Moscow celebration, she would lay a wreath at the tomb of the Unknown Soldier in the Kremlin's Alexander Gardens with President Putin the following day. This was Merkel's dual message: reluctance to give official endorsement to Vladimir Putin's parade of military might while armed conflict continued in Ukraine but recognition that, because of Berlin's special historical responsibilities toward Moscow, Germany must continue to show respect to Russian citizens for the sacrifices they endured during the war.

Putin's German Supporters

In January 2016, Lisa, a thirteen-year-old Russian-German girl in Berlin disappeared for thirty hours. When she resurfaced, she claimed she had been abducted and raped by Middle Eastern migrants. Russian television and internet sites began broadcasting this news, accusing Merkel of disregarding the legitimate security fears of her citizens. Indeed, Foreign Minister Sergei Lavrov went on television accusing Germany of a "cover-up" and of "whitewashing reality to make it politically correct." Steinmeier called Moscow's reaction "political propaganda."[54] A demonstration of 700 protestors demanding justice for Lisa took place outside the Chancellery in Berlin. The German police conducted an exhaustive inquiry and concluded that Lisa had made up the story because she had quarreled with her parents and spent the night out with a male friend. The police presented all the information to the Russian government, only to have Lavrov appear once more on television and repeat the charges. This deliberate Russian deception infuriated the Chancellery. Some Germans saw this as a Kremlin effort to undermine Merkel herself. Germany's anti-immigrant, anti-Muslim Far Right parties also joined pro-Russian demonstrations, as did the Far Left, reinforcing both the image and reality that the Kremlin was actively engaged in supporting anti-government groups of all political stripes through a coordinated media and social network campaign. This was the "Russian world" in action.

The Kremlin has targeted the "Russian world" inside Germany to undermine Merkel's policies. Following on the wave of patriotic sentiment inside Russia after the annexation of Crimea, the Kremlin appealed to various groups in Germany, particularly Germans of Russian descent. Despite the fact that they had left Russia, many felt like second-class citizens in Germany and had failed to integrate. Russia also played on anti-immigrant feelings in Germany. Many Germans believed that Merkel, by encouraging migrants fleeing the civil war in Syria or the instability in Afghanistan to come to Germany, was endangering the safety of Germans—and taking their jobs.

Germans remain deeply divided about Russia, and the Kremlin has done its utmost to play on these differences. Since the outbreak of the Ukraine crisis, successive groups of current and former German politicians—including former chancellors Helmut Schmidt and Gerhard Schroeder, and former foreign minister Hans-Dietrich Genscher—supported by journalists and prominent academics, criticized Merkel's tough stance on Russia and called for an end to sanctions and a return to close ties with Moscow. Their arguments have been rebutted by those who reject a return to business as usual. In 2016, 64 percent of Germans said that Vladimir Putin's Russia was not a credible partner for Germany, although 38 percent of East Germans thought Berlin's policy was too anti-Russian (the figure was 22 percent for West Germans). Yet despite the growing disenchantment with Russia, 57 percent of those questioned said that German soldiers should not go to defend NATO members Poland and the Baltic states if they were attacked by Russia.[55] The image of Germany as a peaceful power that rejects militarism and can be an honest broker tempering hostility between Russia and the West continues to resonate deeply in German society. Meanwhile, in Russia, just over half the population holds an unfavorable view of Germany, while 35 percent hold a favorable view.[56]

German pro-Russian sentiment is often inversely correlated to German views of the United States. This was vividly illustrated by the Edward Snowden affair. Snowden, the NSA employee who fled to Hong Kong and then to Russia in 2013 with millions of stolen classified files, was given political asylum by Vladimir Putin, who portrayed this as a humanitarian gesture. Snowden claimed that the NSA was spying on US citizens—and also on foreigners. He revealed that 500 million pieces of personal data were intercepted every month in Germany. Worse still, in a country that continues to deal with the dual secret police legacies of Hitler's Gestapo and the East German Stasi, was the revelation that the NSA apparently was also eavesdropping on Merkel's personal cell phone.[57] She was, needless to say, greatly angered by this. Snowden received an award from a prominent German human rights organization, and some of the members of a Bundestag committee looking into NSA activities in Germany recommended that Berlin grant him political asylum. For Putin, Snowden was a gift that kept on giving. Not only did Snowden's revelations cause major strains in the US-Germany relationship, but they also fed into the Kremlin's narrative that the United States was a major human rights violator.

Angela Merkel continues to walk a fine line between keeping the sanctions regime in place and not neglecting entirely German business interests in Russia. The Nord Stream II pipeline represents the essence of this balancing act. In 2015, the Nord Stream consortium, run by Matthias Warnig and in which Gazprom has a majority stake, signed an $11 billion shareholder agreement with five European companies—some of which subsequently dropped out—to build a second gas pipeline that would carry 55 billion cubic meters of gas to Germany and Europe while bypassing Ukraine. This was at a time when gas prices were falling and Nord Stream was operating at 70 percent capacity. The project generated a great deal of controversy. On the face of it, this expansion of the network would appear to involve technical and legal issues. But its geopolitical implications were significant, given the tensions between Russia and Europe and the ongoing fighting in Ukraine. The arguments in favor of the project were that Europe's gas demand would rise by 2020 while domestic supplies decline, and the new pipeline would fill these increased needs. Ukraine had raised transit rates for gas, increasing Russia's interest in building the pipeline. Moreover, the Ukrainian pipeline system is in need of repair and lacks investment, and the Ukrainian energy sector remains corrupt. The arguments against the project were that it contravened the EU's goals of diversification of supplies, it would deprive Ukraine of $2.3 billion of much-needed transit revenues, it would endanger Europe's energy security, and it would cause environmental damage. In the eyes of most Central European states, it was a Russian geopolitical project rather than an energy deal, designed to give Russia greater influence over Europe. While the European Commission considered its relative merits, Merkel took a neutral stance, insisting that commercial factors would ultimately decide whether it went ahead. This was her concession to the business community in return for their continuing support for sanctions. But few view this project as strictly commercial. Indeed, at the July 2018 NATO summit in Brussels, Donald Trump accused Germany of being "captive" to Russia because of Nord Stream.[58]

In September 2017, Germans went to the polls. Unlike in the US, French, and British election campaigns, Russia appears to have refrained from interference, although there were concerns in Germany that it would. The outcome sent shock waves around Europe. Support for traditional parties—including the Christian Democratic Union/Christian Social Union, Free Democratic Party, and Social Democratic Party—fell, while the nationalist, populist, anti-immigrant, pro-Russian Alternative for Germany party gained enough votes not only to sit in the Bundestag but emerge as the largest opposition party. It took eight months of painstaking negotiations for Merkel to cobble together a coalition, returning to the grand coalition model. The new Social Democratic foreign minister, Heiko Maas, sounded a more cautious note on Russia, unlike his predecessors Frank-Walther Steinmeier and Sigmar Gabriel. Maas accused Russia of having become a difficult partner and listed a series of unwelcome actions it had perpetrated beyond its borders. He also admitted for the first time that a recent cyberattack on Germany's foreign ministry had likely stemmed from Moscow. "We will keep up the political pressure on Russia," he pledged.[59]

Will Trump Cause Ostpolitik to Return?

The contrast between US and Russian leaders' treatment of Angela Merkel could not have been more striking. By May 2018, a series of US actions caused serious rifts between the United States and Germany, including levying new tariffs on German goods and withdrawing from the nuclear agreement with Iran, which Germany had worked hard to create and enforce. After a difficult meeting in Washington with Trump, in which he continued to berate her, Merkel traveled to Sochi and was greeted by a beaming Putin, who presented her with a large bunch of pink and white roses—instead of a large dog. The tables had surely turned. Putin and Merkel discussed the need to maintain the Iran agreement despite the US withdrawal; they talked about the situation in Ukraine and about trade and the Nord Stream II pipeline.[60] Commentators speculated about a "new détente" between Germany and Russia.

The advent of the Trump administration and its marked distancing from Germany—as compared to the Obama administration—has led Berlin to reassess its relations with Russia. For Trump, Merkel embodies the liberal global order he despises. Merkel's visits with Trump have been awkward, and Trump has accused Germany of not contributing enough to its own defense and of engaging in underhand trade practices against the US. While Merkel remains wary of Putin's Russia, both she and Putin understand the need for pragmatic cooperation on issues such as Iran, faced with an unpredictable US administration. At their joint press conference in Sochi, Merkel said of their discussions on Iran, Syria, and Ukraine, "I think these major problems can only be resolved if we discuss the topics on which our opinions differ, discuss these topics, analyze them, and try to bridge the gaps, to discuss the facts together and to seek solutions; therefore, the negotiations have been important and we will continue these negotiations later."[61]

Since 2017, the German chancellor has faced the unenviable challenge of balancing between Trump and Putin. Merkel's relationship with Trump deteriorated sharply in 2018 in the wake of the G-7 summit in Canada and the July NATO summit in Brussels. In Canada, he accused Germany of unfair trade practices and of owing the US $1 trillion in back payments for contributions to NATO. In an unprecedented attack at the opening breakfast in Brussels, Trump made an unfounded claim that "Germany is totally controlled by Russia, because they're getting between 60 to 70 percent of their energy from Russia and a new pipeline"[62] (the figure for gas is 37 percent). Merkel responded, "Because of given circumstances I want to point out one thing: I experienced the Soviet occupation of one part of Germany myself. It is good that we are independent today."[63]

The Trump administration's treatment of Merkel had caused much soul-searching in Germany and a recognition that Germany not only can no longer count on its relationship with the United States but may have to devise strategies for dealing with Washington as an adversary.[64] Will that induce Germany to return to acting as a mediator between East and West? For now, Putin will seek to draw Merkel back into his world as she continues to confront her unpredictable American ally.

—5—

THE "MAIN OPPONENT"

Russia and NATO

Question: What did you do as a KGB case officer in Dresden?

Answer: We were interested in any information about the "main opponent" as we called them, and the main opponent was considered NATO. —*Vladimir Putin, 2000*[1]

The headquarters of the North Atlantic Treaty Organization (NATO) lies in a leafy northeastern suburb of Brussels, a futuristic set of buildings flying the flags of the twenty-nine member states. The organization was founded in 1949 to create a common defense against the Soviet Union, ensuring that the United States would remain committed to that defense—and equally ensuring that Western European countries would eschew conflict with each other. One of NATO's founding fathers, Lord Hastings Ismay, in 1949 explained that the collective defense alliance had three main purposes: to "keep the Americans in, the Russians out, and the Germans down."[2] The first two remained as constants, but the third changed once West Germany joined NATO in 1955. From the beginning, it was clear that NATO was designed both to deter any possible future Soviet attack on Europe and to reassure Western Europeans that the United States would protect them.

The foundation of NATO represented a radical transformation of US foreign policy, away from its previous isolationist inclinations, which reached all the way back to George Washington's admonition in his

Farewell Address: "Why, by interweaving our destiny with that of any part of Europe, entangle our peace and prosperity in the toils of European ambition, rivalship, interest, humor, or caprice?"[3] But in the mid-twentieth century, after the war, it was a very different world. Secretary of State Dean Acheson, responding to skepticism from senators who wanted the United States to resume its historic isolationism after World War Two, made both a moral and a practical case for US membership in NATO:

> We were decent people, we could keep our promises, and our promises were written out and clear enough. They were to regard an attack on any of our allies as an attack on ourselves and to assist the victim ourselves and with the others, with force if necessary, to restore and maintain peace and security. Twice in twenty-five years there had been armed attacks in the area involved in this treaty and it was abundantly clear what measures had been necessary to restore peace and security.[4]

What might have reassured the Europeans had the opposite effect on the Soviets. NATO was the first tangible embodiment of George Kennan's policy of containment, which he had enunciated in his famous "Mr. X" article in 1947, in the midst of the Soviet takeover of Eastern Europe. Kennan, then head of the Department of State's Office of Policy Planning, argued that the USSR would, if unchecked, continue to expand its international reach, and his prescription was clear: containment of the USSR. However, he opposed the creation of NATO.

The Soviet takeover of Czechoslovakia in February 1948 was the final act in the consolidation of Moscow's control over Eastern Europe—and was the event that galvanized the United States and Western Europe into forming NATO. On April 4, 1949, the foreign ministers of twelve countries gathered in Washington to sign the agreement establishing NATO. The US Marine Band—perhaps presciently—played two songs from the popular musical *Porgy and Bess*: "I Got Plenty of Nothin'" and "It Ain't Necessarily So."[5] Joseph Stalin, apparently with a straight face, complained about NATO's aggressive character, contrasting it with the ostensibly benign nature of Moscow's intentions.[6]

For the first forty years of its existence, NATO proved itself one of the most successful alliances in history. The United States maintained a quarter of a million troops in West Germany at the height of the Cold War, with substantial deployments in other European countries. NATO and Warsaw Pact troops faced each other directly over the Fulda Gap near Frankfurt, the anticipated Soviet attack route into West Germany. Secretary of State Colin Powell recalled his formative years opposing the Soviets:

> I was just a twenty-one-year-old second lieutenant out of New York, having just finished infantry school. We all knew our jobs. When the balloon went up, my job was to race to our positions at the Fulda Gap and beat the crap out of the Russians as they came through. That was it. We didn't need to know much more.[7]

Six years after the formation of NATO and two weeks after West Germany joined, Stalin's successors met with the leaders of Eastern Europe in Warsaw on May 14, 1955, to sign on to the Warsaw Treaty Organization, their own "collective defense pact" with eight members. Warsaw Pact troops were never used against NATO, only against their own members, including the invasion of Czechoslovakia in 1968 to crush the reformist Prague Spring movement. The pact persisted until Germany reunified and after the collapse of communism in Eastern Europe, when it was rendered obsolete. Indeed, the Soviet ambassador to West Germany Yuli Kvitsinsky described in scathing terms one of the pact's last meetings in June 1990. It was "the most unpleasant negotiating session that I ever remember having to endure. A haze of insincerity lay over the negotiations: people were afraid to name things by their proper names and escaped by wording the document in ambiguous formulas. I felt as if I were participating in a meal where the guests were stealing silver spoons while the host was not looking."[8]

For the Soviets, NATO was the foe because it embodied the Western resolve to resist them, and they spent four decades seeking to exploit rifts between the Europeans and the Americans, and between the Europeans themselves, hoping to weaken the alliance.

What Did Bush Promise Gorbachev?

The fixation with NATO did not end with the Soviet collapse. For a few years after 1991, Moscow modified its view of NATO, but that did not last long. Fast-forward to March 2014, when Putin made his speech announcing Russia's annexation of Crimea. He highlighted the threat that NATO could pose to Russia were Ukraine to join the alliance and station troops in Crimea. Putin has also repeatedly said that NATO is an obsolete organization, so apparently it is seen as both a threat to Russia and irrelevant in the twenty-first century. Russia's 2015 official Foreign Policy Concept cites NATO as a major threat to Russia and also out-of-date as a new global order takes shape.[9]

Moscow has expressed a persistent complaint about NATO: the United States, so this argument goes, promised Gorbachev at the time of German unification that NATO would not enlarge were the USSR to assent to a united Germany remaining in NATO. This claim is repeated both in Russia and in the West, and the alleged violation of this promise is blamed for the deterioration of Russia's relations with the West and is used to legitimize Russia's seizure of Crimea. According to a US academic, "the United States and its European allies share most of the responsibility for the crisis. The taproot of the trouble is NATO enlargement, the central element of a larger strategy to move Ukraine out of Russia's orbit and integrate it into the West."[10]

More than any other issue, the enlargement of NATO to include former communist countries and republics of the Soviet Union has defined the widening split between Russia and the West since 1999. Russia and its supporters in the West put NATO expansion at the heart of the problems between Moscow and the United States and Europe. If only NATO had not expanded, so the argument goes, Russia and the West would have succeeded in working out a productive modus vivendi together. In this view, the West is responsible for the events that produced the war in Ukraine.

In Putin's world, NATO expansion is presented as one of the main reasons for the discord with the West. But does Putin really see NATO as the "main opponent," and if so, why? After all, at the end of the Cold War NATO explicitly modified its mission to promote a "Europe whole and free and at peace" and formed a partnership with Russia. It has sought to work with Russia in a number of fora, but most of these attempts have been unsuccessful. With hindsight, it is clear that the United States and its allies in the 1990s were unable to forge a Euro-Atlantic security order in which Russia had a stake. "Europe whole, free, and at peace" ended up excluding Europe's largest country, Russia.

But did Russia want to be included in this architecture? Should the West have dismantled NATO in 1991 and worked with Russia to create a new security structure whose rules Moscow would have had an equal say in determining? If NATO were now to fade away, as both Donald Trump and Vladimir Putin have proposed, would that usher in a new age of improved relations between Russia and the West? What promises were—or were not—made to Gorbachev and Yeltsin, how has Russia's view of NATO sharpened under Vladimir Putin, and how might the NATO issue be managed going forward?

Much of the controversy about what assurances Gorbachev received stems from a couple of conversations the Soviet leader had in February 1990, three months after the fall of the Berlin Wall, when the United States was discussing how negotiations on German unification would be organized and before East Germany's first free election in March. At this point Gorbachev hoped that the Warsaw Pact might survive and that a united Germany might belong to both military blocs—or to no bloc.[11] In January 1990, West German foreign minister Hans-Dietrich Genscher had given a speech declaring that a united Germany would be a member of NATO, but "there will be no expansion of NATO territory eastwards." On February 9, Gorbachev met with US secretary of state James Baker, who assured him that the United States and its allies would guarantee "there would be no extension of NATO's jurisdiction for forces of NATO one inch to the east," meaning no non-German NATO troops would be deployed on the territory of the former East Germany.[12]

The Soviet and US records of this conversation are largely identical. But even though the participants were talking only about NATO troops not being stationed in the GDR, it is true that the concept of NATO "jurisdiction" not extending to part of the territory of a member state was in fact impractical.[13] During Gorbachev's talks with Chancellor Helmut Kohl the next day, Kohl elaborated on what Baker had said, assuring the Soviet leader that the eastern part of a united Germany could have a "special status" in NATO. Records from these conversations show that at no time did the subject of NATO enlargement beyond Germany ever come up. Gorbachev never received any assurances on this subject, nor did he ask for them.[14] He finally conceded in July at a meeting with Kohl that a united Germany could remain in NATO. But enlargement was not on anyone's mind at that point.

In his memoirs, Gorbachev's subsequent recollection of the conversation with Baker is somewhat different. He recalls saying that any expansion of NATO would be unacceptable.[15] Former US ambassador to the USSR Jack Matlock has also testified that Gorbachev received a "clear commitment that if Germany united and stayed in NATO, the borders of NATO would not move eastward."[16] Since these discussions involved oral, not written, promises, it is impossible to prove or disprove what participants thought they heard. Gorbachev may have subsequently believed he heard from Baker, Bush, Kohl, and Genscher that there would be no NATO expansion, but none of his Western interlocutors were thinking about enlarging NATO during the intense negotiations on German unity. Indeed, in 2014 Gorbachev gave an interview in which he said, "The topic of 'NATO expansion' was not discussed at all, and it wasn't brought up in those years. I say this with full responsibility.... Another issue we brought up was discussed: making sure that... additional forces from the alliance would not be deployed on the territory of the then-GDR after German reunification."[17] Yet myths about what was promised persists, and claims about broken commitments have become more elaborate and extravagant as the relationship between Russia and the West has deteriorated.[18]

The Decision to Enlarge NATO—An Extension of Containment?

Was the enlargement of NATO "the most fateful error of American policy in the post-Cold-War era," as George Kennan claimed?[19] The original architect of containment had changed his mind about Russia after the Soviet collapse, urging its inclusion in the European security order, warning that its exclusion would have unforeseen, dangerous consequences. In 1992, the Warsaw Pact had gone out with a whimper, and the George H. W. Bush administration faced a greatly weakened Russia and a security vacuum in Central and Eastern Europe. The Bush administration's solution was to create the North Atlantic Cooperation Council, a NATO-led forum that included all the post-communist states. It met between 1991 and 1997 and discussed issues related to Russian troop withdrawals, but it had a large membership and diffuse agenda. In 1997, it became the Euro-Atlantic Partnership Council with fifty members. But it was soon clear that the large multilateral body with so many members, even though it met the test of inclusiveness, was not coherently planned nor did it have any real strategy. It was a temporary solution for a far more challenging issue: was it possible to create a new Euro-Atlantic security architecture in which both Russia and Eastern Europe would have a role—and a firm stake?

The countries of Central and Eastern Europe, newly liberated from Soviet control and facing daunting domestic political and economic problems, were beginning to consider the security challenges they would face in the new post-Soviet world. Meanwhile, Russia was facing even greater domestic challenges, together with adjusting to the loss of the Soviet empire. The Russian state emerged in 1992 smaller than it had been in four centuries, and without the defense perimeter provided by the other Soviet republics and the Warsaw Pact countries; it had lost the buffer states the Kremlin believed were vital for the security and safety of the Russian state—and which protected it from NATO.

In retrospect, the United States and its allies seriously underestimated what the collapse of the USSR meant for Russia's perception of its own vulnerability, focusing rather on the insecurities and concerns of the Central European countries. Admittedly, the latter were overtly pro-Western and wanted to join NATO, while the Kremlin, still reeling from the diminution of Russia's international clout, was much more ambivalent about the idea of joining an organization whose rules had been written by its former adversaries. The West was and remains unable to resolve the dilemma of creating a security architecture in Europe that adequately, and at the same time, addresses the concerns of Central Europe, Russia, and the Western post-Soviet states. What assuaged Central European countries' fears heightened Russian concerns, so that NATO enlargement became a zero-sum issue, with countries like Ukraine and Georgia remaining in a no-man's-land.

In 1993, Russia's Foreign Intelligence Service, then led by veteran Soviet diplomat Yevgeny Primakov, put out a report warning against NATO enlargement and staked out what would become the established Russian position. "This expansion," Primakov argued, "would bring the biggest military grouping in the world, with its colossal offensive potential, directly to the borders of Russia.... If this happens, the need will arise for a fundamental reappraisal of all defense concepts on our side, a redeployment of armed forces, and changes in operational plans.... The new Russia," he insisted, "has a right to have its opinion taken into account."[20]

Boris Yeltsin and Opening NATO's Door

Perhaps more important than what was or was not said about NATO to Gorbachev in 1990 was what was said to Boris Yeltsin in 1993, just before the Primakov paper. In October 1993, shortly after Yeltsin had used deadly force to disband opposition groups in the Russian parliament, US secretary of state Warren Christopher visited Moscow to explain the idea of the Partnership for Peace. As the Clinton administration and its allies began to debate how to reorganize European security in the 1990s in such a way that gave Russia a place, it remained committed to retaining NATO. While many Russians and some in the West advocated scrapping the organization as a Cold War relic and replacing it with a pan-European organization that included Russia, Washington, and Brussels, others saw no reason to dissolve a successful alliance in which all members had a stake. And despite Russian complaints, Russia never proposed any positive agenda for redesigning European security architecture. NATO instead decided to create the Partnership for Peace (PfP), a bilateral outreach program for former Warsaw Pact countries focusing on defense and military cooperation and on the democratization of post-communist armed forces. Each country would develop its own program with NATO for PfP, and for some it could become the first step on the path to eventual membership. Some US officials intended for PfP to be an alternative to NATO membership, but for many Central European countries, membership was the goal.

When Christopher explained to Yeltsin that nothing would be done to exclude Russia from "full participation in the future security of Europe," Yeltsin approved. But then Yeltsin asked Christopher to promise him that

PfP meant partnership, not membership, for the participating Central European states. Christopher assured that this was the case. "This is a brilliant idea, it is a stroke of genius," replied Yeltsin. Subsequently, Christopher said that the United States would be "looking at the question of membership as a longer term eventuality," but it is unclear how Yeltsin reacted to that.[21] Russia signed its PfP agreement on June 22, 1994, the anniversary of Hitler's invasion of the USSR.

But others in Moscow from the outset were much more skeptical about PfP. Its great flaw, they argued, was that it offered Russia the same deal as every other post-communist state, meaning that it did not recognize Russia's special status as a great power. Defense Minister Pavel Grachev declared that if Russia were to join PfP, it should have a special role and special relations with NATO. But, he was told, that kind of deal was not on. Russia would sign its PfP agreement on the same basis as everyone else. Two US ambassadors—James Collins and Thomas Pickering—later admitted that Washington reneged on its promises by subsequently offering membership to Central Europe.[22] Yeltsin was correct in believing that explicit promises made in 1993 about NATO not enlarging for the foreseeable future were broken when the Clinton administration decided to offer membership to Central Europe.

Russia had barely absorbed the implications of PfP when the debate about European security leapt forward to planning NATO enlargement. The United States government was divided on this issue, as were the governments of other NATO countries. It is important to remember the context in which these debates took place. The former Warsaw Pact countries were undergoing a painful and contentious transition away from communism. The ghosts of the interwar authoritarian past of most of these countries continued to haunt them. Nativist nationalist parties, seeking to revive their ethnic agendas from the interwar years, were challenging the new democratic parties. There were several unresolved territorial disputes—for instance, between Romania and Hungary—and irredentist groups were agitating to resolve them on their terms. US and

Western European officials feared that without effective structures to combat these movements, the European order could once again be threatened. EU membership was a long way off, and NATO, by imposing strict conditionality—including the resolution of territorial disputes—could serve as a democratizing instrument. Faced with the dilemma of reconciling two contradictory goals—integrating Central Europe into NATO to enhance European security and reassuring Russia that it too had a role to play in expanded Euro-Atlantic structures—the West chose to prioritize the first. Not surprisingly, while Washington told Russia that this was a win-win solution, Moscow viewed NATO enlargement in zero-sum terms.[23]

The Clinton administration embarked on NATO enlargement with the first group of countries—Poland, Hungary, and the Czech Republic—believing it could assuage Russian concerns by offering Russia a series of compensatory incentives. These included joining the G-7 and offering Russia its own agreement with NATO, the Permanent Joint Council, which was signed in Paris in 1997. The PJC was designed to give Russia a unique relationship with NATO, whereby Russia had a voice, but not a veto, in NATO deliberations. In 2002, after the US and Russia had cooperated in the war in Afghanistan, the PJC was redesigned as the NATO-Russia Council. The PJC had operated on the basis of "nineteen plus one," with Russia meeting NATO after NATO's then-nineteen member states had taken decisions of interest to Russia. The NATO-Russia Council was supposed to operate on the basis of "twenty," meaning that Russian officials would meet with NATO officials to make their views known before NATO took decisions, to ensure that NATO took Moscow's interests into account. While Russia has sometimes spoken approvingly of this special relationship with NATO, in practice, the NATO-Russia Council has never worked very well, despite periodic cooperation on issues such as search-and-rescue missions, civil emergencies, and counterterrorism. Russia's ambivalence about interacting with an organization whose agenda it had to accept and its suspicions about NATO's intentions persist, and no amount of NATO attempts to create a more cooperative environment could overcome them.

Three weeks after Poland, Hungary, and the Czech Republic joined NATO in 1999, NATO launched its bombing campaign against Serbia, fulfilling the Kremlin's worst fears. The United States and its allies hailed the enlargement as a victory for freedom and democracy. For Yeltsin, "NATO was making a mistake that would lead to a new confrontation between the East and the West."[24]

The Balkan Wars and Russia's Conflict with NATO

The split between Russia and the West came in the Balkans, the same cauldron of competing ethnicities and religions that had given birth to World War One. Much of Russia's suspicion of and opposition to NATO was rekindled during the Balkan wars of the 1990s. Yugoslavia was a patchwork state made up of historically hostile ethnic groups constructed in 1918 after the breakup of the Austro-Hungarian and Ottoman empires. During most of the twentieth century, it survived as a unitary state, first under the rule of monarchs and then, after the communists took over in 1946, under the iron hand of Marshal Josip Broz Tito. After his death, the presidency rotated among the major ethnic groups, but the system began to break down at the same time as the USSR opened up and Gorbachev unwittingly encouraged greater ethnic self-determination in the USSR.

After the constituent republics of Yugoslavia began to declare their independence, Serbian strongman Slobodan Milosevic supported the Bosnian Serbs, who unleashed an ethnic war against Bosnia's Muslim population, including the massacre of 8,000 Muslim men and boys at Srebrenica in 1995. Initially, Washington hoped that its European allies would intervene themselves and halt the carnage in their backyard. But the Europeans could not agree on the modalities of a possible military operation, and under US leadership NATO intervened to stop the bloodshed in Bosnia in 1995. Russia reluctantly agreed to cooperate with NATO via the Contact Group for the former Yugoslavia, which was created in 1994 and met regularly to discuss the progress of the military operation. The US was determined to include Russia in NATO's planning, although Russian ambivalence was clear. Russia consistently presented itself as the historical ally and defender of the Serbs. After listening to the US arguments about why Russia should support action against the Serbs, Foreign Minister Andrei Kozyrev snapped, "It's bad enough you people tell us what you are going to do whether we like it or not. Don't add insult to injury by telling us that it's *in our interest* to obey your orders."[25]

Moscow invoked its special relationship with the Serbs—their common Orthodox faith and historical and cultural links—but nevertheless at this point agreed the Serbian leader had to be stopped. The diplomat Richard Holbrooke, negotiating the 1995 Dayton peace agreement that ended the Bosnian War, understood the importance of including Russia. What Russia "wanted most was to restore a sense, however symbolic, that they still mattered in the world.... Behind our efforts to include Russia in the Bosnia negotiating process lay a fundamental belief on the part of the Clinton administration that it was essential to find the proper place for Russia in Europe's security structure, something it had not been part of since 1914."[26] The Dayton Accords created a three-headed government based on Bosnia's three ethnic groups: Serbs, Croats, and Bosniaks (Muslims). The peace was enforced by a multinational Implementation Force, in which Russian troops, surprisingly, served directly under an American commander, since they refused to serve under a NATO commander. This unprecedented military cooperation worked well. Yet today Russian officials recall the Bosnian intervention as inimical to Russia's interests with a peace imposed by NATO.

NATO next intervened in the Balkans in 1999, during the Kosovo conflict. At issue was the right of the Muslim Kosovars living in Orthodox Serbia to declare their independence from Serbia and form their own state. At this point Russia's position toward the alliance had considerably hardened, and Yeltsin himself was seriously ailing and facing growing domestic opposition to his policies after the ruble collapsed in 1998, causing an economic meltdown. NATO-Russia tensions in the former Yugoslav states were much more intense during the Kosovo War. Though Russia had been part of the solution in Bosnia, it had no intention of acceding to another NATO military operation to save beleaguered Kosovars from Serbian attacks.

In March 1999, as tensions between the United States and Russia increased, former Soviet intelligence chief and diplomat Yevgeny Primakov, by now prime minister, was on his way to the United States to discuss Kosovo, in the hope of de-escalating tensions. During his flight, he received the news that NATO had begun bombing Belgrade. He immediately turned his plane around midway over the Atlantic and flew back to Moscow in a rage. Yeltsin's opponents were warning him that if NATO could bomb Belgrade, "Today Yugoslavia, tomorrow Russia!" "Wasn't it obvious," Yeltsin wrote, "that each missile directed against Yugoslavia was an indirect strike against Russia?"[27]

Despite vigorous Russian opposition to the Kosovo campaign, former prime minister Viktor Chernomyrdin joined with Finnish president Martti Ahtisaari to broker a peace deal. But even as Chernomyrdin was putting his signature on the agreement, Russia and NATO almost came to direct physical blows at the end of the war. Contrary to the piece of paper Chernomyrdin had just signed, Russian troops rushed to the airport in Pristina, Kosovo's capital, and occupied it, before NATO troops had entered Kosovo. This was in direct contravention of the terms of the cease-fire they had just helped to negotiate. At this point the supreme allied commander in Europe, US general Wesley Clark, was in favor of NATO directly confronting the Russians. But British general Michael Jackson, who was in charge of NATO troops on the ground, told Clark that he was "not starting World War Three for you," and eventually the crisis was defused.

The Kosovo campaign and its aftermath have been a consistent source of Russian criticism, from Yeltsin to Putin. Kremlin leaders have argued that NATO defied international law as enshrined in the United Nations

Charter by bombing Serbia, including the inadvertent bombing of the Chinese embassy in Belgrade, which caused an outcry in Beijing. Russians believe the subsequent history of Kosovo exemplifies the worst excesses of NATO imposing its will on Europe against Moscow's core interests. After the end of the war, Kosovo was administered by a United Nations body. But by 2004, there was renewed violence between Serbs and Kosovars, and Ahtisaari again began to negotiate the difficult issue of Kosovo's future status. Between 2006 and 2008, Moscow blocked UN decision-making on Kosovo, claiming that Serbia's interests were being ignored and highlighting a possible Kosovo precedent for other unrecognized states, including the frozen conflicts in the post-Soviet space. It refused to support the negotiated plan after most Western countries decided that the only solution to the violence was for Kosovo to become an independent state.

Kosovo unilaterally declared its independence in 2008, and the United States recognized it, as did twenty-two out of the then twenty-seven EU member states. Russia declared the independence declaration illegitimate, with Putin warning, "This is a harmful and dangerous precedent.... You can't observe one set of rules for Kosovo and another for Abkhazia and South Ossetia."[28] To prove his point, Russia recognized the independence of those two breakaway regions after the Russia-Georgia War in 2008. Kosovo became a touchstone for Putin. The Kosovo precedent was the gift that kept on giving. In his speech announcing the annexation of Crimea in March 2014, Putin declared: "Our western partners created the Kosovo precedent with their own hands. In a situation absolutely the same as the one in Crimea they recognized Kosovo's secession from Serbia as legitimate while arguing that no permission from a country's central authority for a unilateral declaration of independence is necessary."[29] He also rejected the Western argument that Kosovo's independence was the only way to end ethnic bloodshed and that, in contrast to Russia's actions in Crimea, nobody had annexed Kosovo and incorporated it into their own state. NATO's actions were, therefore, a source of both criticism and legitimacy for Russia's own actions in Georgia and Crimea.

Putin and the "Main Opponent"

Putin had not always characterized NATO as the enemy. When he first took office, he did not rail against NATO. Indeed, he reached out to Western leaders and gave them the impression that he was genuinely interested in developing a more productive relationship with them after the 1999 Kosovo campaign. This included the possibility that Russia might consider joining NATO. The United States and its allies had reiterated that any European country was eligible to join NATO if it met the criteria for membership, and Putin seemed to be testing this claim. He had raised the issue of Russia joining NATO with Bill Clinton,[30] and then with NATO secretary-general George Robertson, who had told him that Russia would have to apply for membership.[31] In a July 2001 press conference, Putin said the alliance could "include Russia in NATO. This also creates a single area of defense security." Senior Russian officials believe that Putin was at that point serious about exploring Russia's NATO membership.[32]

Over the years, officials from various NATO countries have suggested that NATO should invite Russia to join. This would answer the question of where Russia belongs. When the George W. Bush administration came into office, it conducted a review of Russia policy. As part of this review, officials in the Department of State's Office of Policy Planning (including the author) suggested a more creative way of approaching the NATO issue. NATO, they argued, had always been an adaptable, protean organization. The challenges of the twenty-first century led them to conclude: "It is in our long-term interests to have Russia as a partner, not a spoiler." They laid out a road map of how negotiations with Russia should proceed at the same time that NATO was preparing its second round of enlargement to include the Baltic states. According to Richard Haass, then director of the Office of Policy Planning, "Having Russia inside NATO was a big idea. NATO had become a set of discretionary relations, and having Russia close to NATO is not inconsistent with what NATO has become."[33]

Shortly thereafter, former secretary of state James Baker, the man whose assurances to Gorbachev in 1990 had been misinterpreted by many, wrote an article arguing that Russia should be offered NATO membership. He trenchantly reminded his readers that NATO is "a coalition of former adversaries—one sad lesson of the twentieth century is that refusing to form alliances with defeated adversaries is more dangerous than forming such alliances."[34] His authoritative voice should have borne some weight, but the Bush administration did not pursue this track.

Yet how serious was Putin in discussing NATO membership? In a 2000 BBC interview, TV host David Frost asked him, "Could Russia ever join NATO?" To which Putin replied, "I don't see why not. I would not rule out such a possibility—if and when Russia's views are taken into account as those of an equal partner."[35] But beyond Putin's perception of NATO as the "main opponent," there was another problem. Russia would have to accept NATO's rules if it joined. These were rules written in Washington and Brussels. Putin, seeking to regain Russia's position as a great power, bristled at accepting the Western agenda. Russia wanted to interact with the United States as an equal, with the power to co-determine how NATO was run.

The "Big Bang" Enlargement, 2004

Yeltsin had objected to the first round of NATO enlargement, and Putin's attitude toward the second round was similarly critical, even more so. After all, NATO was now proposing to take in seven new members, including three former Soviet republics—Latvia, Lithuania, and Estonia—which some believed would be a red line for the Kremlin. During Putin's visit to Brussels in October 2001, at the height of US-Russia cooperation in Afghanistan, he expressed his dismay at the prospect:

> For example, the NATO enlargement will take place. Some new members will be adopted into that organization. Whose security

> will that action enhance? Which country of Europe, which country of the world and citizens of which country of the world would feel more secure? If you go to Paris or Berlin and ask a person in the street whether he or she would feel more secure after the expansion of NATO, enlargement of NATO, and whether that person from the street would feel secure against the threat of terrorism—the answer most probably would be no.[36]

Nevertheless, he proceeded to discuss further cooperation with NATO in Afghanistan. At that point joint work on defeating the Taliban meant Russia was interacting with the United States and its allies as an equal. There was still the expectation that, as a consequence of this joint action, Russia could indeed secure the "equal partnership of unequals" that it sought.

With hindsight, NATO enlargement to include the Baltic states was undertaken without fully thinking through its implications. Article 5 of the 1949 North Atlantic Treaty that established NATO guarantees the collective defense of each member. If one state is attacked, all the other states will come to its defense. But are the Baltic states defensible? In 2004, few in NATO apparently thought through the possibility that Russia might one day pursue more confrontational policies toward these neighbors. As soon as the Baltic states joined, NATO introduced a system of air policing for the three countries, a defensive, rotational 24/7 surveillance to secure their airspace. Russia was not enamored by the presence of NATO aircraft so near to Kaliningrad, the exclave that is part of the Russian Federation but physically separated from it by Lithuania and Poland. After the onset of the Ukraine crisis, Russia began a campaign of naval and air harassment of the Baltic states, and continued its cyberattacks, which had been going on for some time. A decade after Putin had basically accepted the states' NATO membership, Russia was bent on raising questions about whether indeed NATO would come to their defense. In response to these aggressive moves, President Obama traveled to Tallinn in September 2014 to offer words of reassurance: "We will defend our NATO Allies, and that means every Ally.... And we will defend the territorial integrity of every single Ally.... Article 5 is crystal clear: An attack on one is an attack on all."[37]

Nevertheless, a 2016 RAND study based on a series of war games playing out a Russian invasion of the Baltic states came to a sobering conclusion: Russian forces could reach the outskirts of Tallinn and Riga, the capital of Latvia, in sixty hours. "As currently postured, NATO cannot successfully defend the territory of its most exposed members." The world's most powerful military alliance would face a painful dilemma: either abandon its allies to Russian occupation or face a war with a nuclear superpower. The solution, in response, was to enhance NATO's military posture to better deter a Russian invasion, while recognizing that this could not sustain a longer-term defense of the area.[38] A British former deputy supreme allied commander in Europe wrote a novel describing a Russian invasion of the Baltic states in which NATO is both unwilling and unable to answer with an Article 5 response, and the locals have to rely on their own defense.[39] In ten years, NATO had gone from welcoming seven new members to having Russia actively challenge its credibility as a defense organization.

The Medvedev European Security Initiative and the Bucharest Summit

There has been only one Russian attempt since the Soviet collapse to put forward a positive plan for reorganizing Euro-Atlantic security, and that came in June 2008 at the start of Dmitry Medvedev's presidency. On a visit to Berlin, he proposed a new European security initiative and later produced the draft of a treaty to implement his proposals. In Berlin, his speech was rather vague as he called for a new, inclusive European security system and criticized NATO:

> NATO has also failed so far to give new purpose to its existence. It is trying to find this purpose today by globalizing its missions, including to the detriment of the UN's prerogatives, which I mentioned just before, and by bringing in new members. But this is clearly still not the solution.[40]

For the next year, Russia worked on producing a treaty to formalize the Medvedev ideas. It was published in late 2009.[41] Many of its provisions remained vague. Most Western countries rejected the idea that there was any need for another legally binding Euro-Atlantic super-treaty.

Shortly thereafter, Foreign Minister Lavrov presented the draft of a new NATO-Russia treaty designed to increase Russia's role in NATO decision-making on defense planning and military deployments, especially missile defense deployments, which were of particular concern to Moscow. NATO members raised questions about the contentious issue of whether the steps one country would take to enhance its security could actually harm the security of another state. Since Russia and the West have such different definitions of security, the interpretation of a security threat would be subjective and potentially contentious.[42]

The NATO-Russia relationship, by contrast, experienced a modest improvement under the reset policy of the first Obama administration, but Russia's contradictory attitude toward NATO posed serious obstacles to closer cooperation. At the very same time as Russia and NATO were cooperating to counter narcotics in Afghanistan and piracy off the coast of Africa, Russia's 2010 military doctrine named NATO as the number one external threat to Russia, whereas NATO's new strategic concept talked about the desire for a "strong partnership" with Russia.[43]

While NATO sought to reach out to Russia in the NATO-Russia Council, it made a major mistake in 2008. It mishandled the issue of further enlargement, thereby exacerbating Russian fears and ultimately provoking a military response from Moscow. In 2008, at the NATO Bucharest summit, the Bush administration tried to secure a Membership

Action Plan (MAP) for both Georgia and Ukraine. This issue was contentious within the Bush administration. Secretary of Defense Robert Gates and Secretary of State Condoleezza Rice were both against granting the two post-Soviet states a MAP, which would be the first step toward NATO membership. It was one thing to admit the Baltic states to NATO. After all, the United States had never recognized their incorporation into the USSR in 1940. But Georgia and Ukraine had been integral parts of both the Russian Empire and the USSR, and granting them a MAP would surely raise Russian ire—and countermeasures. Because of this, many of the United States' key allies—most importantly France and Germany—were adamantly opposed to granting the MAPs. Bush insisted to Rice that it had to happen. "I have to deliver this," she realized. "This is going to be really hard."[44]

The Bucharest summit was the most contentious and dramatic NATO meeting ever—that is, until Donald Trump came to power—with the German and Polish foreign ministers hurling thinly veiled barbs at each other. As the deadline for the opening plenary neared, President Bush and his advisers tried to hammer out a compromise that would be acceptable to everyone. Angela Merkel finally broke the deadlock when she proposed the following compromise: Georgia and Ukraine would not receive MAPs. But the communiqué would say: "We agree today that Georgia and Ukraine will become members of NATO."[45]

But what did that sentence really mean? In many ways it was the worst of both worlds. Neither Georgia nor Ukraine were granted the MAP, but Russia could assert that they would eventually join NATO and use this promise as an excuse to undermine both countries. In retrospect, this was an unnecessarily provocative sentence that did little to assuage the security concerns of either Ukraine or Georgia and everything to redouble Russian determination to reassert its domination of the post-Soviet space.

Vladimir Putin arrived in Bucharest the next day for a NATO-Russia Council meeting. It was the first time a Russian leader had attended a

NATO summit. He was angry about the language in the communiqué, particularly the prospect of future NATO membership for Ukraine and Georgia. In a private aside with Bush, he uttered the fateful sentence: "George, you have to understand that Ukraine is not even a country. Part of its territory is in Eastern Europe and the greater part was given to us."[46] Six years later Russia would invade Ukraine to prove this point, and just four months after the summit Russia invaded Georgia. Yet the 2018 NATO Brussels summit communiqué reiterated the promise of NATO membership for Georgia and Ukraine.

From Tbilisi to the Donbas: Putin's Doctrine of Limited Sovereignty

Russia's reaction to NATO's eventual promise of membership for Ukraine and Georgia was to use military force to ensure that neither country would remain territorially intact and that the frozen conflicts in both countries would make it difficult for their governments to function effectively. The West's acknowledgment of the limits of its support for either country in face of Russia's military action against them reinforced the inescapable fact that NATO had no treaty obligations to defend them.

In August 2008, after months of mutual provocations, Russian troops marched into Georgia after Georgian troops attacked the South Ossetian capital Tskhinvali. South Ossetia was a disputed enclave within Georgia—a mélange of ethnicities—that had declared its de facto independence from Tbilisi in the early 1990s. Georgia's president Mikheil Saakashvili was determined to reincorporate it into Georgia. Putin was equally determined that this would not happen, since these unrecognized statelets under Russian protection gave Moscow leverage it wanted to preserve. Saakashvili was also determined that Georgia should join NATO and was apparently backed by the majority of his population.

During this short war, Russian and American troops came closer to facing one another on opposite sides of an armed conflict than at any other time since the Cold War. US military personnel had been training Georgian troops who were fighting in Afghanistan and Iraq. During the war, the White House convened a Principals' meeting to discuss whether the United States should respond to Russia's invasion with military force. The participants in the meeting agreed that the US should not go to war with Russia over Georgia.[47] Although the West would not acknowledge Russia's right to a sphere of influence in its backyard after 1992, it nevertheless recognized that since Georgia and Ukraine were not NATO members, there was little the alliance could do to help them. After defeating the Georgian army, which was no match for the Russian military, Moscow recognized the independence of South Ossetia and Abkhazia, Georgia's other unrecognized statelet. Even though only a handful of other countries recognized their independence, Georgia had now lost its territorial integrity, making eventual NATO membership even more remote.

Russia's actions in Ukraine were more far-reaching and disruptive to the European peace order than those in Georgia. Between 2008 and 2014, Moscow's relations with the West significantly deteriorated. Although the question of further NATO enlargement receded into the background, and Ukraine's president Viktor Yanukovych reaffirmed Ukraine's nonbloc status, Putin and other officials continued to invoke the specter of further enlargement as a threat to Russia's vital interests.[48] When Yanukovych fled the country in February 2014, the NATO threat once again came to the fore. The Kremlin may have feared that, with Yanukovych gone, Ukraine might revisit its bloc-free status.[49] In his March 18, 2014, speech announcing the annexation of Crimea, Putin invoked the NATO threat as one of the reasons for Russia's moves:

> Let me note too that we have already heard declarations from Kiev about Ukraine soon joining NATO. What would this have meant for Crimea and Sevastopol in the future? It would have meant that NATO's navy would be right there in this city of Russia's military glory, and this would create not an illusory but

> a perfectly real threat to the whole of southern Russia. These are things that could have become reality were it not for the choice the Crimean people made, and I want to say thank you to them for this.[50]

Russian actions since the annexation of Crimea have produced a counterreaction by NATO that has significantly escalated tensions between the two players. NATO initially responded cautiously to the seizure of Crimea and to the outbreak of war in the Donbas region. NATO had been working with the Ukrainian military, under the terms of Ukraine's own partnership agreement, to strengthen the Ukrainian armed forces, but it was not obligated to come to Ukraine's defense.

The Kremlin has consistently asserted that it has no regular troops supporting the separatists in the Donbas region—a claim that has been refuted by reliable photographic evidence. The Russian military contracting firm Wagner has sent mercenaries to fight in Ukraine.[51] Putin has admitted only that there were Russian military intelligence officers in the Donbas.[52] The Kremlin says that if Russian soldiers are there, they are fighting on their "vacation" time. Moreover, the Russian NGO Committee of Soldiers' Mothers has described the body bags with hundreds of dead soldiers that have returned to Russia from Ukraine.[53] But Kremlin spokesman Dmitry Peskov has adamantly denied these claims: "We have stated many times that there are no Russian troops on the territory of Ukraine. It is simply an obsession to ascribe Russia a destructive role in the development of the Ukrainian crisis with which we categorically disagree."[54]

NATO's Response to Russia's Wars with Georgia and Ukraine

This Kremlin's insistence on "alternative facts" has increased NATO's suspicions about Russian motivations and future plans, and rendered discussions in the NATO-Russia Council very challenging. NATO's response has been to reverse twenty-five years of drawing down its presence near Russia's borders and recommit to its original goal: defending its members from outside aggression, including from Russia. In 1997, there were 100,000 NATO troops in Europe. In 2014, there were only 25,000. In July 2014, at its summit in Wales, NATO focused on Russia's invasion of Ukraine:

> We condemn in the strongest terms Russia's escalating and illegal military intervention in Ukraine and demand that Russia stop and withdraw its forces from inside Ukraine and along the Ukrainian border. This violation of Ukraine's sovereignty and territorial integrity is a serious breach of international law and a major challenge to Euro-Atlantic security. We do not and will not recognize Russia's illegal and illegitimate "annexation" of Crimea.[55]

NATO subsequently agreed to establish a Very High Readiness Joint Task Force (VJTF), a new allied force that would be able to deploy within a few days to respond to challenges that arise, particularly at the periphery of NATO's territory. It also exhorted its members to meet their commitment to spend at least 2 percent of their GDP on defense, something on which President Trump has insisted to every European leader he has met.

At its Warsaw summit in 2016, the alliance explicitly moved from "reassurance" to "deterrence," a major shift since the more optimistic years after the end of the Cold War. It was clear whom the alliance believed it needed to deter. The symbolism of holding a NATO summit in Warsaw, where the Soviet-era Warsaw Pact was founded, was lost on neither the Poles nor the Russians. One Russian newspaper dubbed it "the first in many years to have such an openly anti-Russian agenda." There was no hint in the official Russian media that NATO was reacting to Russia's ongoing conflict with Ukraine and its military buildup in the Baltic Sea, just as Russian attacks on EU sanctions neglected to explain why the sanctions had been imposed in the first place. This has been a Russian pattern at least since Stalin, who failed to acknowledge that NATO was founded in response to the Soviet takeover of Eastern Europe. Russian leaders are acting as if they had no agency in any of these developments.

NATO agreed to deploy military forces and forward-positioning equipment to the Baltic states and eastern Poland in January 2017 to deter Russia, in response to Moscow's moves in Crimea and the Donbas. The four battalions, totaling between three and four thousand troops, are led by the UK in Estonia, the US in Poland, Canada in Latvia, and Germany in Lithuania. Furthermore, NATO took command of a US-built missile shield in Europe to defend against ballistic missiles from Iran. It also agreed to welcome Montenegro as its newest member. NATO secretary-general Jens Stoltenberg warned about growing Russian activity in the Balkans, discussed earlier. The Balkans has become the latest battleground where the Kremlin seeks to counter southeast Europe's move westward.

The European Deterrence Initiative of the US Department of Defense has enhanced these NATO efforts.[56] To Russian complaints about this new military buildup, Stoltenberg replied: "But this is not an egg and chicken situation because there's no doubt that it was Russia's aggression against Ukraine, annexing Crimea and continuing to destabilize Eastern Ukraine, that triggered the NATO response. Before Russia started its aggressive actions against Ukraine, no one was seriously talking about any enhanced NATO presence in the eastern part of the alliance."[57]

In January 2017, these new NATO deployments took place. The deployment in Poland was the largest infusion of US troops in Europe since 1991. For Germany, sending troops to Lithuania remained a sensitive issue in both Germany and Lithuania, given the legacy of World War Two; but these ghosts of the past were dwarfed by concerns about Russian aggression.

As the new NATO deployments began, Russia threatened retaliation. According to Kremlin spokesman Dmitry Peskov, "We perceive it as a threat. These actions threaten our interests, our security. Especially as it concerns a third party building up its military presence near our borders."[58]

The spiral of reaction and counterreaction in NATO-Russia relations shows no signs of abating. Russia claims that it moved into Crimea because it feared that its security would be threatened if Ukraine joined NATO and the alliance moved up to its borders. NATO in return has beefed up its forces near Russia's borders because the Baltic states and Poland felt threatened. Whereupon Russia announced that it would retaliate militarily to these new deployments. Is it possible to break out of this cycle?

Would Russia's relations with the West have been that different had NATO not enlarged? If NATO had disbanded itself in the early 1990s, what security arrangement might have replaced it? Even in 1992, a weakened Russia reeling from the Soviet collapse still regarded the former republics of the Soviet Union as its "near abroad," not independent countries with sovereign rights. It was more willing to accept that Central Europe had become independent but still was hardly in a position to begin a serious consideration of what it believed a Euro-Atlantic security system should be. And the OSCE—the one existing multilateral security organization that included North America, Europe, Russia, and the post-Soviet states—was not a substitute for a successful military alliance that had kept the peace for nearly five decades. In the 1990s, the United States drastically reduced its military presence in Europe, and NATO explicitly shifted its mission from deterring the Soviet Union to working cooperatively with the former communist countries to create a Europe "whole and free." In the uncertain years after the end of the Cold War, the dissolution of NATO would have led to a dangerous security vacuum in Europe. And Russia was not in a position to suggest or provide alternative arrangements.

Would Russia's NATO membership have been the answer? Strictly speaking, NATO's open-door policy meant that Russia was theoretically eligible to join, although that might have raised questions about whether NATO was ready to come to Russia's defense in a possible conflict with China. But Russia's membership in NATO was probably never a realistic option, as explained by a senior official in the Clinton administration:

> The reason that Russian membership in NATO never became a real possibility was more fundamental—and not always easy to talk about. How one felt about Russia *being* a member depended on how it *became* one, on how its accession was interpreted by both sides. Was membership a matter of geopolitical entitlement, or was it something to be earned? Was Russia to be asked to join because of its power or because it honestly embraced NATO's goals? The way Russia had been whisked into other international institutions did not provide a good model.[59]

Russians, as Bill Clinton once remarked, were "lousy joiners." They did not like joining organizations whose rules they had not designed and had to accept. And many of the organizations in which they had hitherto been members—with the exception of the UN—had been dominated by them because they had written their rules.

In the years since the Soviet collapse, Russia has been very vocal about what it does not like but usually unable to present a positive agenda for change. It has largely been reactive to Western policy, and when it has been proactive, as in Ukraine in 2014, it has often used military and cyber instruments of coercion in its neighborhood and beyond.

Looking back over the past twenty-five years, it is difficult to make the argument that NATO enlargement alone led Russia and the West into a dangerous downward spiral of relations. NATO enlargement offered the post-communist states a security framework in which they have been able to develop and prosper. It is only one of the reasons for the deterioration in Russia's relations with the West. The more important reason is that Russia has not, over the past quarter century, been willing to accept the rules of the international order that the West hoped it would. Those included acknowledging the sovereignty and territorial integrity of the post-Soviet states and supporting a liberal world order that respects the right to self-determination. Russia continues to view the drivers of international politics largely through a nineteenth-century prism. Spheres of influence are more important than the individual rights and sovereignty of smaller countries. It is virtually impossible to reconcile the Western and Russian understanding of sovereignty. For Putin, what counts is power and scale, not rules.

Will NATO Survive Donald Trump?

The election of Donald Trump has raised serious questions about whether the US and Russia will continue to have such opposing views about European security. Indeed, Putin has a new trump card in his campaign against NATO: the American president. During the election campaign, candidate Trump sounded two consistent themes about Russia and NATO. Of NATO, he said, "It's obsolete, first because it was designed many, many years ago. Secondly, countries aren't paying what they should," and NATO "didn't deal with terrorism."[60] Putin's spokesman Dmitry Peskov echoed President Trump's assertion that NATO is "obsolete," saying, "NATO is indeed a vestige [of the past] and we agree with that."[61]

The other consistent *Trump* theme during the US election campaign was that Vladimir Putin is a great leader and the United States and Russia should be friends and jointly fight "Islamic terrorism." An "America first" vision, moreover, is in line with Putin's views about absolute and limited sovereignty more than with the traditional Euro-Atlantic understanding of sovereignty and of the mutual support embodied in Dean Acheson's words in 1949.

Despite the White House's apparent disdain for NATO, Trump's cabinet appointees told a different tale. At the February 2017 Munich Security

Conference, Defense Secretary James Mattis reassured his worried audience that NATO remained the bedrock of transatlantic security, saying the "transatlantic bond remains our strongest bulwark against instability and violence."[62] The stark contrast between the White House and the Department of Defense raised serious questions about what US policy going forward would be. Nevertheless, the prospect of a lessened US commitment to NATO has galvanized the rest of the alliance to recommit to increasing their own defense spending.

The July 2018 Brussels NATO summit exposed the deep rift between Trump and his allies, raising questions about whether NATO is facing an existential crisis. Trump began with a breakfast at which he attacked Angela Merkel for being "captive" to Russia because of Germany's imports of gas: "We're supposed to protect you against Russia, but they're paying billions of dollars to Russia, and I think that's very inappropriate."[63] As he berated his allies, a grim-faced NATO secretary-general Jens Stoltenberg tried to push back politely, pointing out that most allies have already increased the percentage of their GDP they spend on defense. The next day Trump interrupted a session with the Ukrainian and Georgian presidents and insisted at an emergency meeting that the US would pull out of NATO unless all the allies pledged to increase their defense spending immediately. Eventually he claimed victory, saying that they had agreed to do so.[64] In fact, the NATO communiqué to which Trump signed on was very tough on Russia. It contained language about "Russia's aggressive actions," which had adversely affected the European security environment, and committed NATO to further deterring Russia while at the same time continuing the NATO-Russia partnership "based on respect for international law and commitments."[65]

Given the uncertainty about NATO's future, it is quite possible that by the end of Trump's term in office, two fundamental elements of NATO may have been further eroded: the US commitment to Europe and the Euro-Atlantic agreement to defend Europe against aggression from a hostile power. The possibility of European populist parties gaining power or at least leverage to diminish their own governments' investment in NATO could create a radically different European security landscape.

If NATO does survive in its present form, the West has limited options. It can work with Russia while eschewing previous attempts to persuade Russia to sign on to a rules-based order. In that case, the issue will be how the alliance deals with Russian actions in the post-Soviet space going forward. For the time being, NATO serves a useful purpose for Russia. It provides a most convenient main opponent.

—6—

RUSSIA AND ITS "NEAR ABROAD"

How Civilized a Divorce?

> Anyone who doesn't regret the passing of the Soviet Union has no heart. Anyone who wants it restored has no brains.
>
> —*Vladimir Putin, 2005*[1]

> I would like to make it clear to all: our country will continue to actively defend the rights of Russians, our compatriots abroad, using the entire range of available means—from political and economic to operations under international humanitarian law and the right of self-defense.
>
> —*Vladimir Putin, 2014*[2]

The Moldovan president Igor Dodon walked up to the podium at the 2017 Saint Petersburg International Economic Forum plenary. He criticized the European Union and the Association Agreement that Moldova had signed with Brussels in 2014. Then he turned to Putin, who smiled as he declared: "We are different from the Western world. We have got different cultures, we have got different values, we have different customs.... We used to have an anti-Russian foreign policy, but after the presidential elections we decided to rectify this situation."[3] Rarely does the leader of such a small, poor country—population 3.6 million, average per capita income $3,000 per year—have the opportunity to appear on stage at a major international conference with the same status as President Putin and his other guest, Indian prime minister Narendra Modi. But Dodon was there for a specific purpose, to show that Moldova was the "un-Ukraine." It had realized the error of its ways by seeking to turn West and align with the European Union, had repented, and was now returning to Mother Russia. No matter that Moldova's pro-European prime minister shortly thereafter contradicted Dodon, claiming that he had no authority to "declare or make such decisions."[4] For the thousands of conference attendees, Dodon's message was clear: Russia's neighbors were rethinking their international alignments, expressing remorse about their flirtation with the West, and gravitating back to Moscow.

Since Putin's ascension to the Kremlin, domination of the new Eurasia—a vast expanse of territory from the Baltic Sea to the Pacific Ocean—has been an essential component of his main goal of restoring Russia as a great power.

The collapse of the Soviet Union created an unprecedented challenge for Moscow: how to interact with its new neighbors, some of whom had been part of the tsarist empire and the USSR for four centuries. Russia now had fourteen land neighbors. As Putin has pointed out, the United States has only two neighbors, enjoys generally good—if somewhat bumpy—political relations with both of them, and all three have increasingly integrated economies. The same cannot be said for Russia and some of its neighbors. Russia acquired Ukrainian lands in the seventeenth century and began expanding east to conquer all of Siberia by the late seventeenth century. Under Peter the Great, it absorbed the Baltic states. Under Catherine the Great, it acquired parts of Poland, Crimea, and Novorossiya, the lands north of the Black Sea that are the scenes of today's separatist war. Russia moved south to conquer the Caucasus and Central Asia in the nineteenth century. In 1918, the Baltic states became independent—only to be reabsorbed by the USSR in 1940. The three states of Transcaucasia—Georgia, Armenia, and Azerbaijan—declared their independence after the Bolshevik Revolution, only to be reabsorbed by 1920. After World War Two, Kaliningrad and Western Ukraine became part of the USSR. At that point Stalin had achieved something the tsars had never accomplished. The USSR was larger than any other previous Russian state. The historical process of "gathering in the lands" appeared to be complete and unassailable. But Yeltsin's signing of the Belavezha Accords in December 1991 dismantled the USSR with one fell swoop and reduced Russia to the smallest size it had been since 1654.

Russia, Ukraine, and Belarus dissolved the Soviet Union on December 8, 1991, in that Belavezha hunting lodge outside Minsk. They did not invite any other republics to the dissolution ceremony. The Central Asian countries objected, claiming they did not want to leave the USSR. But once the hammer-and-sickle flag was lowered from the Kremlin for the last time on Christmas Day 1991, they had no choice. The USSR was gone. The Soviet dissolution was termed a "civilized divorce" because, unlike in Yugoslavia, it had been relatively peaceful. It is important, more than a quarter century later, to remember that while some republics sought independence, others had independence thrust upon them, and this reluctant statehood has benefited Putin.

The Soviet system was essentially patrimonial—the Kremlin and the rulers of the republics maintained their positions of authority in return for distributing resources to a network of supportive clients scattered throughout the country. All political competition took place informally at the elite level, rather than through elections or political parties. Patronage politics worked particularly well in the clan-based societies of Muslim Central Asia. The "second economy," or black market, that existed throughout the USSR was prevalent in the agricultural sector in Central Asia, with local producers and party officials colluding to falsify statistics and set up alternative networks of exchange for their products. Indeed, the system worked so well that, in contrast to other parts of the USSR, there was little public demand for reform in Central Asia under Gorbachev, hence the resistance to embrace independence.[5]

Imperial Russia colonized the territories it conquered by sending Russian officials into its far-flung corners, seeking to assimilate local elites into Russian imperial structures. This process was quite successful in the Ukrainian lands but less so in other areas. Hence Lenin's appeal to the non-Russian ethnic groups in the multinational empire. After the Bolshevik Revolution, Stalin, as commissar of nationalities, drew the borders of the new Union of Soviet Socialist Republics seeking to prevent one single ethnic group from dominating each of its fifteen constituent republics, with the exception of the Russian republic. In his native republic of Georgia, for instance, he included as autonomous subunits the territories of South Ossetia and Abkhazia, both of which held historical grievances against the Georgian people. This ensured friction, which eventually erupted into armed hostilities in the late 1980s when central authority was weakened. Every republic in the USSR was a multiethnic patchwork, and it was only the iron hand of the communist authorities that kept the peace and suppressed interethnic violence. During the entire Soviet period, a superstructure of Russified communist political institutions was superimposed on local customs and political cultures, which, after lying dormant for seventy-four years, reasserted themselves after 1991. The Kremlin has benefited from this Soviet legacy of ethnic resentments and contested borders, and has encouraged the frozen conflicts in the post-Soviet space.

Creating viable countries where none existed at the time of the Soviet collapse was a great challenge for the new states. Moreover, the transition from an imperial power to a post-imperial power—to accepting the independence of its neighbors—has been particularly challenging for Russia over the past quarter century. But rather than see Putin's Russia as seeking to restore the USSR, it is more accurate to say that the Kremlin would like the outside world, and particularly the West, to treat it as if it were the Soviet Union: a nuclear superpower whose interests are as legitimate as any other great power, a country to be respected—and still feared. This means accepting that Russia has a right to a sphere of privileged interests in the post-Soviet space. As one Russian observer put it, "Accept us as we are; treat us as equals; and let's do business where our interests meet."[6] But Russia is realistic enough to understand that it cannot re-create the USSR, nor would it want the economic burdens that would accompany an imperial restoration. Russia is today what might be called a "postmodern empire, in which many of the physical features of empire have disappeared, but where the imperial spirit is still present and even resurgent."[7]

Russia feels a sense of entitlement toward its neighbors based on shared history, language, and culture, what Foreign Minister Lavrov has called "civilizational commonalities" in the post-Soviet space. It believes that it has a *droit de regard* in its neighborhood. Russia's national identity extends spatially beyond the current border of the Russian Federation to the borders of the USSR—minus the Baltic states.[8] The very words Russians used to describe the former Soviet states—the "near abroad"—conveys that Moscow does not view Minsk or Yerevan or Astana as foreign capitals but as capitals of semi-independent entities with which Russia should enjoy a relationship that differs from that of "far abroad" powers. These outside powers should not treat Russia's neighbors as they treat other, fully independent countries. There is also an important security dimension to these concerns. The Kremlin views the post-Soviet countries as part of its own defense perimeter and believes that it must control the strategic space in which they are located. Hence they must not join Western security organizations that are deemed hostile to Russia's core interests—primarily NATO.[9]

Russia's ability to exert influence in its neighborhood has been facilitated by the persistence of the "post-Soviet syndrome" in all of the former Soviet republics—except the Baltic states. This syndrome exists on a continuum and is most pronounced in Central Asia and less so in some of Russia's Western neighbors. Nearly three decades after the Soviet collapse, the rule of law, transparent governance, real political competition, and democratic institutions have barely taken root in most of the post-Soviet states, and their political systems resemble that of Russia far more than those of Europe or the United States. Post-Soviet countries are run by small groups of political and/or family clans, where nominally competitive elections are in fact managed and their outcomes often predetermined. As a Kazakh official said, "In Central Asia, people need a clear leader and controlled modernization." Personal ties and informal networks are more important than institutions of governance, which are weak. The rule of law is also weak. There are few transparent succession mechanisms. The economy is controlled by a small elite with close ties to the political leadership, and together they control most of the country's assets. Corruption and nepotism are rife. Freedom of expression is curtailed, and the electronic media are state run or controlled by magnates close to the leadership. Commercial ties between Russian oligarchs and wealthy business magnates in the post-Soviet states reinforce the influence of Russian ways of doing business. However, Ukraine, Georgia, Armenia, and Moldova do not exhibit all the features of the post-Soviet system. They have competitive elections whose outcomes cannot be predicted, and they permit greater freedom of expression. In most post-Soviet countries, the ties that bind are often stronger than those that divide Russia from many of its neighbors. Moreover, Russia, unlike the US or the EU, never criticizes its neighbors for democratic deficits.

Under Putin, Russian policy in Eurasia has had three main goals. The first is to pursue the economic and political integration of its neighbors via the newly-created Eurasian Economic Union and through upgrading the existing Collective Security Treaty Organization. The second is to expand Russian influence in the region through the use of "soft" power instruments, such as the organization Russky Mir (Russian World) and the World Congress of Compatriots Living Abroad, which promote Moscow's interests through Russian-language teaching and Kremlin-friendly electronic media. The third is using economic (mainly energy) or military pressure against those states seeking to exit Russia's influence and integration via the frozen conflicts or direct military aggression, as in Ukraine. Remittances are another form of leverage. More than 25 percent of the GDP of Kyrgyzstan and Tajikistan comes from remittances from migrant labor in Russia, and the economies of Uzbekistan, Armenia, Moldova, and Georgia also depend on remittances from Russia.[10] Under Putin, the Kremlin has viewed Western activity in the post-Soviet states as a major security risk and has sought to benefit from its neighbors' vulnerability to Russian influence via the frozen conflicts.[11]

Core Interests and Challenges in the Post-Soviet Space

The Russian Diaspora

When the USSR collapsed, about 22 million Russians lived outside the Russian Federation. Completely accurate figures are hard to come by, because the word "Russian" can mean ethnic Russian or someone who may be partly Russian, speaks Russian, or identifies with "civilizational" Russia.[12] The largest diaspora—12 million—was in Ukraine, with 1.7 million in Crimea. The next largest diaspora was in Kazakhstan, with 8 million Kazakhs and 4 million Russian speakers, mainly in the north. There were also large diasporas in Uzbekistan, Belarus, Estonia, and Latvia, and smaller ones in the rest of the fifteen newly independent states. They had been sent there decades earlier by the Soviet regime to ensure as much Russification and conformity to official Communist Party programs as possible. They also went there to assist in the economic development of the republics. Stalin sent some to gulags in different republics. In most of the fifteen union republics, the first party secretary was from the majority ethnic group, but the second party secretary was Russian. In 1992, these Russians were suddenly non-citizens in new countries seeking to cast off the Soviet legacy. How was Russia to deal with them?

In contrast to other diasporas, the Russian diaspora never organized into a coherent group across the former Soviet space. Russians barely were able to organize into a lobbying organization inside the countries in which they lived. While Moscow made halfhearted attempts to push the idea of dual citizenship or offer Russian passports to diaspora Russians, most of them realized that it was more prudent to accept a civic—as opposed to ethnic—definition of citizenship. Eventually, most diaspora Russians became citizens of the countries in which they lived. Some left and returned to Russia, and out-migration was greater from Central Asia than from other countries. The situation in the Baltic states was particularly complicated. Latvia and Estonia had large Russian populations, and they initially introduced very restrictive citizenship tests for Russians, hoping that many of them would leave. But despite constant accusations from Moscow of discrimination against ethnic Russians in the Baltics, very few have "voted with their feet," including those pensioners who served in the Soviet military in Narva, Estonia. Under pressure from the European Union, which they joined in 2004, the Baltic states have modified their citizenship laws, and protests by Russians have diminished.

In 1992, Yeltsin and his foreign minister Andrei Kozyrev introduced the term "compatriots abroad," referring to people who live outside the borders of the Russian Federation but feel they have cultural and linguistic ties to Russia, irrespective of their citizenship. A series of state programs was created to promote ties with compatriots, but under Putin, things have become more organized and better funded. Outreach to the diaspora has become more dynamic, with active participation by the Russian Orthodox Church, designed to enhance Russia's role as a newly restored great power. Putin is now the champion of the global diaspora. In 2007, the Kremlin funded the new organization Russky Mir (Russian World), to appeal to compatriots. According to a member of its board, there are 300 million Russian speakers globally.[13] The foundation has three goals: to promote the Russian language in the former Soviet space, to promote Russian as a second language globally to rival English and Chinese, and to ensure that Russian remains a world language.[14] As Putin said in his 2007 Address to the Federal Assembly:

> The Russian language not only preserves an entire layer of truly global achievements but is also the living space for the many millions of people in the Russian-speaking world, a community that goes far beyond Russia itself. As the common heritage of many peoples, the Russian language will never become the language of hatred or enmity, xenophobia or isolationism.[15]

Putin has built upon the compatriot idea to justify the annexation of Crimea and to defend the rights of Russians living in Ukraine. He now portrays himself as the guarantor of security for the Russian world and claims the right to intervene wherever Russians feel threatened.[16] Since the annexation of Crimea, the Russian world is now described as a "state civilization" situated on a distinctive territory struggling with other civilizations for resources. The concept is now a justification for "re-collecting the Russian lands," for Russian revanchism, defined as the desire to recover not territories per se but past position, power, and status.[17] Diaspora politics have become an important geopolitical lever.

Military Security and Counterterrorism

For a brief moment after the Soviet collapse, Yeltsin and his advisers hoped to create a military force that included other post-Soviet states, but that idea was stillborn. Each new country wanted its own armed forces, and yet Russia felt vulnerable because it defined its security perimeter as the border of the former USSR. As early as 1993, Russia's military doctrine said that suppression of Russians in the near abroad represented a military threat to Russia.[18] So the Kremlin worked out arrangements with some of its neighbors to station its troops on their territory. In the last years of the Gorbachev era, fighting broke out in the areas that are now frozen conflicts: Nagorno-Karabakh, Transnistria, South Ossetia, and Abkhazia. These are unrecognized entities that separated from the central authority after an armed conflict and are supported by Russian troops, which remained there after the Soviet collapse and during its tumultuous aftermath. Russia's union treaty with Belarus in 1996 allowed Russia to station troops there to protect its western flank. Later, during the Tajikistan Civil War, Russia became heavily involved in ending the hostilities and retains troops there. Today Russia has a military presence in eight of the fifteen former Soviet states: Armenia, Belarus, Georgia, Kazakhstan, Kyrgyzstan, Moldova, Tajikistan, and Ukraine. This enables it to project military power effectively in its neighborhood. Each of the post-Soviet states has its own armed forces, but the Russian military is far stronger than that of any of its neighbors.

The Kremlin is deeply worried about the terrorist threat largely emanating from Central Asia. Russia has worked bilaterally with its neighbors on these issues but also multilaterally with both China and the United States. Its perspective on terrorism differs from that of the United States and its allies. It focuses on the threat to Russians, as opposed to any broader global threat. Russia's main concern in Central Asia is that the secular authoritarian governments of the region could be destabilized, leading to the radicalization of Muslims in the Russian Federation, which has suffered from numerous terrorist attacks.

Although Yeltsin did not succeed in retaining a Russia-dominated integrated Commonwealth of Independent States military force in 1992, he created the nucleus of a multilateral military alliance, which became the Collective Security Treaty Organization (CSTO) in 2002. Putin aspires to develop CSTO into the equivalent of a Eurasian NATO, but it remains a pale replica of NATO. Unlike NATO, CSTO does not have an Article 5 committing its members to come to each other's collective defense should one be attacked.[19] Indeed, Russia has never invested in creating the structures required to underpin such a commitment. CSTO members are Russia, Armenia, Belarus, Kazakhstan, Kyrgyzstan, and Tajikistan. Its secretary-general until 2017 was Nikolai Bordyuzha, a former secretary of the Russian Security Council.[20] The new head is Yuri Khachaturov, ex-head of the Armenian general staff.

CSTO's members are divided into three groups: Western (Belarus and Russia), Caucasus (Russia and Armenia), and Central Asian (Russia, Kazakhstan, Kyrgyzstan, and Tajikistan). CSTO has also created a rapid reaction force of 22,000 troops, of which 10,000 are Russian, but not all members participate in the force. Moreover, CSTO's credibility was seriously eroded during the outbreak of ethnic violence in Kyrgyzstan in 2010—resulting in more than 400 casualties—when, despite appeals by the Kyrgyz president for the CSTO to intervene, Moscow refused to get involved and deploy peacekeeping forces.[21] The CSTO's effectiveness is also hampered by lingering mistrust among its members that Russia is trying to limit their sovereign decision-making and by tensions between individual members. For instance, Armenia would like its allies to commit to supporting it in its conflict with Azerbaijan, but they have demurred.

Moreover, Putin's repeated attempts to have NATO recognize the CSTO and develop a partnership with it have been rebuffed. In the words of a US official opposing formal ties between the two organizations, the CSTO "is an organization initiated by Moscow to counter potential NATO and US influence in the former Soviet space."[22] So while NATO cooperates with individual members through their Partnership for Peace programs, there is little prospect of Brussels being willing to work with the CSTO itself. CSTO member states, especially those in Central Asia, would like the organization to serve as a bulwark against color revolutions—by political opponents or religious extremists—but ultimately their mistrust of each other and doubts about Russia's commitment to back them up in the face of a public uprising highlight the limits of Russia's Eurasian integration projects.

Ramzan Kadyrov, the Chechen Ruler

Concerns about the dangers of Islamic extremism extend from Central Asia to Russia itself, particularly to Chechnya. Because of these threats, Moscow's goals in the near abroad are inextricably linked to what has been called Russia's "inner abroad," the North Caucasus.[23] These six multiethnic Muslim-majority republics are part of the Russian Federation but far less integrated into it than its other eighty territorial subjects. They have presented a major challenge to the Kremlin since the Soviet collapse because a combination of separatism and religious fundamentalism has created a persistent low-level insurgency and terrorism in Russia's south. The most problematic republic is Chechnya, with whom the Kremlin has fought two wars since the Soviet collapse. Indeed, Putin's rise to power in 1999 was facilitated by his launch of the Second Chechen War in 1999. Justifying his actions then, he famously said of his Chechen opponents, "Pardon my language, if we catch them in the toilet, well, then we'll whack them in the outhouse."[24]

Two of the most lethal terrorist attacks in Russia were the 2002 seizure of the Dubrovka Theater in Moscow by Chechen terrorists, which resulted in 130 deaths, and the 2004 seizure by Chechen and Ingush terrorists of an elementary school in Beslan, North Ossetia, in which 331 people perished, 186 of them children. There also have been terrorist attacks carried out by Chechens and Central Asians in the Moscow and Saint Petersburg subways and at Moscow's Domodedovo Airport.

Today Chechnya is ruled by Ramzan Kadyrov, a strongman who runs his fiefdom with an iron hand. He apparently enjoys an extravagant lifestyle. According to a leaked US diplomatic cable, his exploits include attending a thousand-person wedding in neighboring Dagestan, where he "danced clumsily with his gold-plated automatic stuck down the back of his jeans," after which he showered guests with hundred-dollar bills.[25] Putin and Kadyrov made a deal after the end of the Second Chechen War. Kadyrov promised to pacify the republic if he were allowed to run it without interference from the Kremlin. Today, with extensive financial subsidies from Moscow, Chechnya is quiet, but the laws of the Russian Federation barely extend to its territory, where Kadyrov's draconian and capricious interpretation of sharia law prevails. Kadyrov has sent Chechen battalions to fight on Assad's side in Syria and to join the separatists in the Donbas—although there are also Chechens supporting the Ukrainian side.[26] A substantial number of fighters who have joined the Islamic State in Syria and Iraq are Chechens too, an estimated three to four thousand.[27]

Kadyrov is outwardly hyper-patriotic. "We say to the entire world that we are combat infantry of Vladimir Putin," he has announced. Kadyrov and his supporters have been linked to the assassination of opposition leader and Putin critic Boris Nemtsov in the shadow of the Kremlin, and so far the Chechen who pulled the trigger has been convicted, but not the person who ordered the murder. Some Russians believe that Putin has made a Faustian bargain with Kadyrov to maintain the peace in Chechnya, the consequences of which could one day come to haunt him. Kadyrov, in this view, has considerable leverage over Putin. But others believe

Kadyrov serves a useful purpose for Putin because he can threaten Putin's opponents without the Russian leader having to do it himself. According to Alexei Venediktov, editor-in-chief of Russia's last remaining independent radio station, Echo of Moscow, and a target of Kadyrov's wrath, "Just like anyone with unlimited power, who faces no borders at all, he tries to expand his influence as much as possible."[28]

Frozen Conflicts

Frozen conflicts in the post-Soviet space began before the USSR collapsed and persist today. They are areas where fighting has waned but no peace treaty or other political framework has resolved the situation to the satisfaction of the combatants. The conflicts have created four unrecognized statelets in which Russia continues to exercise influence. Vladimir Putin did not create the frozen conflicts in Eurasia, but he has used them to enhance Russia's leverage in the post-Soviet space. Their persistence means that none of the three states of the South Caucasus—Armenia, Azerbaijan, and Georgia—fully controls its own territory, and neither does Moldova, which shares a border with Romania and Ukraine. The four frozen conflicts resulted from the wars of Soviet succession. Although the Soviet breakup itself was relatively peaceful, ethnic strife in these regions broke out under Gorbachev and intensified after 1992 to produce four unrecognized entities. The failure to bring the conflicts to an end guarantees that these statelets will remain weak and beholden to Russian economic largesse and military support in the absence of international recognition.

Nagorno-Karabakh

The first of the disputes to erupt was in Nagorno-Karabakh, an Armenian-majority enclave within Azerbaijan. It is the longest-running secessionist conflict in Eurasia. In 1989, the ethnic Armenians—representing 80 percent of the enclave's inhabitants—complained of cultural discrimination and economic underdevelopment, and demanded that the enclave be

transferred from Azerbaijan to the Armenian Soviet Socialist Republic. Christian Armenians view Muslim Azeris—whose language is Turkic—as being closely allied to Turks, and they associate them with the Armenian Genocide under the Ottoman Empire. The ethnic enmity between the two groups was suppressed under the Soviet system but reemerged as soon as Gorbachev began his liberalization program.

In 1992, armed hostilities between Armenians and Azeris intensified, and eventually a cease-fire was brokered by the OSCE in 1994. The war resulted in 25,000 deaths, and the displacement of 700,000 Azeris and 400,000 Armenians. The Armenians declared their own state in Nagorno-Karabakh and de facto control it, but a peace treaty has never been signed and the Azeri government does not accept that the enclave is no longer part of Azerbaijan. Fighting periodically erupts, and in April 2016 there was a four-day "mini war" that raised fears of renewed conflict. Since 1992, the OSCE has led the Minsk Group, which meets regularly to try to find a solution to the problem; its co-chairs are Russia, the United

States, and France. Russia has also periodically sought to bring the Azeri and Armenian sides together to broker a peace agreement but so far has failed. Nagorno-Karabakh represents the essence of the dueling narratives in the post-Soviet space: Armenians base their claim for Nagorno-Karabakh's independence on the principle of the right to national self-determination. Azeris base their claim to Nagorno-Karabakh on the right to territorial integrity.

Hostilities between the two countries are such that when Turkey reached out to Armenia to normalize relations in 2009 and began to explore the possibility of opening its border with Armenia, Azerbaijan vigorously objected and the Turkish overture was stillborn.[29] As a result, only Armenia's borders to Georgia and Iran are open, which has increased its economic dependence on Russia, although it does not share a border with Russia. Russia continues to supply arms to both Armenia and Azerbaijan. After the annexation of Crimea, Armenia supported Russia in the UN General Assembly, while Azerbaijan voted to condemn the annexation, mindful of what the precedent could mean for Nagorno-Karabakh. Armenia and Azerbaijan remain in a state of war with each other and have no diplomatic relations, but both have extensive ties to Russia.

A careful examination of Russia's actions shows that, in this frozen conflict, Russia has played a generally constructive role over the past twenty-five years and has coordinated its bilateral efforts with the United States and France.[30] Yet it is debatable whether Russia is indeed interested in seeing this conflict end, because the lack of resolution provides it with ongoing leverage over both Armenia and Azerbaijan—which it might lose were the two sides to come to an agreement.

In April 2018, Armenia underwent an unexpected "velvet" popular uprising against the government. Long-term ruler and strongman Serzh Sargsyan was replaced by opposition anti-corruption activist Nikol Pashinyan as prime minister. To the surprise of many, Russia's reaction was muted. The Russian Foreign Ministry's Maria Zakharova complimented the Armenian people's unity in a difficult situation: "Armenia, Russia is always with you!"[31] Pashinyan made it clear that Armenia would continue to be allied with Russia and was not seeking to move toward the EU. That is the litmus test for the Kremlin.

Transnistria

Transnistria, the second frozen conflict, is a breakaway region of Moldova that the Russian military and heavy Russian economic subsidies help to sustain. It is a landlocked self-proclaimed state (population 475,000) that lies between the Dniester River and Moldova's border with Ukraine. Only Nagorno-Karabakh, Abkhazia, and South Ossetia recognize it as a state. It is the only secessionist conflict in the post-Soviet space that remains "frozen" inasmuch as, unlike in Nagorno-Karabakh and Georgia, both sides agree on the boundary line and there is no ongoing fighting. Nevertheless, the war in Ukraine has raised new questions about Russia's future intentions in this conflict.

As is the case in Ukraine, changing historical borders and complex national identities have facilitated Moscow's involvement. In the early

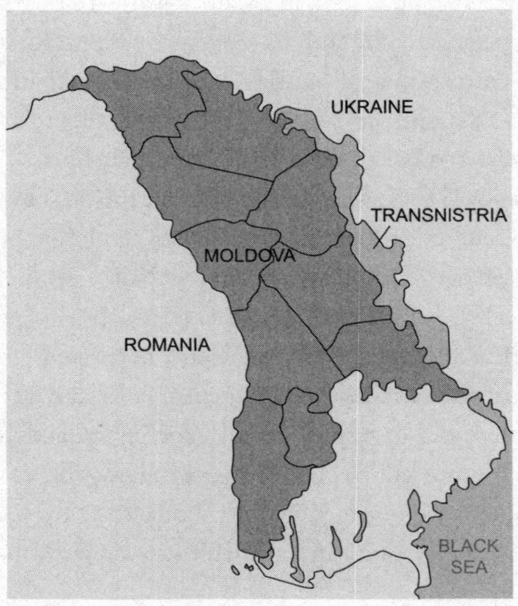

nineteenth century, Russia took what is present-day Moldova—then called Bessarabia—from the Ottoman Empire. But after the Bolshevik Revolution, most of Bessarabia became part of the Kingdom of Romania. In 1924, the USSR created the Moldovan Autonomous Soviet Socialist Republic out of the territory it still controlled, which is today's Transnistria. As a result of the Molotov-Ribbentrop Pact, Stalin acquired Bessarabia, and after the end of the war, the USSR regained control over all of today's Moldova. Moldovans are essentially Romanians, their language and culture are very similar to that of Romania, and the Soviet attempt to create a separate Moldovan ethnic identity only partially succeeded.[32]

As the USSR unraveled and Moldovans declared their independence, the population of Transnistria objected. Their seven decades under Soviet rule had given them a different identity. They were bound to Russia by strong ties in the military-industrial complex, by the Russian language, and by ties to the Russian 14th Army stationed there. At the time of the Soviet breakup, there was talk of Moldova reuniting with Romania, and the pro-Russian population in Transnistria feared they would be marginalized. They declared their independence from Moldova, and hostilities broke out in 1992 between the new Moldovan armed forces and Russia's 14th Army. Eventually a cease-fire was signed, and Transnistria emerged as a de facto autonomous state protected by Russian troops, although it is internationally recognized as part of Moldova.

Since the end of hostilities, the OSCE has led a five-plus-two mediation process, consisting of representatives from the OSCE, Russia, Ukraine, the EU, the US, Moldova, and Transnistria, but the group meets only intermittently. Today 75 percent of Moldova's population of four million is ethnically Romanian, and 6 percent is Russian. In Transnistria, roughly 30 percent is Russian. The area has its own flag, currency, and border guards. It is best known as a haven for smuggling and illicit trafficking of goods and people. But like the other frozen conflicts, it survives not only because of Russian support but also because the authorities in the capital of the region have done quite well from business deals with the separatists.[33]

In 2003, the Kremlin decided to intervene actively to resolve the

Transnistrian issue by suggesting a plan for federalization of Moldova similar to proposals Putin has put forward more recently for Ukraine. The Kozak Memorandum provided for the settlement of the Transnistrian conflict and the reunification of Moldova with a plan for an asymmetric federation. Some of the most important governmental powers—minority rights, customs, energy, the national bank, law enforcement, federal taxes and budgets, and electoral law—were to be shared equally between the federal government and the two federal subjects: Transnistria and Gagauzia, a region populated by the Russian-speaking Orthodox Turkic Gagauz ethnic group, which had also declared its independence from Moldova. This plan would have given Transnistria a virtual veto over national government policies—including moving closer to the EU and NATO—and would have compromised Moldova's ability to function as an effective state. It also would have permitted the Russian military to remain in Transnistria. For this reason, the OSCE, the EU, and the United States opposed the memorandum, but Moldovan president Vladimir Voronin was prepared to sign it. Putin announced that he would fly to Chisinau, the capital, to witness the signing. Reporters and television cameras assembled to film the historic moment. But demonstrators gathered in the streets in Chisinau to protest the agreement, and as they were waiting, television screens suddenly went live, broadcasting from Georgia the Rose Revolution, showing President Eduard Shevardnadze being carried out of the parliament to safety as mobs of angry Georgians protested a falsified election. If the president could be overthrown by protestors in Tbilisi, why not in Chisinau?

Shortly before Putin was to board his plane, EU high representative Javier Solana called President Voronin with a blunt message: "If you sign this memorandum, you can say goodbye to your hopes for European integration." Hours of frenzied negotiations trying to salvage the agreement followed, but in the end, Voronin called Putin to say he would not sign. Dmitry Kozak, author of the memorandum, denounced Voronin's "political irresponsibility," and Putin was reportedly furious and accused George Bush personally of derailing the settlement. The failure of the

Kozak Memorandum reinforced Putin's belief that the West was directly competing with Russia for influence in the near abroad and that this was indeed a zero-sum game to which Russia had to respond robustly.[34] There was now no incentive to resolve the conflict.[35]

Since 2003, the Kremlin has pursued a two-pronged policy. It supports the Transnistrian government in Tiraspol and maintains an active military presence there. But Russia has not recognized Transnistria's independence, nor has it responded positively to its requests to become part of the Russian Federation. Its real aim is to maintain and solidify its influence in the breakaway region as a source of leverage over Moldova.

In 2014, Moldova resisted Russian pressure and signed a Deep and Comprehensive Free Trade Agreement (DCFTA) with the EU. In 2016, Transnistria joined the agreement and benefits economically from it. Moldova also cooperates closely with NATO, although membership has never been officially on the table. Still, the Kremlin remains concerned about Moldova's future direction. Russia has benefited from persistent governmental dysfunction and ongoing corruption scandals in Moldova, including the disappearance of $1 billion from three Moldovan banks, representing 12 percent of the country's GDP.[36] As a result of continuous political turmoil, Igor Dodon—an academic turned politician—was elected president in 2016, promising to clean up corruption and move Moldova closer to Russia, as he told Putin in Saint Petersburg. He has proposed reviving the idea of a federal state and granting special status to Transnistria similar to what Russia and the separatists in Ukraine are demanding for Luhansk and Donetsk: a People's Republic. Some question whether Moldova is seriously interested in reintegrating Transnistria, with all its economic problems. Meanwhile, Putin will no doubt continue to encourage Dodon to move his country closer to Russia.

Georgia's Abkhazia and South Ossetia

The final two frozen conflicts—Abkhazia and South Ossetia—are no longer frozen, inasmuch as Russia has recognized them as independent states after defeating Georgia in a brief war and has signed alliance treaties with both of them. In the Soviet period, both regions were part of the Georgian Soviet Socialist Republic and opposed Georgian domination, while the Georgians resented Russian domination. The Abkhaz are divided between Orthodox Christians and Muslims. The Ossetians are predominantly Christian with a Muslim minority. To complicate matters further, ethnic Ossetians are divided between the republic of North Ossetia, which is part of the Russian Federation and in which 450,000 Ossetians live, and South Ossetia, where 65,000 live (out of a total population of 98,000).[37] As the USSR disintegrated, both Abkhazia and South Ossetia sought independence from Georgia and were engaged in civil wars with the new leaders in Tbilisi. When the fighting was over, 250,000 Georgians had been ethnically cleansed from Abkhazia, and Russian peacekeeping troops remained in both areas. In both wars, Russia played an ambiguous role, alternately supporting different sides during a period when the Yeltsin government was not in full control of its military. Fighting would periodically erupt in both regions, but they remained under nominal Georgian control. And then came the 2003 Rose Revolution and Mikheil Saakashvili.

Eduard Shevardnadze, Gorbachev's foreign minister, had ruled Georgia since the end of the civil wars. Greatly admired in the West for his role in ending the Cold War, he was increasingly unpopular in his own country with its dysfunctional political system. Georgia had become a weak and corrupt state. Younger Georgians chafed under his leadership, and in November 2003, a falsified parliamentary election brought protestors into the streets, and Shevardnadze had to flee. The new president, Mikheil Saakashvili, was tall, charismatic, and eloquent in several languages, having been educated in Ukraine and the United States. A Clinton administration official who became his staunch advocate described him as "flamboyant, brash—a swashbuckling figure in a region that had produced a disproportionate share of bigger-than-life personalities."[38]

This was the first of the color revolutions in the post-Soviet space, and its implications were not lost on Putin: a disgruntled populace, incensed about corruption, repression, and falsified elections, had deposed an unpopular leader. Nevertheless, Putin initially tried to work with Saakashvili, although Saakashvili was unwilling to show the Russian president the respect he felt he deserved. Relations soon began to fray as Saakashvili cultivated close ties with George W. Bush, sought integration with the EU, advocated Georgia joining NATO, and pledged to regain control over South Ossetia and Abkhazia. It did not help that he was known to have referred to Putin as "Lilli-putin," an unflattering reference to the Russian leader's height compared to his own.[39]

The Russia-Georgia relationship deteriorated rapidly after Saakashvili abruptly and publicly expelled Russian spies in 2006. Russia imposed a ban on imports of Georgian wine and mineral water for "sanitary" reasons, and they suddenly disappeared from Russian stores. Military tensions between the two countries increased in the summer of 2008. Headstrong and unrealistic about his ability to reunite Georgia and resist the Russians, Saakashvili ignored repeated warnings from George W. Bush, Condoleezza Rice, and EU leaders not to act recklessly. But others in Washington, including in the office of Vice President Cheney, sent contradictory messages, encouraging the man they considered the standard-bearer of freedom against Russia. On the night of August 7, 2008, Georgia launched a "massive artillery attack" against the South Ossetian capital of Tskhinvali, which killed Ossetians and the Russian forces protecting them.[40] Russian troops then marched into South Ossetia from North Ossetia, and over the course of the next five days, 40,000 Russian troops entered Georgia. At the same time, Georgia was subject to a massive coordinated cyberattack that disabled all the major government and financial sites and obstructed the conduct of military operations. Although the Russian army's equipment was antiquated—officers used cell phones to communicate with their men—the Russians soon overwhelmed the much weaker Georgian army.

French president Nicolas Sarkozy, representing the EU, came to negotiate a cease-fire with the Kremlin. The Russians left Saakashvili in office, but he was rejected by his disillusioned electorate in 2012, left Georgia under threat of arrest, and made his way to Ukraine after the ouster of Viktor Yanukovych, where Petro Poroshenko appointed him governor of the Odessa region. He then quarreled with Poroshenko, lost his Ukrainian citizenship, and sought political asylum in the Netherlands.

At the end of the war, the independence of Abkhazia and South Ossetia was recognized by Russia, followed by Nicaragua, Venezuela, Nauru, and Vanuatu.[41] The former two have close ties to the Kremlin. The latter are tiny, impoverished Pacific island nations that apparently were well compensated for their recognition.[42] Not one other post-Soviet state followed suit, concerned about the precedent of rewarding ethnic separatist groups for their own country. Russia now occupies 20 percent of Georgian territory. This was the first time Russia had broken its commitment to respect post-Soviet borders, but the Kremlin blamed the West for the war. As Putin later said, "[Saakashvili] would never be bold enough to do that on his own. In any case, no one tried to stop him."[43] Putin justified Russia's actions in the name of self-determination, invoking the Kosovo precedent, even though the parallels were questionable. Russia has been in violation of the Sarkozy-brokered peace agreement since the day after its signing. It has moved the Russian border further into South Ossetia, encroaching even more on Georgian territory, and thereby taking over parts of the Baku-Supsa oil pipeline, which transports oil from Baku through the Georgian Black Sea port of Supsa to Europe.[44]

The Kremlin's actions were designed to weaken the Georgian state and complicate its attempts to join the West, especially NATO. Russia established military bases in both South Ossetia and Abkhazia, provides them with significant economic support, and plays an active role in their domestic politics. Both unrecognized states rely on Moscow for their future survival.

In August 2017, Putin pointedly visited Abkhazia to celebrate the ninth anniversary of its independence from Georgia—a week after US vice president Mike Pence visited Georgia to pledge support for Georgia's struggle to regain control over Abkhazia. "We reliably guarantee the security, self-sufficiency, and independence of Abkhazia. I am sure that will continue to be the case," said Putin.[45] In recognizing Abkhazia's and South Ossetia's statehood, Russia has achieved three goals: making it difficult for Georgia to function effectively as a state, perpetuating the post-Soviet dependence syndrome, and forcing the West to acknowledge the limits of its influence in Russia's neighborhood. The current Georgian government is seeking a less antagonistic relationship with Russia while maintaining its Euro-Atlantic aspirations, but there is little prospect that Tbilisi will regain control over its occupied territories.

Key Eurasian Relationships

Belarus

Russia's only true ally in the near abroad is Belarus, the "last dictatorship in Europe." And even that relationship is awkward and at times antagonistic. Stanislau Shushkevich, the westward-looking leader who signed the Belavezha Accords with Yeltsin, did not last long. In 1994, Belarusians elected Alexander Lukashenko as their president, and he remains in office to this day, having altered the constitution to accommodate his political ambitions. A former collective farm director, Lukashenko was the only member of the Belarusian legislature to vote against independence from the USSR. He is an idiosyncratic and repressive leader, unofficially known as *Bats'ka* (Daddy), and has enough support in the rural areas to remain in power. Early on he decided to ally with Russia, while the other post-Soviet states sought to escape Moscow's embrace. He has sought to maximize his leverage by playing Russia and the West off against each other: "Belarus has been both an indispensable ally and ward of the Kremlin, depending on Russian subsidies to keep its economy afloat and an important buffer zone for the West against the Kremlin's growing military aggressiveness."[46]

In 1996, Russia and Belarus signed the first of several treaties committing them to closer ties, culminating in the 1999 creation of the Union State. The treaty's goals were ambitious—including setting up a common market and a common legal system, and coordinating foreign and defense policies. Lukashenko had a grand design: to take over from Yeltsin at the end of his term in 2000 and rule the joint Russian-Belarusian state. But Lukashenko was disabused of this ambition when Yeltsin named Putin as his successor. Once in the Kremlin, Putin was cautious about drawing too close to Lukashenko, especially during his first years in office, when he was reaching out to the West. The far-reaching plans for integration were never implemented. Nevertheless, Belarus joined the Customs Union, the Collective Security Treaty Organization (CSTO), the Eurasian Economic Union (EEU), and other Russia-dominated multilateral organizations. Russia views Belarus as its westernmost line of defense against NATO. After all, Belarus was on the historical invasion route taken by both Napoleon and Hitler. Joint military maneuvers are routine; and in 2017, in preparation for the September quadrennial Zapad military exercises that simulate Russia's response to an attack by a NATO country, it deployed large numbers of troops to Belarus, raising speculation about its future intentions toward Minsk.

There are tensions between the two countries, most notably about energy. Belarus depends on Russia for most of its oil and gas, which it purchases at heavily subsidized prices. Russia has used oil and gas supplies as a form of economic and political leverage with Belarus, cutting off gas supplies in 2004 and oil supplies in 2007 because of its displeasure with Lukashenko's policies. Eventually Belarus had to make concessions to secure continuing energy supplies. Under pressure from the Kremlin, Belarus sold 50 percent of its gas transit monopoly Beltransgaz to Gazprom, leading Lukashenko to complain that the relationship with Russia is periodically "poisoned by gas."[47] The two countries continue to argue about energy prices and Belarus's $425 million debt to Russia. Things came to a head in December 2016, when Lukashenko boycotted a joint CSTO-EEU summit in Saint Petersburg, apparently the result of disagreements over energy and trade but also because the director of a Kremlin-affiliated think tank denied there was a separate Belarusian identity and language and criticized Lukashenko for conducting overly independent policies.[48] Just as some Russians question whether Ukrainian is more than a dialect of Russian and whether Ukrainians are a different nationality, identical challenges are raised about Belarusian identity and language.

Belarus remains an indispensable but quirky partner for Russia; it is essential to Russia's post-Soviet integration projects, but it is led by a man who is a challenge to control. Its presence sustains the mythology of a distinct post-Soviet space with a Slavic core, and it has been one of Russia's few supporters over the past decades.[49] Were Lukashenko to be replaced by a more Western-leaning leader, Putin might well reassess the current relationship whereby Russia guarantees Belarus's security but does not interfere in its domestic politics.

Kazakhstan

In July 2018, the Astana International Financial Center opened with great pomp and circumstance. Political and business leaders from China, Russia, the United States, Europe, and the Middle East gathered in the capital to hear President Nursultan Nazarbayev address the crowd as flashing colored lights and columns of smoke hailed the inauguration of the center. The AIFC is designed to become a regional financial and investment hub and will be governed by British law. Indeed, Kazakhstan has recruited a group of retired British judges to adjudicate AIFC cases. The inauguration of this center highlighted Kazakhstan's main aspirations: to become Central Asia's economic leader and to balance maintaining good relations with China, the United States, and, above all, Russia.[50]

Indeed, Russia's other key ally in the near abroad is Kazakhstan, with which it shares a 7,000 kilometer border, the second longest in the world after the US and Canada. Kazakhstan is the richest and most important Central Asian partner for Russia as it pursues four main sets of goals in the region: military security, regime consolidation, protection of ethnic Russians and the Russian language, and economic integration via the Eurasian Economic Union.

In the nineteenth century, the Russian Empire conquered Central Asia—a region populated by both sedentary and nomadic tribes—and dispatched Russians to colonize the sparsely populated lands. During the Soviet period, the Kazakh Soviet Socialist Republic had the largest ethnic Russian population in the USSR outside the Russian republic. In 1954, Nikita Khrushchev launched his ill-fated Virgin Lands Campaign, dispatching two million enthusiastic young Slavs to Northern Kazakhstan to dramatically boost agricultural production and solve the USSR's food crisis—ultimately an unsuccessful and costly fiasco.

During World War Two, ethnic Germans and Jews were relocated to Kazakhstan, and together with the populations of the various gulags in the area, they became the nucleus of a new intelligentsia after Stalin's death, making the Kazakh Soviet Socialist Republic a leader in science and medicine. During the Soviet period, a majority of Soviet nuclear tests were carried out at Kazakhstan's Semipalatinsk site, creating serious health and environmental consequences for the local population and leading post-Soviet Kazakhstan to become a champion of nuclear nonproliferation. Indeed, in August 2017, the International Atomic Energy Agency opened the world's first low-enrichment uranium bank in Eastern Kazakhstan to discourage new nations from trying to enrich their own uranium.[51] Kazakhstan also houses the world's first launch site, at the Baikonur Cosmodrome, for joint Russia-US flights that launch US astronauts into space.

In 1989, Nursultan Nazarbayev became the last communist leader of Kazakhstan, and he has remained in office since then, exchanging the symbols of Soviet socialism for secular Islam. Kazakhstan is the only post-Soviet state not to have undergone a leadership transition. With the title of Leader of the Nation, he can remain in office until 2020, and in the 2015 election he won 98 percent of the vote, albeit in a contest that the OSCE depicted as flawed.[52] He has carefully constructed a Kazakh national identity based on a multi-ethnic and multi-confessional state, and has moved the capital from the Soviet-era more cosmopolitan Almaty to Astana, located in the interior, a planned city with elegant boulevards and a gold-domed monument to the leader. Aware of the risks of living in a landlocked country in a dangerous neighborhood, which was part of the nineteenth-century Great Game between the British and Russian empires, he has deftly crafted productive ties to Russia, China, and the United States, positioning his country as an honest broker in a number of conflicts, a crossroads between East and West. His regime appears stable, but the threat of Islamic extremism is an abiding concern—several hundreds of Kazakhs have gone to fight with ISIS and other indigenous Central Asian terror networks. Moreover, in 2011, labor unrest in the western city of Zhanaozen led to violent clashes between disgruntled oil workers and police, resulting in more than one hundred casualties.[53] As he approaches eighty, the issue of succession—and Russia's potential role in the process—raises questions that have been exacerbated by the Ukrainian conflict. There are concerns that Russia could take advantage of any instability accompanying the succession and seek to annex Northern Kazakhstan, where most of the Russians live. In April 2018, Kazakhstan—which had a rotating seat on the UN Security Council—abstained on the Russian-originated vote to condemn the US and its allies for their air strike in Syria following a chemical weapons attack. The Russians were greatly displeased that the Kazakhs had not voted with them and made veiled threats to Astana.[54]

Russia views Kazakhstan as its most reliable and useful partner in the near abroad. As early as 1994, Nazarbayev was proposing a Eurasian Union with Russia and other ex-Soviet states, and Kazakhstan is an active member of both the CSTO and the EEU. Moreover, Kazakhstan, unlike its neighbors Uzbekistan and Kyrgyzstan, did not offer a military base to the United States after the 9/11 attacks. It has signed a series of bilateral treaties with Russia, the latest being the 2013 Treaty on Good-Neighborliness and Alliance.

Kazakhstan is also a key energy partner for Russia. The birthplace of the Russian oil industry is Baku, in Azerbaijan, but Kazakhstan has become the key Caspian oil producer, on a par with Norway, and Central Asia's largest energy producer. As a landlocked country, it is dependent on other countries to transport the 1.8 million barrels per day of oil it produces for export. Its major export pipeline passes through Russia, but it has also built pipelines to China. Its vast energy resources have enabled the nation to become a major international player, attracting investment from western majors like Chevron and ExxonMobil and from China. But Nazarbayev has also been careful to maintain close energy relationships with Russia. The private energy company Lukoil is the largest Russian investor in Kazakhstan, participating in seven projects there. Yet, beyond energy, the bilateral Russian economic relationship with Kazakhstan is quite modest. The EU is Kazakhstan's largest trading partner.

Despite these close ties, the annexation of Crimea and launch of the war in Ukraine have caused tensions in the Russia-Kazakhstan relationship. Although there has been significant out-migration of Russians from Kazakhstan back to Russia, roughly one-third of the population remains Slavic, largely concentrated in the north. Nazarbayev's policy of Kazakhization means that few ethnic Slavs remain in high positions in government structures, and some Russians have complained of discrimination in the workplace.

The Kazakh leadership was disturbed by the Ukrainian events and did not support Russia's annexation of Crimea in the UN General Assembly. Putin raised Nazarbayev's ire at a press conference in 2014 when he paid him a distinctly backhanded compliment. "[Nazarbayev] created a state on territory where no state had ever existed. The Kazakhs had never had statehood. He created it. In this sense, he is a unique person for the former Soviet space and for Kazakhstan too."[55]

The response was swift. Kazakhstan promptly announced plans to celebrate the 550th anniversary of the Kazakh Khanate, dated to 1465. While Nazarbayev acknowledged that the khanate "may not have been a state in the modern understanding of the term," the symbolism was impossible to miss.[56] The elaborate celebrations in September 2015 included traditional costumes, dances, displays of cultural artifacts in the yurt (the nomadic dwelling), and a triumphal parade through the streets of Astana.[57] Nazarbayev has also begun the process of shifting from the use of Cyrillic to Latin characters in the Kazakh language.

Since the onset of the conflicts in Ukraine and Syria, Nazarbayev has provided support to Putin by seeking to broker dialogue between the warring factions. He—along with Lukashenko—was present at the Minsk II negotiations on Ukraine and is a constant voice urging reconciliation. He hosted talks in 2015 between Iran and major world powers over Tehran's nuclear program. He offered to serve as a mediator when Russia and Turkey broke off relations after the Turks shot down a Russian aircraft on its way to Syria, flying over Turkish territory, and he visited Erdogan to show support after the 2016 attempted coup. He has hosted several rounds of peace talks in Astana with the warring factions in the Syrian conflict. All these activities enhance Kazakhstan's international standing as a conflict mediator and strengthen Nazarbayev's position domestically, but Nazarbayev is also generally supportive of Russian policies. Moreover, the Kazakh population receives much of its news coverage from the state-run Russian media and tends to believe the Kremlin's version of events. Putin and Nazarbayev meet often, and even if one discounts some of the more extravagant rhetoric of their mutual praise, they remain indispensable partners.[58]

The Eurasian Economic Union

Kazakhstan is Russia's key partner in the EEU, Putin's major project during his third term. Nazarbayev is credited with being the "godfather" of the EEU because he first floated the idea in 1994. But in reality this is

Putin's grand design to enhance economic integration of the post-Soviet area to solidify Russia's political dominance of the region. It is also a cornerstone of Putin's plan to create the institutions of a new, non-Western global order—and a defensive move to contain expanding Chinese and European Union influence in the near abroad. In 2011, as part of his election campaign, Putin announced his initiative building on an existing Customs Union to create a regional integration mechanism within the post-Soviet space that would mimic the European Union and bring its members into a "Greater Eurasia." It would not be a re-creation of the Soviet Union, he wrote: "It would be naive to attempt to restore or copy something from the past. However, a stronger integration on a new political and economic basis and a new system of values is an imperative of our era."[59] At this time the EU was negotiating with Ukraine, Armenia, Georgia, and Moldova to sign comprehensive free trade agreements, which involved renouncing sovereignty over external tariffs.

Although Putin has portrayed the EEU as a primarily economic organization, its members—Russia, Kazakhstan, Belarus, Armenia, Kyrgyzstan, and (prospectively) Tajikistan—all understand that Moscow views this also as a geopolitical project. Putin has said that the EEU would offer a chance for the post-Soviet space "to become an independent center for global development, rather than remaining on the outskirts of Europe and Asia."[60] The Kremlin conceives the EEU as a counterweight to Euro-Atlantic structures—the EU and NATO—expanding their reach into Russia's backyard but also as a way to temper the range of Chinese integration projects in Eurasia, such as the ambitious Belt and Road Initiative connecting China to Central and Southeast Asia and on to Europe. While Putin's ultimate goal is to create a "Greater Eurasia," including the post-Soviet space, China, India, and Pakistan, much of this remains aspirational. It is clear, however, that the non-Russian members of the EEU, while they are suspicious of Western democracy promotion and human rights advocacy, are also determined to resist Russian attempts at political integration, such as a joint parliament or common currency.

Putin's initial goal was to have all post-Soviet states join the EEU.

Ukraine was the most important prospective member, given its size and economic interdependence with Russia. Hence the pressure put on Yanukovych not to sign the agreement with the EU. Both the EEU and EU demand a single external tariff, so it was impossible to belong to both. But Poroshenko signed the EU agreement, as did Georgia and Moldova. Armenia also planned to sign the EU agreement, but after considerable pressure from Moscow in 2013, culminating in a "heart-to-heart" conversation with Putin, the Armenian president changed his mind and Armenia agreed to join the EEU. Given its security dependence on Russia because of the Nagorno-Karabakh conflict, it had no choice. But this is hardly an organization of equals, since Russia represents 86 percent of the GDP of the EEU, with Kazakhstan coming next at 10 percent, Belarus at 3.5 percent, and Armenia and Kyrgyzstan at less than 1 percent together. This means the other members are heavily dependent on the health of the Russian economy.[61] Moreover, the EEU countries make up only 6.6 percent of Russia's international trade (the figure for the EU is 49 percent).

Each member has its own agenda in the EEU. Belarus's energy dependence on Russia is its paramount concern, as are its agricultural exports to Russia. Lukashenko has ceded elements of Belarusian sovereignty to Russia in exchange for favorable energy prices, arguing, "sovereignty is not an icon one needs to pray before."[62] For Kyrgyzstan, migration is the paramount issue. The country has one of the highest rates of reliance on labor migration and remittances in the world. As much as 30 percent of its GDP has come from remittances sent by its citizens working in Russia. The EEU guarantees preferential visa treatment for migrants from member states, which Kyrgyzstan needs. For Kazakhstan, the agenda is different. It sees the EEU as a way to contain Russia within a rules-based organization.[63]

For all its ambitious aspirations, the EEU has struggled from the beginning. It came into existence in January 2015, an inauspicious time for the Russian economy, following the Ukraine crisis, Western sanctions, a precipitous drop in oil prices, and the devaluation of the ruble after a December currency crisis. The Russian economy was hit hard, and since all the EEU members are dependent on the health of the Russian economy, the contagion effect was immediate. Kazakhstan found that cheap Russian goods were flooding its market, and it had to devalue its currency. In Kyrgyzstan, there was a 45 percent drop in remittances from Russia. Trade inside the EEU fell by 26 percent in 2015. Russia's economic recovery in 2017 and 2018 and rising oil prices may eventually create more favorable conditions for the other EEU members, but so far Putin's goal of creating a vibrant economic bloc that will serve as a separate pole of the new world order seems some way off.

Post-Soviet Futures

The creation of the Commonwealth of Independent States (CIS) in 1991 was intended as a "civilized divorce," a way for Russia and the former Soviet republics to go their separate ways and avoid the turmoil and bloodshed engulfing a disintegrating Yugoslavia. With the exception of the fighting between Armenia and Azerbaijan and within Georgia, the USSR's breakup was nonviolent. But the Soviet divorce remains a work in progress. Nor has it been entirely civilized. With the exception of the Baltic states, it has proven very difficult for the post-Soviet countries to emerge from centuries of Russian imperial rule and seventy years of Soviet control with full independence and sovereignty. Russia continues to dominate its near abroad and retains considerable economic, military, and political leverage over most of its neighbors, in part because none of them has succeeded in constructing the institutions of modern governance and political resilience that would make them less vulnerable to Russian pressure. Twenty-five years is a short time span in the history of centuries of Russian dominance and the divorce will take much longer to be finalized. Meanwhile, most of Russia's neighbors, including those with whom Russia has alliances, continue to regard it warily, understanding their ongoing dependence on Moscow but determined to limit its ability to interfere in their internal politics or to dictate their external relationships. Nevertheless, the prevalence and sophistication of Russian-language electronic media in the post-Soviet space ensures that the Kremlin's version of reality will continue to influence the ruling elites.

Putin has accepted that the USSR cannot be resurrected, but he is determined to create Eurasian integrative structures that will bind the post-Soviet states and form the nucleus of a post-West order. These organizations will also support the larger objective of restoring Russia as a great power with a seat at the table on all important international decisions. Ukraine and Georgia may at present be lost causes, but their internal weaknesses may yet provide opportunities for Russian influence. Russian soft power—particularly through language, culture, and media—continues to bind the citizens of the post-Soviet space.

In June 2017, Alexei Navalny, the Russian opposition politician who constantly criticizes Putin but also appeals to Russian nationalists, remarked on a TV show, "Yes, it goes without saying that nobody in Uzbekistan knows who Pushkin is." The response on Facebook was instantaneous. Uzbek adults explained that Tashkent has a monument to the Russian poet, has streets named after him, and Uzbeks study all of Russia's great poets. Young Uzbek children posted endearing videos of themselves reciting Pushkin verses. One man chided Navalny, telling him he really does not know anything about Uzbekistan and should visit the country.[64] In short, the power and attraction of Russian culture should not be minimized.

Russia's influence is greatest in Central Asia, with the exception of Turkmenistan, which exists largely in its own orbit. Faced with China's ever-expanding economic presence, Central Asian countries look to Moscow to balance Beijing. But, as the Kazakh case shows, they also assiduously guard their domestic autonomy, seeking to limit Russia's ability to interfere in their succession processes. The next test will come in Kazakhstan, when Nazarbayev departs the political stage, but as in most post-Soviet countries, the succession process is opaque. Russia's relations with Belarus are close but sometimes adversarial, and Putin has at times indicated his exasperation with the mercurial Lukashenko. Moreover, the

Kremlin's preference for grand framework agreements, such as the EEU, should not be confused with sustainable and effective integration mechanisms in a time of economic stringency in the post-Soviet space. But the ongoing frozen conflicts will continue to provide Russia with opportunities to influence Eurasian outcomes until the Kremlin decides it is in its interest to have them resolved.

After 1991, the mantra in the West was that it was crucial to support the independence of the post-Soviet states and disabuse Russia of the notion that it had a sphere of interest there. More than twenty-five years later, there are serious questions about how realistic this is. Neither the United States nor Europe is prepared to become involved in this part of the world to an extent that would seriously challenge Russia's predominant role as has been clear in Ukraine. Eurasia represents an intermittent, as opposed to a core, interest for the West. Indeed, as the war in Afghanistan winds down, the US is withdrawing from Central Asia and leaving it to China and Russia to work out their modus vivendi. The EU has grown weary of its attempts to promote reform in Belarus. It will continue to engage Moldova, Georgia, and Ukraine and encourage them to implement their Association Agreements, but it will not offer them a membership perspective. And while the EU and NATO will continue to rebuff Russian attempts to secure formal agreements with the EEU and CSTO, they will periodically rethink how to engage these organizations in a more limited way. The West is not ready to recognize a Russian sphere of influence in the near abroad, but there are limits to which it will go to challenge Russia's interests in the region.

A wary Armenian official of the Eurasian Economic Union pithily summed up the current reality: "This independence thing has not worked out that well."[65] Putin does not wish to restore the USSR, but he will continue to seek to exploit the vulnerabilities of his neighboring states as they struggle to move beyond the post-Soviet syndrome, knowing that the West's response will be restrained.

7

"THE PAST IS ALWAYS CHANGING"

Russia and Ukraine

> Imagine Crimea is yours and the wart on your nose is no more.... This deed will win you immortal glory greater than any Russian Sovereign. Crimea assures dominance of the Black Sea.... Russia needs paradise!
>
> —*Prince Grigory Potemkin in correspondence with Empress Catherine the Great*[1]

Two competing banknotes begin to tell the story. The Russian thousand-ruble note has a picture of Yaroslav the Wise (978–1054), Grand Prince of Kiev, a venerated ruler of Kievan Rus. His father, Vladimir (Volodymyr in Ukrainian), was baptized as an Orthodox Christian in Crimea and accepted Christianity as the religion of Rus. Yaroslav stands sideways with his full beard in the tradition of Muscovite rulers, holding a scepter. The Ukrainian two-hryvna note also has a picture of Yaroslav the Wise. This Yaroslav's face—with a Ukrainian Cossack-style mustache but no beard—looks straight ahead with no adornments. Both Russia and Ukraine claim Yaroslav as their sovereign, the first to give them a code of law. Was Yaroslav a Russian or a Ukrainian ruler? Was Kievan Rus indeed the origin of the Russian state, as many historians have argued, or was it the cradle of the original Ukrainian nation? For centuries, both Russians and Ukrainians have claimed him as their own. Indeed, the competition for Yaroslav has been so fierce that in 1943, with the Soviet army advancing, Ukrainian clergy removed his remains from the cathedral in Kyiv where he is buried and allegedly moved them to New York, to prevent them from being taken to Moscow.[2]

Vladimir Putin does not accept that Russia and Ukraine are two different nations. As he told the documentary filmmaker Oliver Stone, "I'm deeply convinced that the Ukrainian people and the Russian people are not simply close relatives. They are almost the same."[3] Moreover, he does not believe that Ukraine is really a separate state, as he told George W. Bush in 2008.

These are hardly just debates about history. The dueling narratives have, in the past few years, become deadly. As a result of Russia's annexation of Crimea and support for an ongoing conflict in the Donbas region in Southeastern Ukraine, more than ten thousand people have died, more than two million have become refugees and displaced persons, and Ukraine's statehood has been under constant pressure. The events of 2014 were a turning point, precipitating a breakdown of the post–Cold War consensus that accepted the borders of the former Soviet republics as the borders of the newly independent states. They have caused many Europeans to question Russia's commitment to a stable, secure Europe. The Kremlin views Ukraine's international orientation as an existential question. It claims that if Ukraine were to join the West, this would represent a direct threat to Russia's heartland. Ukraine in turn views Russia as an existential threat to its continued sovereignty and existence. So far, no resolution to this conflict is in sight. Indeed, Russia's recent actions have helped unify what was until recently a Ukrainian identity divided between East and West. Why has Russia essentially refused to accept Ukraine's right to self-determination since the Soviet collapse? What is the Kremlin's game plan for dealing with Ukraine going forward? Can Russia and Ukraine ever find a peaceful modus vivendi?

The Shadow of Kievan Rus

As the old Soviet joke put it, in a system where interpretations of history are protean, "the past is always changing." In the case of Russia and Ukraine the past has noticeably changed since the Soviet collapse.

Moreover, the argument about identity is not only between Russians and Ukrainians but among Ukrainians themselves. Russian and Ukrainian historians have long been engaged in "a struggle for the exclusive possession of the supposed legacy of Kievan Rus."[4] Where did the words "Rus" and "Ukraine" originate? The word "Rus" has Scandinavian roots and was first used to describe Vikings who populated Eastern Europe. A Kievan chronicler first used the word "Ukraine" around 1187 to describe the steppe borderland from Pereiaslav in the east to Galicia in the west. The word "Ukraine" means "borderland," but it soon fell into disuse as a term for a specific territory and was not revived until the early nineteenth century. We know that Kievan Rus was a polity inhabited by different tribes, among them Eastern Slavs, whose center was in Kyiv, and it encompassed part of today's Western Russia and Ukraine. It was not a state in the modern sense of the word and had no centralized government.[5] It came into being sometime in the mid-tenth century and ended on December 7, 1240, when the invading Mongols took Kyiv. Indeed, the battle of historical accounts continues with different narratives about life under the Mongols. Russians talk about the "Tatar yoke" and Mongol oppression; Ukrainians portray them as less intrusive.[6]

After the Mongols retreated, today's Ukraine became part of the Polish-Lithuanian Commonwealth and remained under its rule until 1648. The commonwealth was a multinational state, and its population fluctuated with waves of different migrations, including those of the Ukrainian Cossacks. A French military engineer who served in the Polish army described these freebooters in 1651 in vivid terms:

> There is not one of them, of any age, sex or rank whatever, who does not try to drink more than his companion, and to outdo him in revelry.... They are sly, crafty, clever [and yet] sincerely generous... they greatly value their liberty, and would not want to live without it.[7]

The First Independence Interlude

It was a Cossack who first led Ukrainians to independence from the Poles—only to change course and unite Ukrainian lands with Russia. Cossack nobleman officer Bohdan Khmelnytsky led the revolt against the Poles and, to his surprise, defeated their armies. Khmelnytsky arranged a triumphant entrance into Kyiv in December 1648, where he was hailed as the new leader of Rus and called "Moses" for delivering the nation from Polish enslavement.[8] But the revolt soon became internationalized, and Khmelnytsky eventually decided to seek a new protector. In 1654, in the town of Pereiaslav, a group of Cossack officers and their leader swore allegiance to the new sovereign of Ukraine, Tsar Aleksei Romanov of Muscovy, the second Romanov tsar. (In 2017, when the separatists in Southeastern Ukraine declared their own independent state, they did so with a replica of Khmelnytsky's banner.[9]) So ended the first, brief period of Ukrainian independence and began the long, complex relationship with Russia. In 1954, the USSR with great fanfare celebrated the tercentennial of Ukraine's "reunification" with Russia. The reality is a little more prosaic. The tsar, unlike the Polish king, was willing to grant the Cossacks privileged status and recognize their statehood. Hence Khmelnytsky's decision to align with Muscovy. What is striking in the complex Russia-Ukraine relationship is the constant inveighing of competing historical narratives.

Ukrainians in the Russian and Austro-Hungarian Empires

Between the late eighteenth century and 1917, people who came to identify themselves as Ukrainians lived in both the Russian and Austro-Hungarian empires. This split historical experience is the basis for Putin's claim to Bush that part of Ukraine is in Eastern Europe while most of it "was given" to Russia. It also explains why the formation of a unified Ukrainian national identity has been such a challenge since independence and why some Ukrainian citizens in the east of the country feel more affinity with Russia than with Ukraine.

A brief period of greater autonomy for the Cossack Hetmanate ended after Peter the Great defeated the Swedes in 1709 at the Battle of Poltava, declared himself emperor in 1721, and renamed the tsardom of Muscovy the Russian Empire, thus signaling the rise of Russia as a major European power. Those Ukrainians living under Russian rule were gradually absorbed into the Russian imperial system and Cossack self-governing units were abolished. Russians began to call Ukrainians "little Russians." In 1768, Catherine the Great went to war with the Ottoman Empire, and for the first time, Russia gained control over what is today's Donbas region in Southeastern Ukraine, the territory seized by Russian-supported separatists in 2014. Catherine called these lands, which included the Port of Odessa, Novorossiya (New Russia). Russia also conquered Crimea for the first time. The peninsula had been under Ottoman rule, and its inhabitants were Muslim Crimean Tatars.

Catherine the Great's lover, Prince Grigory Potemkin, who administered these newly acquired territories, persuaded the tsarina that she should visit her new conquests. In 1787, she set out from Saint Petersburg on a six-month trip to Sevastopol in Crimea, covering more than 4,000 miles by land and water. Potemkin, realizing that the trip had to be flawless, arranged for all the roofs in villages she passed on the Dnieper River to be freshly painted, the streets freshly paved, giving rise to the legend of "Potemkin villages," or "false fronts covering a gloomy reality."[10] Catherine was gratified as she traversed the new lands of Ukraine. A wilderness was waiting to be developed, and Potemkin planned cities on the Black Sea, attracted foreign colonists to settle in them, and began to create the fleet that would be his legacy.

As Russia was conquering Southeastern Ukraine, the Polish-Lithuanian Commonwealth began to break apart, ending in 1772 with the first of three partitions of Poland. Those Ukrainians living in Galicia were now ruled from Vienna and were called Ruthenians in most of the Austro-Hungarian Empire and Rusyns in the Transcarpathia region. By 1795, ethnic Ukrainians were divided between Dnieper Ukraine under the Russian tsars—where 85 percent of them lived—and Austria-Hungary. The social and cultural development of ethnic Ukrainians between the late eighteenth century and the Bolshevik Revolution diverged widely. Galician Ukrainians in Western Ukraine preserved their language and customs more than those Dnieper Ukrainians under imperial Russian rule in the east. They began to develop a distinct national consciousness, participating in the revolutions of 1848 and declaring their autonomy. For the next half century this consciousness grew. In imperial Russia, by contrast, there was little effective political activity on behalf of ethnic Ukrainians, nor was the Ukrainian language well developed. Most Russians did not consider Ukrainians a separate ethnicity. After the 1905 revolution, the first Ukrainian-language journal appeared in Kyiv, and a group of Ukrainians gained a few dozen seats in the new Duma, where they tried to promote Ukrainian causes. But the tsar soon dissolved the Duma and put an end to these endeavors.

Revolution, War, Famine, and War Again

Vladimir Lenin promised the non-Russian ethnic groups living in the empire that, if the revolution came, they would achieve independence. In March 1917, after the tsar's abdication, representatives of Ukrainian political and cultural organizations in Kyiv composed a coordinating body, the Central Rada. The revolution came in October 1917, and the Ukrainians took Lenin at his word. Following the Bolshevik coup, the Rada proclaimed the Ukrainian People's Republic and in January 1918 declared Ukraine's independence. Thus began Ukraine's second, brief period of independence from Russia during the chaotic post-revolutionary period and the civil war. The collapse of the Austro-Hungarian Army and ensuing Russo-Polish War also reunited Dnieper and Galician Ukrainians and led to the proclamation of an independent Ukrainian state of former Russian- and Austrian-ruled parts of the country in 1919. But the collapse of the Austro-Hungarian Empire also created a new, independent Polish state.

As the Russo-Polish War intensified, Lenin's long-term goal of world revolution was subordinated to the imperatives of military victory over the Poles. Without Ukrainian bread and coal, that would be very difficult. Ukraine's rich black earth and abundant grain supplies were indispensable for Russian victory. In 1920, the Poles defeated the Russians and seized lands the fledgling Ukrainian state had sought to incorporate. By the terms of the March 1921 Treaty of Riga, Poland took back Galicia, and Ukraine was once again divided—this time between Russia, Romania, Poland, and Czechoslovakia. The question of why Poland and Czechoslovakia were able to achieve independence after 1918, while Ukraine was not, is partly answered by the weakness of the Ukrainian national movement and the different historical trajectories of Galician and Dnieper Ukraine.[11]

Under Stalin's rule, Soviet Ukraine experienced a brief cultural renaissance—with increased use of the Ukrainian language in educational institutions. This was soon followed by a dark decade of famine and violence during collectivization and the purges. When Stalin began his campaign of forced collectivization of the Soviet countryside, and many peasants throughout the USSR burned their crops and slaughtered their livestock in acts of resistance against being herded onto collective farms, the regime singled out Ukraine for especially harsh treatment. Between 1932 and 1934, increasingly unrealistic grain requisition quotas were levied on Ukrainian peasants. Altogether, close to four million people in the Ukrainian Soviet Socialist Republic perished as a result of the ensuing famine.[12] Ukrainians refer to this man-made famine as the Holodomor, a premeditated act of genocide during which Stalin deliberately targeted Ukrainians for elimination. Many Russians dispute this narrative, claiming that Stalin was essentially an equal-opportunity killer and that there were Soviet-made famines in other parts of the Soviet Union during collectivization.

Ukrainians had barely recovered from the famine and Stalin's purges when Germany invaded Poland under the secret terms of the 1939 Molotov-Ribbentrop Pact, followed shortly thereafter by the USSR invading Eastern Poland and acquiring the Galician Ukrainian population. In June 1941, Hitler scrapped his agreement with Stalin, launched Operation Barbarossa, and invaded the USSR—through Belarus and Ukraine. Ukraine was, for the Nazis, the ultimate *Lebensraum* (living space), a territory where racially pure Germans could escape from the "unhealthy urban society" and build a racially pure society. This meant, of course, removing the local Slavic population, who they considered *Untermenschen* (subhumans). The *Reichskommissar* for Ukraine, Erich Koch, was a particularly brutal leader.[13] Nevertheless, given many Ukrainians' antipathy toward Soviet rule, some of them initially welcomed the Nazi invaders as liberators and collaborated with them. This, plus the fact that one of their nationalist leaders, Stepan Bandera, initially allied his organization with the Nazis, has fueled the current Russian narrative about "Ukrainian fascists" running the government in Kyiv. Other Ukrainians joined the resistance to the Nazis. By the time Lieutenant-General Nikita Khrushchev led Red Army troops to recapture Kyiv in November 1943, Bandera and others had grown disillusioned with the Germans.

The territorial settlement at the end of World War Two reunited Galicia and Dnieper Ukraine in the new Ukrainian Soviet Socialist Republic. Stalin had managed to secure Roosevelt's assent to allow Ukraine to have its own delegation at the United Nations, which gave it international status. His successor, Nikita Khrushchev, in a seeming act of generosity, made that decision in 1954 whose consequences he could not possibly have foreseen. In honor of the 300th anniversary of the Treaty of Pereiaslav, and celebrating the "great and indissoluble friendship" of the Russian and Ukrainian people, he transferred Crimea from Russian to Ukrainian jurisdiction, making it part of the Ukrainian Soviet Socialist Republic.[14] At that point Khrushchev was involved in an ongoing power struggle and he wanted to improve his support among Ukrainian elites. He did this not just for symbolism and sentiment but also for practical economic reasons, hoping that Ukraine was in a better geographic position to help Crimea's struggling economy. After all, Ukraine and Crimea were connected by land, whereas Russia had no access by land to Crimea.[15]

In the years between Khrushchev's rise and Gorbachev's coming to power, Ukrainians were well integrated into Soviet society, with a disproportionately high percentage serving in the Soviet armed forces. Much of the Ukrainian intelligentsia was Russified and co-opted into the Soviet system. A quarter of the Soviet military-industrial complex was located in Eastern Ukraine. Periodically nationalist currents would assert themselves, but they would be suppressed. Mikhail Gorbachev himself embodied this Soviet reality, with a Ukrainian mother and a Russian father. When he came to power, his calls for glasnost were not immediately taken up by the more conformist Ukrainian party leadership. But events soon changed that. In 1986, the nuclear explosion at Chernobyl—including the initial cover-up that may ultimately have cost hundreds, if not thousands, of lives in Ukraine and the subsequent admission of guilt by the Soviet authorities—mobilized public opinion.[16] Between 1986 and 1991, different Ukrainian nationalist groups organized themselves, pressuring for greater autonomy and, ultimately, for independence. Although much of the Ukrainian party ruling *nomenklatura* were reluctant nationalists, they were caught up in an accelerating process of state collapse as Soviet citizens took Gorbachev at his word and insisted on self-determination.

When asked at a lecture in the Library of Congress some years after the Soviet collapse what his greatest mistake had been, Gorbachev paused and said, "I underestimated the nationalities question." Ever since the tsarist empire began to expand, eventually comprising more than one hundred different ethnic groups, the rulers' challenge was to maintain centralized control over this complex mosaic of languages, cultures, and religions. The default instinct was Russification—the imposition of Russian language and culture on the population—which produced a counter-reaction and mobilized non-Russian groups to join the Bolsheviks. Eventually history repeated itself seventy-four years later. Like Soviet leaders before him, Gorbachev believed that the federal Soviet state, which had existed since 1922, had resolved the national question by granting limited cultural autonomy to different ethnic groups. This was especially true of Ukraine, viewed as the cradle of Russian history.

But in the end, Ukraine was instrumental in the collapse of the USSR. Throughout 1990 and 1991 Gorbachev sought to negotiate a new union treaty that would have held the USSR together by granting more autonomy for the union republics. How different things might have turned out had he succeeded. But just before the vote on a new treaty, a group of disgruntled hard-line officials staged a coup against Gorbachev while he was on vacation in Crimea. Shortly after the August 1991 putsch collapsed, Ukraine's top legislative body the Supreme Soviet, under the leadership of party chief Leonid Kravchuk, declared its independence, much to Gorbachev's dismay.

He was not the only official to oppose the Ukrainian move. President George H. W. Bush did everything he could to keep the Soviet Union alive. The US was very concerned about the security implications of a potential Soviet collapse because of the USSR's vast nuclear arsenal. Just before the coup, in a speech in Kyiv, Bush admonished Ukrainians: "Freedom is not the same as independence. Americans will not support those who seek [independence] in order to replace a far-off tyranny with a local despotism. They will not aid those who promote a suicidal nationalism based upon ethnic hatred."[17]

In December 1991, the Ukrainian people voted in a referendum for independence: 90 percent supported independence, including 83 percent in the Donetsk region and 54 percent of the population of Crimea. Shortly thereafter, Boris Yeltsin met with Kravchuk and Belarusian leader Stanislau Shushkevich in the hunting lodge in the Belavezha Forest outside Minsk. What happened at that meeting? What promises were made? Revisionist interpretations of this meeting have fueled the current Russian narrative about Crimea. While the Russian delegation arrived with proposals for a reformed Slavic union, Kravchuk was determined that

Ukraine emerge from the meeting with its independence. On the first night, dinner was dominated by a vigorous debate about whether some form of union could be preserved. Kravchuk argued with Yeltsin about whether the USSR should be completely dissolved. In the end, after two days of intense discussions, the three leaders emerged with a handwritten document (there were no typewriters in the hunting lodge) that dissolved the USSR. The Agreement on the Establishment of a Commonwealth of Independent States (CIS) consisted of fourteen articles. The three leaders agreed to recognize the territorial integrity and existing borders of each independent state. So ended seventy-four years of Soviet rule. Andrei Kozyrev, Yeltsin's foreign minister, called George H. W. Bush to give him the news. As for Gorbachev, he was furious: "What you have done behind my back with the consent of the US president is a crying shame, a disgrace," he told Yeltsin.[18]

Almost from the beginning, Russians began to question the legality of the hastily written agreement. They hinted that a secret addendum would have permitted changes in borders were the local population to decide this by referendum. What is indisputable is that Kravchuk's refusal to sign a new union treaty led to the Soviet Union's demise. For that reason, some Russians blame Ukraine for precipitating what Putin has called "a major geopolitical disaster of the twentieth century."[19]

Russia and Ukraine Under Yeltsin

The three signatories to the treaty that ended the USSR termed it a "civilized divorce." But as the 1990s wore on, the Russian-Ukrainian divorce became increasingly acrimonious. Yeltsin's main objective in convening the meeting that dissolved the USSR had been to oust Gorbachev from the Kremlin. He had not thought through the implications of ushering in an independent Ukrainian state. Four years later, it became clear that Yeltsin was having second thoughts about the security implications of the Soviet breakup. A September 1995 presidential decree, laying out Russia's security interests in the CIS and the imperative of protecting the rights of Russians living there, stated that "this region is first of all Russia's zone of influence."[20] Almost from the beginning, Russian officials sought to reinforce that decision by using the extensive financial, trade, personal, political, and intelligence networks that bound the two societies together to undermine Ukrainian sovereignty and strengthen dependence on Moscow. The Russian Duma, even in its early, more pluralistic incarnation, intervened on several occasions to declare that Crimea was Russian, backed by Moscow's powerful and outspoken mayor Yuri Luzhkov, who had extensive personal investments on the peninsula. Domestic developments inside Ukraine served to facilitate these Russian endeavors. In the 1990s, Ukraine developed a more pluralistic political system than that in Russia but one ruled by corrupt, oligarchic clans that failed to build transparent institutions of government and law strong enough to resist Russian meddling. The energy sector was particularly corrupt, with opaque middlemen—both Ukrainian and Russian—amassing fortunes from the transit system that carried Russian gas to Europe via Ukraine.[21]

Three issues dominated Russia-Ukraine relations in the 1990s: nuclear weapons, the disposition of the Black Sea Fleet, and Crimea. When the USSR collapsed, Ukraine was the world's third largest nuclear state after the United States and Russia, with one-third of the Soviet nuclear arsenal and significant capacities in design and production. It had 2,000 strategic nuclear warheads and 2,500 tactical nuclear weapons. Immediately after the Soviet collapse, the fate of Ukraine's nuclear arsenal became an urgent matter for US policy makers. The prospect of "loose nukes" set off alarms in the White House. The issue dominated Washington's policy toward Ukraine during the last year of the George H. W. Bush administration and the first years of the Clinton administration.[22] The United States was determined that Russia be the only nuclear state in the post-Soviet space. That meant Ukraine, Belarus, and Kazakhstan (the latter two also had nuclear weapons on their territories) should transfer their warheads and delivery systems to Russia, which would destroy them. Initially, Washington wanted Russia to handle the negotiations with its three post-Soviet neighbors, but that proved impossible. So in the end the United States negotiated with all four states to accomplish denuclearization.

At the end of the USSR, acrimonious rhetoric was exchanged between Ukrainian and Russian officials, parliamentarians, and commentators; there was a concern that war—perhaps even a nuclear conflict—might break out. Hence the urgency the West felt to move the nuclear weapons out of Ukraine. The new Ukrainian government, suspicious of Yeltsin's longer-term intentions, asked the Americans to give it security guarantees similar to those of NATO members—namely that the United States would come to Ukraine's assistance were it attacked by another power. But American officials realized that was impossible and proposed that Russia also provide Ukraine with security assurances. And so, after an arduous negotiation process, the US insisted on using the word "assurances" instead of "guarantees" in the legal document that accompanied Ukraine's denuclearization. "Assurance" implies a lesser commitment than "guarantee." Here is where translation fails. The problem is that both Russian and Ukrainian use the same word for guarantee and assurance, leaving room for misinterpretation.

In January 1994, Bill Clinton had to twist the arms of both Yeltsin and Kravchuk to sign a trilateral agreement on the disposition of Ukraine's nuclear weapons.[23] He met with them in Moscow wearing a button that read "Carpe Diem" (Seize the Day).[24] In December of that year, the deed was finalized in Hungary with the new Ukrainian president, Leonid Kuchma. The Budapest Memorandum on Security Assurances was signed by the United States, the United Kingdom, and Russia. The three signatories agreed to "respect the independence and sovereignty and the existing borders of Ukraine," "to refrain from the threat or use of force against the territorial integrity or political independence of Ukraine," and "to seek immediate United Nations Security Council action to provide assistance to Ukraine... if Ukraine should become a victim of an act of aggression."[25]

In June 1996, two trains carrying the last strategic nuclear warheads departed Ukraine and arrived in Russia, where the warheads were delivered to a dismantlement facility. Ukraine had given up its nuclear weapons in return for security "assurances" from Russia, the United States, and the United Kingdom. Just how credible these were became clear in March 2014, when neither the United States nor the United Kingdom came to Ukraine's assistance after Russia's military incursion into Crimea and later into the Donbas region. Nor was the United Nations able to intervene, because of Russia's veto in the Security Council. The Budapest Memorandum was a dead letter, a lesson not lost on either advocates of nonproliferation or states aspiring to become nuclear powers. Giving up nuclear weapons makes a country vulnerable to outside aggression.

The Black Sea Fleet was the second most contentious issue between Russia and Ukraine. The former jewel in Russia's naval crown, created by Prince Potemkin and headquartered in Sevastopol, Crimea, was, in the words of the nineteenth-century London *Times,* "the heart of Russian power in the East." The fleet had 350 ships and 70,000 sailors at the time of the Soviet collapse.[26] Russia was determined to maintain its naval presence in Crimea. Ukraine, which had a $3 billion debt to Russia, mainly to Gazprom, was not in a strong bargaining position. Although Yeltsin himself understood that a compromise had to be found, he was battling his Supreme Soviet, which called for "a single, united, glorious Black Sea Fleet."[27] In the immediate post-Soviet years, the situation was tense, as Russian and Ukrainian commanders challenged each other by raising—and then taking down—each other's flags on their ships. Ukraine did not have the wherewithal to take over the fleet completely, and Russia would never have acquiesced to that. After a series of protracted negotiations, Yeltsin and Kuchma eventually signed an agreement in 1997 dividing the fleet. Russia agreed to lease basing facilities in Crimea, principally in Sevastopol, for its Black Sea Fleet until 2017 and would pay for the lease by forgiving part of Ukraine's debt. When Viktor Yanukovych was elected president in 2010, he extended the Russian lease until 2042.

Closely tied to the Black Sea Fleet issue was the dispute over Crimea. At the time of the Soviet breakup, ethnic Russians constituted 60 percent of the peninsula's population and 70 percent of the population in Sevastopol, home to the Black Sea Fleet. For the first half of the 1990s, Russian lawmakers would vote to reincorporate Crimea into the Russian Federation, and local leaders in Crimea would declare independence from Ukraine. In May 1992, the Russian parliament declared illegal Khrushchev's 1954 transfer of Crimea to Ukraine, and the Crimean legislature scheduled an independence referendum—with Moscow's approval. Eventually, Crimea was granted the status of an autonomous republic inside Ukraine with considerable self-rule powers. But the peninsula began to suffer from economic neglect. "The Palm Springs of the Soviet Union has now become the Coney Island of Ukraine," said a US official.[28]

In 1997, Yeltsin and Kuchma signed the Treaty of Friendship, Cooperation, and Partnership Between the Russian Federation and Ukraine. The treaty codified the border, and both sides agreed to work toward a strategic partnership. It was Yeltsin's first official visit to Kyiv as Russian president, and he sounded a conciliatory note: "We respect and honor the territorial integrity of Ukraine."[29] At this point Russia appeared to have reluctantly reconciled itself to the independence of a Ukraine that included Crimea. The treaty in retrospect represented the high point of Ukraine-Russia relations in the post-Soviet era. Once Putin came to power, things began to change.

Putin and Ukraine: From the Orange Revolution to Gas Wars

When Putin entered the Kremlin in 2000, Ukraine's president, Leonid Kuchma, was steering a careful course between Russia and the West. Putin traveled to Kyiv shortly after becoming president and praised the relationship with Ukraine while pointedly noting Kyiv's outstanding gas debt to Russia. The two presidents traveled to Sevastopol, boarded flagships of both their navies, and Putin acknowledged Ukraine's sovereignty over both Sevastopol and Crimea. It appeared to be a promising start to relations. Privately, however, Ukrainian officials expressed wariness about this unknown Kremlin leader with a KGB past.[30]

Ukraine's domestic situation under Kuchma suited Moscow. Economic reform had stalled, oligarchic capitalism and corruption were on the rise, and the gas trade was arguably the most corrupt element in a system that united Russian and Ukrainian magnates. Eighty percent of Russia's gas exports to Europe went through Ukraine. The gas trade, including gas purchased from Central Asia and then re-exported to Europe via Ukraine, was in the hands of an opaque middleman company jointly owned by Russians and Ukrainians, RosUkrEnergo (RUE). There was no "us versus them" in the gas trade, and both Russians and Ukrainians amassed large fortunes from RUE.[31] Ukraine's weak institutions, floundering economy, and corrupt political system left it vulnerable to Russian influence. Moreover, financial and intelligence networks from the Soviet period that connected Ukrainians and Russians had survived the Soviet collapse. When Kuchma was implicated in the murder of investigative journalist Georgiy Gongadze, the United States demanded an unbiased inquiry. The Kremlin never criticized Kuchma for undemocratic practices.

But the people of Ukraine had a different view. They became increasingly frustrated with their government and its lack of accountability. In the lead-up to the 2004 presidential election, they were determined to choose a more accountable leader. Kuchma's chosen successor was Viktor Yanukovych, a former juvenile delinquent from the Donetsk region who represented the pro-Russian part of Ukraine and spoke Russian. His main rival was Viktor Yushchenko, former central bank governor with an American wife, whose first language was Ukrainian and who represented Ukraine's pro-Western forces. Unlike in Russia, elections in Ukraine were not "managed" and the outcome was not predetermined. The election campaign became a contest between Russia and the West. Ukraine occupied a key place in Putin's foreign policy priorities, and he was determined that Yanukovych win. The Kremlin also mistakenly believed that tactics that had worked well in manipulating Russia's own elections would be equally effective in Ukraine. But, in the words of outgoing president Kuchma, "Ukraine is not Russia."[32]

In July 2004, Putin effectively endorsed Yanukovych in a meeting with Kuchma. Indeed, during a visit with Putin in May, Secretary of State Condoleezza Rice was introduced to Yanukovych and the implication was clear: the Russian leader was communicating that he had the power to choose the next Ukrainian leader.[33] Shortly thereafter, Gleb Pavlovsky, a Kremlin-connected "political technologist" established a "Russian club" in Kyiv aimed at promoting Yanukovych and denigrating Yushchenko through aggressive media tactics. The Kremlin also offered a series of economic and political concessions to convince the Ukrainian people of the importance of cooperation with Russia.[34]

The US government, by contrast, did not endorse either candidate but stressed the importance of a fair, free, transparent election. Nevertheless, US NGOs, in cooperation with European civil society groups, were involved in training Ukrainian groups in activities such as parallel vote counting and election monitoring. Many US officials and democracy-promotion organizations saw the Ukraine election as a test case for political transformation in the post-Soviet space, and the Kremlin understood this as a direct challenge to its influence in this neighborhood. The Soros Foundation contributed $1.3 million to Ukrainian NGOs, and USAID gave $1.4 million for election-related activities, including training the Central Election Commission.[35] Russian commentators—betraying a profound misunderstanding of how the US system worked—later conflated Soros and George Bush as jointly promoting regime change in Ukraine, apparently not realizing that in 2004 Soros was spending large sums of money in the US to defeat Bush in the upcoming US election. But US public relations firms were also working to burnish Yanukovych's credentials. Paul Manafort, Trump's campaign manager in 2016, who resigned after his Ukrainian and Russian connections were exposed and was subsequently jailed as part of the Mueller investigations into the 2016 US election, was hired by Yanukovych in 2004 to assist in his election campaign.[36]

The results of the first round of elections were inconclusive. During the interim between the first and second round, Putin personally campaigned for Yanukovych. The day after the second round, on November 22, 2004, Putin congratulated Yanukovych on his win—before the results were announced. He was duly proclaimed the winner. But all the exit polls and NGO parallel vote counting pointed to a rigged vote count, indicating that the real victor was indeed Yushchenko. Thousands of Ukrainians began congregating in sub-zero temperatures in Kyiv's snow-covered central Maidan Nezalezhnosti (Independence Square), demanding a rerun of the election. Protestors blocked access to government buildings, effectively shutting down the government for weeks. The stalemate ended when US secretary of state Colin Powell chose sides for the West and announced, "We cannot accept the Ukraine election as legitimate."[37] Thereafter, Polish president Alexander Kwasniewski and Lithuanian president Valdas Adamkus led a mediation process that resulted in a rerun of the election and Yushchenko's victory. Four months after his installation as president, he visited Washington, spoke to a joint session of Congress, and received a standing ovation.

Moscow's candidate had lost and Washington's had won—at least that is how the Kremlin saw the Orange Revolution. Putin had invested personal and political capital in backing Yanukovych but had not prevailed. For Putin, Ukraine now represented a double challenge—to Russian foreign policy interests and to the survival of the regime itself. Yushchenko's desire to move toward the West threatened Russia's political and economic ties with and influence over its most important neighbor. But equally threatening was the specter of the Ukrainian people protesting against a corrupt, repressive government and bringing it down. Hence it was convenient to blame the United States for pursuing regime change in Ukraine. For example, Sergei Markov, one of the Kremlin's "political technologists," told an international audience in May 2005, "The CIA paid every demonstrator on the Maidan ten dollars a day to protest."[38] The Kremlin made similar comments a decade later when the next major Maidan upheaval occurred. As Putin told the friendly American filmmaker Oliver

Stone, after the Orange Revolution, "We saw the West expanding their political power and influence in those territories, which we considered sensitive and important for us to ensure our global strategic security."[39]

Putin's relationship with Yushchenko and Yushchenko's one-time ally and then opponent Yulia Tymoshenko remained tense for the next five years. The battle of historical narratives between Russia and Ukraine resurfaced, challenging the legitimacy of Russia's claims. The new government revived all the arguments about Ukrainian historical identity, introducing a far more critical stance toward Russia's role. The Holodomor—Stalin's man-made famine in the early 1930s—was commemorated as a Soviet genocide against the Ukrainian people. Stepan Bandera, the wartime Nazi collaborator, was posthumously and controversially designated a "Hero of Ukraine." Yushchenko spent much of his time traveling to Europe, seeking assistance from the EU and NATO, and promising economic and legal reforms. His conflicts with Prime Minister Tymoshenko ultimately led to a stalemated reform agenda and increasing Ukrainian and Western frustration with his government. Meanwhile, many of the old ties between Russian and Ukrainian oligarchs and security service personnel remained. Ukrainians who had flocked to the Maidan became disillusioned with the Orange government because its leaders spent more time abroad or quarreling with each other than implementing real reforms. When Yushchenko came into office, Ukraine rated 122nd on Transparency International's corruption perception index. When he left office, it was ranked at 146th, on a par with Zimbabwe.[40]

Throughout this period, Russia retained a major source of leverage over Ukraine: the gas trade. After Yushchenko's election, Gazprom engaged in tough negotiations with Kyiv over the price it would pay for Russian gas. Ukraine has one of the least energy-efficient economies in the developed world. Gas from Russia was heavily subsidized, and Kyiv paid one-third the price for Russian gas as Europe. As Putin said in 2005, if Ukraine wanted to join the West, why should Russia subsidize its energy? As the December 31, 2005, deadline for agreeing on a new price approached, the Ukrainians refused Gazprom's latest offer. On

January 1, 2006, Gazprom turned off the gas tap to Ukraine without informing its customers in Europe, leaving many along the pipeline route without heat in freezing temperatures. But the Kremlin miscalculated. Ukraine siphoned off supplies destined for Europe, and the Europeans blamed Russia for their shortages. Three years later, in 2009, Gazprom repeated the cutoff after another price dispute, but Europe was better prepared this time, having stored gas reserves. Nevertheless, Russia's energy leverage over Ukraine continued to limit Kyiv's freedom to maneuver throughout the Yushchenko presidency.

Yanukovych's Return, Crimea's Seizure, and the Break with the West

In January 2010, Ukraine went to the polls in a presidential election viewed as a referendum on the Orange Revolution. Tymoshenko and Yanukovych were the main contenders, and Yanukovych emerged victorious after the second round. With the Obama administration pursuing its reset with Russia, Washington had no desire to have Ukraine as a contentious issue in US-Russia relations and decided to try to work with the new Yanukovych government. The Kremlin, needless to say, welcomed Yanukovych's election, particularly since he said that his first priority was to improve ties to Russia and that Ukraine would not seek NATO membership. During his first months in office, he reversed Yushchenko-era policies that angered Moscow, such as the designation of Holodomor as a genocide, the praise for Bandera and his colleagues, and the de-emphasis on the Russian language. From Putin's point of view, Russia now had an opportunity to reassert its influence over Ukraine.

But Yanukovych was not an easy client. He also continued to seek closer ties with the European Union, something the oligarchs from Eastern Ukraine—who supported him—favored because they wanted better access to European markets for their metals and industrial equipment. The Obama administration decided to scale back its involvement in

Ukraine and let its European allies focus on encouraging Ukraine to commit to a reform program. After Yanukovych became president, he began negotiations with the EU for an Association Agreement and a Deep and Comprehensive Free Trade Agreement. The EU bureaucrats who carried out these negotiations focused on technical details, perhaps failing to comprehend the broader geopolitical impact of their actions, so there was little consideration given to how Moscow might react. It is also true, however, that Moscow rebuffed several EU attempts to bring it into these discussions. Initially, the Kremlin appeared to be indifferent to these talks. But as the negotiations neared their conclusion in 2013, the Kremlin began to focus more intensely on the content of the EU agreements. A critical point came when it realized they were much more far-reaching than Russia had originally understood. If Ukraine signed them, it could not join the Eurasian Economic Union and its economic relationship with Russia would be disrupted. The economies of Russia and Ukraine—especially Eastern Ukraine—are quite interdependent, and the EU was offering Ukraine a deal that involved a great deal of economic pain while reforms were implemented in return for a more prosperous economy somewhere further down the road.

Once the Kremlin understood the full implications of the EU deal, it sprung into action. Russia used a mixture of sticks—including preventing Ukrainian trucks from crossing the border to deliver goods into Russia—and carrots to dissuade Yanukovych from signing the Association Agreement. They worked. On November 21, 2013, Ukraine announced that it had suspended its talks with the EU.[41] At the November 28–29 EU summit in Vilnius, Lithuania, where Ukraine had been expected to sign the agreement, Yanukovych pulled out.[42] Soon thereafter, it was announced that Moscow would loan Ukraine $15 billion to bail out its faltering economy. The Kremlin breathed a sigh of relief. It had stopped Ukraine moving closer to the EU.

But Putin had not reckoned with the Ukrainian street, which almost a decade earlier had mobilized to oust Yanukovych. Since his election in 2010, his administration had become increasingly corrupt. Symbolic of the regime's excesses was his palatial estate north of Kyiv, which housed a zoo with wild boars and a mansion with ornate furnishings, marble staircases, and vintage automobiles.[43] Even though the palace was only opened to the public after his flight from Ukraine, Ukrainians understood the scale of corruption under which they were living. For them, signing an agreement with the EU meant committing to a more democratic, less corrupt Ukraine. So when they once again poured into Kyiv's central square in protest, they called their movement EuroMaidan. Three days after Yanukovych's announcement, 100,000 protestors went out into the streets of Kyiv.

For the next three months, the number of protestors in Maidan grew to 800,000, demanding that Yanukovych change course. Protestors ranged from pro-Western liberals to right-wing nationalists, and as the demonstrations continued, the government's response became more violent.[44] US assistant secretary of state for European and Eurasian affairs Victoria Nuland and Senator John McCain both visited the protestors in the Maidan and offered food and support. US secretary of state John Kerry expressed "disgust with the decision of the Ukrainian authorities to meet the peaceful protest in Kyiv's Maidan Square with riot police, bulldozers, and batons rather than with respect for democratic rights and human dignity."[45] "Yanukovych," wrote one eyewitness, "claimed to the Western media that Maidan was filled with fascists and anti-Semites—while telling his own riot police that the Maidan was filled with gays and Jews."[46] Things came to a head between February 18 and 20, 2014, when Ukrainian special forces and Interior Ministry snipers launched an attack on the Maidan, eventually killing one hundred people and wounding hundreds more. Today the Maidan commemorates the Heavenly Hundred with a permanent exhibition of their photographs and biographies lining the outer perimeter of the square.

Two days later, the German, French, and Polish foreign ministers arrived to try to broker a settlement between Yanukovych and opposition politicians. Russia sent former diplomat Vladimir Lukin to take part, but he did not sign the agreement negotiated by his colleagues. On February 21,

Yanukovych and the leaders of three opposition parties agreed that presidential elections would be moved up to December 2014, that constitutional reform would be undertaken, and that there would be an independent investigation into the slaughter in the Maidan. The EU officials left convinced they had negotiated a compromise that would de-escalate the crisis. They were, therefore, stunned to find out the next day that Yanukovych had fled Kyiv during the night, eventually turning up in Rostov in Southern Russia a week later.[47] Apparently his security detail had abandoned him when they realized he would soon be out of power and no longer able to protect them, and he feared for his safety. It was subsequently ascertained that he had begun packing his belongings a few days earlier. Shortly thereafter, opposition politicians announced the formation of a new government and set new presidential elections for May. In what was a provocative gesture, they also voted to deprive the Russian language of its official status—although that unwise decision was soon reversed.

The issue of how and why Yanukovych fled inflamed relations between the Kremlin and the West. Russia's version of the facts differed radically from that of the West. Given that the Kremlin controlled all major Russian news outlets, it served a unitary and consistent diet of news. A "fascist junta" had taken over in Kyiv, illegally ousting a democratically elected president. Russian media excoriated the appearance of posters in Kyiv bearing the picture of Stepan Bandera. Russians consistently speak of a "coup" in Ukraine, orchestrated by the US and EU. The truth is more prosaic. Yanukovych was not overthrown. He simply fled. While Putin was known to hold Yanukovych in contempt, he was demonstrating that, unlike Obama—who had abandoned such allies as Egypt's Hosni Mubarak during the 2011 revolution in Egypt—he would stand by his allies and welcome them to Russia.

Nevertheless, Putin was convinced that the United States and its allies were responsible for Yanukovych's ouster. Actions by US officials reinforced this view. Nuland was overheard on a phone call leaked by the Russians bluntly discussing with the US ambassador in Kyiv which of Yanukovych's opponents they should support. Since Putin was already convinced that Washington was out for regime change in the post-Soviet space, he viewed Yanukovych's ouster as a direct threat to Russian interests. It is also likely that he feared the next Ukrainian president might renege on the deal for the Black Sea Fleet. Moreover, to have not reacted to the Maidan events and to Yanukovych's ouster would have left him looking weak.

A few days after Yanukovych fled, and just after the Sochi Winter Olympics had ended, President Putin ordered surprise military exercises of ground and air forces on Ukraine's doorstep. Suddenly hundreds of troops with no insignia ("little green men") began appearing in Crimea. The decision to invade was made by Putin in consultation with only four advisers: his chief of staff, the head of the National Security Council, his defense minister, and the head of the Federal Security Service (FSB). Foreign Minister Lavrov was apparently not consulted.[48] In the name of protecting Russians in Crimea from oppression by the "illegal fascist junta" in Kyiv, unidentified militiamen took over Sevastopol's municipal buildings, raising the Russian flag, and then proceeded systematically to repeat these moves around Crimea and intimidate the Ukrainian naval forces in Sevastopol. Ukrainian forces in Crimea, on the advice of the United States, remained in garrison and did not challenge the Russians. The Russian military soon controlled the whole peninsula. After that, events moved very quickly. Crimea held a referendum in which 96 percent of the 82 percent of the eligible population who went to the polls voted to join Russia.[49] On March 18, Putin walked into the Kremlin and announced, to thunderous applause, the reunification of Crimea with Russia, proclaiming, "In people's hearts and minds, Crimea has always been an inseparable part of Russia."[50]

The stealth annexation was masterfully executed and took the world by surprise. The post–Cold War consensus on European security was at an end. The leaders of the G-8 countries were scheduled to hold their annual summit in Sochi in June. But the meeting was cancelled, and the seven other members voted to expel Russia from the group. The luxury hotel built especially for the G-8 in the picturesque Caucasus Mountains

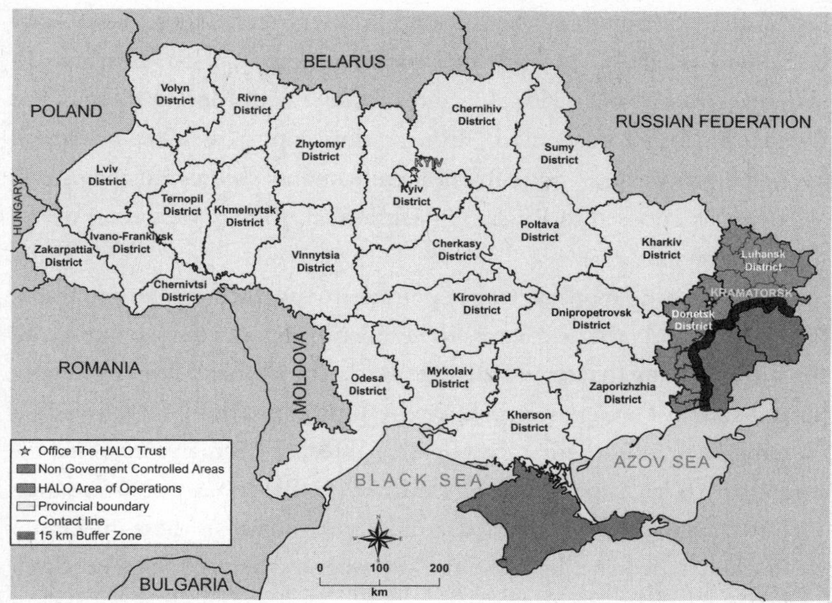

in Krasnaya Polyana above Sochi stood empty. A year later, at the annual Munich Security Conference, a stone-faced Sergei Lavrov claimed that the reunification of Crimea with Russia via a referendum was more legitimate than German reunification: "Germany's reunification was conducted without any referendum, and we actively supported this."[51] He was greeted with boos.

Putin was now emboldened to mobilize separatist groups in the Donbas region who resented Kyiv and favored closer ties to Russia, just as Russia had done in Transnistria, South Ossetia, and Abkhazia. No sooner had Crimea been annexed than new groups of little green men—a motley assortment of Soviet Afghan veterans, Russian intelligence agents, mercenaries, disgruntled pro-Russian Ukrainian citizens who felt neglected by Kyiv, Cossacks, Russians from Transnistria, and Chechens dispatched by their leader Ramzan Kadyrov—began to appear in Southeastern Ukraine, particularly Donetsk and Luhansk, and repeated the Crimean scenario, systematically taking over municipal buildings. They were called separatists because they supported secession from Ukraine, but they were in fact insurgents armed by Moscow and led by often feuding Russian and Ukrainian warlords, yet with one common ambition: to wrest Southeastern Ukraine from Kyiv's rule and reunite it with Mother Russia. The Donbas has had a particularly difficult time coping with the aftermath of the Soviet collapse and many of its inhabitants still regard themselves as Soviet, as opposed to Russian or Ukrainian, so they were receptive to these insurgents.

In the ensuing months, Russia poured troops, funding, ammunition, heavy arms, and other aid across the border to support the separatists, all the while denying that they were there at all. The Donetsk People's Republic and Luhansk People's Republic were proclaimed early in April 2014. Harking back to Catherine the Great's eighteenth-century conquests, the separatists referred to this region north of the Black Sea as Novorossiya. The first separatist leader and paramilitary organizer in these operations was a Russian, Colonel Igor Girkin, who went by the nom de guerre Strelkov (Rifleman). Apart from his previous combat experience in various wars, he enjoyed participating in historical battlefield reenactments.

Unlike in Crimea, however, the Ukrainian army fought back this time. The armed forces were weak, because much of the Western assistance given to train and strengthen the military had previously disappeared into the black hole of corruption. There were also private paramilitary groups, such as the Azov Battalion, which played a major role in recapturing territory from the separatists and was eventually incorporated into the Ukrainian National Guard. In May 2014, in the midst of what was now a full-fledged war in Southeastern Ukraine, Petro Poroshenko, a confectionery magnate and former prime minister known as the "chocolate king," was elected president. One of his first acts was to go to Brussels and sign the Association Agreement that Yanukovych had spurned. As the fighting raged in the Donbas, disaster struck in the air. On July 17, a Malaysia Airlines flight took off from Amsterdam's Schiphol Airport bound for Kuala Lumpur. It was shot down over the war zone in Southeastern Ukraine. Many of its 298 passengers were traveling to a major AIDS conference in Canberra and one of the world's leading AIDS researchers was on board.

Local residents described pieces of debris and body parts hurtling out of the sky onto fields covered with sunflowers. Everyone on board perished. The once bucolic landscape was now a killing field guarded by heavily armed separatists, who initially prevented any access to the crash site.

Who or what brought MH-17 down? Immediately the tragedy became part of the information war between Russia and the West. Reconnaissance photography showed that the plane was shot down by a sophisticated Buk anti-aircraft missile and the missile had been transported from Russia.[52] The Ukrainian government had recordings of separatist leaders reporting to their Russian superiors that they had mistakenly shot down a plane they had believed to be a Ukrainian Antonov military transport, not a commercial airliner.[53] Russia vigorously denied that it had anything to do with the tragedy and blamed the Ukrainian army. The majority of victims were from the Netherlands, and the anger of the Dutch people at constant Russian prevarications was such that Putin's elder daughter, Maria, who was living with her Dutch partner in Amsterdam at the time, had to return to Russia after a Facebook campaign revealed her address.[54] Several inquiries into the cause of the crash have been hampered by the lack of Russian cooperation. Like so many issues connected to the Ukraine crisis, the Kremlin continues to deny any involvement, a source of endless frustration to those seeking a solution to the conflict and restitution for the lives lost.

The Ukrainians continued to battle the separatists and, by August 2014, appeared to be in sight of regaining control of the Donbas. But by late August, regular units of the Russian army crossed the border, attacked the Ukrainian forces, and regained separatist territory. In September, a cease-fire agreement was signed in Minsk by Germany, France, Russia, and Ukraine, but by December heavy fighting had resumed. Another cease-fire, Minsk II, was signed in February 2015 and remains the only basis for a settlement on the table. But even in the three days between its signing and implementation Russian and separatist forces launched a major assault on a key Ukrainian transport junction between Donetsk and Luhansk and captured it. By the terms of the Minsk agreement, each side was required to withdraw its heavy weapons behind the line of contact, to exchange all prisoners and hostages, and to allow OSCE officials to monitor the implementation. Foreign forces and equipment were to be withdrawn, there was to be constitutional reform in the disputed region, and Ukraine was to regain full sovereignty over its border with Russia.[55] The Minsk II agreement applies only to the war in the Donbas. It does not mention Crimea. There is a tacit consensus in the West that, although the West will refuse to recognize Crimea's annexation, it will be a very long time—if ever—before Crimea is reunited with Ukraine. Only a handful of countries—including Cuba, North Korea, and Syria—have recognized its incorporation into Russia.

Since February 2015, fighting in Ukraine has continued intermittently, and the OSCE has been constantly thwarted by the separatists in its attempts to monitor the cease-fire. The Minsk II agreement has barely begun to be implemented. Russia and Ukraine disagree on the sequencing of implementation because the agreement itself is vague on that score. Moscow says Kyiv must introduce far-reaching decentralizing reforms and special status to the Donbas—which would give the region a virtual veto over Ukraine's foreign policy—before Ukraine can regain control over its own border. Kyiv says it will not begin to introduce constitutional reforms until the Russians have withdrawn behind the border. Germany, France, Ukraine, and Russia meet regularly at various levels, and all agree that Minsk II must be fulfilled—but virtually nothing happens. The United States has had its own bilateral channel with Russia to discuss Minsk II implementation with Vladislav Surkov, Putin's close colleague and author of the "sovereign democracy" concept, who manages the separatists. Many observers fear that the situation in the Donbas has already turned into a frozen conflict similar to those in Georgia and Moldova, where Russia supports separatists who make it impossible for the governments in the titular state to have full control over their territory. Others question how "frozen" the conflict is. In July 2017, Kurt Volker, newly appointed Trump administration special envoy for Ukraine, said after visiting Southeastern Ukraine, "This is not a frozen conflict, this is a hot war, and it's an immediate crisis that we all need to address as quickly as possible."[56]

Meanwhile, the Kremlin has abandoned the idea of creating a Novorossiya as it was in Catherine's time. Instead, in July 2017 the separatists proclaimed a new state of "Malorossiya" (Little Russia), which would encompass most of Ukraine. Russian officials disavowed this move, highlighting the opaque nature of Moscow's control over the separatists. Some Ukrainians and their supporters in North America have begun to question whether it really is in Kyiv's interest to try to regain control over the impoverished, battle-scarred, unruly Donbas. Since the beginning of the conflict, so this argument goes, Kyiv is "no longer obliged to sustain a rust belt that once drained its coffers, endure the region's corrupt oligarchs, political elites, and criminal gangs, or appease its pro-Soviet and pro-Russian population."[57]

Russia has suffered economically from its invasion of Ukraine. After the annexation of Crimea, the United States imposed sanctions on individuals close to Putin. But the more serious financial sanctions came after the MH-17 crash. The new sanctions, imposed by the US and Europe, sharply restricted access for Russian state banks to Western capital markets, a major source of foreign lending. Under the sanctions, EU and US firms were barred from providing financing for more than thirty days to the country's key state-owned banks. This has severely limited the banks' ability to finance major projects. Russia's energy sector was also targeted. Sanctions prohibited access to certain energy technologies and participation in deep-water Arctic oil shale development, ending Rosneft's collaboration in the Arctic with ExxonMobil. In retaliation, Russia imposed counter-sanctions on European agricultural imports, and the Kremlin used this to encourage domestic production of high-end agricultural products. Indeed, at the 2017 Saint Petersburg International Economic Forum, in what became known as the "cheese ambush," a Russian farmer accosted the US ambassador John Tefft and proudly handed him a large cheese wheel, explaining that he had been able to produce it because of the ban on competing cheeses from Europe. The ambassador, though taken by surprise, was a consummate diplomat and explained that he was from the cheese-producing state of Wisconsin and graciously accepted the gift.

Can the Ukraine Crisis be Solved?

At the 2014 G-20 summit in Brisbane, Australia, Putin endured hours of criticism from Western leaders about Ukraine and left the summit early. Yet it was, of course, impossible to isolate him, given Russia's relationship with China and other countries. And his calculation—proven correct—was that he could ride out this initial wave of ostracism, knowing full well that in the end the West would have to deal with him. The Russian leader has patience. The West would have to seek him out again, particularly after Russia launched its air strikes in Syria in September 2015. The 2017 Hamburg G-20 meeting proved him right. He was center stage, sought out by most leaders, held a two-and-a-half-hour meeting with President Trump, and attended many other bilateral meetings.

The Ukraine war has been particularly challenging for the West because Russia repeatedly denies that it is directly involved. Ukraine is a new type of "hybrid" war, combining cyber warfare, a powerful disinformation campaign, and the use of highly trained special forces and local proxy forces. The Russians sought to mask the reality of what was happening by having "little green men" invade Crimea and the Donbas, claiming that the Russian soldiers who were observed fighting in the Donbas were "on vacation," asserting that trucks going to and from Ukraine were carrying "humanitarian supplies" instead of weapons and men, accusing Ukraine of shooting down MH-17, and burying dead Russian soldiers in unmarked graves without informing their families.[58] Ukraine and the West understand that Russia is dissembling and that there have been as many as tens of thousands of Russian troops in the Donbas, but the constant barrage of state-run Russian television news tells another story, not only to Russia's own population but to those around the world. In Oliver Stone's four-hour television interview with Putin, for instance, the narrative is Putin's. The audience is told that the separatists are fighting alone, mobilized by the "coup d'état" in Kyiv, and Putin questions whether MH-17 was indeed shot down.

In May 2018, the Australian and Dutch governments published a report detailing the results of their years-long investigations into the MH-17 downing. Its conclusion was unambiguous: "The Netherlands and Australia hold Russia responsible for its part in the downing of flight MH-17."[59] A Dutch police official went further. The investigative team, he said, "has come to the conclusion that the Buk TELAR by which MH-17 was downed originated from the 53rd Anti-Aircraft Missile Brigade from Kursk, in the Russian Federation. All of the vehicles in the convoy carrying the missile were part of the Russian armed forces."[60] The report did not specify who fired the missile, but several media outlets named a high-level Russian GRU officer tied to the downing.[61] Russia continues to deny that it had anything to do with the crash.[62] When Putin was asked at the Saint Petersburg International Economic Forum about whether a Russian missile had downed the plane, he replied, "Of course not!"[63]

There are few signs that Russia is interested in resolving the Ukraine crisis. Continuing conflict makes it difficult for the Poroshenko government to function, and the Kremlin wants a weak, divided Ukraine. Russia and the West have discussed the possibility of deploying UN Peacekeeping troops to the Donbas, but there is no agreement on where these troops should be stationed or what their remit would be. Western sanctions are tied to Minsk II implementation, but although Putin would like sanctions lifted, he apparently is not willing to moderate Russian policy toward Ukraine. Former secretary of state Rex Tillerson suggested that the US administration should not be "handcuffed" if Russia and Ukraine can work out their differences bilaterally outside the Minsk II structures.[64] But prospects for such a deal also appear remote. Putin has indicated that Russia might withdraw to its side of the border if both the Donetsk and the Luhansk People's Republics are granted wide-ranging autonomy, including leverage over foreign policy decisions made in Kyiv. But Poroshenko does not have the votes in the Rada to pass such legislation, even if he wanted to. Thus Moscow blames Kyiv for failing to implement Minsk II, and Kyiv blames Moscow. Meanwhile, all sides realize that the Crimean issue will not be resolved for a very long time.

Russia has also indicated that a precondition for Ukraine regaining sovereignty over its territory would be a pledge not to seek NATO membership and revert to the "non-bloc" status it had until Yushchenko came to power. However, Poroshenko in July 2017 committed Ukraine to seeking NATO membership by 2020. It is not at all clear that NATO wants Ukraine. The idea that Ukraine should "Finlandize"—that is, accept a status similar to that of neutral Finland during the Cold War—has been advocated by two US statesmen who often did not agree with each other: the realist Henry Kissinger and the more ideological Zbigniew Brzezinski.[65] Viktor Pinchuk, prominent Ukrainian oligarch and son-in-law of Leonid Kuchma, has also argued that Ukraine must give up its aspirations to join the EU and NATO if it wants the war to end.[66] In fact, neither EU nor NATO membership is on offer for Ukraine, nor will they be for the foreseeable future. But the specter of the United States, Russia, NATO, and the EU agreeing to keep Ukraine neutral is disconcerting. It resurrects the ghosts of Yalta and the division of Europe into great power spheres of influence, with limited sovereignty for the countries that lie in the EU's and Russia's common neighborhood. It would signal that the post–Cold War international order, which Russia seeks to undermine, is indeed over. There is also no guarantee that such an agreement would curb Russia's appetite for increasing its influence in the post-Soviet space and continuing to undermine Ukraine's ability to function as an independent state.

Nevertheless, it is undeniable that Russia's stake in Ukraine is far greater and more compelling than is that of the United States or many members of the EU. Ukraine is an existential question for Russia, as Russia is for Ukraine.

Kyiv is 5,000 miles away from Washington, and until now Ukraine has not been considered a core interest for the United States. There is not much ambiguity there. The US and its allies will continue to support

Ukraine's independence, territorial integrity, and political and economic development, but they will draw a line at taking actions that would involve any military conflict with Russia. Berlin is only 750 miles from Kyiv but will continue to oppose any NATO membership for Ukraine. So despite the tensions in Russia's relations with the West that have increased since 2014, Putin knows there is a limit to how far the West will go to counter Russian actions, as the reaction to Russia's seizure of the Kerch Straits showed.

No short-term solution to the Ukraine crisis appears to be on the horizon. Disillusionment with the lack of reforms and persistence of corruption has largely soured the people who came to the Maidan in 2013. Both the EU and the United States continue to deal with the "Ukraine fatigue" that periodically emerges when Ukrainian leaders make verbal promises to reform but do not act on them. But Russia's actions have also served to integrate the heirs to Dnieper and Galician Ukraine. Ukrainian national identity has become more unified in reaction to the Russian invasion and occupation of their country. The West may be dealing with a frozen conflict that sometimes becomes hot for some time to come—but that appears the preferred option in Putin's world.

—8—

RUSSIA AND CHINA

Duo of the Willing?

> Russian-Chinese ties have now probably reached a peak in their entire history and continue developing. The partnership between Russia and China is based on sincere friendship and sympathy between our peoples, on deep respect and trust, consideration for each other's key interests, and commitment to make our countries flourish.
>
> —*Vladimir Putin, 2015*[1]

> "President Putin is the leader of a great country who is influential around the world. He is my best, most intimate friend."
>
> —*Xi Jinping, 2018*[2]

Moscow's embassy in Beijing spreads out over 40 acres of elegantly landscaped gardens and fountains, complete with a newly renovated Orthodox Church with gleaming gold onion domes, an ornate pagoda, and spacious reception rooms. It is the largest Russian embassy in the world, built on the site of the original Russian mission to Beijing in 1658. For the three and a half centuries since, the relationship between Russia and China has fluctuated between periods of cooperation and conflict, but today the rhetoric and reality reflect a strong bilateral partnership reinforced by growing wariness of the West. The Russian embassy was first established after the settlement of armed clashes on the Amur River, which forms the border between the Russian Far East and Northeast China—the first of many such border clashes over the succeeding centuries. It initially housed forty-five families, and it was the first foreign mission in China and the only one for over a century.[3] Today its walls are covered with photographs of Russian and Chinese officials, showing meetings between the two presidents, their foreign ministers, military officials, and business executives.

Since the start of the Ukraine crisis, Putin has energetically promoted ties with China to balance Russia's troubled relationship with Europe and the United States. In 2015, Western leaders snubbed the annual May 9 World War Two Victory Day Parade in Moscow because of Russia's invasion of Ukraine. Xi Jinping was one of the few world leaders who did attend, and Putin reciprocated by participating in China's ceremonies to mark seventy years since the end of World War Two in Asia in September 2015. The two leaders' strong ties are based on a mutual interest in challenging a world order led by the United States, and in maintaining domestic stability and preventing "color" revolutions at home. Putin and Xi share a conviction that their countries were unfairly treated in the past, and they are critical of the current Western-dominated international political and economic order.

It was not always this harmonious. Indeed, Russia and China have experienced several centuries of conflicts and confrontations over borders. From the north and west, an expansionist Russian Empire sought to pry loose China's vast hinterland and incorporate it into Siberia.[4] Borders fluctuated over the decades, with intermittent military skirmishes and rising tension. In 1969, the USSR and China, two "fraternal communist" countries, engaged in a brief shooting war over the contested Damansky Island on the Ussuri River, which runs through the Russian Far East and part of Northeast China. Film footage from the time shows People's Liberation Army soldiers pointing their rifles at Soviet soldiers with one hand and brandishing the Little Red Book of Chairman Mao Tse-Tung's quotes in the other.

A few years before Mao had said to a group of Japanese socialists, "There are too many places occupied by the Soviet Union.... About a hundred years ago the area to the east of Lake Baikal became Russian territory, and since then Vladivostok, Khabarovsk, Kamchatka, and other areas have been Soviet territory." He added ominously, "We have not yet presented our account for this list."[5]

The contrast between armed hostilities and ideological saber rattling a half century ago and today's "strategic partnership" between Russia and China is quite remarkable. For much of the Cold War period, Beijing and Moscow were at loggerheads not only over borders but also as competitors for influence in the developing world. Each claimed to be the true standard-bearer of Marxism-Leninism and communism and denigrated the other. Now they support each other on major international questions. Does this new relationship represent a genuine alliance of like-minded great powers or is it, as one observer has argued, an "axis of convenience" that falls short of strategic cooperation?[6] How much does the weight of the Russian-Chinese past affect Moscow's ability to work with Beijing? And how does this partnership affect the West's relations with Russia?

Unequal Treaties and Two Revolutions

Russia and China had little contact before the middle of the seventeenth century. It was only as the tsars began their eastward expansion into Siberia that Russians and Chinese encountered each other. They both sought to control the same territory, and yet they also began to trade with each other. The Treaty of Nerchinsk in 1689—the first China signed with any foreign power—delimited the Russo-Chinese border and remained in force for nearly two hundred years. The treaty recognized China's right to large swaths of land in today's Eastern Siberia.[7] But the development of Chinese-Russian relations was hampered by the lack of a common language, mutual ignorance, and the Chinese inclination to treat the Russians as they treated other "barbarians" from whom they sought tributes and deference, which the Russians rejected. The Chinese believed theirs was the "central" kingdom and that other countries were, by definition, peripheral and removed from the cultural center of the universe.[8]

The Romanov tsars continued to push the Russian Empire farther into

Central Asia while the Chinese conquered neighboring Xinjiang. Overall, Russia grew stronger while China grew weaker. By the middle of the nineteenth century, Russia was a major player in the European concert of powers, while China under the Qing dynasty was in decline as a result of the Opium Wars and domestic atrophy. In 1847, Tsar Nicholas I named Nikolai Muravyev to be governor of Siberia. Muravyev saw himself as an empire builder and believed that the US and Russia should jointly rule the Pacific. He told the tsar, "It seems natural for Russia, if not to own all Asia, at any rate to control the whole Far Eastern coast." Russia took advantage of China's troubles to take back territory it had ceded in 1689. Subsequent treaties gave Russia the north bank of the Amur River and secured the maritime provinces east of the Ussuri River, enabling Russia to build a new naval base in Vladivostok (which means "Ruler of the East").[9] As a result of these "unequal" treaties and a series of Russo-Chinese military skirmishes prior to the 1905 Russo-Japanese War, the Chinese lost 600,000 square miles of territory to Russia.[10]

"Taking a Bath in a Toilet": Chinese and Soviet Communists in the Interwar Years

The fall of the monarchies in China and Russia ushered in a period of political unrest and civil wars. In 1911, the Qing dynasty collapsed, China's central authority was fractured, and the country descended into chaos. In 1917, the Bolsheviks overthrew the Romanov dynasty, which had ruled Russia since 1613, and Russia was engulfed in a civil war, which lasted until 1921. Meanwhile, China was also in the throes of a decades-long civil war, between the Kuomintang (KMT), led by Chiang Kai-shek, and the communists, led by Mao Tse-tung. During the interwar period Soviet-Chinese relations were complicated and sometimes contradictory. Some 200,000 anti-communist Russians fleeing the Bolshevik Revolution escaped to Harbin and Shanghai, plotting to overthrow the Bolsheviks. The Soviet communists, on the other hand, became involved in China via the Communist International (Comintern) and its chief emissary Mikhail Borodin. One of his main qualifications was that he had lived in Chicago for many years and spoke English—enabling him to communicate with the Republican leader Sun Yat-sen—but he did not speak Chinese. Borodin worked both sides of the street, with the Chinese communists and the nationalists, and this caused severe strains with Mao's followers. Indeed, the Comintern decreed that "the Communist Party of China must exert all its efforts directly in alliance with the Left Kuomintang," to which the Chinese communists replied, "Such an order is like taking a bath in a toilet."[11] The USSR had entered into an alliance with the KMT, and in 1927, Chiang's forces took Shanghai with the help of the communists, only to turn on them and slaughter them. The Shanghai Massacre's lasting lesson to Mao was that Stalin pursued his own interests, and fraternal solidarity with communist comrades was not his priority.

As the civil war intensified from 1945 to 1949, Stalin continued to hedge his bets, supporting both Chiang Kai-shek and Mao Tse-tung. A unified China under one ruler, in his view, could represent a potential challenge to Soviet interests. But in the end Mao succeeded in 1949 in forcing Chiang and the KMT to flee to the island of Taiwan, while Mao now ruled all of mainland China. He still admired Stalin as the leader of the international communist movement. The USSR was the first country to recognize the People's Republic of China. But Stalin was ambivalent about Mao and, more than that, suspicious of his intentions. Thus began forty years of difficult and sometimes tense Sino-Soviet relations.

The Cold War Legacy

After his victory, Mao hoped to be recognized by Stalin as his equal, having won a long and brutal war and having created another communist great power. But Stalin took his time inviting him to Moscow. Mao finally arrived in December 1949, two months after the proclamation of the People's Republic of China. On his way to Moscow, in a state of tension, he suffered a severe anxiety attack at the Sverdlovsk station.[12] When he disembarked from the train in Moscow he was met not by Stalin but by Foreign Minister Vyacheslav Molotov, an obvious slight.[13] Later that night the entire Politburo greeted him.

But things did not go smoothly. Mao wanted Stalin to abrogate the treaty the USSR had signed with Chiang Kai-shek, and Stalin was reluctant to do so. So he sent Mao to his own dacha outside Moscow for two weeks to cool his heels. As it turned out, Mao remained in Moscow for nearly two months while the Soviets negotiated in a dilatory fashion. He was isolated. According to Nikita Khrushchev, "During Mao's stay, Stalin would sometimes not lay eyes on him for days at a time... and since Stalin neither saw Mao nor ordered anyone else to entertain him, no one dared go and see him."[14] Mao was humiliated and became increasingly furious. At last, Stalin allowed negotiations to begin. On February 14 the two countries finally signed a Treaty of Friendship, Alliance, and Mutual Assistance in case of an attack by a third power. But Stalin offered a niggardly amount of economic assistance to his fraternal ally. Nevertheless, relations remained outwardly cordial—at least while the Soviet dictator lived.

When Stalin died in 1953, Mao assumed he would now be recognized as number one, the leader of the communist world. After all, he was not only a guerrilla leader but also a prolific author of theoretical texts on the Chinese road to socialism. To his surprise, the uneducated (in his view) peasant Nikita Khrushchev managed to maneuver himself to become Stalin's successor. Khrushchev had no intention of ceding leadership of the communist world to Mao. Worse still, in 1956 Khrushchev denounced Stalin and his crimes at the Twentieth Party Congress without warning his Chinese comrades of what was about to happen. Foreign communists were not allowed in the room when Khrushchev made his speech, and they had to read the speech's text from Chinese translations of the *New York Times*.[15] Mao and Khrushchev ended up scorning each other. Interviews with the Soviet and Chinese translators who interpreted for the two leaders during their fraught summits depict two men who looked down on each other and believed the other to be reckless.[16] At the end of the 1950s, the Soviets abruptly withdrew 1,400 technical specialists from China and ceased giving the PRC assistance for its nuclear program, leaving 600 scientific projects unfinished and forcing the Chinese to fend for themselves and build their own nuclear arsenal.[17]

Although the Soviet Union viewed the United States as its main antagonist during the Cold War, China also represented a threat, albeit of a different kind. The United States, as the other nuclear superpower, was economically far stronger than its rival. It had alliances with the major European countries and Japan. It offered a competing ideology—capitalism and democracy—to that of Soviet socialism. China was much weaker militarily and economically than the Soviet Union. But it represented an ideological challenge. At the height of Maoism, China questioned the legitimacy of the Soviet Union as a socialist state, claiming that Beijing's version of socialism was the only authentic one, whereas the USSR had abandoned socialism for state capitalism. "However hard Khrushchev tries to serve the US imperialists," said one Chinese publication, "they show not the slightest appreciation.... They continue to slap Khrushchev in the face and reveal the bankruptcy of his ridiculous theories prettifying imperialism."[18] China appealed to countries in the third world and even within the Soviet bloc, claiming that Beijing, not Moscow, should lead the global revolutionary movement.

The Sino-Soviet split produced escalating mutual polemics—especially during the most acute phase of the Cultural Revolution from 1966 to 1969—border clashes, and the freezing of relations, culminating in a mini war on the Amur River in 1969.[19] Thinly veiled racism was evident on both sides. The USSR engaged in a substantial buildup of nuclear forces near the Chinese border. According to Khrushchev's memoirs, Mao claimed China would survive a nuclear war with the USSR and would soon start reproducing its population and taking back the territories in the Soviet Far East that rightfully belonged to Beijing. Periodic attempts by the Soviets to ease tensions were largely unsuccessful until Mikhail Gorbachev came to power in 1985.

Gorbachev's Common Asian Home

As part of his goal of enhancing the USSR's standing in the world, Gorbachev realized that it was incumbent on Moscow to take the first steps toward improving ties with China. Gorbachev's rapprochement efforts culminated in a trip to Beijing in May 1989, the first Sino-Soviet summit in thirty years. A decade earlier, Deng Xiaoping had become China's leader, and he too had begun a major economic reform program and was open to improving Sino-Soviet ties. Mao was long gone, and his successors were committed to working with the USSR. Deng had set several preconditions for normalizing Sino-Soviet relations, including a reduction in Soviet troop presence on China's northern border and the withdrawal of Soviet troops from Afghanistan and of Soviet-backed Vietnamese troops from Cambodia. Gorbachev agreed to all of China's demands and traveled to Beijing on Deng's terms.[20]

But Gorbachev's visit came at the worst possible time. China was in turmoil, and it was the height of the student pro-democracy movement. A welcoming ceremony in Tiananmen Square, in sight of Mao's mausoleum, had to be cancelled because of the thousands of protestors camped out on the square. Worse still for the Chinese hosts, the protestors saw Gorbachev as their hero because of his commitment to glasnost. Notwithstanding, talks between the eighty-four-year-old Deng and fifty-eight-year-old Gorbachev went well.[21] The historic enemies had been reconciled.[22] Shortly after Gorbachev left, Chinese troops took up their positions in Tiananmen Square, and two weeks later, the Chinese authorities cleared the area.

During Gorbachev's last years in office, Sino-Soviet ties continued to improve. Talks on regularizing the 2,600-mile border produced results. But the past was always present. During a trip to China to sign border agreements, Foreign Minister Eduard Shevardnadze met with Deng Xiaoping, by then an elder statesman. After praising the border agreement, Deng led the Soviet foreign minister into a room where a map of China lay on the table. The map showed Outer Manchuria, which forms the Russian Primorsky Krai province, as Chinese, not Russian, territory.[23]

Gorbachev remains an ambivalent and controversial figure in China. He took the necessary steps to defuse tensions and end the Sino-Soviet split on Chinese terms. But his reform policies and the collapse of oil prices and the economy led to the disintegration of the USSR and of Soviet socialism. Indeed, during the three-day August 1991 coup attempt against Gorbachev, the Chinese supported the anti-Gorbachev putschists. Deng's verdict was that Gorbachev had not done enough to preserve state and party power.[24] In 1992, a Chinese leader described the Soviet collapse as "like the aftermath of an explosion—shock waves in all directions."[25]

The Chinese remain determined that this will not happen to them. They believe Gorbachev's cardinal error was opening up society politically and loosening the reins of control instead of focusing on economic reforms. China took the opposite course and by now has a far larger and more successful economy than does Russia, while the Communist Party remains in full control. Vladimir Putin agrees. He has said that the USSR should have done what China did and introduced economic reforms before opening up politically. The implication is that if Gorbachev had followed that path, then maybe the USSR would still exist.[26]

In 1949, Stalin told one of Mao's top lieutenants, Liu Shaoqi, "I sincerely hope that one day the younger brother will catch up with and surpass the elder brother. This is not only the hope of my colleagues and me; this is the historical rule: the latecomers will eventually surpass the advanced ones. Let's toast to the younger brother surpassing the elder."[27] The younger brother has indeed overtaken the elder brother, as Stalin predicted.

Normalization Continues—The Yeltsin Years, 1992–1999

Boris Yeltsin's main foreign policy focus was on the West. Nevertheless, the new Russian leadership soon accepted that it had to continue on the path toward normalization with Beijing.[28] The Russian leadership realized that it had to accept the one-China policy even as it sought to improve economic links with Taiwan. During Yeltsin's tenure, the border issues that continued to plague the relationship were gradually settled, and economic ties—including military sales—increased. Russia was at first wary of fully endorsing China's calls for a multipolar world. But when Yevgeny Primakov became foreign minister in 1996, Russia's foreign policy focused more on balancing between West and East, and China began to occupy a more prominent place in the Kremlin's priorities. But the new pluralism and decentralization of the Yeltsin era also posed new challenges for the Kremlin's China policy: officials in the Russian Far East were wary of what were called Chinese "shuttle traders," who came across the border and began to dominate the local market. Once the border opened up, the number of Chinese laborers in the Far East ranged from 300,000 to 1 million, depending on whose estimates one believed.

Yeltsin made his first presidential visit to Beijing in December 1992, although he had to cut it short because of a political crisis at home when acting prime minister and chief economic reformer Yegor Gaidar was ousted. Joking that the number of bilateral agreements they did sign during their truncated meeting might qualify for the *Guinness Book of World Records,* Yeltsin announced, "We agree that the long period of artificial cold war is now over, and we are now entering a new stage of de-ideologized relations."[29] Russia and China pledged not to enter into alliances or treaties that would hurt the other's "state sovereignty and security interests." Indeed, this first visit set the foundation for the relationship going forward.

This new bilateral relationship focused on economic ties, regulating border issues, and noninterference in each other's domestic affairs. China and Russia both faced separatist challenges—Tibet and Xinjiang for China and Chechnya for Russia. Beijing supported Yeltsin's Chechen campaign, saying the Russian leader had to wage war in order to preserve the country's unity.

The Chinese remained wary of the unpredictability of the early

Yeltsin years and of its pro-Western policies. But the newly porous borders required attention. As PRC president Jiang Zemin noted, "When a door is opened, people can come into a room, but flies can get in too. We must go about this in such a way that there will be fewer flies." The delimitation of the Russo-Chinese border was achieved through a series of arrangements in the 1990s. But the collapse of the USSR had left China with a series of new Central Asian neighbors too. China also faced the challenge of dealing with extremism and Islamic movements emanating from the Uighur population in Xinjiang, which shares a border with Russia and several Central Asian countries. In 1996, Russia, China, Kazakhstan, Kyrgyzstan, and Tajikistan—the "Shanghai Five"—signed a border pact and pledged not to attack each other. This was the beginning of multilateral cooperation and an attempt to regulate Sino-Russian relations in Central Asia. For the newly independent nations of Central Asia, the need to navigate relations with their two large neighbors would be a permanent challenge.

Russia's relations with China were always linked to its fluctuating ties to the West. After Yevgeny Primakov became foreign minister, he advocated creating a "strategic triangle" among Moscow, Beijing, and New Delhi to counterbalance the transatlantic alliance. In 1997, Yeltsin and Jiang signed the Joint Declaration on a Multipolar World and the Establishment of a New International Order.[30] This declaration contained themes that have become the standard talking points of Sino-Russian relations since then: equal partnership, strategic cooperation, a multipolar world, and the need to develop a "new and comprehensive form of security." Although neither the United States nor NATO is explicitly mentioned, it was clear at whom this declaration was directed.

As ties with the United States soured over NATO's intervention in the Balkan wars, Yeltsin's own pronouncements also began to reflect greater criticism of the West and more praise for China. During the Kosovo War, US planes mistakenly dropped five bombs on the Chinese embassy in Belgrade, killing three people and causing an outcry in Beijing and beyond. The Chinese did not believe it was a mistake. Both Russia and China loudly condemned NATO's actions in Serbia.[31]

This new anti-American dimension of Russia's China policy was on full display during one of Yeltsin's last public appearances as president. On a visit to Beijing in December 1999, he lashed out at President Clinton, who had criticized Russia for launching the Second Chechen War, saying of the US president, "He evidently forgot for a second, a minute, or half a minute just what Russia is, and that Russia possesses a full arsenal of nuclear weapons....A multipolar world—that's the basis of everything. That's what we agreed on with Jiang Zemin." Interestingly, his heir-apparent then prime minister Vladimir Putin felt it necessary at that point to correct Yeltsin and deny that there had been any cooling in US-Russia relations.[32]

Sino-Russian Relations Under Vladimir Putin: A Cautious Embrace

The Lure of China

The year 2001 represented a milestone in Russian-Chinese relations inasmuch as it produced an agreement codifying the strategic partnership. And the two leaders spoke the same language. The Chinese president Jiang Zemin had worked in the Stalin Automobile Works in Moscow in the 1950s, had passable Russian language skills, and could do a rousing rendition of a favorite Soviet song, "Moscow Nights" ("*Pod Moskovskie Vecheram*"). The Russian-Chinese Treaty of Good-Neighborliness and Friendly Cooperation is a twenty-year agreement laying out in broad brushstrokes the major elements of the relationship, including in the economic and military spheres. Since Vladimir Putin entered the Kremlin, he has consistently sought to maintain and improve ties with China. This is a result of Russia's perceived need to offset its deteriorating relationship with the West but also of an appreciation of the advantages of allying oneself with a rising power who also happens to be a neighbor—and a large market with multiple sources of capital. Neither China nor Russia—both supporters of the concept of "absolute sovereignty"—is committed to an alliance that would limit its freedom of maneuver. A pragmatic partnership based on a shared interest in a multipolar world and maintaining authoritarian control at home is what both countries seek. Since the onset of the Ukraine crisis, Moscow has sought to intensify the relationship, but China retains its instrumental and clear-eyed view of its ties to Russia and will not take actions that might jeopardize its strong economic links with Europe and the United States. Nevertheless, the relationship has enabled Russia to avoid the international isolation the West has sought to impose after the Crimean annexation. Moscow can point to Beijing's support for—or at least neutrality toward—actions the West has condemned. China is willing to validate Russia while the West criticizes it.

The Russia-China relationship has significant bilateral dimensions, including trade and energy, border regulation, (the border demarcation was completed between 2004 and 2008), and military-to-military cooperation. Both sides reject Western criticisms of their human rights records and support each other's domestic policies. Russia supports the Chinese positions on Taiwan and Tibet. The relationship also has an important multilateral agenda, including regulation of relations in Central Asia via the Shanghai Cooperation Organization and coordination at the United Nations Security Council over issues such as Iran, Syria, and North Korea. Strikingly, there are no major international issues on which Russia and China disagree, unlike Russia's vexed relationship with the West. For their first foreign trips as president, both current Chinese president Xi and his predecessor Hu Jintao (2002–2012) chose Moscow. Putin visited China early on in his first presidency.[33] He likewise went to China soon after his 2012 reelection,[34] after cancelling a planned trip to Washington for the G-8 summit a month earlier, saying he was "too busy."[35]

The bilateral and multilateral agenda has greatly expanded under Putin. Nevertheless, the relative asymmetry between the "elder" and "younger" brother has noticeably grown over the past fifteen years. China's GDP is $14 trillion, whereas Russia's is $1.28 trillion. Russia has a population of 142 million, China has a population of 1.3 billion. China is a dynamic, rising power, its economy projected to overtake that of the United States by 2030. Russia is not a rising power. Its economy is in decline, as is its population, particularly in the Far East region bordering China. Russia exports hydrocarbons and military hardware to China in return for imports of Chinese manufactures, including electronic goods. Unless Russia modernizes its economy, it will remain a raw materials and weapons supplier for China's advanced industrial economy.

The New "Yellow Peril"?

The danger of hordes from the East invading Russia and subjugating its population is a centuries-old trope in the Russian historical narrative. Genghis Khan and his twelfth-century marauders imposed the Mongol yoke that oppressed the Russian people for centuries, so the story goes. Fast-forward to the 1800s, and Chinese immigrants into the Russian Far East led to the first Russian warnings about the "yellow peril." Tensions between the local Russian population and Chinese workers ebbed and flowed. In 1900, in retaliation for a Chinese attack on a Russian outpost, Russians in the border town of Blagoveshchensk drove all 3,000 Chinese then living in the city into the Amur River, where most of them drowned.[36]

A 1911 pamphlet summed up Russian fears about the Chinese:

> It is well-known that the yellow peoples nourish an organic hatred towards Europeans, and to us Russians in particular.... They dream... of conquering the world.... Invasion by the yellow races of the rich region of Siberia has already begun.[37]

When the Sino-Russian border opened up after the Soviet collapse, new fears about a twenty-first century "yellow peril" reemerged as Chinese migrant laborers flocked to the Russian Far East. There are 6.3 million Russians in the areas bordering China, facing 109 million Chinese on the other side of the border.[38] Opinion polls show that the Russian population in the Primorsky Krai border region fear Chinese laborers less than they did ten years ago, but a sizeable number believe that border clashes similar to those in 1969 are still possible. They remain suspicious of the Chinese, who often dominate local commerce. They also are wary of China's designs on their land.[39]

Indeed, a 2015 Russian government proposal to lease 1,000 square kilometers of land to the Chinese was abandoned after the local population and their leaders objected.[40] The contrast between the Chinese side of the border (with large, modern hotels and urban infrastructure) and the Russian side (with sparse and often dilapidated buildings) is striking. In 2007, both countries agreed to build a rail bridge across the Amur River, to be a symbol of their friendship. The Chinese have built their section of the bridge. The Russians only began construction in 2016.[41]

Trade and Energy

Since 2009, China has been Russia's largest trading partner. But their bilateral trade is less than one-tenth the size of US-China trade. For all the lofty words about how good the relationship is, in fact the economic relationship is comparatively modest. China is a much more important trade partner for Russia than vice versa. Before the Ukraine crisis and Russia's subsequent economic difficulties due to falling oil prices and Western sanctions, bilateral trade amounted to $88 billion. It fell by 25 percent in 2015, and recovered to its previous level by 2018. The structure of trade largely resembles that between a developing and a developed country. Mineral products and hydrocarbons make up 73 percent of Russian exports. Machinery and transport equipment constitute 52 percent of Chinese exports, with textiles and footwear at 15 percent.[42] One exception is advanced weaponry. China is the second largest buyer of Russian military hardware. Russia was initially careful not to sell China its most sophisticated arms, because China has a habit of reverse engineering Russian military hardware and selling it on the world market. But in 2015, as part of the post-Crimea intensification of ties, Russia agreed—in a $3 billion deal—to sell China Su-35S fighter jets and S-400 surface-to-air missiles, which will upgrade China's missile defense capabilities and could jeopardize Taiwan's aerial defenses.[43] The deliveries began in 2018.

As China has modernized and become much richer, its demand for energy has grown exponentially. Russia has plentiful oil and gas reserves, but most of its energy exports went to Europe in the Soviet era. Since the Soviet collapse, Russia has worked on diversifying its energy exports, although energy relations with China have proven quite challenging, due to the vagaries of Russian politics and tough Chinese negotiating. The project of building the Eastern Siberia–Pacific Ocean oil pipeline (ESPO) took over a decade and went through many permutations. For a time, it looked as if the first Russian oil pipeline to Asia would go via Japan, but eventually the Chinese route prevailed. Russia began its deliveries of crude oil to China in 2011, part of a bilateral "loans for oil" deal whereby Beijing provided Moscow with a $25 billion loan in exchange for oil deliveries until 2030.[44]

Russia is the world's leading gas exporter and began early on to negotiate with China to build a pipeline.[45] But Gazprom and China National Petroleum Corporation were unable to agree on a price, so China turned to Central Asia, concluding a deal for a Turkmenistan-Uzbekistan-Kazakhstan-China pipeline. What changed the equation was Russia's seizure of Crimea and launch of a war on Eastern Ukraine in 2014. After the United States and its allies imposed sanctions on Russia, the Kremlin decided that it had to turn to China. In May 2014, Russia and China signed a $400 billion deal to build a gas pipeline, the Power of Siberia. It is assumed that Beijing was in a favorable position to achieve most of the goals it had pursued for some years: a cheap price and equities in the deal, including ownership of part of the pipeline infrastructure.[46] As of 2019, pipeline construction was proceeding apace, after a slow start.[47]

Central Asia and the Shanghai Cooperation Organization

In addition to regulating their bilateral economic and political relations, Russia and China have worked hard to manage ties in their challenging and dangerous common neighborhood. The five states of Central Asia—Kazakhstan, Uzbekistan, Kyrgyzstan, Tajikistan, and Turkmenistan—must balance relations with their two large neighbors. The least developed of the Soviet republics, they struggled to create viable states after the Soviet collapse and have all remained authoritarian polities in which clan politics are paramount. Two of them—Kazakhstan and Turkmenistan—have substantial oil and gas reserves. Until the precipitous decline in oil prices in 2014 and 2015, Kazakhstan was relatively prosperous and focused on modernizing its economy. The subsequent oil price rebound has been reflected in renewed economic growth in Kazakhstan. In addition to the challenge of poverty, interethnic conflicts produced a five-year civil war in Tajikistan and continuing tensions in the Fergana Valley in Kyrgyzstan, where armed conflict between Uzbeks and Kyrgyz has also erupted several times, most recently in 2010.

Another major challenge to the area comes from Islamic fundamentalism. Groups such as the Islamic Movement of Uzbekistan and Hizb ut-Tahrir are designated as terrorist organizations that threaten Central Asia and beyond. Thousands of Central Asians have joined Islamic State and other extremist groups. The ongoing conflict with the Taliban in Afghanistan has exacerbated these problems. Since Beijing has to deal with Uighur separatism and fundamentalism, and Russia faces the ongoing threat of terrorism from the North Caucasus region, both China and Russia are united in supporting Central Asian governments in combating extremism.

For all these reasons, the Shanghai Cooperation Organization (SCO), established in 2001, has become an important pillar of the Sino-Russian relationship. It has recently broadened its reach. India and Pakistan became members in 2017, and Iran, Mongolia, and Afghanistan may follow suit. Its eight members account for 80 percent of Eurasia's landmass, 43 percent of the world's population, and a quarter of global GDP. In terms of geographic coverage and population size, it is the largest regional organization in the world.[48]

While the SCO was initially founded to manage Russia-China relations in Central Asia, it has expanded not only in membership but in ambition, as a multilateral organization from which the United States is explicitly excluded. By including India, it has the world's largest democracy, which is intended to diminish the SCO's reputation as an alliance of autocracies. However, tensions between Russia and China over enlargement remain. India and China continue to have border disputes. India and Russia have traditionally enjoyed close ties, while China and Pakistan have been aligned. This enlargement could add to existing rivalries between Moscow and Beijing and their respective partners.[49] Indeed, the India-Russia relationship has apparently impacted the personal outlook of the Russian leader. At the end of the 2015 joint summit SCO-BRICS (Brazil, Russia, India, China, South Africa), Putin reiterated a promise he had made earlier to Indian prime minister Narendra Modi about learning yoga: "They say yoga is the transition from the physical to the spiritual. I am already at the physical, so you can say I am halfway there."[50]

So far, Russia and China have successfully managed their rivalry in Central Asia. Russia retains predominant political influence over the area, given the enduring linguistic, cultural, and personal ties between Moscow and many in the Central Asian elites. But China has become the predominant economic power in Central Asia, given its energy needs, its markets, and investment projects. The Chinese, like the Russians, were wary of the United States' entry into Central Asia in the 1990s as US companies pursued economic (and especially energy) projects in the region and NATO developed partner relations with several states. Then came the terrorist attacks of September 11, 2001, and Putin's decision to facilitate the establishment of US military bases in Uzbekistan and Kyrgyzstan, without consulting China.[51] For a while, it looked as if the rapprochement between Moscow and Washington in 2001–2002 might have longer-term effects on ties between Beijing and Moscow. But the Putin reset ended with the US invasion of Iraq.[52] Until recently, Russia was content to see China expand its economic presence in Central Asia as long as Moscow remained the main security provider. With the US withdrawal from Afghanistan, it appeared that Russia's military role in Central Asia would be strengthened. It has bases in Kyrgyzstan and Tajikistan and conducts regular military exercises with its partners in the Collective Security Treaty Organization.

The Belt and Road Initiative

China's dynamic economic growth and Russia's economic problems, as well as the impact of Western sanctions, have raised questions about China's future role in Central Asia. Putin's major project for his third term, the Eurasian Economic Union, was launched in January 2015. As discussed previously, Russia's economic difficulties and their impact on its neighbors have hindered the development of the EEU. China in 2013 announced its intention to construct a Silk Road Economic Belt, subsequently known as Belt and Road Initiative (BRI). This ambitious project will eventually link China with Europe and will involve a network of transportation and construction projects, including multibillion-dollar investment deals in Central Asia. In 2014, the Silk Road Fund was launched with a starting capital of $40 billion for a projected network of railway lines, highways, and energy pipelines leading to and from China. While the Central Asian countries were generally enthusiastic about these projects, Russia was more reticent, until Xi and Putin signed an agreement on the integration of the EEU and BRI projects in May 2015.[53] However, the two initiatives are quite different. BRI transportation corridors will bypass Russia to the south, so it is unclear how Russia will benefit from this massive infrastructure project.[54] However, Russia and China have now agreed that the Northern Sea Route through the Arctic Ocean falls under the BRI project and indeed the Chinese now call it the Polar Silk Road. The BRI is designed to promote globalized trade, financing, and infrastructure and provide markets for Chinese goods. It will inevitably expand Chinese geopolitical influence—all under the rubric of "connectivity." The EEU is a far more inward-looking trade integration project designed to cement Russia's influence in Central Asia.

In May 2017, Xi hosted twenty-nine heads of state or governments and the heads of the International Monetary Fund and the World Bank as well as the UN secretary-general at the first Belt and Road Forum in Beijing.[55] Putin gave a keynote speech in which he praised the initiative: "We welcome China's One Belt, One Road initiative. By proposing this initiative, President Xi Jinping has demonstrated an example of a creative approach toward fostering integration in energy, infrastructure, transport, industry, and humanitarian collaboration."[56] The Russian ambassador to China stressed that Russia and China were equal partners in this endeavor and that the BRI would not be detrimental to Russian interests.[57] However, it remains unclear what Russia will gain from this ambitious project. The author attended two Russia-China conferences organized by the Russian International Affairs Council in 2016 and 2017, where the Chinese side went to great lengths to present elaborate PowerPoint slides on a wide range of BRI projects that would involve and benefit Russia. The Russian side remained skeptical.[58] Indeed, the Chinese have rejected forty infrastructure projects proposed by the Russians.[59] Nevertheless, the BRI appears to be a protean concept, broad enough to encompass Chinese investment in Russian energy and infrastructure projects. So far, the Chinese have built a dry port in Khorgos in Kazakhstan and plan more investments in Central Asia. They also have completed projects in Hungary, Pakistan, Iran, and Sri Lanka.

The reality is that once China has constructed these ambitious projects, it will inevitably become more involved in the security of the countries through which its highways, railways, and pipelines pass. The previous "division of labor" between Russia and China in Central Asia will change.

The countries of Central Asia have learned over the past twenty-five years to balance their ties with Russia and China and fine-tune their economic and political relations with both large neighbors. In general, they are more familiar with Russia than with China, given their centuries of shared history. Their elites still receive much of their news from state-run Russian television channels. They are less familiar with China, its language and its culture. Nevertheless, they need Chinese investment and trade. If China largely steps in to fill the wider vacuum left by the US withdrawal from Afghanistan and the closing of its military bases there, that might disturb the current balance and raise tensions in the area. But for now, China is careful to calibrate its activities in Central Asia so as not to arouse Russian concerns.

Ultimately, Russia, China, and the states of Central Asia share fundamental ideas of what stability in the region looks like and how to maintain it. They are a group of authoritarian states dedicated to maintaining themselves in power and to ensuring that no Islamist or color revolutions threaten their rule. Whereas they view with great suspicion any Western attempts to open up their societies, Central Asian elites welcome Russian and Chinese support of the status quo.

The United Nations Security Council

In its ongoing quest for sovereignty, Russia has been able to exercise influence internationally far beyond what its constrained capabilities would suggest. A major reason for this is its permanent seat—and veto—on the United Nations Security Council. China has been an enabler of Russian actions in places like Syria and Ukraine, reinforcing the exercise of Russian influence by coordinating its Security Council votes with Moscow on important international matters. Indeed, Russia's and China's support for each other has led them to derail a number of Western projects designed to bring humanitarian relief and punish those who promote ethnic violence. The major areas where they have supported each other—and often thwarted the West—are the Balkans, Iran, North Korea, and Syria. Both countries insist that the principles of sovereignty and noninterference in the internal affairs of other countries take precedence over Western concepts of humanitarian intervention—except, in the Russian case, when they apply to defending the rights of Russians living in post-Soviet states, such as Ukraine. Russia and China differ with the West on the interpretation of several of the foundational principles of the United Nations, such as the responsibility to protect and humanitarian intervention. Russia and China have worked together to block or modify resolutions that the United States, Britain, and France have proposed before they ever come up for a vote, so that they do not have to use the veto.

In the past decade, Russia and China have vetoed resolutions criticizing human rights violations by authoritarian leaders, such as Zimbabwe's Robert Mugabe and Myanmar's military junta. In the Zimbabwean case, they claimed that Mugabe's actions did not threaten international security and they refused to support an arms embargo. They repeatedly vetoed resolutions that would have imposed penalties on the regime of Syria's Bashar al-Assad and its use of chemical weapons against its own people as the Syrian Civil War unfolded. However, China has been more cautious in votes on Ukraine, because it has reservations about Russia's actions there. It abstained rather than rejected the General Assembly's condemnation of the annexation of Crimea, and it left Russia alone to veto a Security Council resolution calling for the establishment of an international tribunal to investigate the 2014 downing of the MH-17 airline in the Donbas. Indeed, China maintains active political and economic ties to Ukraine. On other issues, they have coordinated their votes. China has usually followed Russia's lead on issues involving Iran's nuclear program, and Russia has followed China's lead on issues involving North Korea's nuclear program.

Sino-Russian cooperation in the United Nations is a manifestation of a broader commitment to reject an international order imposed by the West. But what does a new order look like? The breakdown of Russia's relations with the United States and Europe following the annexation of Crimea provides some indications.

A Post-Ukraine Pivot to China?

Since the March 2014 annexation of Crimea and the deterioration of Russia's ties with the West, Putin has consistently praised the Russia-China partnership, implying that it is a preferable alternative to the vexed relationship with the United States and Europe. China has not publicly criticized Russia's policy in Ukraine, and its vice premier has said, "China categorically opposes the sanctions the United States and Western countries have taken against Russia."[60] Although China has not sanctioned Russia, it has been careful not to take actions that contravene those sanctions, especially in the financial field. The Bank of China has given Gazprom a loan of $2 billion, and two development banks have provided some loans to Russia. But the big four Chinese banks have complied with Western sanctions. Given the choice between increasing their presence in the high-risk Russian market and the opportunity to strengthen their position in the large and stable markets of the EU and the United States, China has opted for the latter.[61] Russian business people have been disappointed by China's cautious approach to investing in their country. As one of Russia's most successful entrepreneurs said, "There was a certain level of optimism regarding Chinese companies. It was thought they were coming to the Russian market to spend big money. But the Chinese turned out to be very rational and very good businesspeople, so they wouldn't give money away for nothing."[62]

Some Western officials express concern that the China-Russia relationship has entered a qualitatively new stage, one that poses a potential political and military threat to the West.[63] Has the axis of convenience evolved into a genuine alliance? The evidence is decidedly mixed because of the asymmetry in the stakes. As Bobo Lo, author of the axis-of-convenience argument, subsequently wrote, "Beijing and Moscow work together in many areas, challenging US leadership, opposing Western liberal interventionism, and developing economic ties. But progress has been incremental rather than transformative."[64] Nevertheless, Sino-Russian military cooperation has markedly increased. In 2018, 3,500 Chinese troops took part for the first time in Russia's "Vostok" (Eastern) military exercise of 300,000 troops, the largest Russian military exercise since 1981.[65] Earlier, a Chinese official had said that China "has come to show Americans the close ties between the armed forces of China and Russia."[66]

China remains wary of the unpredictability of Russian foreign policy. It does not share Putin's view of Russia as a global power equal to the United States or China. For Russia, however, the partnership with China represents a geopolitical equalizer, counterbalancing the predominant power of the United States. This disparity in the two countries' views of each other limits the nature of their embrace.

China has become the focus of Russia's post-Ukraine, anti-Western policy. This partnership is designed to reinforce Russia's role as an independent center of global power, one of Putin's key foreign policy goals. It is also intended to confer success by association from a rising China to a Russia experiencing serious economic problems. China's support for Russia has served to legitimize Moscow's actions in Ukraine and Syria. China also offers a geo-economic alternative to Europe both as a trading partner and an energy consumer. The two leaders appear to enjoy a close working relationship, enhanced by a mutual aversion to domestic dissent and to Western attempts to promote democracy and human rights, which could undermine their rule. But Russia's strategic dependence on China is much greater than China's is on Russia, and although they both reject the current global order, they do not agree on what a future world order should look like.

Russia is a useful partner for China because it supports China on all major foreign policy issues and does not interfere in China's domestic affairs. While Chinese experts may privately express criticism of Russia's actions in Ukraine, publicly officials have adopted a stance of neutrality. In return, Russia has not commented publicly on China's activities in the South China Sea, although these actions have irked Russia's other Asian partners, such as Vietnam. But Moscow has inveighed against the "internationalization" of the South China Sea disputes and has condemned US "freedom of navigation" activities in the area.

Ultimately, while the Kremlin seeks to overturn the US-led global order and promote a tripolar world order, Beijing prefers to reform the existing order to suit China's economic and geostrategic interests, and it regards the United States as its only true global counterpart. Nevertheless, China's support for Russia has enabled Moscow to avoid the international isolation that the United States and Europe sought to impose on it after the Crimean annexation. In this way, China has acted as a facilitator of Russia's military activities in Ukraine and Syria, which have enabled Russia to raise its international profile and forced the West to resume dealing with Moscow. Despite potential Sino-Russian rivalries in Central Asia or the Arctic, a shared normative approach toward the international arena and suspicion of US intentions and policies will continue to bind the two countries together for the foreseeable future. But it will remain a relationship dominated by official contacts, with far less interaction between entrepreneurs and civil society than is the case for Russia and Europe. As one Russian explained:

> In our relations with countries like Italy or Germany, there are lots of small- and medium-sized enterprises [that] have a presence here and employ many Russians. There is a multi-layered fabric of human contacts that has grown over years with cultural exchanges, mixed marriages. With China, we have very little of that.[67]

This underscores the fact that Russia still defines its foreign policy with Europe and the United States as its main reference points. The men in the Kremlin understand the West better than they do China.

Another reality check against which to assess the rhetoric of close Chinese-Russian ties is to look at where the Chinese send their children to study. In 2017, there were upward of 350,000 Chinese university students in the United States, a fivefold increase in a decade, pouring $9 billion into the US economy. By contrast, there are 25,000 Chinese university students in all of Russia.[68] Even fewer Russian students go to

China—15,000—while 100,000 US students go to China and 900 go to Moscow. This shows clearly that the Chinese are highly pragmatic about where they can secure the best education for their children without this changing moderating political attitudes toward the US.

Russia and China in the Age of Trump

During the 2016 US presidential election campaign, candidate Donald Trump suggested that it was important for the United States to improve relations with Russia because closer US-Russia ties might induce Moscow to join Washington in pressuring Beijing to change its policies. In the Cold War years, "playing the China card" became a central aspect of the Nixon-Kissinger opening toward Beijing at the same time as Washington pursued détente with Moscow. In the strategic triangle of that era, the United States appeared to hold all the cards, because China and the Soviet Union feared—and even fought—each other, and both sought improved ties with the US as a hedge against each other. Today the balance of power in that strategic triangle has dramatically shifted, and China holds most of the cards. As a senior Chinese official put it, "Relations among China, Russia, and the United States currently resemble a scalene triangle, in which the greatest distance between the three points lies between Moscow and Washington. Within this triangle, Chinese-Russian relations are the most positive and stable."[69]

Ties with China have protected Russia from the full impact of Western sanctions and have provided it with continuing international legitimacy at a time when the West has sought to isolate it. Would Russia have acted differently in Ukraine or Syria had there been no Chinese alternative? It is, of course, impossible to answer that question, but Beijing has remained neutral as Russia has destabilized Ukraine and used military force to keep the Assad regime in power in Syria. In the age of Trump and the fraying of traditional alliances, the dynamics of Sino-Russian relations could change were the United States to intensify both its trade war with China and its nascent rapprochement with Russia. But Trump is more likely to continue to upend the international order than to consolidate a durable new partnership with either Russia or China.

China represents a key pillar of Putin's world. It offers Russia a partnership with a rising power and reinforces both countries' drive to create an alternative global order. But it is unlikely that the relationship will blossom into a full-fledged alliance any time soon. The sprawling Russian embassy in Beijing, with its historical roots going back to 1658, is a testimony to the longevity and significance of the relationship between Russia and China and its many changes. For now, the "elder" brother will continue to seek closer ties to his "younger" brother, even as the junior sibling surpasses him.

—9—

WARY NEIGHBORS

Russia and Japan in the Shadow of World War Two

Relations between the two countries during the last 150 years have been relations of war, semiwar, prewar, or postwar. Japan usually is regarded as a hostile country,... whereas... the Japanese public considers the Soviet Union as a most unpleasant country.

—Mikhail Kapitsa, Soviet deputy foreign minister, 1991[1]

I like Japan very much—Japanese culture, sport, including judo, but it will not offend anyone if I say that I like Russia even more.... We believe we have no territorial problems at all. It is only Japan that believes it has territorial problems with Russia.

—Vladimir Putin, 2016[2]

The return of the four islands has been our strong national wish. It has been a shared wish across a wide spectrum of the Japanese. Giving up is not a political option.

—Senior Japanese official, 2017[3]

In the early morning hours, Tokyo's bustling Tsukiji fish market—the largest in the world—comes to life. Workers careen around the vast aisles filled with tuna, salmon, and sea urchin in three-wheeled electric cars, sending spectators scuttling in all directions to avoid a collision. Visitors can watch the daily auctions and then repair to one of the unprepossessing-looking cafés in the outer market for an exquisite sushi breakfast of fresh fish. The 150-year-old SushiBun café, with its simple wooden benches and tables, has a skilled chef who serves up each new piece of sushi with a dramatic flourish. It also has a unique distinction. On its wall hangs a testimonial signed by Russian foreign minister Sergei Lavrov. Lavrov likes to visit the café and sample different fish during his visits to Tokyo, which have become more frequent in recent years. But one of the key topics never changes. For more than seventy years, Russia and Japan have been trying to sign a peace treaty and normalize their relations, but they have not succeeded yet. World War Two has so far not ended for Tokyo and Moscow. Indeed, history plays a more important role in this relationship than in many other parts of Putin's world, and both countries remain trapped in the past. The current prime minister, Shinzo Abe, is determined to improve ties and has pushed for an accelerated negotiating schedule. So this gets Lavrov to the fish market more often now.

Excellent sushi, of course, cannot overcome history. The Japan-Russia relationship has for over a century been fraught and frosty. Ever since Japan defeated Russia in the 1905 Russo-Japanese War, Russians have been wary of the Japanese—and the feeling is mutual. At the end of World War Two, the USSR occupied four islands that had previously been Japanese. Since then, Tokyo has insisted they must be returned, and Russia has refused to return them. Successive attempts to normalize relations have foundered on the islands in question. Today, facing a rising and more assertive China and a dangerous and unpredictable North Korea, the Japanese leadership is convinced that it is essential to improve ties with Russia. The Kremlin has responded favorably to Japan's overtures. Yet Moscow may well continue to rebuff Tokyo's proposals for territorial concessions. Might Japan be willing to renounce the islands? How might a genuine rapprochement between Russia and Japan alter the geopolitical landscape in Northeast Asia and beyond? This chapter will explore ties between a Japanese leader determined to make progress and his Russian counterpart whose devotion to Japanese martial arts has given him a unique perspective on this difficult relationship.

From Nicholas II to World War Two

The twentieth century began with a shock for imperial Russia—whose population numbered 130 million at the time—when it was defeated by Japan, with a population of 46.5 million but with a superior navy and fleet.[4] In February 1904, Japan launched a surprise torpedo attack on Russia's Far Eastern Fleet in Port Arthur, Manchuria, leaving a cruiser and two battleships damaged. The attack was the culmination of tensions that had begun in the early 1890s. Russia had already occupied half of the then-Japanese island of Sakhalin in 1875. The tsarist empire was expanding eastward, and the 1904–1905 war was fought over control of railroad and port facilities in Manchuria and over the political domination of the Korean Peninsula, which until then had been under Chinese control.[5] Japan had been willing to negotiate a spheres-of-influence agreement with Russia on the Korean Peninsula, but its efforts were rebuffed.

The Russians, who were militarily unprepared for this war, had seriously underestimated the Japanese. The Russian legation in Tokyo was sending back reports to Saint Petersburg that the "new model" Japanese conscript army was highly effective. But the Russian imperial court and the military brass discounted this information. They still viewed the Japanese as "little people who lived in paper houses and wasted hours on flower arrangements and tea ceremonies." Ignorant of real Japanese military prowess, Tsar Nicholas and his courtiers referred to the Japanese as "monkeys" and their army as "infantile." In fact, Japanese sailors were literate, while most Russian sailors were not, and most Japanese sailors had grown up on or near the coast, whereas most Russian sailors had not seen the sea until conscription.[6] This was the first victory in modern times of an Asian power over a European empire.

The Russo-Japanese War was economically, politically, and militarily costly for both countries. Japan faced a payments crisis, and the public in Russia grew increasingly incensed by the toll the war was taking. Russia incurred 31,000 casualties and lost almost its entire Baltic and Far Eastern surface fleet after the decisive Battle of Tsushima.[7] Japan lost 49,000 lives. Defeated by the Japanese, Russia signed a peace treaty with Japan in August 1905 in Portsmouth, New Hampshire. President Theodore Roosevelt brokered the treaty, for which he received the Nobel Prize. Tsar Nicholas sent his top adviser, Count Sergei Witte, to negotiate, telling him he wouldn't "pay a kopek or cede an inch of territory."[8] But that was not the case. Russia was forced to recognize Japan's interest in Korea, which Japan annexed in 1910. Russia ceded to Japan the southern half of Sakhalin, together with Port Arthur and Dairen and extensive rights in Manchuria.[9] Russia retained a sphere of influence in northern Manchuria and Outer Mongolia. Although Witte publicly praised Roosevelt's gifts as a leader, his memoirs convey a different impression. He found the US president "selfish and totally without ideals," a vulgar contrast to the "gentlemanly" Japanese.[10]

Russia's defeat by Japan also had a profound impact domestically. It precipitated the first act in a revolutionary movement that eventually led to the Bolshevik uprising a little more than a decade later. The peasants and workers had for some time harbored a number of serious economic and political grievances, but unrest caused by Russia's faltering fortunes in the war exacerbated these problems and precipitated the first Russian revolution in 1905. On January 9, a crowd of peaceful demonstrators gathered outside the Winter Palace in Saint Petersburg to protest their privations. Military units fired on them, killing and wounding more than a thousand. "Bloody Sunday," as it came to be known, led the tsar to introduce limited political reforms and establish for the first time a legislative assembly with limited suffrage: the State Duma. Vladimir Lenin called this 1905 revolution the Great Rehearsal for the Bolshevik seizure of power in 1917.

Russo-Japanese relations improved after the war's end, only to deteriorate after the Bolshevik Revolution in October 1917. Faced with the collapse of state authority in Russia's Far East and suspicious of the Bolsheviks, Japan intervened militarily in Russia's civil war that followed the revolution. At the height of their intervention, 70,000 Japanese troops were deployed across the Russian Far East. Japan supported the anti-Bolshevik White Army—especially its forces deployed in Siberia. But once the Red Army had defeated its White opponents, the Japanese began to negotiate with the new Soviet government, and in 1925 a treaty of recognition was signed, with the Soviets accepting the terms of the 1905 Portsmouth treaty.

In the interwar period, relations between the USSR and Japan remained strained. Yet, unexpectedly, Stalin was able to reach an agreement with Japan that saved the USSR from a two-front war. In April 1941, Japanese foreign minister Yosuke Matsuoka visited his allies in Berlin, and although he was given hints about the forthcoming German attack on the Soviet Union, Hitler said nothing about the need for Japan to move against the USSR as well.[11] He then went to Moscow, where Stalin put on a charm offensive, greeting him as a fellow Asian. "You are Asiatic. So am I. We are all Asian."[12] Two months before Germany invaded the USSR, Moscow and Tokyo signed a five-year neutrality pact. Dubbed a "strange neutrality," the pact would mean that two countries that would soon be fighting in opposing coalitions in a world war nevertheless refrained from attacking each other. The nonaggression pact with Japan was a great coup for Stalin's diplomacy. Stalin was seemingly unaware that within weeks Hitler was to launch Operation Barbarossa and invade the USSR—with which Germany had signed a nonaggression pact two years earlier.[13] But Japan and the USSR observed the neutrality pact for four years—until the victorious Soviet Union broke the pact, invaded Manchuria in August 1945, and reoccupied Sakhalin and the Southern Kuril Islands. Thus the stalemate that persists today.

The Kurils or "Northern Territories"

Russians call them the Kuril Islands. Japanese call them the Northern Territories. The disputed volcanic islands covering 5,000 square kilometers are literally and figuratively shrouded in mists for much of the year. A Russian sea captain who approached the islands in 1811 complained of the "excessively thick fogs."[14] Nevertheless, "these unattractive pieces of real estate carry symbolic associations that matter a great deal to many."[15] In the late eighteenth century, a Russian naval expedition reached the Kuril Islands with their Japanese inhabitants, but Russia and Japan had yet to demarcate borders in the Sea of Okhotsk. Eventually, in the 1875 Treaty of Saint Petersburg, Japan gave up its rights in Sakhalin in exchange for sovereignty over all of the Kuril Islands. At this point both Russians and Japanese lived on the islands, and their respective rights were guaranteed. But ambiguity over the territorial demarcation of these islands persisted, and Soviet foreign minister Vyacheslav Molotov unsuccessfully tried to have them returned to the USSR as part of the Soviet-Japanese neutrality pact.

On the eve of the February 1945 Yalta Conference, President Roosevelt

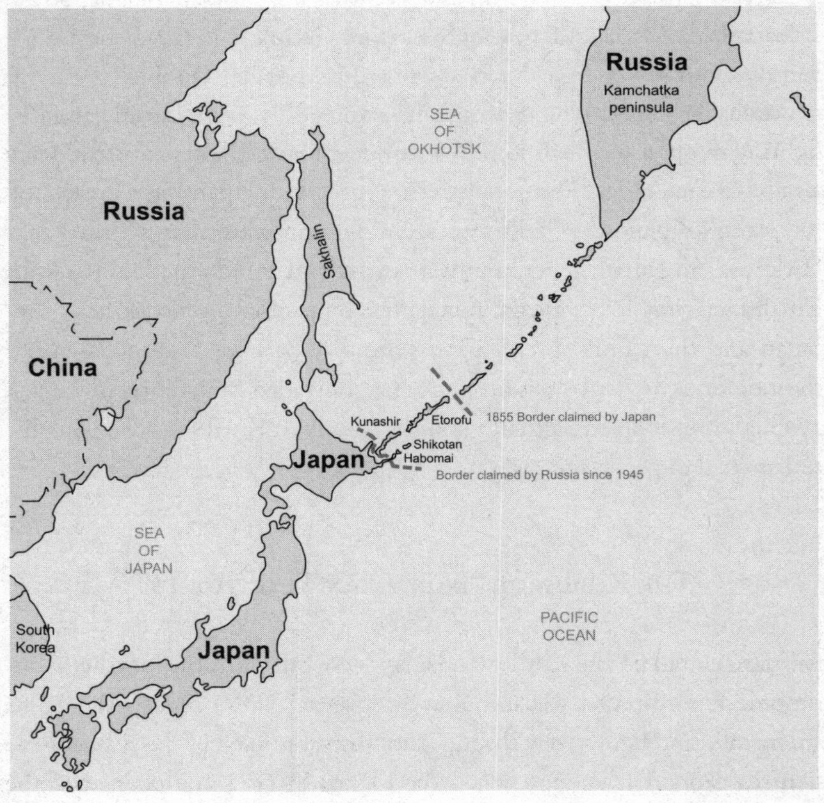

was given a State Department briefing paper emphasizing that these four islands were acquired legally by Japan and belonged to Japan—but he apparently failed to read the paper.[16] By the terms of the Yalta agreement, the USSR was to enter the war against Japan three months after the end of the war in Europe. The secret amendment to the Yalta treaty states: "The Kuril islands shall be handed over to the Soviet Union."[17] By the time the USSR took the four Kuril Islands—the Habomais, Shikotan, Kunashir, and Etorofu—Japan was a defeated nation, and the Soviet Union's allies, the United States and Britain, did not object. In his September 1945 Victory Speech, Stalin declared that the islands would serve "as a direct means of communication between the Soviet Union and the ocean and a base for the defense of our country against Japanese aggression."[18] The four islands were strategically located on the outer edge of the Sea of Okhotsk, providing access for the Soviet Pacific Fleet to the Pacific Ocean, and they also were an economic prize, with a significant fish population.

When the USSR abrogated its neutrality pact with Japan and commenced its offensive against the crumbling Japanese army in Manchuria, it captured 640,000 Japanese soldiers. These prisoners of war were subject to forced labor to construct the Baikal-Amur Railroad, and 62,000 of them perished. The surviving POWs returned to Japan in 1956, when diplomatic relations between the two countries were restored.[19]

In 1956, after difficult negotiations, the USSR and Japan signed a joint declaration whereby the USSR agreed to "transfer" to Japan the two smaller islands—Shikotan and the Habomais.[20] However, this would occur only after the conclusion of a peace treaty between the two countries.[21] Indeed, the Soviets were preparing to hand back the two islands, but the Japanese side would not compromise and insisted that all four islands be returned. Subsequently, the Soviets hardened their position, saying they would not transfer the islands until all foreign (i.e., American) troops were withdrawn from Japan. But the 1956 agreement remains the only deal on the table. Putin has regularly said that Russia is prepared to negotiate with Japan on the basis of this agreement, but the Japanese constitution explicitly ties the conclusion of a peace treaty to the return of all four islands. Moreover, the two islands the Russians have offered are much smaller than the two Moscow would have retained. So, more than seven decades after the end of World War Two, Russia and Japan have not signed a peace treaty because of a dispute over four small but strategically located islands.

The Gorbachev Non-Breakthrough

When in the 1980s Mikhail Gorbachev proclaimed a need for New Political Thinking, it appeared to open the door for progress in the stalled Russia-Japan relationship. In his memoirs, he wrote: "It was very important to me that relations with this large neighbor be normalized and improved." Gorbachev made a major speech in the summer of 1986 in Vladivostok calling for a recalibration and improvement of the USSR's ties with Asia, particularly China. But according to the Soviet leader, Japan displayed a "cool and suspicious reaction" to his speech.[22] The Japanese Ministry of Foreign Affairs was initially reluctant to respond to Soviet overtures. Moreover, Gorbachev had to postpone his planned visit to Japan several times because of the tumultuous international situation he faced as the Soviet bloc began to crumble. Perhaps if he had gone to Tokyo in 1989—as originally planned—he would have been in a stronger position domestically to make compromises. But a variety of domestic pressures, especially the rise of his archrival, Boris Yeltsin, made this very difficult.

Gorbachev's long-awaited visit—the first to Japan by any Soviet or Russian leader—was an anticlimax.[23] It came in April 1991, three months before the coup by inept hard-line plotters that nearly ousted him. By this time Gorbachev was facing mounting pressure from both right- and left-wing opponents. In an important gesture of reconciliation, Gorbachev stopped in Khabarovsk on his way to Tokyo and laid a wreath at the graves of Japanese POWs. He also handed over to the Japanese government a list of the dead. When he and his wife, Raisa, arrived, they were whisked away from the airport to meet the emperor, but their route was changed to avoid the thousands of right-wing demonstrators protesting his visit and demanding the return of the islands.

On the face of it, an economic-political deal might have been possible. The USSR's economic situation was deteriorating, with declining growth rates and an economy hit hard by the 1986 collapse in oil prices. Japan could have been a significant source of investment and trade, in return for a possible political compromise from the Soviet side. But economic incentives were apparently insufficient to overcome the Kremlin's resistance to a territorial deal. Little progress was made on the island question. Gorbachev argued with his Japanese interlocutors about who was responsible for the "illegal" seizure of islands. Nor did Gorbachev come away with any major new economic cooperation projects, although this was one of his key goals. He failed to close the deal he sought: guarantees for private investment in the Soviet Union and official loans. In the final joint communiqué between the two countries, the Soviet side for the first time acknowledged that a territorial dispute existed, the islands were named, and both sides agreed to work together to establish a visa-free regime for visits by Japanese to the four islands.[24] Gorbachev also promised to reduce the Soviet military presence on the islands. But beyond that, little concrete was accomplished.

The Yeltsin "No Necktie" Summits

After Yeltsin replaced Gorbachev, a familiar pattern in Russo-Japanese relations emerged. Each new Russian or Japanese leader would come into office determined to find a more productive way to normalize relations, and there would be an initial period of raised expectations, followed by disappointment and mutual recriminations. After Russia joined the G-8 group of advanced industrialized countries in 1997, for the first time it had Japan as a partner in this kind of organization—until Russia was thrown out in 2014 following the annexation of Crimea. The Japanese side insisted on linking the political and economic aspects of bilateral relations, whereas the Russians tried to separate them. A vicious circle developed, whereby Russia's reluctance to discuss territorial issues prevented Japan from offering economic assistance to Russia's struggling economy, and that in turn strengthened nationalistic forces in Russia that opposed territorial concessions.[25]

Yeltsin had announced that he would visit Japan in 1992, hinting that a territorial deal might be in the cards. But four days before his planned trip, Yeltsin abruptly telephoned Prime Minister Kiichi Miyazawa and called off his trip, leaving the Japanese reeling from a "big shock."[26] Why did Yeltsin get cold feet? The ostensible reason was safety concerns. Yeltsin cited "domestic circumstances" in Russia, Japan's rigidity over the Kuril question, and Japan's inability to ensure the Russian president's safety in the face of extremist demonstrators in Japan.[27] Yeltsin's Security Council reportedly overrode his decision to make the trip, although he took sole responsibility for the cancellation. The Japanese government was furious, and anti-Russian sentiment was on the rise.

But Yeltsin persisted and eventually made it to Tokyo in October 1993, shortly after he had eliminated a major source of domestic opposition by firing on the Russian parliament—whose members had vowed armed resistance to his policies. Yeltsin announced his intention to visit Tokyo a few weeks after the assault on the parliament, and its timing suggests he wanted to demonstrate that he was once again in full command after prevailing over his opponents who had threatened violence. As it turned out, violence awaited him in Tokyo. The protests began before he arrived: black trucks with mounted loudspeakers drove through Tokyo's streets, shouting anti-Yeltsin diatribes and demanding the return of the Northern Territories, and smoke bombs were tossed into the Russian embassy compound. Ten thousand riot-geared officers surrounded the Russian embassy as Yeltsin arrived.[28]

But he came with a message of conciliation. Yeltsin went further than Gorbachev to acknowledge the cruel treatment of Japanese POWs after 1945. "On behalf of the Russian people and the government, I would like to express my apology for these inhuman acts," he told Prime Minister Morihiro Hosakawa, blaming the "totalitarian regime" for these acts. He offered "deep condolences" to the emperor. Hosakawa praised Yeltsin's words as the "foundation for the spiritual and psychological reconciliation of our two peoples." Moreover, Yeltsin went on record as admitting the existence of a territorial dispute and again promised to withdraw the remaining Russian troops from the islands. But, to the consternation of his hosts, he would not acknowledge Japanese sovereignty over the islands.[29]

Despite Japan's disappointment over the meager results of this summit, four years later Prime Minister Ryutaro Hashimoto launched a new initiative. Determined to improve ties with Russia, he made a major speech in 1997 to a business audience in which he acknowledged that of all the key relationships in the Asia-Pacific region, "only Russo-Japanese relations have lagged behind." He proposed a new approach to dealing with Russia based on "mutual trust, mutual benefits, and a long-term perspective."[30] He proposed that the two leaders deal with each other informally and hold a "no necktie" summit.

In November 1997, Hashimoto and Yeltsin met for the first informal summit in the Siberian city of Krasnoyarsk—exactly halfway between Tokyo and Moscow. In his memoirs, Yeltsin describes how the two men set off in a cutter to fish in a remote location along the Yenisei River. It was rainy, windy, and cold, and "the fish fled instantly." After an hour, the two shivering leaders gave up and repaired indoors to eat fish soup. "Only vodka could have warmed me up," Yeltsin ruefully notes, "but I was forbidden to drink at that time." Yeltsin understood the stalemate the territorial issue had created for the Japanese. "They were unable to make concessions on this matter. They are raised on the issue; it's as though they consume it with their mother's milk." But Russia, he emphasizes, could not give up territory. So the two leaders agreed not to link the islands question to economic collaboration nor to the conclusion of a peace treaty.[31] At their joint press conference, they agreed—to the surprise of their aides—to conclude a peace treaty before the year 2000—in a mere three years.[32] They had one more "no necktie" summit in 1998, but as the year 2000 approached, Yeltsin's health deteriorated, and Russian officials walked back the idea that a peace treaty would be signed in 2000.

Putin and the Judo Factor

As he entered the Kremlin, Putin described the role judo had played in his life. Admitting he had been a "hooligan" as a child, he claimed, "It was sports that dragged me off the streets." He began by studying sambo, a Soviet mixture of judo and wrestling, and then switched to judo. As a student in the Leningrad State University's Faculty of Law, Putin continued to compete on the judo team of the original club that had trained him as a schoolboy, rejecting the university's attempts to get him to join their team. He became a master in the sport in 1973 and competed in regional championships.

Judo apparently taught him discipline and a specific outlook on life:

> Judo is not just a sport, you know. It's a philosophy. It's respect for your elders and for your opponents. Everything in judo has an instructive aspect. You come out onto the mat, you bow to one another, you follow ritual. It could be done differently, you know. Instead of bowing to your opponent, you could jab him in the forehead.[33]

Putin's prowess in judo has opened doors for him in Japan that no previous Russian or Soviet leader has managed. During his first official visit to Japan in September 2000, Putin was granted the honorable sixth dan rank by the Kodokan Judo Institute, which was established in 1882 by the man who founded judo. In 2003, Prime Minister Junichiro Koizumi met Putin in the Saint Petersburg judo hall where Putin had learned martial arts in his school days.[34] On a visit to Japan in 2005, Putin won several rounds on the mat—until a young boy managed to throw him to the ground. Nevertheless, despite his knowledge of and respect for Japanese martial arts, Putin has barely moved an inch toward the Japanese position on the Kurils.

Political Ties

Before arriving in Tokyo for his first official visit in 2000, Putin symbolically visited Sakhalin Island, whose governor was adamantly opposed to any territorial concessions. The centrist daily *Kommersant* exhorted Putin not to "sell out the Motherland."[35] When asked by his Japanese hosts about his legal obligations toward his predecessor's pledge, he replied caustically, "*Ia iurist*" (I am a lawyer). Nevertheless, he did privately acknowledge the legal validity of the 1956 Joint Declaration.[36] At their next summit in 2001, Putin rejected a Japanese proposal to separate negotiations on the islands into two tracks—those that would be returned and those that would not—because that would have implied Russia was indeed prepared to return two.

The Russia issue in 2002 became embroiled in a government shake-up, revealing how sensitive the island issue remained. A politician named Muneo Suzuki alleged, at a meeting at the Japanese Ministry of Foreign Affairs, that Tokyo really did not need the islands and that the dispute only continued for reasons of national prestige. As a result, the new foreign minister Yoriko Kawaguchi eventually fired thirty employees of the Foreign Ministry, including a group of Russia experts allied with Suzuki who were willing to compromise on the islands question. She insisted on Russia recognizing Japanese sovereignty over all of the islands and accused Foreign Minister Igor Ivanov of not briefing journalists correctly over the issue.[37] In response, Russian media accused Japan of "McCarthyism."[38] Suzuki was also named in a major corruption scandal tied to a government organization charged with disbursing assistance to Russia and other post-Soviet states.[39] So the Japanese push to normalize relations with Russia and complete a peace treaty that began in 1996 ended on the floor of Japan's National Diet amid accusations of corruption and undue political influence.[40]

During Putin's second term, Russia at various points revived the 1956 proposal of a return of two islands, but the question of sequencing was never resolved. The Russians wanted a peace treaty followed by territorial adjustments. The Japanese insisted on the return of two islands before signing a peace treaty. Nevertheless, Putin has reiterated that the 1956 agreement is still on offer—under the right circumstances.

The Medvedev interlude presents a paradox in Russian-Japanese relations. While he is normally associated with a more Western-leaning and conciliatory policy, Dmitry Medvedev was apparently a hawk when it came to Japan. He was the first Russian leader to visit the Kuril Islands, and he has done so several times. The initial visit was to Kunashir—less than fifteen miles from Japan—in 2010.[41] He toured a geothermal power plant and a construction site, and spoke with representatives of the fishing industry. Some speculated he was doing this to cultivate an image as a strong leader. Others argued this visit was also aimed at Beijing—to project a tough image and remind the Chinese that Russia had several options in Northeast Asia. Needless to say, the Japanese government protested strongly, describing the visit as an "unforgivable outrage."[42] To which Foreign Minister Lavrov retorted, "The president of Russia doesn't discuss with anyone what region of the Russian Federation he will select for his visit. We don't need any advice from Japan on that."[43] In 2015, Medvedev, now prime minister, visited Etorofu, declaring that the Kurils were part of Russia. He posted selfies with a youth group in front of a large Russian flag to mark Russia's Flag Day.

Energy, Investment, and Trade

The Russian Far East (RFE) remains relatively underdeveloped, underpopulated, and in need of investment, and Putin has gradually made this a priority. It is also an area in which China has historically had territorial claims. Japan, conversely, is an island with few natural resources and has a keen interest in Russia's abundant energy supplies. Japan is a natural investment partner for this region. At various junctures, the Japanese government has used the unresolved Kuril Islands territorial issue to dissuade its companies from investing in Russia. For some time this was convenient for the Japanese companies because of their reluctance to do business in Russia without the rule of law and predictable conditions. As time has passed, however, much of this reluctance has waned, and Japanese interest in the Russian market has grown.

The Japanese desire to engage in joint energy projects with Russia has been thwarted both by geopolitics and growing Russian resource nationalism. The first project involved Sakhalin Island. In 2003, Russia and Japan signed a contract for the construction of the world's largest liquefied natural gas (LNG) plant, the Sakhalin-II project, originally led by Shell and two Japanese corporations. The project was designed to have a positive impact on the economy of the Russian Far East. The LNG was to be transported to Japan. But the project ran into trouble in 2006 over the strong-arm tactics of the Kremlin and its Gazprom ally when Shell announced that it had incurred significant cost overruns and the Russian government began to pressure it to sell its stake to Gazprom. Then minister of natural resources Yuri Trutnev weighed in and announced that the production sharing agreement should never have been signed. And environmental official Oleg Mitvol suddenly discovered the project would have serious negative consequences for the wildlife on the island. Shell was forced to halve its ownership in the $22 billion project, cutting its stake from 55 percent to 27.5 percent. Until the very last moment, the Russian authorities tried to pressure Shell into retaining an even smaller share in the project. Gazprom stepped in, buying Shell's share plus half the stakes owned by Japanese partners Mitsui and Mitsubishi, for just $7.5 billion. A Shell spokesman described this as the equivalent of "paying to enter on the ground floor, as if they were a shareholder at the beginning."[44] Once Gazprom took over the majority share, Putin declared that all the environmental issues had miraculously been resolved. Shell executives took this as a message from Putin to other officials that they should desist from further pressuring Shell and other foreign oil companies in this way.

The second major issue was the route of a proposed Russian oil pipeline to Asia. Whereas traditionally most Russian oil and gas has been exported West, Putin was determined to diversify Russia's exports and build pipelines that went east. But who should the first beneficiary be, China or Japan? Putin was initially wary of the China route via Daqing in Northwest China and preferred the Japanese pipeline route, which would have gone from Angarsk to the port of Nakhodka on the Sea of Japan.[45] The Japanese would have imported the oil by tanker. In 2004, Koizumi offered $5 billion to finance the project, and it appeared it would go forward. But in 2005, the Russian government changed its mind and committed to the Chinese pipeline route, to the disappointment of the Japanese. Apparently both cost factors and geopolitics had prevailed, and the Kremlin decided it was more important to strengthen the relationship with Beijing than with Tokyo.

The Abe Factor and Ukraine

Russia's relations with Japan, like those with other major powers, have been heavily influenced by the leaders of both countries. So when Shinzo Abe was elected Japanese prime minister in 2012 and Putin returned to the Kremlin, there were new possibilities for improving relations because of Abe's determination to resolve the Kuril Islands issue. It was a personal mission for him. His father, Shintaro Abe, foreign minister from 1982 to 1986, had worked with Gorbachev and Shevardnadze to achieve a breakthrough in Russo-Japanese relations. Abe had visited Moscow and laid the initial groundwork for Gorbachev's visit to Tokyo in 1991. On his deathbed, he expressed to his son the wish that a peace treaty be signed and the islands be returned. Seeking rapprochement with Russia became, as one Japanese expert put it, a "family business."[46] Moreover, during his reelection campaign in 2011, Putin had ordered Japanese and Russian officials to follow the judo command "*Hajime,*" or "Start."

Abe has prioritized normalizing relations with Russia and is domestically strong enough to continue to push this agenda despite nationalist opposition. He believes he is better placed than any previous prime minister to accomplish this because of his strong power base and influence over the right wing. He also has explicitly delinked the economic and political aspects of the relationship. Concerns about a rising China, Sino-Japanese conflict over the Senkaku Islands (*Diaoyu* in Chinese) in the South China Sea (Japan's other territorial dispute), a disagreement with South Korea over some islets, and the threat from North Korea—all these have reinforced Abe's determination to improve ties to Russia. He is particularly concerned to prevent the formation of a stronger Russia-China alliance. Moreover, the impact of the 2011 Fukushima Daiichi nuclear power plant accident added urgency to the need to diversify Japan's energy supplies. Abe focused on cultivating personal ties with Putin. He began the process of rapprochement as soon as he took office, traveling to Russia in 2013—the first visit by a sitting Japanese prime minister in a decade—and laying the groundwork for a Putin visit to Japan. Abe and Putin created a two-plus-two dialogue, involving foreign and defense ministers to begin negotiations on an eventual agreement. Moreover, Kremlin officials said that Russia would not take sides in the Senkaku Islands dispute with China.

When the Winter Olympics opened in Sochi in February 2014, Abe was one of the few Western heads of state to attend. The others boycotted the games over Russia's legislation penalizing homosexuality and other human rights issues. Then, a few weeks later, Russia annexed Crimea and helped launch a war in Eastern Ukraine. This placed Abe in an awkward position. For the Japanese, Ukraine is far away and not a pressing issue. When the US expelled Russia from the G-8 and imposed sanctions—first over Crimea and then following the July 2014 downing of the Malaysian airliner over Eastern Ukraine—Japan faced a dilemma. As an ally of the

United States and a member of the G-7, it felt obligated to impose sanctions. But imposing sanctions could jeopardize the rapprochement with Russia and set back a possible settlement. Moreover, many in the private sector shared the opinion of one prominent businessman: "Why impose sanctions? They are ineffective. Why does the US care about Ukraine? East Ukraine belongs to Russia."[47]

Reluctantly, Japan imposed financial and technology sanctions similar to those imposed by the United States and Europe. Immediately following the annexation, it suspended talks on investment and visa reform and condemned Russia's actions. After the MH-17 downing, it imposed more sanctions, including freezing assets of those supporting Crimea's annexation, and financial sanctions for new projects in Russia in line with those of the European Bank for Reconstruction and Development.[48] However, this did not satisfy the Obama administration. US officials sought to dissuade Abe from continuing his personal meetings with Putin—but to no avail.[49] This increasingly became a source of US-Japanese friction. Meanwhile, Russia sharply criticized Japan's imposition of sanctions. Abe continued to travel to Russia to pin down a date for a Putin visit to Japan. Japan hosted the 2016 G-7 summit, and Abe unsuccessfully tried to secure an invitation for Putin—after Russia had been ousted from the organization. "We need the constructive engagement of Russia," Abe said. "I believe appropriate dialogue with Russia, appropriate dialogue with President Putin is very important."[50]

It is not surprising, therefore, that as soon as Donald Trump was elected, Abe hoped for a change in the US position on Russia. He visited Trump in New York shortly after his election and apparently met no pushback when he explained why Japan wanted to improve ties with Russia. After Abe's second visit with Trump—this time at the White House and golfing in Mar-a-Lago—Abe affirmed that the US president had encouraged him to improve ties with Russia: "President Trump understands Japan's policy to promote dialogue with Russian President Vladimir Putin to resolve the territorial issue." Moreover, he described Putin as "a man who keeps his promises."[51]

Putin's Visit to Japan and Its Aftermath

Putin finally visited Japan in December 2016, eleven years after his previous trip, this time to Nagato, Abe's hometown in the Yamaguchi Prefecture. Before his departure, an open letter signed by local Sakhalin officials and scholars reminded Putin that the Russian constitution precluded any territorial concessions. "Dear Vladimir Vladimirovich [Putin], we hope that in the course of your talks with the Japanese side you will not depart from the position of the inviolability of the Russian sovereignty over the Kuril Islands."[52] Once Putin was in Japan, right-wing activists in trucks mounted with loudspeakers circled the streets not far from where the two leaders were meeting, blaring "Return the islands" and "Putin go home," similar to what they had done when Gorbachev and Yeltsin visited.

Putin arrived three hours late, and his attitude toward Abe was more distant than previously. Putin had refused the offer of a male mate for his female Akita dog, which Abe had given him in 2012. And he turned down opportunities both to sample the hot springs and to demonstrate his judo skills, in contrast to previous visits. During the summit, it was all business and how to move toward a peace treaty. Eighty economic agreements that could bring Russia up to $2.5 billion were signed, including joint economic projects for the Kurils. However, no substantial Japanese loans were on offer because these would have contravened Western sanctions.

Before he went to Japan, Putin said in an interview with Bloomberg, "We don't trade territories." He went on to explain why ceding the Kurils would be completely different from ceding the island Russia gave back to China in 2004 as part of the final settlement of their mutual border. "The Japanese issue arose as a result of World War II and is set out in international documents linked to the results of the Second World War."[53] This is key to understanding how Putin has approached the Kuril Islands question. Presenting the Great Patriotic War as the crowning achievement in recent Russian history whose results cannot be questioned has been the foundation of Putin's national narrative. To admit that there was something unsettled or unjust in the Soviet occupation of the Kurils would be to challenge the fundamental legitimacy of Russia's claim to be a great power—its victory in World War Two.

In the first half of 2017, there was another Putin-Abe summit and a resumption of the two-plus-two talks. The situation in North Korea was a major topic. Although Russia and Japan agree that North Korea should not have nuclear weapons, they do not see eye to eye on how to deal with Kim Jong-un, particularly in the military sphere. Russia has opposed the deployment of the US THAAD missile defense system in South Korea and would also oppose Japan acquiring the Aegis Ashore missile defense system. But in face of North Korea's increasingly provocative nuclear tests, influential lawmakers are urging Tokyo to develop its own long-range preemptive-strike capabilities. Moreover, Japan has its own unresolved issue with North Korea: the abduction of possibly hundreds of Japanese citizens by North Korea between 1977 and 1983, most of whom have disappeared.[54]

Despite Putin's more conciliatory stance toward Japan, there has been a steady military buildup on the Kuril Islands in the past few years, casting further doubt over Russia's interest in resolving the territorial issue. This military buildup is a growing problem for Japan. Russia deployed 10,000 extra troops on the islands in 2017. It held a military drill in February 2018 that greatly irritated the Japanese. It is also stationing new coastal missile systems as well as missile defense systems and has hinted that it will enhance its naval presence too. Given the financial constraints on the military, it remains to be seen whether this buildup is sustainable, but it certainly indicates that Moscow has no intention of scaling back its presence on the islands. At the 2017 Saint Petersburg International Economic Forum, Putin explicitly linked the buildup on the Kuril Islands to US missile defense deployments in Europe and Asia: "As for the boosting of our military capabilities in the Russian Far East and the [Kuril] Islands in particular, this is not Russia's initiative," portraying the Russian deployments as a defensive response to the United States' own buildup around Japan. He then argued that, were the islands returned to Japan, the US military would no doubt appear in force on those territories.[55] This was hardly a reassuring message for Abe.

For now, the Japanese are focusing on the joint economic development of the islands, which essentially means that Japanese money will support the modernization of what are by all accounts underdeveloped territories. However, the legal questions may prove challenging. Will Japanese companies operate under Russian law? If so, that implies a Japanese recognition of Russian sovereignty over the islands. Japan is now proposing to establish a special set of legal norms by which Japanese firms can invest in the Kurils, but there is opposition to that in the Diet. Meanwhile, Japan's Ministry of Economy, Trade, and Industry has an official in charge of economic relations with Russia. Japan now has an active economic modernization program in Russia involving pharmaceuticals, energy efficiency, tourism, wind power, and aquaculture.

Abe's frequent meetings with the Russian leader attest to his conviction that if he continues to build trust, Putin's stance on the islands may change. The Japanese hope is that in his fourth term Putin will have a freer hand to make a deal and hand back the Habomais and Shikotan. This would happen after a peace treaty was signed. Others in Japan and Russia are far more skeptical that this will happen given Putin's repeated statements that Russia does not give back territory. Indeed, just before the opening of the Saint Petersburg International Economic Forum in 2018, presidential national security adviser Yuri Ushakov told the Japanese to "get over" their fixation on the islands, stressing that Japan had to recognize the results of World War Two and accept the islands belonged to Russia.[56] Abe joined Putin in the plenary, and in his speech to the Forum, proposed that the islands become a symbol of cooperation.[57]

Nevertheless, in Japan, Russia is seen as far less of a threat than is China. The fear of a Russo-Chinese "united front against Japan" will continue to drive the Japanese overtures toward Russia.[58] Japan views the rise of China with deep apprehension. Indeed, the 250,000-strong Japanese Self-Defense Forces have reoriented their focus from a Cold War–era preoccupation with Russia to a rising China. Tokyo's relationship with

Beijing is multifaceted and complex. The shadow of history—particularly the harsh Japanese occupation of China during World War Two—is ever present. The Chinese have asked Tokyo to stop "whitewashing Japan's militarist past." When Abe first came into office, he visited Tokyo's Yasukuni Shrine to Japan's war dead—a potent nationalist symbol—enraging the Chinese. Since then, he has not gone on a repeat visit. Moreover, on the seventieth anniversary of the end of the war in 2015, he made statements reiterating a 1995 admission of Japanese contrition and guilt. Nevertheless, a contentious past continues to influence the relationship.

Irrespective of history and politics, however, trade remains a linchpin of the relationship. China is Japan's number one trading partner by far, and Japan is China's second largest trading partner after the United States. Despite this, so far Japan has declined to join China's Asian Infrastructure Investment Bank—the only country in East Asia (apart from North Korea) that opted out. But the close economic ties between the two countries have not mitigated tense political relations as China rises. Indeed, those tensions are increasing.

As China has become more assertive in claiming territory in the South China Sea, the dispute with Japan over the Senkaku Islands has come to dominate Tokyo's political ties with Beijing. Japan administers the islands and does not acknowledge that Beijing also claims them. According to a Japanese observer, "China has come to pose a physical threat to Japan.... Japanese get the impression China wants to revive the Chinese empire and an ancient order in Asia."[59] In 2014, a public opinion poll found that 53 percent of Chinese believed China would go to war with Japan, whereas only 29 percent of Japanese believed this to be the case.[60] Russia has tacitly supported Chinese claims to these islands.

What are the prospects that the seventy-year-old Russia-Japan territorial dispute will be resolved and a peace treaty finally signed? On the face of it, Putin is surely strong enough domestically to make a deal, especially since the population of the Russian Far East might accept a territorial compromise if it brought them substantial economic benefits. But therein lies the problem for the Kremlin. What does Russia stand to gain economically from giving up territory beyond what the Japanese government and companies are already offering? Abe appears to want a peace treaty and the return of two islands more than Putin does, and Russia has more leverage. Of course, if Russia normalized relations with Japan, Russia could emerge as a more powerful player in Northeast Asia. It could be a broker in a neighborhood beset by rivalries and tensions. Japanese concerns about China and North Korea have created greater urgency for a resolution of this dispute in Tokyo than in Moscow. So Russia might well find it useful to remind the Chinese that it has a variety of options in Asia, including closer ties with Japan. Nevertheless, since the Ukraine crisis, relations with China have become more important for a Russia seeking to create a post-West order. As long as relations with the United States and Europe remain adversarial, it is useful for Russia to cultivate ties with a Japan dedicated to promoting better relations. But it is unlikely that Putin will make any territorial concessions. At the 2018 Valdai meeting, in response to a Japanese questioner, Putin asked with some exasperation, "Is that about the islands again? Not interested."[61]

What are the prospects that Japan might revise its stance on the islands and agree to a peace treaty that leaves the Kurils as part of the Russian Federation? After all, it is more than seventy years since they were part of Japan and surely a younger generation cares less about this issue. Just as questioning anything connected to the Soviet victory in World War Two is taboo in Putin's Russia, so too is the questioning of Japan's sovereignty over the Kurils. For both countries, the persistence of national narratives and myths is an essential part of the fabric that unites their societies. Given these realities, the fate of the islands will remain shrouded in a fog of uncertainty for some time to come.

10

THE NEW POWER BROKER

Russia and the Middle East

Russian policy in the Middle East is aggressive, flexible, and cognizant of its limits.

—*Senior Israeli official, 2018*[1]

Our main aim in Syria is to make sure that our citizens who went there [to fight with ISIS] never come back. For Russia, intervention in the Middle East is a matter of defending our own security. All the rest is details.

—*Vyacheslav Nikonov, Duma member and grandson of Soviet foreign minister Vyacheslav Molotov*[2]

In December 2017, Putin made a surprise visit to Hmeimim, Russia's air base in Syria. He hugged Syrian president Bashar al-Assad, declared victory over Islamic State, announced that Russia was withdrawing some of its troops from Syria, and praised the Russian pilots who had enabled him to declare their success: "You are victorious, and you are going home to your families, parents, wives, children, and friends. The fatherland is waiting for you, my friends. Have a safe trip home. I am grateful for your service."[3] From Syria, he flew to Cairo, met with Egyptian president Abdel Fattah al-Sisi, and signed a $21 billion deal to build a nuclear power plant. Then he flew on to Ankara, met with President Recep Tayyip Erdogan, and the two leaders vowed to strengthen ties between their two countries. They also condemned the Trump administration's decision to recognize Jerusalem as the capital of Israel. "Naturally, the focus was placed on the

Middle East situation [and peace process] that has deteriorated dramatically and on Syrian affairs, where our countries are closely cooperating," Putin told journalists after the talks with Erdogan.[4] In the span of twenty-four hours, Putin had sent an unmistakable message to the rest of the world: Russia is back in the Middle East as the go-to power to tackle the region's most pressing problems. Nothing will get resolved without Russia's participation.

Since Putin's return to the Kremlin in 2012, a steady stream of Middle Eastern heads of state have visited Russia. Leaders from Syria, Egypt, Jordan, Iran, Turkey, Kuwait, Saudi Arabia, and the United Arab Emirates have journeyed to Russia to confer with Putin, as has Israel's Benjamin Netanyahu—the latter several times a year. Indeed, Russia is the only great power that talks to the Shia states, the Sunni states—and the Israelis. It has replaced the United States as the go-to player in a fractured and violent area of key global strategic importance.

Indeed, Russia's return to the Middle East after the withdrawal that followed the Soviet collapse is one of Putin's major foreign policy achievements. He began to restore ties—and build new ones—early on in his tenure in the Kremlin. But it was Russia's military intervention in Syria in September 2015 and the Obama administration's ambivalence about America's role there that gave Putin the opportunity to break Russia out of its post-Crimea isolation and insert it in the region in a forceful way. And in contrast to Soviet times, when Moscow's client states in the Middle East were largely chosen on ideological grounds, Russia's engagement with regional partners today is pragmatic and nonideological. This gives it much greater freedom of action. Russia has been able, remarkably, to establish cooperative ties with the region's main protagonists—and antagonists: Israel and the Palestinians; Israel and Iran; Iran and Saudi Arabia; Turkey and the Kurds; both Libyan governments; and Hamas and Hezbollah.

How and why has Putin succeeded in reestablishing Russia as a major Middle Eastern player, in some cases edging out the United States, and in areas where the USSR was never before present? The story of Russia's return to the Middle East exemplifies Putin's most successful modus operandi: capitalizing on opportunities provided by US inaction and preexisting regional rivalries, and skillfully exploiting them to resurrect Russia as a respected player in a number of key conflicts.

The Soviet Legacy

Imperial Russia and the Ottoman Empire were great power rivals. After Russia was defeated in 1856 by the Turkish-European coalition in the Crimean War, it was determined to regain lost territories in the Caucasus. This it did after its war with Turkey in 1877. Russia also presented itself as the protector of Christians in the Ottoman Empire, particularly of the Armenians. The collapse of both the Russian and Ottoman empires at the end of World War One led to a realignment of Russia's ties with the Middle East. But in the interwar years the USSR's foreign policy focused mainly on Europe and China. The Comintern appealed to anti-colonial groups in the British and French empires—including those in the Middle East—but it was wary of nationalists who wanted independence but rejected communism.

It was only after World War Two and the wave of decolonization that the USSR began to focus on opportunities in the Middle East. Prior to 1948, its influence in the region had been minimal. The 1948 war that established the state of Israel was the first major opportunity for Moscow to become a player. Despite a long history of Russian and Soviet anti-Semitism and an official opposition to Zionism, the Kremlin viewed the Jewish struggle against the British Empire favorably. From Moscow's viewpoint, a Jewish state in the midst of the Arab world would provide a constant source of conflict between the West and the Arabs, and would offer the USSR opportunities in an area from which it had been excluded.[5] So, with Soviet assent, Czechoslovakia supplied the Jewish underground with arms in their struggle against the British Mandate for Palestine. Indeed, the Soviet Union was the first country to recognize Israel de jure (the United States was the first country to recognize Israel de facto; de jure recognition came in 1949).

The Soviet friendship with Israel was, however, short-lived. Soon domestic factors intervened to derail the relationship. In 1948, Golda Meir, Israel's first envoy to the USSR, who was born in Kyiv, came to Moscow and received a tumultuous demonstration of affection during her visit to the Choral Synagogue. This was abhorrent to the Kremlin. Stalin was deeply suspicious about the true loyalties of the USSR's Jewish citizens (calling them "rootless cosmopolitans") and equated their attachment to a foreign country with treason. In the last year of his life he accused a group of Jewish doctors of murdering several prominent Soviet officials and of intending to poison him. The doctors were slated for execution. He was planning a mass deportation of Jews just before a fatal stroke felled him in March 1953. Moreover, Israel had supported the US-led UN force fighting the Korean War and, from Moscow's point of view, was siding with the West on the international stage.

Moscow focused instead on developing ties to the newly emerging anti-colonial and anti-Western Arab countries, even though many of them persecuted communists at home. The first prize was Egypt, which remained the focus of Soviet policy until 1973. The Kremlin was initially skeptical about the officer coup in 1952 that brought Gamal Abdel Nasser to power and overthrew the monarchy. But it soon developed strong ties with Nasser, trained the Egyptian military, and supplied it with advanced weaponry. Similar ties with Iraq and Syria soon developed, as the region became a focus of US-Soviet Cold War rivalry. The USSR was now seen as the main protector of the Arabs against US-backed Israel. Hence the blow to both Moscow and its client states when Israel defeated them in the June 1967 Six-Day War. It was, according to Moscow's man in the Middle East Yevgeny Primakov, "a turning point, not only in Egypt's history, but for the entire world. The magnitude of the Arab defeat seriously traumatized Arabs everywhere."[6] Egypt, Syria, and Jordan all lost territory to Israel, which now controlled all of Jerusalem, the West Bank, the Sinai Peninsula, and the Golan Heights. After the war, the USSR broke off diplomatic ties with Israel, not to be restored until 1991.

The relationship with Egypt deteriorated after 1967 when Nasser's successor, Anwar Sadat, accused the Soviets of falling behind in their promised weapons deliveries. In 1972, he abruptly expelled 21,000 Soviet military advisers. Nevertheless, in the run-up to the Yom Kippur War, the weapons deliveries increased. In October 1973, a coalition of Arab states was, once again, unable—despite the advantage of a surprise attack and success on the battlefield—to defeat Israel during the war. After it was over, Sadat began to draw closer to the United States and eventually made a historic journey to Jerusalem to normalize relations with Israel. But Moscow retained its close military, economic, and political ties to Syria, Iraq, and other Arab states. The Middle East remained one of the top priorities for Soviet foreign policy, and the USSR backed the Arab and Palestinian cause against Israel and the United States.

The USSR's relationship with Iran was complicated. In the months right after World War Two and during what proved to be the first Cold War crisis, the USSR refused to withdraw its troops from Northern Iran, which shared a border with Soviet Azerbaijan and which it had occupied during World War Two. Under UN pressure, Moscow pulled out and eventually developed a profitable economic relationship with Iran under Shah Mohammed Reza Pahlavi, while at the same time supporting the Tudeh Communist Party. After the shah's 1979 overthrow and the emergence of the Islamic Republic of Iran, ties became strained. The new clerical government of Ayatollah Rullohah Khomeini denounced the communist Soviet Union as a "little Satan," as opposed to the "great Satan," which was the United States. Moreover, the Soviet invasion of Afghanistan galvanized Islamic anti-Soviet sentiments. After the Soviet withdrawal from Afghanistan in 1989, ties with Tehran began to improve, with the focus on arms sales.

It was only when Gorbachev came to power that the USSR's zero-sum approach to the Middle East began to change. As part of his New Political Thinking, he sought cooperation with the United States on a number of issues, including the Middle East. Despite Primakov's efforts to avoid a conflict with Iraq after it invaded Kuwait (he personally made three trips to Baghdad to try to persuade Iraqi leader Saddam Hussein to withdraw from Kuwait), Gorbachev and his foreign minister Eduard Shevardnadze eventually supported the US-led coalition in the 1991 First Gulf War to liberate Kuwait. This was a major turning point. Moscow had abandoned a client state into which it had poured billions of dollars in military and other assistance. Gorbachev also realized that in order to join the United States in seeking to achieve an Arab-Israeli peace agreement, the USSR would have to restore ties to Israel. This it did in 1991. Indeed, one of the final foreign policy acts of the USSR was the October 1991 Madrid Conference on the Middle East, which sought to broker an Arab-Israeli deal. Sponsored by the US, USSR, and Spain, it represented the first time Moscow and Washington had jointly organized a Middle East peace conference. Shortly after the meeting, the USSR collapsed, and with it came a diminution of Russian influence in the region.

During the 1990s, Russia had neither the resources nor the commitment to cultivate its relations with the Middle East. While economic ties and arms sales continued, the Yeltsin administration was mainly focused on its relations with the West. It lacked any broader strategic vision of what it wanted to achieve internationally. However, while the Kremlin was preoccupied with ties with the West, a number of former and current officials were freelancing, focusing on lucrative economic opportunities in Iran and Iraq—including in the nuclear field. In 1992, much to the consternation of the United States, Russia concluded an agreement to construct a nuclear power plant in Bushehr in Iran—a deal that originally had been signed by the shah with German and French companies. Moreover, it was becoming clear that various Russian entities were involved in building up Iran's nuclear program and that Russian institutes were training Iranian missile scientists. The US and its allies suspected that the development of a nuclear power program was a cover for what could become a nuclear weapons program. Throughout the 1990s Russia's involvement in the Iranian nuclear program raised questions about who was in control of Russian foreign policy and about Russia's attitude toward nonproliferation.

Russia's policy toward Iran was also driven by domestic considerations under Yeltsin, as it is under Putin. Post-Soviet Russia has a population of twenty million Muslims, who are not immune to the influence of fundamentalism, and the Kremlin sought to ensure that no outside power—be it Iran, Saudi Arabia, or Turkey—would try to export radical Islam to the restive North Caucasus. As one Russian observer explained the drive toward Russian-Iranian cooperation, "Today a hostile Tehran could cause a great deal of unpleasantness for Russia in the North Caucasus and in Tajikistan if it were really to set its mind to supporting the Muslim insurgents with weapons, money, and volunteers."[7]

When Chechen separatists declared their independence and Moscow sent troops to crush their movement, Iran opted not to aid them and supported Russia's territorial integrity. Tehran also cooperated with Moscow to end the civil war in Tajikistan, whose population is largely Shia. Iran worked with Russia to support the forces of the Northern Alliance in Afghanistan, who opposed the Taliban. These pressing domestic and regional concerns argued for a cooperative relationship with Iran.[8]

Vladimir Putin had launched the Second Chechen War in 1999 when he was prime minister under Yeltsin, and his presidency began with a focus on managing Russia's Muslim population. His Middle East policy has been informed by the domestic imperative to contain and prevent future separatist and terrorist movements emanating from the North Caucasus. He has also worked to foster comity with Russia's Muslims. He has on several occasions stressed that, unlike Europe or the United States, where Muslims are immigrants, Russia's Muslims are indigenous. In 2003, he attended the summit of the Organization of the Islamic Conference in Malaysia and declared that "Muslims are an inalienable part of the people of Russia."[9] In 2005, Russia was granted observer status at the organization and remains an active participant. In a 2005 speech to the Chechen parliament, Putin stated: "Russia has always been the most faithful, reliable, and consistent defender of the interests of the Islamic world."[10]

Under Putin, Russia steadily began to restore its ties with the Arab world, as it also built up its relationships with Israel and Turkey. In 2002, it became part of the Quartet on the Middle East—consisting of the United States, Russia, the EU, and the UN—formed to find a solution to the Arab-Israeli dispute. The group has met only intermittently, and Russia's role has never been as prominent as that of the United States, but it remains a formal player in this process. For Russia, stability in the Middle East is a major concern because of the Middle East's ability to export instability to Russia and its neighbors.

During Putin's first term, the most contested aspect of Russia's Middle East policy was its decision to oppose the US-led invasion of Iraq and side with Germany and France in condemning US actions. Russia's relationship with Iraq was deep and complex, involving lucrative oil and arms contracts, and Moscow also saw Saddam Hussein as a bulwark against the growing influence of Iran and of Shiite fundamentalism. Russia had always argued, contrary to the United States, that Iraq did not have weapons of mass destruction and had urged a peaceful solution to the Iraqi problem. In the run-up to the war, the United States apparently assumed that Russia would support its position and spent little time consulting with Moscow about its plans. Three weeks before the invasion, Putin, seeking to prevent any military action, sent Primakov to Baghdad to try to persuade Saddam to step down from the presidency and call elections. Saddam responded with a series of accusations against Russia and walked out of the room.[11]

Still hoping to broker a deal that would avoid war, Putin sent Alexander Voloshin, head of the presidential administration, to Washington to explain the Russian position to US officials. He concluded that Washington mistakenly believed Russia's only interest in Iraq was economic, because American officials combined their briefings on Saddam's alleged WMD programs with offers to compensate Russia for economic losses it might sustain as a result of the invasion. Voloshin tried to explain to his hosts that Russia feared an invasion of Iraq could destabilize Russia's southern neighbors and fuel extremism and terrorism—which, in hindsight, was quite prescient.[12] When it became clear that the Bush administration was determined to pursue regime change in Iraq, Russia responded to German and French overtures and joined the "coalition of the unwilling" in opposing a UN resolution authorizing the use of force against Saddam. Putin denounced the military campaign as illegal, accusing the United States and its allies of replacing international law with "the law of the fist."[13] The invasion of Iraq and the subsequent military campaign adversely affected Russia's economic interests in the country. It also ultimately led to the rise of Islamic State (IS). By disbanding the Iraqi army, the US created a disgruntled group of armed Iraqis searching for revenge—and IS became their haven. But for Putin, the most troubling aspect of the invasion was the US commitment to regime change in the name of democracy. It was a short distance from Saddam's execution to the outbreak of Middle Eastern color revolutions and to the Arab Spring.

The Arab Spring

On December 10, 2010, Tunisian police seized a fruit-seller's cart—and his livelihood. He set himself on fire to protest government repression and corruption, and the flames he ignited sparked a popular uprising against the Tunisian government. One month later, the dictator who had ruled Tunisia for twenty-three years had fled, and in the blink of an eye, the regional status quo began to collapse. Popular discontent against authoritarian leaders and the poverty their corruption inflicted on their citizens erupted all over the Middle East. In February 2011, after only eighteen days of protests in the central Tahrir Square, Egypt's president Hosni Mubarak, who had ruled Egypt for thirty years, resigned under pressure from the United States. After a hastily arranged election, he was subsequently succeeded by Mohammed Morsi, leader of the Muslim Brotherhood. Libya followed suit with protests erupting in February 2011. Seven months later, Muammar Gaddafi, the eccentric leader who had ruled Libya for forty-two years, was dead, shot by an angry mob as he emerged from a sewer. Also in February 2011, a gaggle of schoolboys in a Syrian border town decided to play a prank and used red paint to spray the slogan "The people want the downfall of the regime" on their schoolyard wall. After they were arrested and beaten, outraged citizens demanding change began to protest all over the country. By the time Gaddafi was dead, the popular uprising against Syria's Bashar al-Assad had developed into a full-scale civil war. A region that, prior to 2010, was ruled by autocrats who had maintained relative stability for decades with an iron hand, was in the throes of rebellion against the status quo.

From the Kremlin's point of view, this was no Arab spring, but an Arab winter. Popular protests had brought down long-serving autocrats, and fundamentalist groups were on the rise. The precedent of color revolutions toppling corrupt authoritarian regimes was disconcerting. Moreover, the fact that these revolts were largely carried out in the name of Islam had potentially serious implications for Russia's own Muslim population. And the prospect of instability in a region of strategic importance to Russia increased Moscow's concerns about instability in its immediate neighborhood, in the predominantly Muslim countries of Central Asia that until 1991 had been part of the Soviet Union. Privately, Russian officials expressed not merely disbelief but incomprehension that the United States had abandoned its long-time ally Hosni Mubarak in favor of unknown and potentially dangerous Islamists.

From Putin's point of view, one of the most disturbing aspects of these upheavals was what happened in Libya. Russia had a considerable economic stake in Libya. After forgiving Tripoli's Soviet-era $4.5 billion debt in April 2008, Russian firms signed new oil and construction deals amounting to $10 billion, and arms sales continued to be an important part of the relationship. Moscow had traditionally been reluctant to jeopardize its influence in this part of the world by taking punitive actions against its partners. But during the Medvedev interregnum and the US-Russia "reset," there appeared to be more flexibility in the Russian position. The West was growing increasingly concerned about the turmoil in Libya and the mounting casualties. Vice President Joseph Biden sought to convince Medvedev to support the anti-Gaddafi forces in order to end the bloodshed.

And so, in March 2011, Russia abstained from voting for UN Security

Council Resolution 1973 instead of vetoing it.[14] The resolution authorized member states to use "all necessary means" to protect civilians. It established a no-fly zone, which also permitted all necessary means to enforce its observance. In practice, that meant the UNSC—with Russia's assent—had consented to the use of air power against the Libyan regime to protect the civilian population. Shortly after the resolution was passed, NATO intervened to provide military support to the rebels. Half a year later, Gaddafi, who had been on the run for months, was killed.

In March 2011, the outside world witnessed one of the few public disagreements between Vladimir Putin and his protégé Dmitry Medvedev. Shortly after UNSC Resolution 1973 passed, Putin described it as "deficient," claiming it permitted interference in the internal affairs of other countries, resembling "a medieval summons to a crusade, when someone would call someone to go to a particular place and liberate something."[15] He also criticized NATO's actions. Immediately after his statement, Medvedev gave a press conference in which he said, "Under no circumstance is it acceptable to use expressions that essentially lead to a clash of civilizations—such as 'crusade' and so on."[16] Some present-day Kremlinologists have argued that Medvedev's Libya abstention persuaded Putin that he should not be allowed another term as president. They also say that Putin—who called the Libyan dictator's death "barbaric"—has watched the video of Gaddafi's bloody and humiliating end as a reminder of what can happen if opposition movements are not nipped in the bud.[17] On the other hand, it is difficult to imagine that Medvedev would have made the decision to abstain on the vote without first consulting with Putin. Putin's conclusion from the Libyan debacle was that, as he said, "the West is not to be trusted—once they pocket your concession, they ignore you."[18]

In the aftermath of Gaddafi's overthrow, Russia's economic interests were adversely affected and there was concern about future arms deals. But as the political situation in Libya deteriorated and two rival governments were established, new opportunities opened up. In 2017, Libyan military commander Khalifa Haftar was in Moscow, seeking to secure military supplies and support for his attempts to assert control over all of

Libya. He was feted aboard the *Admiral Kuznetsov,* Russia's lone aircraft carrier. Russia now has ties with both Libyan governments—in Tripoli and Tobruk. It is also back in the arms supply and energy business in Libya, has signed an agreement to build two military bases there, and Rosneft has negotiated new energy contracts. Moreover, after the initial consternation over the fall of Mubarak and his replacement by the Islamist Morsi, the situation in Egypt has become much more favorable for Moscow. Morsi was ousted in 2013 by General Abdel Fattah al-Sisi, and since then, Russian-Egyptian relations have considerably improved and arms, energy, and construction deals have been signed. In the aftermath of the mainly failed upheavals in the Arab world, the Kremlin has found new ways to increase its presence in the Middle East, nowhere more starkly than in Syria.

Syria

On September 30, 2015, with a mere one-hour warning to US military personnel, and to the surprise and shock of the United States and its allies, Putin ordered a squadron of Russian jets to deploy to the Hmeimim airbase near Latakia, home to those loyal to embattled President Bashar al-Assad. It was Russia's first military foray outside the former Soviet borders since the 1979 invasion of Afghanistan. Within a few days, some thirty Russian warplanes had begun to turn the tide of the four-year-old civil war in Assad's favor. Even though this was a relatively small deployment, it represented a pivotal moment in Putin's determination to reestablish Russia as a major player in the Middle East.[19] Suddenly Russian planes were flying in the same airspace as those of the United States and its allies, who were battling Islamic State. Since the US-led coalition had much stricter rules about minimizing civilian casualties than did the Russians, Russia flew more sorties and hit more targets than did the coalition.

Russia's partnership with Syria dates back to the Soviet times, when Assad's father, Hafez al-Assad, had developed close ties with the Kremlin.

Although the KGB considered him nothing less than "a petit-bourgeois chauvinist egomaniac," he was a useful egomaniac and partner.[20] The Assad family is part of the Shia Alawite minority that rules the Sunni-majority country. When the younger Assad succeeded his father, he made his first state visit as president to Moscow in 2005, and Putin received him warmly. At that point Syria had a $13.5 billion debt to Russia. The two leaders signed a "joint declaration on friendship and cooperation," and Russia agreed to write off nearly 75 percent of Syria's debt. From 2007 to 2010, the value of Russian arms deals with Syria more than doubled to $4.7 billion.[21] Syria was a reliable client for Russian arms and one of the few countries in the region over whom Russia had some influence. Moreover, Russia's only naval base outside the former Soviet Union and Russia's only warm-water port is at Tartus, on the Mediterranean in northern Syria. In 2011, it was rather dilapidated with a skeleton staff.

Syria's civil war had begun in 2011. Several opposition groups were fighting Assad's forces, ranging from the secular Free Syrian Army to the more religious Jabhat al-Nusra, which eventually expressed loyalty to Al-Qaeda. The United States, backed by a coalition of Arab states, spearheaded military intervention to assist the non-IS rebels. In 2012, Obama had warned the Syrian leader not to cross the "red line" on using chemical weapons against his own people, as his father had done in Hama in 1982. But in August 2013 came the news of a sarin gas attack in a rebel suburb of Damascus that killed more than 1,400 people. The Russian Foreign Ministry issued a statement saying that the "purported" gas attack could have been "staged by the rebels."[22] The Obama administration debated conducting air strikes against the Assad regime but ultimately demurred.

Putin seized the opportunity provided by the apparent disappearance of the "red line" to publish an op-ed in an unusual platform for him—the *New York Times*—warning that a US military strike against Syria would "unleash a new wave of terrorism" and "could throw the entire system of international law and order out of balance." He added, echoing his 2007 Munich speech, "Millions around the world increasingly see America not as a model of democracy but as relying solely on brute force, cobbling coalitions together under the slogan 'you're either with us or against us.' "[23] And then, appropriating an offhand remark previously made by John Kerry, he proposed a joint US-Russia effort to destroy Syria's chemical weapons stockpile, which worked—until Syria again used chemical weapons on its population in April 2017 and Russia once again vetoed a UNSC resolution condemning it. The pattern repeated itself in 2018, when the Assad government unleashed chemical weapons in another suburb of Damascus.

Yet back in the summer of 2015, it appeared that Assad's forces were in retreat, despite their support from the Iranian Revolutionary Guards, after a war that had claimed as many as half a million lives. Millions of refugees had fled Syria, straining Europe's ability to absorb them. By that time, Russia made the decision to intervene to ensure that Assad stayed in power. Putin had been shunned by the West after the annexation of Crimea, and the Syrian Civil War provided a welcome opportunity for Russia to reassert itself and to force the West to recognize Russia's role as a great power. The Russian military operation in Syria is not only the biggest combat mission of Russia's armed forces abroad since the Afghan War. It also represents a new kind of expeditionary warfare. Russia is fighting in a country with which it has no common border, and this is predominantly an air war.[24] It has allowed the Russian military to train its forces and test under combat conditions the capabilities of troops and of new equipment.

Putin justified Russia's entry into the Syrian Civil War as part of an effort to reduce terrorism by shoring up the Assad regime: "The collapse of Syria's official authorities will only mobilize terrorists. Right now, instead of undermining them, we must revive them, strengthening state institutions in the conflict zone."[25] He presented Russia as a supporter of governments in power, upholding the status quo, as opposed to the United States, which had supported regime change during the Arab Spring. But Putin also admitted there were reasons closer to home for the intervention: "There are thousands of militants originating from the former Soviet republics and from Russia who are fighting there. And they can get back to Russia. And we should prevent that from happening."[26] Putin has said that at least 4,000 Russians—including Chechens—and

Central Asians who live in Russia have joined terrorist groups in Syria. More Russians are fighting with terrorist groups in Iraq and Syria than citizens from any other country.[27]

The United States, which believed the civil war would end only when Assad was no longer in power, opposed Russia's intervention, as did its allies. Europe was already challenged by an unprecedented refugee crisis, with millions of people seeking asylum there. Russia's intervention exacerbated the situation. It also necessitated coordination with the United States to "deconflict" air and ground operations, so that US and Russian planes and troops would avoid direct confrontation with each other. Russia's definition of who was a terrorist differed from that of the US-led coalition. Moscow defined all opponents of Assad as terrorists, including those groups supported by the US. It often appeared that the Kremlin—despite what it said—was less interested in targeting IS than in killing members of secular opposition groups fighting for Assad's ouster. During 2016, Secretary of State Kerry held regular meetings with Sergei Lavrov to try to resolve the conflict and bring the different sides together, but to no avail. While the US reiterated that Assad "had to go," it did not do what would have been necessary to ensure his ouster.[28] Russia, by contrast, said that Assad must remain in power, and did everything it could to secure this outcome.

By the time the Trump administration came in, the United States had accepted that Assad would remain in power, and it focused on maintaining what is known as the "deconfliction channel," an ongoing communication between the two militaries. Every day, a US Air Force officer in Qatar calls a Russian officer at an air base in Latakia to head off, or "deconflict," potential problems in Syria's air space. In April 2017, the US ordered air strikes on Syria in response to Assad's chemical weapons attack, which killed eighty people.[29] Putin called the strikes "aggression against a sovereign state in violation of international law, and under a false pretext."[30] In 2018, responding to another chemical weapons attack, the US, the UK, and France carried out targeted air strikes against Syrian weapons facilities—after coordinating with Russia to ensure there were no Russian casualties.

By 2018, the Russian foray into Syria had paid off. Assad appeared to be firmly in power, the US no longer called for his ouster, and President Trump signaled that the US would begin withdrawing from Syria. Russia had become the go-to country for anyone seeking an end to the war. Putin summoned Assad to Sochi in November 2017 and gave him a bear hug, announcing that the war was ending and Russia would sponsor peace talks to initiate a political process of reform and reconciliation. "We still have a long way to go before we achieve a complete victory over terrorists," Putin told Assad. "But as far as our joint work in fighting terrorism on the territory of Syria is concerned, this military operation is indeed wrapping up."[31] The next day the leaders of Iran and Turkey traveled to meet Putin to participate in these talks. Considering that Erdogan had bitterly opposed Assad and Turkey was home to two million refugees from Syria, this represented a notable turnaround and success for Putin. He called Trump, Netanyahu, the Saudi king, the Egyptian president, and other leaders to discuss his peace plans with them.

Russia had initiated a series of meetings to discuss peace in Astana to which the United States sent a low-level representative. There are now three parallel tracks seeking to resolve the Syrian conflict: the multilateral Geneva talks brokered by the United Nations; the Sochi talks led by Russia, with Turkish and Iranian participation; and the Astana talks in Kazakhstan hosted by President Nursultan Nazarbayev. Moscow is effectively the only link among the three sets of actors involved in the Syria crisis and sees them as complementary to each other, although the Astana process has become more important to Moscow than the Geneva process. The US is present only in Geneva.

So Putin not only has succeeded in keeping Assad in power and expanding and modernizing Russia's once fading naval base at Tartus and air base at Hmeimim. He has forced the United States and Europe—and the countries of the Middle East—to recognize Russia's importance as a regional player. For the time being, Assad will remain in power and Russia will have a say in ensuring that his successor remains friendly to Moscow.

Meanwhile, the situation in Syria remains precarious. An incident in

February 2018 highlighted the danger of having so many parties with different agendas fighting at close quarters. Russian mercenaries working for the private contract group Wagner, owned by an oligarch close to Putin, tried to seize an oil field at Deir el-Zour in eastern Syria near a military base under the control of US-backed rebels and their US military advisers. A four-hour firefight ensued, and the American-backed troops killed "a couple of hundred" Russians.[32] Both the Kremlin and the US Department of Defense played down the incident, but it showed clearly how quickly an unanticipated accident could escalate with unforeseen consequences. Indeed, Russia's use of private military contractors goes back to Tsar Ivan the Terrible. The current activities of Wagner—both in Syria and Ukraine—and the Kremlin's habit of denying they have anything to do with the official Russian military, have raised the stakes in the Syrian conflict.[33]

At the July 2018 Helsinki summit between presidents Putin and Trump, there was apparently agreement to work together on Syria.[34] As the civil war winds down, Putin's goal is to secure a stable and friendly internationally recognized regime that will guarantee Russia's permanent military presence there and enable Russia to project naval and air power into the Mediterranean. Russia will seek Western assistance in reconstructing postwar Syria. By intervening to keep Assad in power, Putin has reestablished Russia as a major power in the Middle East and achieved one of his major goals: ensuring Russia has a seat at the table on all major international decisions.

Turkey

Russia's commitment to the Assad regime has complicated its relations with other countries in the region, most notably with Syria's neighbor Turkey. Russia and Turkey have shared a long and turbulent history. The tsarist and Ottoman empires were often at war with each other between the sixteenth and twentieth centuries. Several of the Russo-Turkish wars led to Russia acquiring territory from the Ottomans and gaining access to the Black Sea. After the collapse of the two empires, Kemal Ataturk's Republic of Turkey and the new Bolshevik state began to work together. However Turkey's accession to NATO in 1952 placed the USSR and Turkey on opposite sides during the Cold War. After the Soviet collapse, Russia grew concerned that Turkey would become a competitor in the post-Soviet space, appealing to the Turkic-speaking countries in Central Asia and promoting the teaching of Islam. But Turkey never succeeded in exercising the influence in Russia's neighborhood that Moscow initially feared it might. Economic ties began to flourish. Russia became Turkey's most important trading partner, and Turkey became the second largest market for Russia's energy resources. Turkey also emerged as the leading destination for Russian tourists and shuttle traders, and private business investments across both countries expanded. And as the long drawn-out membership negotiations between Turkey and the European Union stalled and Brussels's doubts about Ankara's suitability for membership grew, Turkey increasingly turned to Russia.

Russia's relations with Turkey have also seen difficult periods under Putin but have considerably strengthened since the attempted coup against President Erdogan in 2016. Today those relations have deepened due both to the personal relationship between the two leaders and to regional and global developments that have pushed the two countries closer together. Since Erdogan became prime minister in 2003—and president in 2014—he and Putin have developed a close partnership and good personal relations, punctuated by a short period of hostile relations. Both leaders rule as strongmen who have built highly centralized political systems characterized by crony capitalism, strict control over the media and civil society, and an aversion to popular expressions of opposition. Both view the US and EU with suspicion and believe that Western leaders would like to see them ousted. Both are allergic to Western lecturing about universal values and human rights. Turkey and Russia form an axis of the excluded: "states with histories of conflict, deep structural differences and divergent views, which seem to have come together more out of frustration with the United States than a new strategic vision of world affairs."[35]

Nevertheless, Turkey and Russia started out on opposite sides of the Syrian Civil War. Erdogan opposes the Assad regime and its Shia Iranian backers and has taken in more than two million refugees from Syria. He also opposes Russian support of the Syrian Kurdish YPG militia, which has been fighting Islamic State and controls a swath of territory in northern Syria. Ankara sees the YPG as an extension of the Kurdistan Workers' Party, outlawed in Turkey, which it considers to be a terrorist organization.

After Russia stepped up its support for Assad in September 2015, tensions with Turkey escalated. In November 2015, Turkish forces shot down a Russian Sukhoi Su-24 fighter jet that, Ankara claimed, had briefly strayed into Turkish territory, the first time in fifty years that a NATO member had shot down a Russian plane.[36] The pilot was killed. Russia denied the plane had flown into Turkish airspace and said it was flying over Syria. Erdogan voiced "sadness" over the incident but did not apologize. The Kremlin's reaction was swift. Russia imposed harsh economic sanctions on Turkey and forbade Russian tourism companies from selling any vacation packages that included a stay in Turkey. The annual $30 billion Turkey-Russia trade decreased by almost 50 percent, although Russian gas still flowed to Turkey. Erdogan went overnight from being a valued Russian partner to being an enemy and was demonized in the Russian media. As Dmitry Peskov, Putin's press secretary, put it, "The circumstances are unprecedented. The gauntlet thrown down to Russia is unprecedented. So naturally the reaction is in line with this threat."[37]

For months the standoff continued and the invective sharpened. Both sides accused each other of trading oil with Islamic State.[38] Putin charged Erdogan with "Islamizing" his own society. During his December 2015 annual marathon press conference, whose audience included the dead pilot's widow, Putin went further: "Probably, Allah decided to punish Turkey's ruling clique by depriving it of its sense and reason."[39] Eventually one leader had to blink. And that was Erdogan. In June 2016, increasingly isolated internationally, he wrote a letter to Putin offering the

1. Peter the Great: One of Putin's heroes was the first modernizing Tsar, who founded St. Petersburg to be "Russia's window on the West." Traveling incognito as "Peter Mikhailov" to Europe to learn its ways in the late seventeenth century, Peter on his return said, "We need Europe for a few years. Then we will turn our back on it."

2. Catherine the Great: Catherine, the German princess who became the Tsarina and took Crimea from the Ottomans, understood Russia's security dilemma: "That which stops growing begins to rot," she said. "I have to expand my borders to keep my country secure."

ПОБЕДИТЕЛИ СПАРТАКИАДЫ

ПОЧЕТНЫЙ ТИТУЛ

В ленинградском спорте нет почетней титула чемпиона городской спартакиады. К этому званию стремится и опытный мастер, и дебютант.

Нет нужды лишний раз представлять пловца Андрея Смирнова. Это имя хорошо знакомо любителям спорта в нашей стране и за ее пределами. Воспитанник заслуженного тренера РСФСР В. Б. Митрофанова владеет сейчас всесоюзными рекордами в комплексном плавании, в прошлом году стал трехкратным чемпионом VI Спартакиады народов СССР. А главные достижения девятнадцатилетнего мастера спорта международного класса — серебряная и бронзовая медали мирового первенства.

Старший тренер сборной команды СССР С. М. Вайцеховский так охарактеризовал нашего лидера: «Андрей Смирнов может завоевать золотую медаль на Олимпиаде в Монреале. Я верю в него. Почему? В любой ситуации, в тяжелейших условиях он всегда показывает абсолютно все, на что способен».

Ценнейшая черта характера. В полной мере проявил ее Андрей Смирнов и на летней спартакиаде Ленинграда.

Дзюдоист Владимир Путин пока мало знаком широкому кругу специалистов и болельщиков. Завершившийся финальный турнир спартакиады впервые возвел его в ранг чемпиона.

Владимир тренируется в спортклубе «Турбостроитель» у А. С. Рахлина. Занятия дзю-до с успехом совмещает с борьбой самбо.

А. СОКОЛОВ,
мастер спорта

На снимках: А. Смирнов, В. Путин.
Фото В. ГАЛАКТИОНОВА

3. Putin the "Judoist": In May 1976, the Leningrad evening paper hailed the 24-year-old "judoist Vladimir Putin" who had won a prestigious competition. Although he was "little known to the wider circle of specialists and fans," his judo prowess had elevated him to the rank of champion.

4. The Young KGB Case Officer: Putin was sent to Dresden in East Germany in 1985 to "work with people and information," but the fall of the Berlin Wall in 1989 ended that phase of his career and left him with little more to show than the washing machine with which he drove back to Leningrad.

5. All Smiles: French President Emmanuel Macron, seeking better ties to Russia, beams as the French team wins the World Cup games in Moscow in 2018.

6. Russian Energy for Europe: Dmitry Medvedev signs the Nord Stream I pipeline carrying Russian gas under the Baltic Sea to Germany. The United States seeks to prevent the construction of a second line.

7. Angela Merkel and Koni: During one of his first meetings with German Chancellor Angela Merkel, Putin—knowing about her fear of dogs—allowed his Labrador Koni to greet her as she looked warily on. She never forgot the incident.

8. All Friends and Flowers: In 2018, Putin turned on the charm with Merkel, after Donald Trump had repeatedly criticized her and Germany. Putin sought to persuade her to back away from Germany's commitment to the sanctions regime imposed after Russia's annexation of Crimea and launch of a war in Ukraine's Donbas region.

9. "The Main Opponent": The new NATO headquarters in Brussels. Putin has described NATO as "the main opponent"—both a danger to Russia and an obsolete organization.

10. From Prison to Poison: Russian-Western relations reached a new low in 2018 after the attempted murder of former GRU double agent Sergei Skripal and his daughter Julia when they ingested the deadly nerve agent Novichok in Salisbury, England. Skripal had been part of an exchange for ten Russian "sleeper agents" in the United States, and the US expelled sixty Russian diplomats in response to the poisoning.

11. The Shanghai Cooperation Organization: Founded by Russia, China, and Central Asian states, originally designed to manage Sino-Russian relations in their common neighborhood—and pointedly excluding United States and Europe from membership.

12. Dueling Banknotes: The Ukrainian two-hryvna and Russian thousand-ruble notes both carry a picture of Yaroslav the Wise, whom both Moscow and Kyiv claim as their founding father. Note the difference in facial hair: the traditional Russian beard versus the Ukrainian Cossack-style mustache.

13. The Annexation of Crimea: "Little green men" from Russia with no insignia on their uniforms seized Ukrainian installations in Crimea in late February 2014. Shortly after, Russia annexed the peninsula, violating the 1994 Budapest agreement guaranteeing Ukraine's sovereignty and territorial integrity. Moscow claimed the agreement was void because of what it called a "coup" in Kyiv.

14. Let's Make Bliny: After President Xi Jinping declared Putin his "new best friend" the new Russian-Chinese partnership was on full display in 2018 in Vladivostok, as the two leaders cooked Russian pancakes together.

15. Vostok 2018: In September 2018, Chinese troops participated for the first time in the Russian Vostok (East) military exercises—the largest war games in the Soviet space since the Cold War days of the early 1980s.

16. Vostok 2018: Putin watches the maneuvers with the Chinese defense minister Wei Fenghe, saying Russia is "ready to protect its sovereignty, security, and national interests." The joint maneuvers represent a tightening of the Russian-Chinese strategic partnership.

17. The Politics of Judo: Putin's prowess at judo has given him a unique relationship with Japan. Here he gets ready to "hajime"—to spar with Japanese judo students.

18. New Middle Eastern Partners: Putin with Saudi Arabia's King Salman on his first visit to Moscow. The two countries, which had no diplomatic relations during the Cold War, agreed to coordinate oil production and cooperate on investments.

19. Another New Partner: Israel. Benjamin Netanyahu, frequent visitor to Moscow, marches in the "Immortal Regiment" parade with Putin on Victory Day, May 9, 2018, both holding photographs of World War Two veterans—in Netanyahu's case, a Soviet emigré to Israel.

20. The Syrian Operation: Russia began its military campaign in Syria in 2015 to support Bashar al-Assad, who depends on Russia and Iran to keep him in power.

21. Putin the Peacemaker? Putin meets Iranian President Hassan Rouhani and Turkish President Recep Tayyip Erdogan to discuss the war in Syria.

22. Russian Soldiers in Syria: As a result of its intervention, Russia has modernized its two military bases in Syria—the air base in Khmeimim and the once-dilapidated naval base in Tartus—but seeks to "deconflict" with the US in the crowded air space above Syria.

23. Putin's "Super Weapon": In his Address to the Nation, Putin unveiled several new weapons, including a hypersonic missile—5 times the speed of sound—that could evade US missile defenses and reach Florida within minutes.

24. Putin Passes the Ball: At the July 2018 Helsinki summit, held the day after the World Cup ended, Trump and Putin agreed to improve ties, but the toxicity of "Russia" in domestic US politics and investigations into Russian meddling in US elections blocked that move.

25. Putin's Versatile "Chef": A busy man, Evgeny Prigozhin (l) owns top-flight restaurants. He also owns the St.Petersburg–based Internet Research Agency—indicted by Special Counsel Robert Mueller for meddling in the 2016 US presidential election—and the military contractor Wagner, whose troops have clashed with US forces in Syria.

26. Putin's Role Models: On Church Day in Moscow, Putin speaks under the giant statue of his namesake Prince Vladimir, who converted Kievan Rus to Christianity.

27. And in front of the statue of his hero Peter the Great on Navy Day in St. Petersburg, where Putin announced plans for 26 new warships.

apology the Russian leader had demanded after the jet was downed.[40] A month later, there was an attempted coup by disaffected military officers, who accused Erdogan of abandoning Turkey's secular, Kemalist heritage and eroding democratic freedoms. In the ensuing hostilities, 300 people were killed, but Erdogan prevailed, and the coup was defeated. Putin was the first leader to call Erdogan offering support, prompting the Turkish president to say, "It was very important from a mental perspective, this kind of psychological support."[41] Erdogan accused cleric Fetthulah Gulen, an exiled erstwhile ally who lives in Pennsylvania and leads an Islamic movement, of orchestrating the coup with help from the CIA and unsuccessfully demanded that the Obama administration extradite him.

Putin has not officially backed Erdogan's claims about Gulen's involvement but used the occasion of the coup to normalize relations with Turkey. He visited Ankara in August, praised "our friend President Erdogan," and announced that both sides had agreed to set up de-escalation zones in Syria. Since then, the two leaders have met several times, Russian tourists are back in Turkey, and economic ties have been restored. The on-again, off-again TurkStream gas pipeline project that would carry gas from Russia to Turkey appears to be on again. When a disgruntled Turkish police officer assassinated the Russian ambassador to Ankara in revenge for Russia's bombing of the Syrian city of Aleppo, the Russian response was restrained. Despite its opposition to the Assad regime, Turkey appears to have accepted that, with Russia's help, Assad will remain in power for the time being. In May 2017, Turkey discussed the possible purchase of Russia's advanced S-400 missile system, an altogether unprecedented move for a NATO member. The $2.5 billion deal was reportedly finalized in December 2017.[42] After Turkey shot down the Russian plane, NATO worried about being dragged into a conflict with Russia. A mere eighteen months later, it began to question whether Turkey was reconsidering its own NATO membership.

Putin has managed effectively to bind Turkey closer to Russia as Erdogan's resentment of the United States and the EU have grown. Since the attempted coup, 80,000 people in the military, judiciary, media, and education sectors have been purged, and both the US State Department and the EU have criticized Turkey. When President Trump met with Erdogan in September 2017, by contrast, he praised him as "a friend of mine. He is running a very difficult part of the world."[43] Nevertheless, the Trump administration has not extradited Gulen. Putin has never criticized Erdogan for his continuing crackdown and has encouraged his talk of Turkey's Eurasian vocation, which could involve joining the Eurasian Economic Union.[44] He has seized the opportunity to appeal to Erdogan's suspicions of the West and to reinforce them. This remains an instrumental relationship, which could deteriorate again but for now represents "an ideology of sovereign values as a union of the deceived against the West."[45]

Israel

More so than with Turkey or other countries in the region, Russia's new role as a go-to player is demonstrated by its relationship with a country that itself is often at odds with Turkey: Israel. The most striking change in Russian policy in the Middle East in Putin's world has been the warming of ties with Israel. Israelis describe the relationship as "the best ever." Although geopolitical factors can explain much of this shift, Putin's personal experiences have also driven this rapprochement. Given Russia's long history of official and nonofficial anti-Semitism, and the USSR's hostility toward the Jewish state, the cordial ties between the two countries are all the more striking. Indeed, Israeli diplomats were conveniently absent the day the United Nations General Assembly voted to condemn the Russian annexation of Crimea. The Foreign Ministry was on strike.[46] Since then, Israel has maintained a neutral stance on the Ukraine crisis and has not joined the Western sanctions regime, although it maintains economic and political ties with Ukraine.

Putin's family shared its Leningrad communal apartment with a religious Jewish family. In his autobiography, published when he first came to power, he says, "I got along very well with the elderly couple, and often played on their side of their apartment."[47] His high school German teacher Mina Yuditskaya emigrated to Israel in 1973. When Putin visited the country in 2005 to commemorate the sixtieth anniversary of the end of World War Two with veterans of the Red Army who had emigrated, she met with him. He subsequently arranged to buy a new apartment for her, fully equipped with the most modern appliance. Reached by journalists to confirm this, she replied, "Putin is a very grateful and decent man."[48] The Russian embassy in Israel took care of her funeral arrangements when she passed away in December 2017 and Putin inherited her apartment.

The situation for Jews in Putin's Russia is probably the best it has ever been—at least from the perspective of the ability to practice their religion freely. The Chabad-Lubavitch organization predominates in the post-Soviet space, and its rabbis have a privileged relationship with the Kremlin as the official representatives of the Jewish faith. Chabad rabbis focus strictly on religious affairs and avoid politics. Chief Rabbi Berel Lazar has praised Putin on many occasions and has attended events celebrating the annexation of Crimea.[49] With encouragement from the Kremlin, a $50 million Jewish Museum and Tolerance Center opened in Moscow in 2012, chronicling the complex and tragic history of Jews in Russia. Putin even contributed one month of his salary to it.[50] Since 2008, Russians and Israelis do not require visas to visit each other's countries.

Russia's relations with Israel have been significantly influenced by the 1.4 million Israelis whose families emigrated from the former Soviet Union—one-sixth of Israel's population. Many of them still retain close ties to Russia. When Putin was deputy mayor of Saint Petersburg, in charge of foreign economic contacts, he began working with some of these emigrés and apparently developed good relations with them. As he told one of the Valdai Discussion Club members, he regards these compatriots as "our boys," adding that he would like to bring them back to

Russia. He downplayed the idea that, given the historical experience of tsarist pogroms and Soviet repression, they might not want to return.[51]

Business ties between the two countries have flourished, and Israel is even negotiating an association agreement with the Eurasian Economic Union. Scientific and technical cooperation in the high-tech sector, such as in nanotechnology, is rapidly developing. Russia is one of Israel's main oil suppliers, and Gazprom has expressed interest in investing in offshore Israeli gas fields. Israel also sells military hardware to Russia, including drones, in return for Russian pledges not to sell advanced weapons to Iran or Syria that could be used against Israel.[52] Israel Aerospace Industries has been engaged in a $400 million project with Russian Oboronprom for Russian-based production of unmanned aerial vehicles. And Israel has continued its agricultural exports to Russia, benefiting from the fact that Russia sanctioned EU agricultural imports in the wake of the Ukraine sanctions.

Russia and Israel have also seen eye to eye on using harsh measures to deal with extremists and terrorists. They both view radicalized Muslims as their common enemy. Israel never criticized Russia's wars in Chechnya, and Russia largely refrains from commenting on how Israel deals with Palestinians. As one Russian scholar points out, "Russian and Israeli politicians and generals share a no-nonsense, hard-nosed realpolitik-based view of the world."[53] However, while Israel regards Hamas and Hezbollah as terrorist organizations, Russia does not. As the Russian ambassador to Israel explained, "The Supreme Court [of Russia], following an appeal by the prosecution, defines terrorist organizations as such when they intentionally conduct acts of terror in Russian territory, or against Russian interests abroad."[54] Russia maintains ties to both Hamas and Hezbollah. As a member of the Quartet on the Middle East, it has criticized Israeli settlement expansion in the West Bank and upholds the need for a two-state solution to the Israeli-Palestinian dispute.

The Russia-Israel relationship has been nurtured by the good personal ties between Prime Minister Benjamin Netanyahu and Putin, who both have been in power for many years. Netanyahu's frosty relations with

President Barack Obama, who publicly criticized Israel for its policies toward settlements and toward the Palestinians, led him to seek closer ties to Russia. Since Donald Trump came into office, US-Israel relations have improved, but this has not affected Netanyahu's attitude toward Russia. This is largely because of the Syrian Civil War, which has necessitated close Israeli-Russian cooperation. While Syria and Israel remain in a state of war because of Israel's occupation of the Golan Heights, the two countries have developed a modus vivendi, and the Israelis prefer Assad on its border to more radical Islamist anti-Assad groups. The Syrian Civil War remains one key driver of Russian-Israeli relations, the other being Iran and its support for Hezbollah.

From Israel's point of view, Iran is an existential threat and the main regional enemy, and it is supporting Hezbollah, which threatens Israeli territory. Since Israeli planes are in the skies combating Hezbollah's actions in Syria, Jerusalem and Moscow have to carefully deconflict their air operations to ensure there are no Israeli-Russian air accidents similar to that between Turkey and Russia. Netanyahu visits Russia several times a year to see Putin and requests that Russia influence Iran to rein in Hezbollah. Israel has also been extremely critical of the Iran nuclear deal, in which Russia played a major part. In August 2017, Netanyahu came to Sochi with his Mossad chief to present evidence of "sensitive, credible, and very disturbing detailed intelligence" on Iran's military presence in Syria.[55]

Concern about Iran has pushed Netanyahu closer toward Putin. On May 9, 2018, Netanyahu was one of only two world leaders to visit Moscow and stand next to Putin during the Victory Day Parade.[56] He wore the orange Saint George ribbon symbolizing Crimea's reunion with Russia and marched in the Eternal Regiment parade, in which people carry photos of their relatives who fought in the war. The Israeli parliament had made Victory Day a national holiday on May 9, in line with Russia, as opposed to Europe and the US, which commemorate the victory on May 8.[57] Israel had just attacked Iranian assets in Syria, after Iran had attacked Israel. In their private meeting, Netanyahu and Putin discussed their close military coordination in Syria to avoid any unintended clashes, and Putin told his Israeli guest that Russia would not sell S-300 missile systems to Syria.[58] But Russia may not have the influence over Iran that Israel believes it does. The Israelis hope Russia will eventually curb Iranian influence in Syria, but it remains to be seen whether Moscow can or will seek to diminish the Iranian presence there, other than persuading the Iranians to pull back from the Israeli border.[59]

From the Kremlin's point of view, the burgeoning relationship with Israel has cemented Russia's role as a regional power broker, replacing the United States. Putin was able to benefit from the frosty Obama-Netanyahu relationship as well as Washington's aversion under Obama to dealing with Avigdor Lieberman. Former foreign minister and former defense minister, Lieberman has extremely hawkish views on Arabs and hails from Moldova, has praised Putin and can literally speak his language. Nevertheless, the United States still provides the lion's share of Israel's economic and military assistance. Since Donald Trump came into office, the situation has changed, and the US is far more supportive of Israel and less critical of its settlements. It also has taken the unprecedented step of recognizing Jerusalem as Israel's capital, a move Putin has criticized. But Israel continues to pursue close ties with Russia because of Russia's key role in its dangerous neighborhood.

In Soviet times, the USSR was a major backer of the Palestine Liberation Organization (PLO). Moscow continues to maintain active relations with the Palestinian National Authority, whose president Mahmoud Abbas received his candidate's degree from the Patrice Lumumba University in Moscow. The title of his thesis was "The Other Side: The Secret Relationship Between Nazism and Zionism," in which he claimed that accounts of the Holocaust had been greatly exaggerated. But post-Soviet ties to the Palestinians are not as robust as those with the Israelis. Having formally recognized the State of Palestine in 1982, Moscow maintains a diplomatic presence in Ramallah. After the 2006 elections that brought Hamas to power in Gaza, the Kremlin took a pragmatic stance toward the intra-Palestinian dispute between Hamas and the PLO and has tried to promote reconciliation talks between the two groups. The Russian

Foreign Ministry recognized East Jerusalem as the capital of a future Palestinian state and affirmed, "In this context we view West Jerusalem as the capital of Israel."[60] No less remarkable than the turnaround in relations with Israel has been Moscow's recent rapprochement with Saudi Arabia, for decades an adversary of Russia.

Saudi Arabia

Eighty-one-year-old King Salman of Saudi Arabia emerged from his plane at Vnukovo Airport in Moscow in October 2017, stepped out onto the golden escalator he had brought with him, and began to descend. But the escalator malfunctioned, the king paused, and then he had to walk down the stairs, to the consternation of his security detail. Meeting him at the bottom of the stairs was Dmitry Rogozin, the brash deputy prime minister in charge of the defense industry. Later, Putin received Salman in the great hall of the Kremlin, and the leaders got down to business, signing multiple agreements. These included the Saudi purchase of Russian S-400 air-defense missiles, the transfer of several advanced Russian military technologies to Riyadh, and a Saudi pledge to invest in the Russian energy sector. The two leaders also agreed to continue their pact to keep oil production down to levels that would support oil prices and prevent further price declines.[61] The king brought with him an entourage of 1,500 people plus his own furniture, carpets, chefs, and food, and the Saudis took over two of Moscow's most luxurious hotels.[62] It was indeed an impressive first visit ever by a Saudi monarch to Russia. This represented another—and a most striking—milestone in Russia's return to the Middle East. The rapprochement between Russia and Saudi Arabia marks a noteworthy success for the Kremlin in its quest to become the region's new power broker.

The USSR was the first non-Muslim country in 1926 to recognize what a few years later would officially become the Kingdom of Saudi Arabia, because it hoped the new state would become a leader in the anti-imperialist movement. But relations soon soured, and Stalin closed the Soviet embassy there in 1938. The Soviet diplomats who had labored so hard "to convert the Arabs to the Marxian creed" returned to Moscow, where they were promptly executed. Relations between the two countries remained cool, while US-Saudi relations flourished. In 1945, the US-Saudi relationship was cemented when President Roosevelt met the Saudi king, and the kingdom became a reliable, if sometimes difficult, US ally. Its role as the world's largest oil exporter and the custodian of Mecca and Medina established its unique importance. Saudi Arabia worked with the United States to arm the mujahideen fighting the Soviet Union in Afghanistan. Diplomatic relations between Moscow and Riyadh only resumed after the Soviet collapse.

At the same time, the Kremlin became increasingly wary of the influence of what is called Wahhabism—Saudi Arabia's austere form of Islam—on its restive North Caucasus. Indeed, the Saudis encouraged the growth of Islam in the post-Soviet countries, built mosques and madrasas in Central Asia, and expressed support for the Chechens during their war with Moscow in the 1990s. The Russians blamed Wahhabism for the rise in religious extremism in Russia and its southern neighborhood, and they viewed Saudi support of Islamic education in Central Asia as a potential domestic threat.

Nevertheless, Saudi Arabia was becoming more important in Russian foreign policy calculations for a number of reasons. As the leading oil producer and key player in OPEC, it had a major impact on the price of oil, and Russia's interests as another major oil producer did not always coincide with those of Saudi Arabia, which it viewed as a competitor in global oil markets. Indeed, there are some Russians who blame Saudi Arabia for contributing to the collapse of the USSR because, they allege, it colluded with the United States to deliberately drive down oil prices in the mid-1980s. And during Putin's tenure there were also suspicions that the Saudis flooded the market with oil to keep prices down and weaken Russia. Conversely, the Saudis from time to time believed Russia sought to sabotage both the oil market and Saudi leadership by not cutting back on its production when OPEC restricted its own. The Saudis were also a major player in the Middle East and a foe of Russia's partner Iran, and they were suspicious of Moscow's dealings with Tehran. Moscow's support for an ally of Iran—Syria—even before the outbreak of the 2011 civil war, was another factor complicating the relationship.

Putin traveled to Saudi Arabia in 2007, the first Russian leader to make an official visit to the kingdom. He went there the very next day after delivering his blistering attack on the United States at the Munich Security Conference, when Russia was seeking more investment opportunities. The Saudi king welcomed him, saying, "Both countries enjoy great economic capabilities, good natural resources, numerous investment opportunities, and a distinct cultural heritage."[63] The two leaders signed a number of commercial agreements and discussed the Israeli-Palestinian problem, Iraq, and other regional issues. After that, trade grew at a modest pace, and the Saudis began to consider Russia as an alternative arms supplier to their traditional ally, the United States.

Prior to Russia's military intervention in Syria, Saudi Arabia's relationship with the Obama administration came under strain for several reasons. The Saudis could not understand why the United States had abandoned its long-term ally Hosni Mubarak after the outbreak of the Arab Spring in Egypt—only to facilitate the election of the head of the Muslim Brotherhood, which the kingdom had designated as a terrorist group. The Saudis were also disappointed by the US's weak response to the uprising against Assad and its failure to intervene more decisively against the Iran-backed Syrian president. And it was suspicious of Washington's negotiations with Tehran over a nuclear deal. Ironically, it was Syria—and falling oil prices—that drove Russia and Saudi Arabia closer together, even though Russia remains a staunch backer of both Iran and Syria. But it is precisely because the Kremlin has influence in both countries—along with its impact on oil prices—that the Saudis believed it was in their interest to improve ties with Putin in order to better understand and possibly affect Russian policies.

In 2014, oil prices began to fall from their $110 a barrel level. Russia was already suffering from financial and other sanctions imposed by the

West after the onset of the Ukraine crisis. It was hit hard by both the fall in oil prices and the falling ruble. In November 2014, it refused to cooperate with OPEC to support prices. Over the year, oil prices fell to $50. But as the economic pain mounted, Moscow began to rethink its previous reluctance to coordinate production levels with OPEC and, specifically, Saudi Arabia. It had previously toyed with the idea of collaborating with OPEC but had demurred, preferring to retain sovereignty over its production decisions rather than have to debate with a group of countries how much it could produce. Its growing economic problems forced a reappraisal of its aversion to cooperation with OPEC, and in the autumn of 2016, Russia and Saudi Arabia for the first time agreed to work together to limit output and tackle the global oil glut.

In December 2016, OPEC countries, led by Saudi Arabia, and non-OPEC exporters, led by Russia, agreed on cutbacks that succeeded in raising oil prices. Putin subsequently met with the rising star and key decision-maker Deputy Crown Prince Mohammad bin Salman (MBS), describing him as a "very reliable partner with whom you can reach agreements, and can be certain that those agreements will be honoured."[64] During a visit to Moscow, the Saudis had signed memoranda of understanding to invest $10 billion in Russia—the largest single foreign investment pledge ever made. In the run-up to the 2018 Russian presidential election, it was important to sustain the Russian budget, and oil prices were a key factor. The OPEC/non-OPEC oil production agreement—bolstered by strong global demand—was renewed in 2017. Subsequently, MBS called for a ten- to twenty-year agreement with Russia to regulate oil production.[65]

Yet while Russia and Saudi Arabia were able to cooperate on oil prices, the Saudis became increasingly incensed after Russia moved in militarily to bolster Assad. Iran's support of Assad—together with that of Russia—threatened to weaken Saudi influence in the Middle East. The Saudis backed Syrian opposition groups but were angered by the United States' reluctance to give more robust support to these groups. However, as it became increasingly clear that Russia would make sure that Assad stayed in power and prevailed over his opponents, the Saudis, like the Turks, apparently calculated that it was better to establish closer links with Russia than continue to support a losing cause. As the then thirty-one-year-old MBS said, "The main objective is not to have Russia place all its cards in the region behind Iran."[66] Thus Russia has been the beneficiary of regional rivalries in the Middle East that long predate its reentry into the area after 2000.

After Donald Trump's election, the Saudis went out of their way to woo the new US president. They succeeded, and his first foreign trip after his election was to the kingdom. During his stay he was lavished with extravagant royal pomp, including participation in an elaborate sword dance. The Saudis signed a memorandum of understanding for a large arms deal, and the US-Saudi relationship seemed to be reinvigorated. A few months later, the aging king made his historic visit to Russia. His son and heir to the throne had launched his ambitious Saudi Vision 2030 program for modernizing the kingdom, designed to turn it from an oil exporter into a regional powerhouse with a diversified economy. Forging a partnership with Russia was part of this grand design. This was also an opportunity for the Kremlin to build a relationship with a traditional US ally. The possibility to use the leverage it derived from its close ties to Saudi Arabia's archrival, Iran, was very welcome, as its relations with the West continued to deteriorate. Russia is now an important interlocutor for two countries that officially are antagonists but who are united in their antipathy toward Iran and their desire to have Moscow use its influence to pressure Tehran—namely Saudi Arabia and Israel.

During King Salman's October 2017 visit to Moscow, the Saudis signed an agreement to purchase Russian S-400 air-defense missiles (Iran has only the older S-300 version) and to transfer Russian technology to the kingdom for the production of several advanced Russian weapons systems. The Saudis in return agreed to invest $1 billion in Russian energy projects, and Russia will build a $1.1 billion petrochemical plant in the kingdom.[67] While the Saudis may have few illusions that they can split Tehran from Moscow, they understand that Russia now plays the role of great power balancer in the region. They, like the Turks, have come around to accepting that they must work with Russia on Syria. As one regional expert said, "The Saudis now realize that the Russians could be the only party that can settle the Syria conflict. . . . They don't have a problem with the idea that the regime can stay."[68]

Putin has succeeded in cementing ties with Saudi Arabia in a relationship focused on energy and Iran. Indeed, Iran remains a key partner in Putin's world.

Iran

The Iran-Russia relationship has historically been quite fraught. After all, in the eighteenth and nineteenth centuries, the Russian and Persian empires fought four wars, as a result of which Persia lost the three South Caucasus states and Dagestan to Russia. The USSR also supported secessionist movements in Iran in the 1920s and occupied Northern Iran after World War Two. During the Soviet Afghan War, more than two million Afghan refugees fled to Iran, putting great strain on its budget. And Moscow's support for Saddam during the Iran-Iraq War further alienated the new Islamic republic. Relations improved after the fall of the Soviet Union. But they entered a more intense phase after Putin became president and determined to reprioritize Moscow's ties to Tehran. The countries have grown closer since Russia entered the war in Syria and since Donald Trump's election.

In the early part of Putin's tenure in office, Iran's nuclear program not only was the focus of Russian-Iranian relations but was also a major issue in US-Russia relations. Russia remained committed to building the Bushehr reactor, asserting that Iran was not seeking to acquire a nuclear weapons capability, while the US and the EU were far more concerned about longer-term Iranian nuclear ambitions. Russia appeared to accept the prospect of a nuclear Iran with relative equanimity. As one of Russia's top Middle East experts put it, "A few years back, I heard one of our diplomats say: 'A pro-American Iran is far more dangerous for us than a nuclear Iran.' "[69] During the Bush administration, Russia was reluctant to yield to US pressure not to build Bushehr. The construction of the reactor brought needed revenues and the promise that, once it was completed, orders for more nuclear power plants would be forthcoming. Putin has prioritized Russia's nuclear power industry. Bushehr was to be the flagship project that would advance Russia's global role as a leading exporter of nuclear power plants.

However, in 2004 the International Atomic Energy Agency (IAEA) found that Iran was hiding information about its nuclear activities and reneging on agreements it had already made. Russia began to delay the completion of the reactor, much to Iran's annoyance; it was finally completed in 2011. Russia also vacillated between cooperating with the United Nations Security Council to censure Iran and arguing that Iran was not violating its IAEA obligations. Moscow too came under pressure from the West not to supply Tehran with the S-300 surface-to-air missiles it had agreed to sell in 2007, a deal that would have netted Russia $800 million. When Medvedev became president, he froze the deal.

Indeed, Medvedev supported much tougher UN sanctions against Tehran after President Obama showed him evidence of Iran's secret uranium enrichment facility near Qom. These punitive sanctions helped bring Iran to the negotiating table with the five permanent members of the UN Security Council, plus Germany and the EU. These negotiations resulted in the 2015 Joint Comprehensive Plan of Action (JCPOA), which commits Iran to greatly reducing the number of centrifuges it has and to not engaging in significant uranium enrichment for ten years. President Obama praised Russia for its help in ensuring the deal was completed. Candidate Trump insisted that the United States would pull out of the deal were he to win the White House, and in May 2018, he followed through on that promise, to the dismay of Russia, China, and the European co-signatories. Russia accused the United States of "trampling upon the standards of international law" and committed itself to working with the other JCPOA signatories to saving the deal.[70]

Since the signing of the JCPOA, Russia has significantly increased its military cooperation with Iran. Russia and Iran have signed wide-ranging agreements in military education, anti-terrorism, and modernization of Iran's air force. Iran is also interested in buying a broad range of Russian military hardware, but so far progress on signing deals has been modest. In 2014, Russia signed agreements to build another eight nuclear reactors in Iran, although the timetable for these deals is, at best, unclear. Beyond these arms and nuclear energy deals, Iranian-Russian economic relations are quite modest.[71] After the UN sanctions against Iran were lifted, Iran and Russia signed deals worth $40 billion, compared to Iran and China signing a twenty-five-year road map that envisages bilateral trade rising to $600 billion.[72] And it is the United States, France, and the UK—not Russia—that have educated many Iranian politicians and intellectuals, including its current president, foreign minister, and former chief weapons negotiator.

Russia's intervention in Syria has created conditions in which Iran has become an even closer partner for the Kremlin. Iran had long backed Assad, partly because Syria has given it access to Hezbollah, a Shia Islamist party and militant group based in Lebanon that Iran strongly supports. Once Russia intervened militarily to bolster Assad, Iran and Russia were allied. Russia's intervention also strengthened the role of Iran's Islamic Revolutionary Guard Corps fighting there. Iran controls up to 70,000 men on the ground in Syria.[73] In an unprecedented and domestically controversial move, Iran allowed Russia to use its Shahid Nojeh air base to launch air strikes into Syria. Both countries support Assad remaining in power to prevent the breakup of the country. While Russia is willing to contemplate a future federal structure in Syria, Iran favors a centralized country, but these differences are much less important than both countries' determination to keep the current regime in power.

Iran's strengthened relationship with Russia is a product both of the war in Syria and of Donald Trump's election. His criticism of the Islamic Republic and withdrawal of the US from the JCPOA have reinforced Tehran's decision to draw closer to Moscow. During Putin's November 2017 visit to Tehran, both Russia and Iran criticized the United States for questioning the deal, saying that it was working well.[74]

On other issues, however, Russia and Iran differ. For nearly three decades they were unable to agree on the demarcation of the Caspian Sea. The USSR and Iran had an understanding, but after the Soviet collapse, there were five littoral states: Russia, Iran, Azerbaijan, Turkmenistan, and Kazakhstan. They were unable to agree whether to divide the sea equally among all five states, which Iran favors, or according to the size of each country's coastline, favored by the others. They finally came to an understanding about delimitation in August 2018.[75] And Iran is wary of Russia's ties to Saudi Arabia and, above all, to Israel, especially the constant Russian-Israeli coordination over air operations in Syria. Iranians remain divided on how far they should align with Russia, with some groups warning of excessive dependence on Russia and favoring a more concerted opening to the West.[76]

Russia's relations with Iran are, therefore, on one level close but also complex. The fact that the Kremlin supports Iran on a number of issues has enhanced its international leverage, because most of Iran's neighbors view it with suspicion and believe that if they want to contain Iranian power, they need to seek out Moscow's support. Whether Russia really has the power to influence what Iran does is unclear. Once the Syrian Civil War is over, Russia might well seek to limit Iran's presence in Syria, although Assad has become dependent on the Iranian Revolutionary Guards for the survival of his regime. Israel and Saudi Arabia will continue to seek Russia's help with Iran as long as they view the Islamic republic as an existential threat.

Russia's Middle Eastern Future

How did Russia achieve this spectacular and rapid return to the Middle East? Putin's success is a product of shrewd tactics, determination, and skillful use of opportunities provided by uncertain US policy. The US may remain the most important player in the region for some time to come, but Russia's advantage is that it talks to virtually all the parties arrayed on different sides of conflicting issues in this difficult neighborhood. Its appeal as an opponent of regime change and supporter of existing governments endears it to all governments in the area, authoritarian and democratic. It has largely succeeded in neutralizing external threats to its own Muslim population, although IS and Islamic extremism remain a major challenge. Russia also has succeeded in breaking the US monopoly of influence in the region and has earned the respect of all the major regional players. Nevertheless, Putin has focused much more on increasing Russia's presence in the region rather than contributing toward the solution of any of the Middle East's most pressing problems. The United States has chosen sides in the Middle East, while Putin's Russia has not, which gives it leverage. Many of the regional players have an instrumental view of Russia, yet they understand that it will not replace the United States for a long time. Russia can be a useful balance against the US, but it will continue to behave opportunistically in the region.

Putin's new status as a Middle East power broker was on display in a marathon of diplomatic activity just before he met with President Trump for their Helsinki summit. Netanyahu once again flew to Moscow to impress on his Russian interlocutor the need to restrain Hezbollah's and Iran's activities near the Golan Heights, after Israel had responded to Iranian military provocations. Putin subsequently suggested that Iranian forces withdraw 100 kilometers from the Golan Heights, a proposal Israel rejected.[77] As soon as Netanyahu had left, Putin welcomed Ali Akbar Velayati, a senior Iranian adviser, seeking to persuade Iran to withdraw from the border with Israel and Jordan in return for economic incentives. With the US retreating from the Middle East, all eyes are on Moscow.

Putin has become the chief shuttle diplomat in the Middle East. One difference to past shuttle diplomacy in the Middle East is that, in addition to Putin's own travels, many of the region's leaders flock to see him in Moscow. Russia is back in the Middle East in a way the Soviet Union never was and is there to stay.

11

THREE FAILED RESETS

Russia and America Before the Trump Era

> Today we are witnessing an almost uncontained hyper use of force—military force—in international relations, force that is plunging the world into an abyss of permanent conflicts. . . . One state and, of course, first and foremost the United States, has overstepped its national borders in every way.
>
> —*Vladimir Putin, 2007*[1]

> The Russians can't change or significantly weaken us. They are a smaller country, they are a weaker country, their economy doesn't produce anything that anybody wants to buy, except oil and gas and arms.
>
> —*Barack Obama, 2016*[2]

In February 2007, Putin attended his first Munich Security Conference in the stately Bayerischer Hof hotel. The conference is an annual gathering of European and US foreign and defense ministers and other international officials and experts who meet to discuss the world's most pressing security issues. It is the most influential of the many security conferences held around the world. Putin's address was eagerly anticipated. Less than a year before, Vice President Dick Cheney had delivered a blistering attack on Russia in Vilnius, Lithuania, criticizing Russia's domestic system and its treatment of its neighbors, and the US-Russia relationship had become increasingly contentious.[3] There was standing room only in the Munich conference room, with Chancellor Merkel and her colleagues in the front row sitting next to leading US Congress members. Putin, looking stern, walked up to the lectern and began by warning that his speech might be "unduly polemical."[4] Indeed it was. He had only one target in his speech: the United States.

Putin began by criticizing the idea of unipolarity: "It is a world in which there is one master, one sovereign. And at the end of the day this is pernicious not only for all those within this system but also for the sovereign itself because it destroys itself from within. And this certainly has nothing in common with democracy.... Incidentally, in Russia we are constantly being taught about democracy. But for some reason those who teach us do not want to learn themselves." Putin then went on to lambast the United States for its aggressive and destabilizing foreign policy and concluded with a plea for multipolarity and a greater role for the United Nations.[5]

His audience sat in stunned silence and then offered scattered and restrained applause. Putin had thrown down the gauntlet and put the United States on notice that there could be no more business as usual as Washington defined it. But newly appointed US defense secretary Robert Gates, a veteran of the CIA, chose not to respond in kind. Saying "One Cold War was quite enough," he added he would travel to Russia soon because "Russia is a partner in [our] endeavors."[6] The White House described Russia as a "valued ally." The Bush administration, knowing that Putin had only one year left in office, preferred to believe that the speech was domestically oriented in the lead-up to a presidential succession.

Although the Munich speech was indeed partly designed to appeal to Putin's supporters at home, in retrospect it marked the beginning of a new phase in Russia's relations with the West—and particularly with the United States. After seven years of rising oil prices and growth rates of 7 percent per annum, Putin felt emboldened to deliver a strong message: Russia was no longer willing to accept an agenda set by the United States. Instead of showing respect, so the Kremlin felt, the United States had taken a series of steps inimical to Russia's interests, including expanding NATO, invading Iraq, supporting color revolutions in Russia's backyard—and constantly criticizing Russia for its democratic deficits. Russia had had enough.

Why have US-Russia relations gone so badly wrong, given that, unlike during the Cold War, there is no formal ideological confrontation and Russia is integrated into the global economy? What are the origins of the challenges—and the opportunities—inherent in a relationship central to global stability? Even though the Cold War ostensibly ended in 1991, its legacy continues to cast a long shadow over the relationship.

Moscow and Washington during the Cold War

The US-Russia relationship has always been a study in contrasts. As a young man, George Kennan, who would become America's most astute observer of Soviet Russia in the twentieth century, learned Russian in Riga, Latvia, the United States' listening post in the years before diplomatic recognition in 1933. He declared his "love for this great Russian language—rich, pithy, musical, sometimes tender, sometimes earthy and brutal, sometimes classically severe—that was... an unfailing source of strength and reassurance in the drearier and more trying reaches of later life."[7] He called on that strength, if not reassurance, in 1947, when he published a seminal article that defined US policy toward the USSR for the next forty years. He depicted Soviet communism as a lethal combination of traditional Russian nationalism and an expansionist Marxist-Leninist ideology that depicted the West as the main enemy. His solution was stark and clear: "the main element of any United States policy toward the Soviet Union," Kennan wrote, "must be that of a long-term, patient but firm and vigilant containment of Russian expansive tendencies."[8]

Kennan in many ways embodied the complexities of US views about the USSR: antipathy toward communist ideology at home and abroad, determination to contain Soviet expansionism, disapproval of the Kremlin's repressive rule, and belief in the superiority of the American way of life. But there was also an appreciation for Russian culture and a belief that if one could move beyond the political leadership, the two societies might be able to interact more productively. Indeed, Kennan said as much after advocating containment of the Soviet Union. Should communism one day collapse, he argued, the United States should be prepared to welcome Russia back into the community of nations.

The Soviet view of the United States was no less complicated. On the one hand, the United States was the capitalist enemy, out to destroy the USSR. On the other hand, there was admiration for America's economic achievements. The United States was the "other," often vilified, yet the only country that could validate the USSR's importance by treating it as an equal even if the US was the "main enemy." Throughout most of the twentieth century, the belief in the superiority of Soviet socialism over the evils of Western capitalism coexisted with a deep-seated inferiority complex about the USSR's relative backwardness and inability to innovate compared to the United States. This was clear when Nikita Khrushchev visited the United States in 1959, the first Soviet leader to do so. Before he came, he vowed to show the Americans that "we will not allow anyone to push us around or to sit on our necks." Moreover, he was resolved "not to be amazed by the grandeur of America, not to appear an envious provincial." During his thirteen-day tour, the Soviet leader tried to downplay how impressed he was by what he saw—everything from the homes of ordinary Americans to a dinner with the patrician New York elite at the Upper East Side residence of W. Averell Harriman, wartime US ambassador to the USSR. He was particularly galled that he could not visit Disneyland because of security concerns. After returning home, he told his colleagues, "I did not come to the USA to beg. I represent the great Soviet state."[9]

For Russians, the best time in US-Soviet relations was the wartime alliance between the US, the USSR, and Britain. From Moscow's perspective—and Putin frequently harkens back to this—it was a time when the United States and Russia were equals, when Washington treated Moscow with respect. They had a clear, common enemy—Adolf Hitler—and together they defeated him. Russians still complain—with some justification—that the West has never given the USSR the credit it deserves for its role in the war, since it bore the brunt of casualties on the European front.

But the wartime alliance was a marriage of convenience rather than a partnership of like-minded leaders. As soon as it was clear that Germany would lose the war, the allies started to disagree about the shape of postwar Europe. The February 1945 Yalta Conference highlighted these differences. Although the allies agreed that there would be competitive elections in every European country after the war was over, they interpreted this clause very differently. From Stalin's point of view, it was a given that the USSR would control the governments of the countries it had occupied in Central and Eastern Europe to ensure they would never again be used as an invasion route from Germany. For Franklin Roosevelt, who hoped to lay the basis for a postwar partnership with Russia, it was clear, as he said in private, that "the Russians are going to do things their own way in the areas they occupy." But he hoped a general framework of collaboration would prevent the Soviet sphere of influence from becoming a sphere of control.[10] Today Putin praises the Yalta agreement, signed seven years before his birth. For many Americans—and, of course, for Central Europeans—it represents a betrayal of the interests of Russia's neighbors that consigned them to forty years of Soviet domination.

For four decades Kennan's advocacy of containment drove US policy toward Russia. Whereas Kennan himself had emphasized political containment, successive US administrations expanded its range to include global military containment of the Soviet Union. The ideological rivalry continued, well after the nationalistic component overtook Marxism-Leninism for the Soviet leadership. By the end of the 1960s, however, there was a new element: the Sino-Soviet split, which opened up opportunities for the new administration of Richard Nixon and Henry Kissinger. As the White House pursued an opening with China, Soviet leader Leonid Brezhnev sought a rapprochement with Washington to strengthen security on his western flank, also seeking to increase economic ties to the US and import Western technology to help modernize the stagnating Soviet economy. Washington responded favorably, hoping that the USSR could help extricate the US from the Vietnam War by facilitating negotiations with the North Vietnamese.

But from the beginning, the US and Soviet understandings of détente were at odds with each other, even though they were both based on pragmatism and realpolitik. Nixon's view was clear: "The Soviet Union will always act in its own self-interest; and so will the United States. Détente cannot change that. All we can hope from détente is that it will minimize confrontation in marginal areas and provide, at least, alternative possibilities in the major ones." Kissinger elaborated further: "Détente is a means of controlling the conflict with the Soviet Union," adding that the US needed to "manage the emergence of Soviet power." On the face of it, Soviet leader Leonid Brezhnev's explanation was similar: "Détente above all means overcoming the 'cold war' and transition to normal, equal relations among states.... Détente means a certain trust and ability to take into account the legitimate interest of one another." Note the stress on equality and legitimate interests. But Brezhnev made it clear that détente "does not and cannot mean forgoing the objective processes of historical development." In other words, better relations with the United States did not constrain Soviet support of national liberation movements around the world.[11]

Détente worked well for a few years. It produced the first major arms control agreement between the two nuclear superpowers in 1972, a bilateral trade agreement, and the 1975 Helsinki Accords. Rhetoric on both sides was positive. But it soon became apparent that the USSR would not forgo opportunities to expand its influence in the third world, becoming involved in civil wars in Angola and Mozambique, where it supported leaders opposed by the United States, and coming close to a nuclear confrontation with the United States at the beginning of the 1973 Yom Kippur War.[12] By the time Jimmy Carter became president in 1976, détente was flailing, and the White House's focus on human rights further alienated the Kremlin.

The 1979 Soviet invasion of Afghanistan was a major turning point. For the West, this appeared to be the first step on Moscow's march to the Persian Gulf. The Soviet invasion was partly based on incorrect information the Politburo had acquired that Afghanistan was about to abrogate its neutrality agreement with the USSR and join the West. A year after the invasion, Ronald Reagan, a dedicated anti-communist, won the US presidential election, and relations deteriorated further. A succession of three old and infirm Soviet leaders following Brezhnev's death in 1982 left bilateral ties at a low ebb.

The Gorbachev Thaw

And then came Gorbachev. Emerging from the Politburo gerontocracy was an energetic, voluble fifty-three-year-old leader from the provinces who was determined to overcome the years of Brezhnev's stagnation and revitalize the Soviet Union. Ronald Reagan, despite his strong anti-communist rhetoric and depiction of the Soviet Union as the "evil empire," was eager to meet the new Soviet leader and size him up.[13] The two met in November 1985 on the shores of Lake Geneva. Despite an acrimonious discussion about the United States' proposed Strategic Defense Initiative, whereby American missiles could intercept Soviet rockets before they reached US soil, and which the Soviets saw as a major threat, they developed a personal rapport. Reagan described the summit in glowing terms: "The world was approaching the threshold of a new day. We had a chance to make it a better and safer place." Gorbachev agreed that the summit was a breakthrough.[14]

The next summit, at Reykjavik in 1986, was more consequential. The two leaders—one an anti-communist former head of the Screen Actors Guild and the other a former provincial ideology secretary for the Communist Party—stunned their respective aides by declaring they had agreed to abolish all nuclear weapons in ten years. A dispute over the wording of the communiqué ultimately meant that the summit failed, but cooperation on many levels continued, and in 1987, both sides agreed to abolish their intermediate-range nuclear weapons and signed the INF Treaty in Washington. Gorbachev got out of his limousine on Connecticut Avenue and shook hands with admiring onlookers. The crowd was enthusiastic. A decade later Gorbachev was nostalgic about Reagan: "Ronald Reagan was the greatest Western statesman with whom I dealt," he said. "He was an intelligent and astute politician who had vision and imagination. We were both committed to ending the arms race, to ridding the world of nuclear weapons. President Reagan was farsighted enough to respond to our initiatives on arms control. Together we made a more peaceful place. The presidents who succeeded Reagan don't have this vision and statesmanship."[15]

Nevertheless, US-Soviet relations continued to improve under President George H. W. Bush—despite the continuing skepticism about Gorbachev among some of Bush's top advisers—during the annus mirabilis of 1989, when Gorbachev let Eastern Europe go. After the fall of the Berlin Wall, Bush was determined to persuade his Soviet counterpart that the United States would not take advantage of the USSR's changed international position. The two met in December 1989 on board the *Maxim Gorky* off the coast of Malta in stormy weather. Bush pledged continuing support for Gorbachev, who was battling domestic foes on all sides—from reformer Boris Yeltsin to the hard-liners who opposed his reforms. US-Soviet relations had improved so much that by 1990 Moscow supported Washington during the First Gulf War. Months later, after hard-liners tried to oust Gorbachev in a failed putsch, the White House continued to support him, preferring Gorbachev over his challenger, the erratic Boris Yeltsin. Bush and his advisers did not want the USSR to collapse because they feared what might succeed it and were concerned about the disposition of its large nuclear arsenal. But in the end, the USSR died from self-inflicted wounds, and the United States was a mere bystander.

The Yeltsin Presidency

The 1990s ushered in a hopeful time in US-Russia relations. Before he took office, Bill Clinton declared that what was happening in Russia was "the biggest and toughest thing out there. It's not just the end of communism, the end of the Cold War. That's what's over and done with. There's also stuff that's starting—stuff that's new. Figuring out what it is, how we work with it, how we keep it moving in the right direction: that's what we've got to do."[16] In retrospect, the US belief that a post-communist Russia would embrace Western-style democracy and capitalism was misplaced, but in the heady days following the Soviet collapse, it appeared that Russian society, having rejected communism, was hungry for change. Yeltsin, although he remained wary of the United States, also hoped the two countries could move beyond the Cold War and forge a new relationship, one in which Russia would be the United States' equal. Yet by the end of the 1990s, a cascade of tensions led Yeltsin to accuse the United States of committing "aggression against Yugoslavia" and to walk out while Clinton was addressing the 1999 Istanbul OSCE summit.[17]

Since the collapse of the USSR, every US administration has come into office determined to "reset" relations with Russia and seek a more productive way of interacting with the Kremlin. The same is true for the three Russian leaders since 1991. Each of these resets has ended in disappointment and mutual recriminations because, simply put, both sides have very different definitions of what a productive relationship would look like. Today the 1990s are viewed in diametrically opposite ways in the United States and in Russia. Many Americans who dealt with Russia during that decade believed the country was moving—albeit erratically—toward a more pluralistic political system that encouraged competition and debate. They also witnessed the development of a unique form of Russian capitalism and the rise of the oligarchs. They welcomed Russia's cooperation—sometimes grudging—on foreign policy challenges. For them, the 1990s was a time of promise, and they believed that despite the disintegration of institutions that followed the Soviet collapse, Russia was developing in the right direction toward a democratic, market-oriented society willing to work with the West internationally.

Today most Russians—encouraged by Vladimir Putin's stark narratives—see the 1990s as a time of Western humiliation of Russia, of poverty, chaos, and the rise of rapacious oligarchs. Russia, in this view, had to accept a foreign policy agenda dictated by the United States that was inimical to its own interests and in which it was very much a junior partner. It was also encouraged to adopt an economic system that exacerbated Soviet-era inequality, particularly after the 1998 financial crash. US democracy-building projects were—and are—viewed as interference in Russia's domestic affairs and an assault on Russian sovereignty. The roots of Putin's attacks on the United States lie in his scathing view of the 1990s—that decade was to propel him from a dropout mid-level KGB case officer to the pinnacle of power in the Kremlin.

Since the Soviet collapse, five baskets of issues have dominated the US-Russia relationship. The first is the nuclear legacy. The United States and Russia are the world's two nuclear superpowers, capable of destroying each other many times over. They bear a special global responsibility unlike that of any other country, and this gives their relationship a unique structure. The Cold War nuclear legacy involves arms control, missile defense, and nuclear modernization. The second, and related, basket of issues involves the nonproliferation of weapons of mass destruction, particularly the nuclear programs of Iran and North Korea. The third relates to Russia's neighborhood and the respective roles of America and Russia in the post-Soviet space, particularly Georgia and Ukraine. The fourth involves European security, including conflict in the Balkans, NATO expansion, and the role of the OSCE. The fifth involves Russia's domestic evolution, US democracy-promotion efforts, and attempts to influence how Russia treats it citizens. Under Putin, three additional sets of issues have come to be added to this list of challenges: the upheavals in the Arab world, the war in Syria, and Russia's interference in the 2016 US election campaign.

The US-Russia relationship is largely determined by the reality of these two countries being the world's two nuclear superpowers. The economic relationship is limited because Russia remains a raw-materials and arms exporter, and the United States, unlike Europe or China, does not need to import Russian energy (except the occasional cargo of LNG), nor does it need to import Russian military hardware. Hence there are few stakeholders in the relationship, and personal ties between the two leaders play a disproportionately important role. When those ties are good—as they were between Clinton and Yeltsin in the early years, between Bush and Putin after 9/11, and between Obama and Medvedev—then the relationship functions better. When they are antagonistic—as they were at the end of Clinton's term, after the invasion of Iraq under Bush, and during Obama's second term when Putin returned to the Kremlin—the relationship can quickly enter a downward spiral. Bill Clinton was effusive after his first meeting with Boris Yeltsin in 1993: "I liked him. He was a big bear of a man, full of contradictions.... Compared to the realistic alternative, Russia was lucky to have him at the helm."[18] Yeltsin returned the compliment: "I was completely amazed by this young, eternally smiling man who was powerful, energetic, and handsome."[19]

From the US point of view, the major successes in relations with Russia under Bill Clinton were in foreign policy: the denuclearization of Ukraine, Belarus, and Kazakhstan, leaving Russia as the sole post-Soviet nuclear successor state; cooperating with Russia in the Balkans (albeit with considerable difficulty in Kosovo); neutralizing Russia's opposition to NATO enlargement; and turning the G-7 group of advanced industrial democracies into the G-8 by admitting Russia as a stakeholder. The problem is that on all but one of these issues Washington had to persuade a reluctant Russian government to support actions it initially resisted. Although Russia favored the denuclearization of Ukraine, Yeltsin was forced to deal with Leonid Kravchuk as the leader of an independent, sovereign Ukraine. Moreover, Russia had to sign the Budapest declaration respecting Ukraine's territorial integrity. Russian willingness to cooperate with the US in the Balkan wars diminished as Yeltsin came under fire from nationalistic opponents. The same was true for NATO expansion and the Permanent Joint Council. By 1999, when Putin became prime minister, US-Russia relations had reached a post–Cold War low ebb in the aftermath of the bombing of Belgrade. The first reset had ended.

The Putin Era

Initial Optimism and then Disappointment

Before the Soviet collapse, Vladimir Putin had very little exposure to the United States beyond what he must have learned about the "main enemy" in the KGB. He had served in the GDR and become the "German in the Kremlin." He did not speak English and probably had little occasion to socialize with the few US exchange students who were at Leningrad State University in the early 1970s. Before 1990, he may never have met an American in a personal context. He first began to work with Americans when he became deputy mayor of Saint Petersburg and was responsible for foreign economic contacts. It is said that he drove Vice President Al Gore around Saint Petersburg when Gore visited. Russia was rapidly opening up for business with the West, and Putin dealt with all Western businesses who needed licenses and real estate to operate in Russia. John Evans, then US consul general in Saint Petersburg, described him as a "law and order man. He was not corrupt, but he was a crime fighter."[20] He was seen as pro-business and open to dealing with all westerners. In 1992, the Center for Strategic and International Studies, a Washington-based think tank, had partnered with Procter and Gamble to create the International Action Commission for Saint Petersburg, whose co-chairs were Henry Kissinger and Mayor Anatoly Sobchak. Through this commission, Putin not only met Kissinger—with whom he developed a rapport and continued to consult into his fourth presidential term—but other influential Americans. There was no evidence, prior to his assumption of the presidency in 2000, that Putin harbored particularly antagonistic feelings toward the United States.[21]

Indeed, he impressed those who first met him when he entered the Kremlin as someone who was interested in developing closer ties with the United States and integrating Russia into the world economy. He met World Bank president James Wolfensohn shortly after becoming president and told him he wanted to modernize his country, pursue economic reforms, and reduce corruption.[22] He presented himself as a leader seeking constructive ties with the West.

Putin's first meeting with George W. Bush gave him an opportunity to display his positive disposition toward the US. They met at the Brdo Castle in northern Slovenia. Bush's first trip to Europe had, until this point, been difficult. He had experienced less than enthusiastic—indeed disparaging—treatment from allies. Putin, by contrast, was respectful and serious, warning Bush about the dangers of Islamic fundamentalism and terrorism emanating from Pakistan and Afghanistan. At their joint press conference, Bush spoke about the importance of "building a constructive, respectful relationship with Russia." Putin rejoined, "We are counting on a pragmatic relationship with the United States." After discussing areas of mutual interest, Bush uttered a fateful phrase he would later come to regret: "I looked the man in the eye. I found him very straightforward and trustworthy.... I was able to get a sense of his soul."[23]

At this point Putin was concerned that the United States had not faced up to the dangers of jihadist terrorism. Hence, when Al-Qaeda attacked the Twin Towers and the Pentagon on September 11, 2001, Putin seized the opportunity to offer Russia as the United States' partner in the fight against terrorism. He was the first leader to call Bush after the attacks, pledging support for NATO's campaign, accepting the establishment of US military bases in Central Asia to launch its war against the Taliban, and providing vital intelligence based on Russia's long involvement in Afghanistan.[24] Indeed, the autumn of 2001 was the high point in US-Russia relations under Putin. Russia viewed the anti-terror fight as a twenty-first-century version of the anti-Hitler coalition. Russia and the United States had a common enemy and were equal partners. Putin came to the United States in November 2001, received a positive welcome in Washington, and ended his trip square-dancing at the Bush ranch in Crawford, Texas.

But it did not last long. US and Russian expectations from this partnership were mismatched, and this became clear after the initial rout of the Taliban. Putin, according to one Russian observer, wanted an "equal partnership of unequals" from the United States. For him, that would have meant US recognition that Russia had a legitimate right to a sphere of influence in the post-Soviet space. There should be no prospect of further NATO enlargement, and the US should refrain from democracy promotion that might bring to power anti-Russia governments in the post-Soviet states. Putin often repeats the same catalogue of grievances to his interlocutors: in 2002 the United States withdrew unilaterally from the Anti-Ballistic Missile Treaty—one of the pillars of US-Soviet arms control—in order to proceed with missile defense; it supported color revolutions in Georgia and Ukraine; it invaded Iraq and pursued a global Freedom Agenda deemed hostile to Moscow; the Baltic states joined NATO; and the Bush administration unsuccessfully sought to persuade NATO to offer membership to Ukraine and Georgia. And Vice President Dick Cheney became increasingly vocal in his criticism of repression in Russia and of the Kremlin's attempts to intimidate its neighbors. Putin's frustration erupted at the Munich Security Conference. The second reset was over.

Although he paid a visit to the Bush compound in Kennebunkport, Maine, later that year for an informal "lobster summit," Putin's view of the United States had irreversibly soured. In 2008, he became prime minister, following the law that permitted only two consecutive terms as president, and installed his protégé Dmitry Medvedev as president. Nevertheless, he continued to run Russia. In August 2008, the Russia-Georgia War brought US-Russia relations to an even lower ebb with Washington cutting off all bilateral contacts above the level of deputy assistant secretary. During the 2008 US election campaign, criticism of Russia featured prominently.

The Medvedev Interlude

When Dmitry Medvedev became president, the outside world was intrigued, puzzling over how this new Kremlin "tandem" would work. Would Medvedev really be Putin's successor and a de facto, as opposed to de jure, president? Dozens of hours were spent in US government offices and Washington think tanks analyzing how the Putin-Medvedev dynamic was working. All that effort could have been spared. By the time Medvedev and Putin swapped places in 2012, there was no doubt that Putin had been in charge all along, a reality the Obama administration was slow to recognize. But that was not evident in 2008, and for a while, Medvedev appeared to have Putin's blessing to reach out to the United States and seek to improve ties.

He found a receptive partner in Barack Obama. The new US president came to office offering a reset with Russia. His vice president, Joe Biden, announced the new US policy at the Munich Security Conference in February 2009, two years after Putin's attack on the US: "The last few years have seen a dangerous drift in relations between Russia and the members of our Alliance.... it's time to press the reset button and to revisit the many areas where we can and should be working together with Russia."[25] Obama himself experienced the difference between Putin and Medvedev when he made his first visit to Russia in July 2009. Meeting with Putin, he asked, "How did we get into this mess?" Putin then delivered a ninety-minute monologue cataloging all his grievances against the United States with Obama sitting awkwardly in a chair that was too small for his tall frame. This first encounter set the stage for what was to remain a wary relationship between the two leaders. By contrast, the Obama and Medvedev families enjoyed a cordial dinner together, and the two presidents, both from a post–Cold War generation, developed a good working relationship. The next year Medvedev visited the United States, opened his own Twitter account in Silicon Valley, and dined on gourmet hamburgers with Obama at the latter's favorite fast-food restaurant in suburban

Virginia.[26] Immediately after Medvedev left, the FBI arrested ten "sleeper spies" who had been operating in the United States and sent them back to Russia, without any measurable damage to the relationship.[27]

The first Obama term and Medvedev's only term in the Kremlin were optimistic and productive years for the US-Russia relationship, at least for the first two and a half years. The reset produced concrete results: a New Strategic Arms Reduction Treaty (New START); cooperation to curb Iran's nuclear program by imposing tougher sanctions; cooperation on the Northern Distribution Network carrying NATO troops and materiel to and from Afghanistan over Russian territory; the establishment of a Bilateral Presidential Committee designed to advance the relationship over a broad front; and Russia's accession to the World Trade Organization (WTO) after nineteen years of negotiations. The Obama administration somewhat retreated from the Bush-era focus on the post-Soviet space. But the US and Russia came no closer to agreeing on their respective roles in Russia's neighborhood. Despite intense discussions on developing a cooperative approach toward missile defense, Washington and Moscow were unable to agree, and the US missile defense program remained a contentious issue. Russia insisted that US missile defenses were aimed at Russia, not at Iran, as the United States claimed. Moreover, although during Medvedev's term there was somewhat greater room for domestic discussion of difficult issues, the United States continued to criticize Russia's democratic deficits.

Obama administration officials had initially believed—erroneously, it turned out—that they could "empower" Medvedev to strengthen his position against that of Putin. Although Putin had been willing to allow Medvedev to act as the more liberal leader who engaged with America, it transpired that there were limits to what he would tolerate. Medvedev's support for a UN resolution that ultimately led to Muammar Gaddafi's brutal demise was apparently one of the factors that influenced Putin's decision to end this four-year experiment in closer ties with the US through the tandem leadership. And that was the beginning of the end of the reset.

In September 2011, US-Russia relations received a sudden jolt. Putin announced that he and Medvedev would swap places, and he would return to the Kremlin in the following year. Tens of thousands of outraged Muscovites, resenting the fact that the Russian people would have no say in deciding who would govern them, took to the streets in December 2011 to protest what they believed were falsified Duma election results and demanded that Putin go. Shocked by this unexpected opposition to his rule, Putin immediately blamed the United States, and specifically Secretary of State Hillary Clinton, for financing the protests. Clinton had expressed "serious concern about the conduct of the elections" and called for a "full investigation of all reports of fraud and intimidation."[28] Putin was outraged. Clinton, said Putin, had sent "a signal" to "some actors in our country.... They heard the signal and with the support of the US State Department began active work."[29] Putin's personal animus against Clinton dates back at least to December 2011, as does his belief that the United States interfered in the 2012 Russian presidential election by financing and supporting his opponents. This was hardly an auspicious way to inaugurate the next phase of US-Russia relations as Putin began his third term.

Putin Redux and the End of the Reset

From the Obama administration's perspective, once Putin was back in the Kremlin, the Russian side appeared disinterested in renewing the relationship and did not respond to overtures to establish an agenda for dialogue. Perhaps Putin was awaiting the results of the 2012 US presidential election. Once Obama was reelected, however, things took a turn for the worse. Russia had entered the WTO in 2012, but the price Congress extracted for granting Russia permanent normal trading status was the Magnitsky Act, a piece of legislation that sanctioned Russian officials complicit both in the death in prison of Russian lawyer Sergei Magnitsky and more generally in human rights violations. In retaliation, Russia ended US adoptions of Russian children. The crisis in Syria, discussed in a previous chapter, placed extra strains on the relationship. But the fissure turned into a great chasm when Edward Snowden, a disgruntled contractor for the National Security Agency, arrived in Moscow from Hong Kong, carrying millions of stolen top-secret files detailing US intelligence operations at home and abroad. The US demanded that Russia return him to the United States. Putin seized the opportunity to turn the tables. He declared that Snowden was a "new dissident" and granted him political asylum in Russia as a "humanitarian" gesture.[30] The US reaction was swift. Obama cancelled a bilateral summit he was to have had with Putin, the first time such a cancellation had happened since 1960. He went on to describe Putin's demeanor this way: "He's got that kind of slouch, looking like the bored kid in the back of the classroom."[31] He dismissed Russia as a "regional power" and called for a "pause" in the relationship.[32] Later that year, reacting to a televised address Obama had given, Putin criticized the idea of American exceptionalism in his op-ed in the *New York Times*: "It is extremely dangerous to encourage people to see themselves as exceptional, whatever the motivation."[33]

Russia and the US did cooperate in 2013 to remove Syrian chemical weapons. However, the unfolding situation in Ukraine, Russia's crackdown on opponents of Putin, and passage of legislation discriminating against the LGBTQ community led to further mutual recriminations. Then came the annexation of Crimea, more US sanctions against Putin associates, the launch of the war in the Donbas, and far-reaching financial sanctions against Russian entities. In 2015, after Russia entered the war in Syria, the US and Russia had to communicate constantly in order to avoid direct conflict between their militaries. But with no progress in Ukraine and a growing mutual wariness, the relationship had sharply deteriorated. As a senior Obama official put it, "It's very hard to build a bridge to Russia if Putin's main goal is to thwart the United States."

And then came the 2016 presidential election campaign. US-Russia relations plunged to a new low as Russia became a toxic issue in American politics, now part of a bitter partisan divide over Donald Trump's unexpected victory.

12

THE RIVALS

Russia and America in the Age of Trump

And to those who in the past fifteen years have tried to accelerate an arms race and seek unilateral advantage against Russia, have introduced restrictions and sanctions that are illegal from the standpoint of international law aiming to restrain our nation's development, including in the military area, I will say this: everything you have tried to prevent through such a policy has already happened. No one has managed to restrain Russia.

—*Vladimir Putin, 2018*[1]

Vladimir Putin addressed an enthusiastic crowd in the Manezh Central Exhibition Hall opposite the Kremlin two weeks before his reelection to a fourth term in March 2018 as he gave his Address to the Federal Assembly. The first half of the speech contained pre-election promises made by candidates in most countries: fix the economy, provide more jobs, improve the country's infrastructure. But in the second half, he dropped several bombshells—almost literally. In bellicose tones, Putin rolled out Russia's new generation of nuclear weapons designed to destroy those of the United States. A video animation showed a new, improved intercontinental ballistic missile (ICBM) taking off from Russia, flying over the South Pole, evading detection by US missile defenses, reaching South Florida, and deploying multiple warheads on a target that looked suspiciously like Mar-a-Lago, President Donald Trump's sprawling estate and golf club.

Putin did not stop there. He went on to describe four new superweapons Russia was developing, including a nuclear-armed cruise missile and an intercontinental undersea drone. He then invited the Russian people to join a competition and send suggestions for naming these new weapons systems to the Ministry of Defense website. The country responded. After the seven million votes had been counted, the ministry announced three names: "Peresvet" for a laser, named after a medieval warrior monk who had battled the Mongols; "Burevestnik," for a cruise missile, named after a storm petrel bird; and "Poseidon" for the underwater nuclear drone, named after the Greek god of the sea.[2]

Putin's message to the United States during his speech was explicit: *You did not listen to us when we objected to your unilateral withdrawal from the Anti-Ballistic Missile Treaty in 2002 or when we opposed NATO enlargement. You disrespected us, treated us as junior partners, and took us for granted. But Russia is back and will respond to any provocation from you. You must, at last, take us seriously now.*

This was a campaign address designed for a domestic audience, to appeal to patriotic pride in an era of economic constraints. It was not clear whether Russia actually possessed any of these new weapons or was indeed developing them. Nevertheless, the tone and content signaled that the arms race was back. The Trump administration had set the stage, several weeks prior to the speech, with a new National Defense Strategy that named Russia (along with China) as one of the main threats to the United States.[3] Its *Nuclear Posture Review,* published shortly thereafter, identified Russia as a key challenge and said the United States had to enhance its own nuclear deterrent to counter the increasing global threats.[4] Moreover, Donald Trump had committed the US to raising the Pentagon's budget for nuclear weapons to counter the growing Russian buildup.

Putin's speech, with its unmistakable Cold War overtones, was a far cry from the scenes the day after Donald Trump was elected, when champagne corks popped in Moscow. But Donald Trump's much-anticipated reset with Russia never happened. Since he entered the White House, US-Russia ties have resembled the two-headed eagle on the Russian flag. One head represents an adversarial relationship similar to that of the second Obama administration, which is supported by most of the executive branch. The other, favored by Trump himself, suggests the aspirational, forward-leaning approach of two pragmatic deal makers who, for their own reasons, would like to improve ties, disregarding what has led the two countries to such an impasse.

The situation is quite unique. The new element in Putin's world since 2016 is that Russia has become part of the US domestic political debate. US-Russia relations have not been this adversarial since before Mikhail Gorbachev came to power, partly because Russia has become a toxic issue in the United States in an unprecedented way. Allegations about both Russian interference in the 2016 elections and improper financial and political ties between the Trump campaign and Russians have hamstrung the president and made it difficult for him to move forward to improve ties. Not since the McCarthy era in the 1950s has Russia been such a divisive political topic.

The 2016 US Presidential Campaign

During the highly polarized US election campaign, government officials became aware that hacking activities involving Democratic Party officials' e-mail accounts and their subsequent leaking to WikiLeaks originated from Russian sources. But the full extent of these actions—and their links to the Kremlin—became public only after the election of Donald Trump, the most unorthodox candidate ever to enter the White House. According to the February 16, 2018, indictment handed down by Special Counsel Robert Mueller, the Saint Petersburg–based Internet Research Agency, run by Russian oligarch Yevgeny Prigozhin, "began operations to interfere with the US political system, including the 2016 US presidential election" as early as May 2014.[5] They exploited social media to create false personas and remotely organized rallies of right- and left-wing groups in Texas and other states from 5,000 miles away. But the Russian interference went beyond exploiting social media to direct cyber interference—hacking e-mail accounts and leaking their contents to WikiLeaks. The major US intelligence agencies published a declassified version of their report *Assessing Russian Activities and Intensions in Recent US Elections* in January 2017. Their conclusions were sobering:

> We assess Russian President Vladimir Putin ordered an influence campaign in 2016 aimed at the US presidential election. Russia's goals were to undermine public faith in the US democratic process, denigrate Secretary Clinton, and harm her electability and potential presidency. We further assess Putin and the Russian Government developed a clear preference for President-elect Trump.[6]

Since the fall of 2016, Russia has come to dominate the US news in a way that never happened during or after the Cold War, because of its role in the presidential campaign. Russia has become part of an increasingly bitter and contested domestic political polarization. If Vladimir Putin wanted the United States to pay more attention to Russia and to be certain that Russia featured prominently in the headlines every morning, then this was surely a success. Yet there also has been a cost for the Kremlin. By actively exploiting divisions within American society and having its activities revealed, the Kremlin has ensured that its longer-term goal of having the US remove sanctions and return to a less confrontational relationship so far has been thwarted.

Why did the Russians interfere in the US election and who was behind it? These questions have in many ways defined the US-Russia relationship since 2016 and have made it challenging to move the relationship forward since Donald Trump's election. Russia's ongoing interference has turned the US-Russia relationship if not into a new Cold War then into a new kind of "frozen conflict" on a grand scale. It will be very difficult to unfreeze.

Both presidential candidates were well known to the Kremlin. Putin had not hidden his hostility to Hillary Clinton, whom he blamed for the 2011 protests in Moscow—and indirectly for interfering in Russia's 2012 election. As he told Oliver Stone in answer to a question about US interference in Russia's elections: "In 2000 and 2012, there has always been some interference. But in 2012, this interference was particularly aggressive."[7] Clinton, in turn, had become increasingly vocal in her criticism of Russian domestic and foreign policy—and of Putin himself. Commenting on Russia's annexation of Crimea, she said, "Now if this sounds familiar, it's what Hitler did back in the '30s."[8] Had she been elected, the Kremlin decided, the relationship with the United States would not improve. But she was a predictable antagonist, and they were prepared to deal with her.

Donald Trump was, however, altogether another matter. It was notable that throughout the election campaign he never uttered a negative word about Vladimir Putin, in contrast to many other world leaders—allies and adversaries alike—whom he criticized liberally. Vladimir Putin returned the compliment. In one press conference, he used the Russian word *yarkii* to describe Trump.[9] Some US media translated that into "brilliant," but its real meaning is "vivid" or "bright." Nevertheless, candidate Trump complimented Putin for calling him "brilliant."

Although Trump and Putin had never met, Trump was well known in some Russian business circles. He had made his first trip to Moscow as a real estate magnate in 1987, when Gorbachev was hoping to open up the Soviet economy to Western investors. (At this point Putin was working in a second-tier KGB outpost in Dresden.) Hoping to build a luxury hotel in Moscow, Trump toured the town, describing his trip as an "extraordinary experience." Nevertheless, although he looked at several sites for potential hotels near Red Square, nothing came of these attempts to conclude a deal in the USSR.[10] When Gorbachev visited New York shortly thereafter, Trump tried to meet with him, but Gorbachev's American hosts vetoed that plan.[11] For the next twenty years Trump continued to go to Russia and work with Aras Agalarov, an Azeri-Russian oligarch. In 2007, the teetotaler Trump launched Trump vodka at Agalarov's annual Millionaire Fair in Moscow. But Trump vodka found few drinkers in Russia.

Although he never succeeded in opening a hotel in Russia, he was back in Moscow in November 2013. He organized the Miss Universe pageant, which he owned, in Moscow, working with Agalarov.[12] This was just prior to the 2014 Sochi Winter Olympics, when Putin was under increasing criticism for his domestic clampdown. Prior to the contest, Trump had tweeted, "Do you think Putin will be going to the Miss Universe Pageant in November in Moscow—if so, will he become my new best friend?"[13] The meeting never took place, but Trump continued to speak about both Russia and its president in positive terms as US-Russia relations deteriorated in the wake of the Ukraine crisis.[14] In 2016, Agalarov's pop musician son Emin would become known to the US public for his role in arranging a meeting between his father's lawyer, Natalia Veselnitskaya, and Trump's son and son-in-law in Trump Tower.

During the 2016 election campaign, the contrast between what candidate Clinton said about Russia and what candidate Trump said was striking. The Obama administration began to harden its policies toward Russia as the campaign progressed, going as far as having a senior Treasury official say publicly that Putin was personally corrupt—a charge the latter's spokesman described as "fiction."[15] The Pentagon, for the first time since the end of the Cold War, named Russia as the number one national security threat. But Trump would have none of it, criticizing both the Obama administration and his rival for their position on Russia during the primary season, claiming that he would be a much better negotiator with Putin: "You want to make a good deal for the country, you want to deal with Russia—and there's nothing wrong with not fighting everybody, having Russia where we have a good relationship as opposed to all the stupidity that's taken place."[16] He reiterated that Putin was a "strong leader." And in his first major foreign policy speech in April 2016, speaking of Russia, he said, "Common sense says that this cycle, this horrible cycle of hostility must end and ideally will end soon. Good for both countries."[17] He also downplayed Russia's actions in Ukraine. His campaign manager, Paul Manafort—who had very close ties to ousted Ukrainian president Viktor Yanukovych—succeeded in having references to assisting Ukraine in its conflict with Russia removed from the Republican Party platform. As the November election approached, Trump's message was clear: he wanted to improve ties with Russia and make a "deal" with President Putin. The details of that deal were never specified, but they appeared to include lifting the sanctions imposed after the annexation of Crimea and the launch of a war in the Donbas region, and possibly agreeing with Putin that Ukraine should remain neutral and within the Russian sphere of influence. It was unclear what the United States would gain in this "deal."

While Trump was running for election, his family and campaign staff—it subsequently emerged—were cultivating their own ties with a variety of Russians with two goals in mind: to arrange a back channel with Russian officials to discuss how US-Russia ties would evolve after the election and to obtain "dirt" on Hillary Clinton, which their Russian interlocutors claimed to have. It appears, in retrospect, that both the Russian and US operatives were inflating their ability to deliver what they promised, and an examination of the details of these various schemes reads like a second-rate detective novel, involving characters such as a mysterious Maltese professor who directed a defunct diplomatic academy in London and claimed to have ties to the Kremlin. But the incident that came to dominate the subsequent investigations into Trump's ties to Russia occurred in June 2016, when Emin Agalarov's rumpled British public relations representative sent an e-mail to Donald Trump Jr., who was a frequent visitor to Moscow. He wrote that a senior Russian official "offered to provide the Trump campaign with some official documents and information that would incriminate Hillary and her dealings with Russia and would be very useful to your father."[18] Trump Jr. replied, "If it's what you say, I love it."[19]

The meeting took place in Trump Tower in New York. Participants included Donald Trump Jr.; his brother-in-law, Jared Kushner; Paul Manafort; and several Russians, the most prominent of whom was Natalia Veselnitskaya, a former prosecutor, now a lawyer in private practice. One of her clients was on the Magnitsky Act list and barred from entering the United States or doing business there. Her apparent goal was to advocate that he be removed from the list should Trump be elected, clearly not understanding that it was the US Congress, not the White House, that determines these issues. Trump Jr. would later say that they discussed adoption, a reference to the fact that the Russians retaliated for the Magnitsky Act by barring Americans from adopting Russian children. It is unclear what, if any, derogatory information on Hillary Clinton the Russians were able to provide. They appear to have had information about a Clinton donor, but not about Clinton herself. The meeting and other contacts were apparently part of a broader effort by the Trump campaign to prepare the ground for an improvement in US-Russia relations in 2017—and possibly for a renewed attempt by the Trump organization to open hotels in Russia were Trump to lose the election. During the 2016 election campaign, the Trump organization was still negotiating a possible real estate deal in Russia. Indeed, Trump's personal lawyer, Michael Cohen, pleaded guilty to lying to investigators about how far into 2016 these negotiations continued.

Central to this effort to improve ties with Russia were the activities of Lieutenant General Michael Flynn, Trump's first national security adviser. A former head of the Defense Intelligence Agency, he had the unusual experience of giving a lecture on leadership at the headquarters of the GRU—Moscow's secretive military intelligence organization—in 2013. Flynn enjoyed his visit: "I was able to brief their entire staff. I talked a lot about the way the world's unfolding. It was a great trip."[20] Flynn had grown disillusioned with the policies of the Obama administration in which he served, because he thought it underestimated the jihadist threat. He believed the US and Russia were natural allies in the fight against Islamic terrorism and that this should override all their other differences. He was eventually fired as head of the DIA by Obama. He returned to Russia in December 2015 to join the celebration of the tenth anniversary of RT, Russia's main television foreign propaganda outlet. He was given a seat of honor next to Putin at the gala dinner. According to Flynn, Putin had "no respect for the United States leadership."[21] Once Trump had won the primaries, he chose Flynn as his national security adviser, and Flynn reached out to Russian ambassador Sergei Kislyak, a former physicist and arms control expert who had served in Washington for nine years. They met in Trump Tower with Jared Kushner, who sought to open a back channel to Russia.

Although Flynn was not yet in the White House, he clearly believed he had the authority to conduct foreign policy. On December 29, Obama announced that in retaliation for Russia's interference in the 2016 election, he was expelling thirty-five suspected Russian intelligence operatives, imposing sanctions on Russia's two leading intelligence agencies, and closing down two recreational diplomatic facilities that, so the government thought, were being used for purposes other than pure recreation.[22] The next day, Putin appeared on television, and contrary to the expected tit-for-tat response, he announced that Russia would not expel thirty-five US diplomats but would wait to see how US policy toward Russia under Trump evolved. Moreover, in an unusual act of conviviality, he invited the children of the US embassy staff in Moscow to a New Year's party in the Kremlin. Trump tweeted that Putin's decision to wait is a "great move," adding that he "always knew he was very smart."[23]

Why did Putin surprise the world and decline to activate the expected retaliation against the US? It subsequently emerged that Flynn called Kislyak numerous times after Obama announced the sanctions and reportedly assured him that if Russia did not retaliate, the Trump administration would reverse the sanctions once it was in office. There were two remarkable aspects to these calls. Firstly, it is illegal for private citizens to negotiate with a foreign power, and at that point Flynn was not a government official. Secondly—and perhaps more surprising—as a former DIA head, Flynn surely must have known that the Russian ambassador's phone calls were being monitored and there would be a record of what he said. Indeed, one did not have to be a former DIA head to suspect this. Shortly after he became national security adviser, someone leaked details of the phone calls to the media. Flynn repeatedly denied that he had discussed sanctions with Kislyak, but after it emerged that he had lied to the vice president, Trump was forced to dismiss him—twenty-five days into the job. In December 2017, Flynn pleaded guilty to lying to the FBI and admitted he had discussed sanctions with Kislyak.[24]

As more and more details emerged about contacts between the Trump campaign and Russians, questions about Trump's own ties to Russia and his consistently positive view of Putin became increasingly tied to the major stories of 2016: Russia's interference in the presidential election and possible collusion between Trump operatives and the Russians.

The Russian Interference Campaign

The Russian interference campaign was a multipronged strategy involving everything from sophisticated cyber operations to the exploitation of social media. It began in 2014 but burst into the public consciousness in 2016. On June 15, a hacker calling himself Guccifer 2.0 posted opposition research and donor documents stolen from the Democratic National Committee (DNC). A cybersecurity firm investigating the breach concluded that Russia was behind it, and later Guccifer was linked to the GRU. Then, in July—a day before the start of the Democratic National Convention—WikiLeaks posted 20,000 e-mails from DNC officials, some of which contained offensive remarks about Clinton's rival Bernie Sanders. The leaks were intended to exacerbate tensions within the Democrats' ranks and raise questions about the legitimacy of Clinton's nomination. WikiLeaks' founder, Julian Assange, holed up in the Ecuadorian embassy in London to avoid arrest on rape charges, held a personal grudge against Clinton. It was subsequently determined that Russians had given the stolen e-mails to WikiLeaks.[25] In addition to a steady stream of leaked e-mails, state-run Russian media RT and Sputnik constantly denigrated Clinton, accusing her of corruption, calling into question her mental and physical health, and intimating she would "steal" the election from Trump.

As if that were not enough, Russia exploited social media to push disinformation to millions of Americans. It created thousands of bots (automated internet accounts) and paid internet trolls to spread false news. According to testimony by Twitter executives on October 2017, more than 30,000 Russia-linked accounts generated 1.4 million tweets during the final months of the campaign.[26] Some of these posts showed telltale signs of faulty grammar and syntax (omitting definite articles, which is characteristic of the Russian language), but apparently no one thought these were generated by foreigners. According to the Mueller indictment, the Internet Research Agency coordinated the social media campaigns. Owner Yevgeny Prigozhin is quite resourceful. Not only do his restaurants feed visiting dignitaries and Kremlin bosses. He also owns Wagner, the major military contracting organization that sends mercenaries to fight in Ukraine, Syria, and elsewhere, and provides the Kremlin with plausible deniability in its hybrid wars. People who worked for the Internet Research Agency traveled to the United States to gather information on US political and social movements, and eventually remotely orchestrated dueling political rallies where opposing groups nearly came to physical blows. Of course, Putin has ridiculed the idea that Prigozhin was involved in hacking:

> Do you really think that a person who is in the restaurant business, even if this person has some hacking opportunities and owns a private firm engaged in this activity—I do not even know what he does—could use it to sway elections in the United States or a European country?[27]

Finally, the US Department of Homeland Security reported that Russia targeted presidential-election connected voting systems in at least twenty-one states, including key swing states, such as Florida, Ohio, and Pennsylvania. With the exception of Arizona and Illinois, which reported that their voting systems had been compromised, the Russian attempts to manipulate and sabotage voter data apparently failed.[28]

This was an unprecedented attack on American democracy. During the Cold War, both the US and USSR had sought to interfere in each other's domestic systems, and the Soviets had funded and promoted anti-American peace movements in Europe. But the scale of this coordinated campaign was qualitatively different from previous actions. In the age of social media and new technology, the possibilities for manipulation and influence are almost limitless. And the United States was caught completely off guard.

What was the Russian goal? The Kremlin was determined to take advantage of the polarization within US society and provoke Americans to question the legitimacy of their democracy. The goal was to relativize everything, question what were really facts, and, as RT and its sister network Sputnik repeatedly argued, show that the United States was no better than Russia.

Some Russians suggest that Putin made the decision to authorize Russian hackers to weaponize the hacked e-mails by giving them to WikiLeaks in response to the publication of the Panama Papers. In April 2016, a multinational group of reporters involved in the Organized Crime and Corruption Reporting Project (OCCRP) published a bombshell report detailing how governments and oligarchs all over the world were using offshore Panama companies for both legal and illegal purposes, including fraud, tax avoidance, and evasion of international sanctions. Russian journalists had identified multibillion-dollar accounts owned by Sergei Roldugin, a cellist and childhood friend of Putin. The articles argued that he had been put in charge of Putin's money. Roldugin denied he was acting for Putin and said that the $2 billion in the accounts had been donated by others for the purchase of musical instruments for young Russians. But Putin was furious. He summoned a meeting of his Security Council, and they reportedly discussed how to retaliate. That was when, it is thought, they decided to leak the hacked DNC e-mails to WikiLeaks.[29]

The first indication of the Russian hacking came in July 2016 with an alert by Dutch intelligence agencies to Washington based on work done by their hackers, who had accidentally penetrated a Russian network from which hackers launched attacks on the DNC.[30] But the full realization of the new reality came in August, when the CIA handed Obama an envelope of information derived from sources inside the Russian government that detailed Putin's direct involvement in the cyber campaign to discredit and disrupt the US presidential election. Only a small number of people have seen this information, and it took until January 2017 for a declassified report about Russian interference to be published.[31]

Obama administration officials were taken by surprise, and it took some time in the autumn of 2016 to put together all the pieces of this complex web of Russian interference. They were, in hindsight, unprepared to deal with a multifaceted cyber and social media campaign of this scale.[32] Obama was in an awkward position. He did not want to appear to be partisan at a time when the consensus was that Hillary Clinton would win, so the administration delayed sharing this information with the public. When officials sought to present a bipartisan response to the interference, they were rebuffed. The Republicans refused to admit to anything that would give the impression that Trump's public appeal was not legitimate. Finally, on October 7, 2016, the administration formally accused the Russian government of stealing and disclosing e-mails from the DNC, other institutions, and prominent individuals, leaving unanswered the question of retaliation. However, the report was in turn overshadowed by the release of a recording of Donald Trump, on which he could be heard making disparaging remarks about women, and by WikiLeaks's publication, an hour later, of thousands of e-mails belonging to Clinton's campaign manager John Podesta.

At the fall G-20 meeting in China, Obama himself had an opportunity to raise the issue with Putin. He bluntly told Putin to "cut it out."[33] On the night of November 8, Donald Trump—to many people's shock—won the election by sweeping the electoral college, losing the popular vote to Clinton by three million. In his last press conference, Obama sought to play down the Russian interference, using language designed to irritate Putin. Obama's problem, one senior official later recounted, was that "he wanted Russia to go away."[34]

But Russia, of course, will not go away. Obama's final act against Russia was the December 29 sanctions legislation. There were also rumors of a cyber response to Russian actions. By the time Obama left office, many Democrats believed that Trump had won the election because of Russian interference. Trump has only occasionally and grudgingly acknowledged that Russians may have interfered in the election because he believes this would detract from the legitimacy of his election victory.

Russiagate

Despite Trump's desire to brush aside the issue of Russian interference, it has dogged him since day one of his presidency and has hamstrung him as he tried to reach out to Putin. The most inflammatory issue is the suggestion of collusion between members of the Trump campaign and Russians. "Russiagate" is about what Russia did in 2014–2016. But it is also about US domestic politics and reflects the deep political divisions within US society. This issue first came to the public's attention in October 2016, when *Mother Jones* published an article claiming that the FBI was investigating claims made in a series of reports written by a former MI6 official. Christopher Steele had been hired by a US firm to look into Donald Trump's ties to Russia. He had concluded that the evidence showed the "Russian regime has been cultivating, supporting, and assisting TRUMP for at least 5 years. Aim, endorsed by PUTIN, has been to encourage splits and divisions in western alliance." It maintained that Trump "and his inner circle have accepted a regular flow of intelligence from the Kremlin, including on his Democratic and other political rivals." It claimed that Russian intelligence had "compromised" Trump during his visits to Moscow and could "blackmail him."[35]

Steele had not been in Russia since his posting there as an intelligence official in the early 1990s, but he had a network of contacts there to whom he subcontracted his research. The original research into Trump's Russia ties had been done on behalf of Republicans seeking to defeat Trump during the primary season. When Trump became the candidate, however, Democrats took over the project and the research continued. Altogether,

Steele produced sixteen separate reports on Trump-Russia ties, which became collectively known as the "Steele dossier."

After BuzzFeed published the dossier, it was immediately attacked by Republicans and has been a subject of controversy since then. It is very difficult to verify the contents of the dossier, but some former intelligence officers argue that many of its claims ring true.[36] Certainly the material about Russia's manipulation of social media to help Trump was confirmed in the Mueller indictment. Steele himself has said he believes that 70 to 90 percent of the material is accurate.[37] Leaving aside the more salacious material about Trump's activities while he was in Moscow for the Miss Universe contest, the dossier details how the Russians had been cultivating Trump and his associates for some years and had shared derogatory information about Hillary Clinton with them. Material about different Trump associates meeting with Russian officials and businessmen has been corroborated. The dossier remains at the center of a bitterly partisan battle inside the US Congress and between the Trump administration and the FBI, with whom Steele shared his material.

No sooner had Trump entered the White House than investigations into Russia's actions in 2016 began. There are two kinds of investigations: one into Russian interference in the election and the other into possible collusion between Russians and the Trump campaign. Special Counsel Robert Mueller, a former director of the FBI, is leading a criminal inquiry for the Department of Justice, the most high-profile investigation. He is examining Russia's actions in 2016 as well as those of the Trump campaign. He has a mandate to pursue any links or coordination between Trump's presidential campaign and the Russian government, including any efforts to obstruct such inquiries. At the same time, both the US Senate and House of Representatives intelligence committees, as well as the US Senate Judiciary Subcommittee on Crime and Terrorism are investigating Russian interference. While Mueller can prosecute individuals for committing federal crimes, congressional inquiries cannot produce criminal prosecutions, unless witnesses lie under oath. In terms of the law, the issue is not collusion—which is difficult to define—but whether people conspired with Russia to break a criminal statute or whether they broke the law themselves.

There already have been several indictments of Americans. General Flynn has pleaded guilty to making false statements to the FBI, and two other Trump associates have pleaded guilty to lying about their contacts with Russians. Paul Manafort—facing multiple counts of conspiracy to launder money and failing to register as a foreign agent—was convicted in one trial and initially pleaded guilty and agreed to cooperate with the Mueller investigation to avoid a second trial.[38] Mr. Mueller has assembled a team of top money-laundering experts and appears to be focusing on financial ties between Russians and people around Trump.

The US public remains sharply divided over Russiagate. A majority of Americans (59 percent) think senior members of Donald Trump's administration definitely or probably had improper contacts with Russia during the presidential campaign, and most believe Mr. Mueller will conduct an impartial investigation. But while 71 percent of Democrats believe the Russia probe is "very important" to the nation, only 19 percent of Republicans believe it is.[39] Trump has denied any collusion, has mostly refused to acknowledge Russian interference, and has not ordered his intelligence agencies to take any action to counter Russian cyber and social media activities, which continued in 2018. Indeed, he has disparaged the FBI and other intelligence agencies throughout these investigations.

Putin has repeatedly dismissed the idea of interference, challenging his audience at the 2016 Valdai Discussion Club meeting: "Does anyone seriously imagine that Russia can somehow influence the American people's choice? America is not some kind of 'banana republic,' after all, but is a great power. Do correct me if I am wrong."[40]

TRUMP AND PUTIN

What did Trump believe he could accomplish with Putin once he entered the White House? On the campaign trail, he gave a few hints. Russia, he said, was a key ally in fighting a common enemy: terrorism. Russia would help solve the Syrian Civil War. It could be helpful with North Korea. And closer US-Russia relations would draw Russia away from its partnership with China. Similarly, Russia might act as a brake on Iran's nuclear and regional ambitions. As K. T. McFarland, who served for four months as deputy national security adviser, wrote in a leaked e-mail after Obama imposed sanctions on Russia in December, "Russia is the key that unlocks the door," adding that the Trump administration should be able to maneuver Russia away from allies such as Iran.[41] This idea—that Russia might be a genuine partner in anti-terrorism and in other global issues—was widespread among Trump's inner circle. But the belief that Russia could be turned away from its deepening partnership with China revealed a profound misunderstanding of the reality of the Sino-Russian relationship. The development of close ties to China was one of Putin's previous foreign policy successes, which he would hardly jeopardize for closer ties with an unpredictable United States.

The Russians welcomed Trump's election. People celebrated in Moscow bars, and state-run media were fulsome in their praise. Putin called to congratulate Trump, expressing hope that they should move beyond the "absolutely unsatisfactory state of bilateral relations" and cooperate on "the broadest possible range of issues."[42] A group of wealthy Russians attended the inauguration, and one of them posted a picture on Facebook of him clutching inauguration memorabilia, writing, "I believe that President Donald Trump will open a new page in American History." It was clear that the delegation of Russian businessmen were hoping Trump's election would lead to a thaw in US-Russia relations and would open up new business opportunities for them after Trump lifted the sanctions imposed by Obama.[43]

During the first four months of his administration, Trump spoke several times with Putin, mainly about Syria, counterterrorism, and North Korea. His first meeting with high-level officials came in May, when he received Foreign Minister Lavrov and Ambassador Kislyak in the Oval Office. He had just fired the head of the FBI, James Comey, whom he considered disloyal because of his pursuit of the Russia investigation. (Mueller then took over the investigation.) Although US media were barred from the meeting, the Russians managed to get their photographer in, so pictures soon emerged of Trump laughing with his Russian guests, with all three men in a jovial mood. Trump said they had had a "very, very good meeting." It was subsequently revealed that he had disclosed highly classified information to the Russians—emanating from Israel—about terrorists trying to use computers to blow up planes.[44]

It was not until July 2017 that the two presidents finally met. During their first encounter at the G-20 meeting in Hamburg, Vladimir Putin and Donald Trump looked relaxed, smiled at each other, and had "positive chemistry," according to former secretary of state Rex Tillerson.[45] The meeting went on much longer than planned, and First Lady Melania Trump was sent in after two and a half hours to remind them that it was time to wrap it up. Trump was effusive in his praise for the Russian leader: "We had some very good talks—we look forward to a lot of very positive things happening for Russia, for the United States, and for everybody concerned. And it's an honor to be with you." Putin returned the compliment: "I am delighted to be able to meet you personally, Mr. President."[46] Putin praised his American interlocutor: "Mr. Trump's television image is very different from the real person; he is a very down to earth and direct person, and he has an absolutely adequate attitude towards the person he is talking with."[47]

During the meeting, the two leaders discussed the conflict in Syria, and when the issue of Russian interference in the 2016 US election was raised, Putin denied that this had occurred. As far as the public was concerned, that was the only Trump-Putin meeting. But it turned out that later that evening, when the dinner was finished, Trump went over to Putin—who had been sitting next to Mrs. Trump—and had a one-hour conversation with him. What was unusual about this was that Trump did not take his interpreter with him, so the only other witness to the meeting was the Russian interpreter, and there is no record of what was said—at least for the US side.[48] After the Hamburg meeting, Trump spoke to a journalist from a major newspaper and told him, "I had Putin eating out of my hands."

All the anomalies of this singular relationship were on display during those few hours in Hamburg: a US president determined to secure a good relationship with a leader he had consistently praised throughout his election campaign and after he entered the White House, despite the mounting evidence of Russian interference in the 2016 election; and a Russian ex-KGB leader intent on reaching out to and flattering the American president, at the same time as he excoriated the United States for a range of sins.

Trump had only one more meeting with Putin during his first year in office—this on the margins of the Asia-Pacific Economic Cooperation summit in Vietnam. According to their joint statement, released after the pull-aside, they reiterated their determination to defeat ISIS in Syria, to maintain their military deconfliction channels in the Syrian war, and to seek a political solution to the crisis.[49]

If Trump had hoped, as he said on the campaign trail, to make an early visit to Moscow, this was not to be. With the Russia investigations swirling and criticism for the praise he had given Putin during their first meeting, he was hamstrung. But Putin continued to leave the door open for better ties. During his speech at the 2017 Valdai Discussion Club forum, after blasting the United States for a range of sins, he chided those in the audience who questioned Trump's performance in office: "He is being disrespected in the country. This is a deplorable, negative aspect of the American political system. You can argue, but you cannot show disrespect."[50]

The domestic impediments to a closer Trump-Putin relationship obscured an important reality: even without a "Russiagate," what was the US-Russia agenda? What did both sides want from each other, and how did they define their respective interests? Whatever the president himself wanted, Trump had appointed a national security team—Rex Tillerson at State, James Mattis at Defense, and H. R. McMaster as national security adviser—who dealt with their Russian counterparts and cautiously sought ways to move the relationship forward. Congress meanwhile was pursuing its own confrontational policy toward Russia. There appeared to be three Russia policies in the Trump administration: that of the White House, that of the rest of the executive branch, and that of the Congress.

The Trump Administration's Three Russia Policies

Russia hoped that Trump's election would usher in a new era of closer US-Russia relations and that Washington would finally give Moscow the respect it had not received since Putin returned to the Kremlin in 2012. Early on in the administration, Putin took the initiative and dispatched Deputy Foreign Minister Sergei Ryabkov to the State Department to propose a sweeping revamp of relations. The reset would involve discussions on cybersecurity, Afghanistan, the Iran nuclear deal, the situation in Ukraine, and the denuclearization of the Korean Peninsula. There would be regular consultations between the two presidents, their intelligence chiefs, and other cabinet officials from both sides. Many of the Obama-era military and diplomatic channels closed after the annexation of Crimea would be reopened. This amounted to a full-scale normalization of relations back to where they had been while Obama and Medvedev were still presidents. But the reset ignored everything that had caused the relationship to deteriorate since then, as if the election interference and the Ukraine crisis had never happened.[51] The US State Department declined to confirm the report of the Russian proposal, but the Russian side did. "Yes, of course, such proposals in various formats were passed to the US," Putin spokesman Dmitry Peskov told reporters. "Moscow consistently came out for the resumption of dialogue, for the exchange of opinions, for trying to find joint resolutions, but, unfortunately, was not met here with reciprocity."[52]

Apparently the Kremlin believed that President Trump and his advisers would be open to these proposals, and that knowledge of their election interference would have little impact on bilateral relations because

Trump had won and would be free to move forward with Russia. It took the Russian leadership some time to understand the full ramifications of its tampering.

It soon became clear that there was a disconnect between President Trump's forward-looking views of Russia and those of his cabinet colleagues and the US Congress, lending a significant degree of incoherence to the United States' Russia policy. Secretary of State Rex Tillerson, like his colleagues at Defense and the National Security Council, was determined to engage Russia cautiously. The former CEO of ExxonMobil had considerable experience dealing with Russia, had been going to Russia since the 1990s, and had received the Order of Friendship from Putin in 2013. He had worked closely with Igor Sechin, CEO of Rosneft and arguably Russia's second most powerful man.[53] Rosneft and ExxonMobil had signed a multibillion-dollar agreement to jointly explore the Arctic, but that deal had been scuttled as a result of the post-Crimea sanctions on energy technology. After his first trip to Russia as secretary of state and meetings with Putin and Lavrov in April 2017, he acknowledged there was a "low level of trust." He subsequently crafted a three-point plan for working with Russia: first, push back against Russian aggressive acts against the United States; second, engage Russia on issues that are of strategic interest to the United States; third, seek to establish "strategic stability" with Russia on a longer-term basis. This strategy was similar to that of the Obama administration after 2015.[54] That is not surprising, given that the issues that dominated US-Russia relations after 2014 had not gone away.

The Trump administration reestablished some channels of communication that had previously been suspended, such as direct talks between the US and Russian chiefs of the general staff, talks between the intelligence chiefs, and talks between Tillerson and Lavrov. A strategic stability channel was established between the US undersecretary of state and the Russian deputy foreign minister. The new Russian ambassador to Washington, Anatoly Antonov, a veteran defense official, sought—with limited success—to reach out to different constituencies in Washington. His counterpart, Ambassador Jon Huntsman, former governor of Utah and former ambassador to China, did likewise in Moscow, seeking to promote business ties—a challenge in an era of cascading US congressional sanctions. Eschewing the idea of resets, Huntsman explained his policy: "Just take the relationship for what it is, clear-eyed and realistically," adding that his work "is completely disassociated from the Mueller investigation because it's work that you just need to get done in a relationship among major powers."[55]

As 2017 wore on, a series of sanctions, counter-sanctions, and diplomatic expulsions continued to fracture the relationship. The US Congress, which took an even tougher approach toward Russia than either the executive branch's national security team or certainly the White House, was determined to impede any reset with Russia that would not hold Moscow to account for its election interference. In July, fearing that Trump might unilaterally lift the Obama-era sanctions on Russia, the Senate passed the Countering America's Adversaries Through Sanctions Act (CAATSA) by a vote of 98–2. The act, among other provisions, imposes sanctions on some energy transactions with Russia. But its potentially most far-reaching impact is contained in a clause requiring the administration to submit to Congress lists of Russian oligarchs and political figures close to Putin who could be personally sanctioned. Trump, whose ability to lift sanctions was severely constrained by this legislation, reluctantly signed the bill, which, he said, contained "clearly unconstitutional provisions."[56] Indeed, Igor Sechin, who had been personally sanctioned in 2014, called the new legislation "sanctions against Trump." When the administration eventually delivered the names of individuals to Congress, it consisted of the *Forbes* list of 96 Russian billionaires and what amounted to the telephone directory for 114 Russian government officials, giving the impression that it did not favor sanctioning anyone. On March 15, 2018, the first round of sanctions began. The Treasury Department sanctioned a group of individuals and organizations for "destabilizing activities, ranging from interference in the 2016 US election to conducting destructive cyber-attacks." The sanctions included individuals listed in the Mueller indictment but extended to actors who "have also targeted US government entities and multiple US critical infrastructure sectors, including the energy, nuclear, commercial facilities, water, aviation, and critical manufacturing sectors."[57]

The Kremlin retaliated to the August sanctions by seizing two US diplomatic properties and ordering the United States to reduce its Moscow embassy staff by 755 people. Most of these people were Russian nationals who provided necessary support for the visa office and many other parts of the embassy. Trump responded by thanking Putin: "I'm very thankful that he let go of a large number of people, because now we have a smaller payroll."[58] Nevertheless, the cuts had an adverse effect on the ability of the embassy and consulates to function efficiently, including issuing visas to Russians in a timely fashion. Some Russians living in Moscow applying for US visas had to travel to the US consulate in Vladivostok—four thousand miles and seven time zones away, and even to other countries—to get their visas. Moreover, the US ambassador lost his chief interpreter and most of his political staff.

The next act in this tit-for-tat round of sanctions was the US closure of the Russian consulate in San Francisco. Perched high on top of a hill with a direct line of sight to the ocean, the building was in the vicinity of Silicon Valley, educational institutions such as Stanford and Berkeley, and a large number of defense contractors and researchers—including two Department of Energy–affiliated nuclear weapons laboratories. US officials had long suspected that the consulate was a focal point for Russian espionage efforts in the United States. Indeed, in the forty-eight hours between the announcement and its actual closure, clouds of black smoke wheezed from the consulate's chimney, presumably because its employees were burning as many documents as possible before they had to evacuate the building.[59] The United States also closed the Russian consulate in Seattle. The Russians retaliated by closing the US consulate in Saint Petersburg.

This pattern—Trump consistently praising Russia while his administration imposed more sanctions on Russia—became more noticeable well into his second year in office. The contrast between Trump and the rest of the executive branch was very much on display as Putin entered his fourth term in the Kremlin. The day before Rex Tillerson was fired by a tweet from the president while Tillerson was in Africa, he criticized Russia more harshly than previously. The United Kingdom had just directly implicated the Kremlin in the attempted murder of Sergei Skripal and his daughter. Tillerson called the Kremlin "an irresponsible force of instability in the world" and expressed solidarity with the British government.[60] Days later, President Trump phoned Putin to congratulate him on his reelection, against the explicit advice of his national security team. "We had a very good call," Mr. Trump told reporters in the Oval Office. "We will probably be meeting in the not too distant future to discuss the arms race, which is getting out of control."[61] The Kremlin concurred: "On the whole, the conversation was constructive and businesslike, with a focus on overcoming the accumulated problems in Russian-American relations."[62]

The next round of sanctions, issued by the Department of the Treasury's Office of Foreign Assets Control (OFAC), came in April. These were directed against seven oligarchs with ties to Putin along with twelve companies they own or control. Sanctions were also imposed on seventeen senior government officials and the state-owned Russian weapons trading company Rosoboronexport, which has longstanding ties to Syria, and its subsidiary Russian Financial Corporation Bank. The White House said these targeted sanctions would help to ensure that Russian oligarchs profiting from the Kremlin's destabilizing activities, including its interference in the 2016 elections, would face consequences for their actions. One oligarch was particularly notable: Oleg Deripaska, the aluminum magnate who had in the past worked with Paul Manafort. As a result of the sanctions, Deripaska's firm Rusal was unable to service its dollar-denominated debt, and its economic difficulties impacted the global aluminum industry. In the end, OFAC had to extend the deadline for dealing with Rusal's creditors, and Treasury Secretary Steven Mnuchin announced that sanctions against Rusal would be reassessed. All of those sanctioned can no longer obtain visas to come to the United States, and any assets they have in the US are frozen.

In June, the Treasury Department imposed a fresh round of sanctions on Russia, this time targeting five Russian companies and three individuals, some of whom are accused of directly supporting Russia's domestic intelligence agency, the FSB. Mnuchin explained, "The United States is engaged in an ongoing effort to counter malicious actors working at the behest of the Russian Federation and its military and intelligence units to increase Russia's offensive cyber capabilities."[63] Congress has signaled that new sanctions are forthcoming in response to continued Russian election interference, including hacking into its members' computers.

On July 13, 2018, three days before Trump met Putin in Helsinki for a summit, Mueller handed down indictments on twelve GRU agents "engaged in cyber operations that involved the staged release of documents stolen through computer intrusions. These units conducted large-scale cyber operations to interfere with the 2016 US presidential election."[64] The US intelligence community had, once again, spoken clearly about Russia election interference. Deputy Attorney General Rod Rosenstein had discussed the indictments with Trump before he left for Europe, and Trump had agreed that these charges could be made public before his meeting with Putin.[65] Yet three days later Trump stood next to Putin in Helsinki and said, "I have great confidence in my intelligence people, but I will tell you that President Putin was extremely strong and powerful in his denial today."[66]

The Helsinki Summit: "Better than Super"[67]

How did Trump persuade his skeptical advisers that he should have a bilateral summit with Putin? By the spring of 2018, his growing self-confidence—especially following his unprecedented meeting with North Korean dictator Kim Jong-un in Singapore—led him to abruptly fire both Tillerson and McMaster, whom he deemed insufficiently loyal. In their places, he appointed CIA director Mike Pompeo as secretary of state and John Bolton as national security adviser. Both of these men were known to have hard-line views on Russia, but they were Trump supporters who were committed to implementing the president's policies. Bolton, who in 2017 had described Russian election interference as an "act of war," in July 2018 described the Mueller investigation as a "witch hunt."[68]

The hastily prepared meeting came at the end of a tumultuous trip to the NATO summit in Brussels and to the United Kingdom. In Brussels, Trump disparaged NATO allies and called into question the United States' commitment to collective self-defense. In the UK, he criticized Prime Minister Theresa May and expressed support for her rival Boris Johnson. But in the presence of Vladimir Putin, he was cordial and deferential. Putin and Trump appear to share a similar worldview, criticizing alliances that limit a major power's freedom of action, supporting the idea of absolute sovereignty, and rejecting the liberal international order in favor of muscular nationalism.

The two presidents held a ninety-minute meeting at which only their interpreters were present—very unusual for such high-level sessions. Hence there is no official record of what was discussed. Although the Russians subsequently released information about a variety of agreements they claimed Trump and Putin had reached, the US side furnished no details on the presidential tête-à-tête. Subsequent interviews with Pompeo and Bolton raised questions about how much either knew about what was discussed. Bolton claimed the meeting had no agenda and was just designed to be an "exchange of views."[69] By contrast, in the days following the summit, Russia claimed there had been agreement on four issues: the establishment of a council of experts to promote "points of contact" between the two countries; the creation of a US-Russia business forum to promote commercial ties; the reestablishment of a counterterrorism working group; and the creation of a cybersecurity working group.[70]

Putin began the Helsinki press conference self-confidently, saying he and Trump had had a "good conversation" and had discussed disarmament, the INF Treaty, strategic stability, counterterrorism, Syria, Ukraine, Iran, and North Korea. Trump, blaming both the US and Russia for the bad state of relations, mentioned few details of what had been discussed.

He called Putin "a good competitor." During the question-and-answer session, Putin was asked whether he had wanted Trump to win the election. "Yes," he replied. "Yes, I wanted him to win." Trump talked at length about his doubts about his own intelligence community's investigations into Russian meddling and collusion.[71] The worst fears of US allies—namely that Trump would say Crimea belonged to Russia or that the US might leave NATO—did not materialize. Indeed, Putin explicitly said that Trump believed that the Crimea referendum was illegal. But the specter of Putin acting as if he were in charge and Trump questioning his own intelligence officials made a strong impression on both the Russian and the American side.

Russian state-run media praised the summit as the first step toward improving ties.[72] US media was much more divided, with former CIA head John Brennan accusing Trump of treason.[73] In the days following the summit, the Kremlin floated two ideas that it claimed also had been discussed in Helsinki: holding a referendum in the Donbas to decide the region's future and having Mueller come to Russia to sit in on interviews with the twelve indicted GRU agents in return for Russian criminal police interrogating former US officials and businessmen connected to the Magnitsky Act list.[74] Both ideas were soon rejected—but it took the White House several days to criticize the latter.

Helsinki was a win for Putin, a significant achievement in Putin's world. After eighteen years in power, he had achieved what he wanted from the United States and what he believed he had not had since his first summit with Bush in Slovenia in 2001: respect and equality. The US president had praised him while publicly criticizing his own officials. Days after Trump returned, he invited Putin to visit Washington. The domestic battle between Trump partisans and opponents intensified in the aftermath of the summit, further polarizing the Russia issue. Some Russians questioned whether Putin would regret having waded into the toxic domestic debate by coming down so firmly on Trump's side.[75] After Helsinki, the disconnect between the president and his key colleagues in their evaluation of Russia continued. But by beginning to restore relations, there was a chance that US and Russian officials would start to work more intensively on the long list of problems that require their urgent attention.

The Agenda for US-Russia Relations in Putin's Fourth Term

Irrespective of where the Russia investigation goes, there are a number of pressing points in the US-Russia relationship. The US-Russia agenda focuses on a few multilateral issues in which the interests of both sides necessitate engagement because of ongoing conflicts. The first is Syria. The air forces of both countries are present in Syria, and coordinating air operations remains important. The Russians are trying to secure promises of US assistance in reconstructing Syria, and the US wants Russia to rein in Iran's activities there. Syria is also an area where counterterrorism cooperation could be deepened, although so far that has proven elusive.

Ukraine is another priority. The US-Russia channel led by Kurt Volker and Vladislav Surkov was supposed to achieve progress on resolving the crisis, but so far the pace of negotiations remains glacial. Putin's suggestion of holding a referendum in the Donbas is a nonstarter as long as Russian troops remain there, and neither side appears interested in fully implementing the Minsk II agreements. Something could change after the Ukrainian elections in 2019, but there appears to be little incentive for ending the ongoing hostilities.

North Korea is another potential area for cooperation. Russia supported tougher UN sanctions on the North Korean regime, but there was also evidence it was increasing its economic ties to the north, as China was cutting back on its trade. There are also substantial numbers of North Korean laborers working in the Russian Far East under very harsh conditions, and Russia refused to repatriate them, as was required by the UN sanctions.[76] So far, Russia has remained a side player in trying to resolve the North Korean denuclearization problem, but Putin hopes to play a greater role going forward.

The most important bilateral US-Russia issue is the state of both countries' nuclear arsenals and the looming expiration or jettisoning of two treaties that for almost half a century have created a predictable and stable arms control regime since Richard Nixon and Leonid Brezhnev signed the Strategic Arms Limitation Treaty (SALT) in 1972: the Intermediate Nuclear Forces (INF) Treaty, signed in 1987, and the New START, signed in 2011. The New START committed each side to reducing its stockpiles of strategic nuclear weapons, and in February 2018, both sides announced they had in fact complied with the provisions.[77] But the US and Russia both maintain some four thousand nuclear weapons—more than ten times the number of any other country.[78] Moreover, both the US and Russia are committed to modernizing their nuclear forces and developing new, more powerful weapons systems. Putin made this clear in his pre-election speech, and Trump has also said, "We must modernize and rebuild our nuclear arsenal."[79] Russia has communicated that it does not want any further reduction in strategic nuclear weapons. So far, attempts at negotiating what comes after New START, which expires in 2021, have not been successful in a time of heightened US-Russia tensions. The treaty could be prolonged for another five years by presidential decree, and this may be the most realistic path to ensure that a strategic arms control regime is preserved. However, a five-year prolongation would at best represent a holding pattern. What is needed going forward is a new framework taking into account emerging technologies, such as enhanced cyber capabilities, outer space, artificial intelligence, and missile defense. If there is no new treaty, the US and Russia will enter into a new, unpredictable, and dangerous nuclear, cyber, and outer space arms race.

The other treaty at risk is the INF Treaty, which committed both sides to eliminate a whole class of intermediate-range weapons. The US claims that Russia has violated this treaty by deploying an intermediate-range ground-launched cruise missile. Russia denies this and argues that the US has violated the treaty by building missile-defense sites in Romania and Poland capable of launching intermediate-range cruise missiles. The INF Treaty is in danger of collapsing unless the two sides can negotiate seriously about how to preserve it. In October 2018 National Security Adviser John Bolton met with Putin in Moscow and told him that the United States intends to withdraw from the INF Treaty, a move that drew widespread criticism in Russia, Europe, and the United States. The imperative to tackle these challenges is compelling because of the dangers of nuclear proliferation. If the US and Russia—which control 90 percent of the world's nuclear weapons—are no longer constrained by arms control agreements, how will that affect the effort to prevent other states from acquiring nuclear weapons?[80]

There are some areas where the United States and Russia continue to cooperate. One of them is space. The US depends on Russian capsules to transport US astronauts to and from space and to launch its satellites. Russia makes money from its space cooperation with the United States, and its cosmonauts have developed productive relations with their American counterparts. Additionally, the Boeing Company has had a close relationship with Russia for decades. Without Russian titanium, it could not build its planes, and it works closely with Russian engineers to design them. The Russian company TMK produces pipes used in the exploration and production of US shale oil.[81] In compartmented public and private spheres, where specialists can work together in an environment largely removed from the political cauldron, America and Russia can cooperate effectively.[82]

Another area of cooperation could be cybersecurity. Ultimately Washington and Moscow should sit down and discuss cyber rules of the road going forward. There are precedents for this. The US and China have a commercial cybersecurity agreement on economic espionage that works reasonably well, despite their very different views of the cyber arena.[83] Moscow has several times proposed opening talks on cybersecurity—most recently in Helsinki—but so far these feelers have been rebuffed because of US doubts about whether Russia would adhere to any new agreement given the continuing Russian interference in US cyberspace, which the Russians continually deny. The fundamental issue, of course, is the absence of trust between the leadership of both countries, which hampers any meaningful engagement in this area. A prerequisite for achieving agreement on a cyber code of conduct would be to begin with small confidence-building measures, but these so far remain elusive.

Even if the US and Russia succeed in establishing working groups to tackle these issues, Congress will exercise its prerogatives and implement the CAATSA. More sanctions on oligarchs deemed close to Putin will be forthcoming, particularly if Russian interference continues through the 2018 midterm elections and beyond. In September 2018 the Trump administration announced new sanctions against individuals and countries that seek to interfere in US elections.[84] So far Russia has managed to overcome the most acute economic effects of the sanctions. It has sought to manage the problem by neutering the sanctions, as opposed to accommodating US concerns. Russia has turned to China for financial support and for energy cooperation. It is also not completely clear what Russia would have to do to get either the Ukraine or election interference sanctions removed. With oil prices rising, the economic pressure has lessened, but the latest US sanctions reduce incentives for Western companies to do business in Russia, given the possibility of their extraterritorial application and the uncertainty of who will next be sanctioned.

How important is repairing relations with the United States for Vladimir Putin? The two major foreign policy successes in his first three terms were the strengthening of ties with China and Russia's return to the Middle East as the key power broker. These resulted from increasing strains in the relationship with the United States and a US retreat from the Middle East. The official Russian state media depicts the United States in extremely negative terms, although, like their president, they continue to praise Donald Trump. Both blame the American people for trying to prevent Trump's rapprochement with Russia. Many attribute the fact that Putin received 76 percent of the votes in the March 2018 election to the perceived threat from the West and his promise to defend the Motherland from enemies.

But Putin faces a dilemma when it comes to the United States. On the one hand, he seeks recognition by the US as an equal to legitimize Russia's status as a great power. He would also like to see US sanctions removed.

On the other hand, the US represents a danger because of its uneven attempts—at least until Donald Trump took power—to promote democracy and the rule of law in Russia, which are seen as direct threats to the current ruling elite. A close relationship with China, which never raises the subject of Russia's domestic politics and has no interest in democracy promotion, is more congenial.

Putin has seized the opportunity presented by Trump's evident desire to have a strong relationship with him. Moreover, the Kremlin sees a West that is in disarray. Donald Trump's denigration of NATO members and his questioning of the utility of maintaining the alliance, combined with his launch of a trade war against the European Union and Britain's exit from the EU, may well accomplish what neither the Soviets nor post-Soviet Russia succeeded in doing: a rupture in the Western alliance. The Kremlin can only sit back and observe these transatlantic quarrels with satisfaction while it seeks to exploit and benefit from them. Putin has apparently concluded that it will be possible to improve ties with Donald Trump's America even if Russia does not change its behavior in Syria, Ukraine, or cyberspace. After all, he secured a summit with Trump four years after the Obama administration sought to isolate Russia for its actions in Ukraine, and yet Russia still supports the separatists in an ongoing war. Its cyber interventions in the United States also continue apace. Putin may well believe that if Russia waits long enough, the United States will reengage and put aside its previous reservations. But that may well prove to be a miscalculation.

An outwardly cordial relationship between Donald Trump and Vladimir Putin should not be confused with concrete progress on real issues. The two leaders can praise each other and pledge to tackle difficult problems in the relationship, but as the contrasting official Russian and American reactions to Helsinki showed, both sides may have different interpretations of what they agreed upon—and what they want to do. Trump returned from Helsinki insisting, "I'm different than other presidents. I'm a dealmaker. I've made deals all my life. I do really well. I make great deals."[85] But what is the deal? Rhetoric aside, while Putin's goals are reasonably clear, Trump's are not. What is it that he really wants from Russia?

In the best of times, the US-Russia relationship is compartmented, with areas of cooperation coexisting with areas of rivalry or conflict. But when it is not the best of times, and the areas of conflict far outweigh those of cooperation, the challenge is to identify issues on which engagement is necessary and proceed with caution and realism. Since their Helsinki meeting, both Trump and Putin have conveyed the impression of forward movement in their relationship. But in reality, US-Russian ties may remain adversarial for many years to come, with all the risks that come from that.

13

WHAT KIND OF ENGAGEMENT WITH RUSSIA?

> Russia is a mixed breed, like someone born of a mixed marriage. He is everyone's relative, but nobody's family. Treated by foreigners like one of their own, an outcast among his own people. He understands everyone and is understood by no one. A half-blood, a half-breed, a strange one. It is now up to the Russian people whether Russia becomes a loner in a backwater or an alpha nation that has surged into a big lead over other nations. It's going to be tough, but Russia faces a long journey though the thorns to the stars. It'll be interesting, and there will be stars.
>
> —*Vladislav Surkov, presidential aide, 2018*[1]

The many dimensions of Putin's world were on full display in one month in the summer of 2018 in a whirlwind display of power. First came the World Cup and the goodwill it produced for both Russian and foreign fans. A day after the final, during which Emmanuel Macron sat with Putin cheering the victorious French team, Putin flew to Helsinki to meet Donald Trump. At their press conference, Putin was in charge, complimenting his American counterpart on their joint accomplishments, as Trump praised him and appeared to disavow his own intelligence agencies. Then it was off to Johannesburg for a BRICS summit, where Putin lauded the organization that Russia co-founded with China twelve years before, one from which the West is explicitly excluded. He reiterated the BRICS commitment to the Iran nuclear agreement, which the Trump administration had jettisoned. Next it was back to the Kremlin, to honor the Russian soccer team, which had performed much better than expected. Putin then took part in a solemn ceremony commemorating the 1,030th anniversary of Russia's conversion to Christianity. He spoke under the giant statue of his namesake, Prince Vladimir (completed in 2016), who converted the Slavs in 988. Standing a stone's throw from the Kremlin, Putin addressed a crowd of priests in gold robes, praising Prince Vladimir, who—to the irritation of the Kremlin—is also claimed by the Ukrainians as their historical sovereign. The next day he was in Saint Petersburg, celebrating Navy Day with an impressive military parade. He complimented Russia's powerful fleet that "defends the Motherland." He did so standing in front of the statue of Peter the Great—one of his heroes—on the Neva River.[2] Within two days Putin had placed himself adjacent to two "founding fathers" of the Russian state: Vladimir, who made Russia an Orthodox Christian nation, and Peter, who turned Muscovy into the Russian Empire and opened Russia to the West. This is Putin's world: meetings with world leaders in fora where Russia is a key player, highlighting Russia's military might, celebrating the Kremlin's close ties to the Orthodox Church, and summoning the great symbols of the past to stand with him as he marks two decades at Russia's helm and approaches the future.

In a new era of strongmen, Vladimir Putin stands out as one of the strongest. During his time in power, Russia has reasserted itself on the world stage, a remarkable feat for a country that experienced such rapid decline in the 1990s, only to accomplish an unexpected resurgence after Putin entered the Kremlin. He has made it his mission to relitigate the end of the Cold War and renegotiate its terms. As he embarked on his fourth term, Russia's relations with the West were the worst they had been since the last years of the Brezhnev period in the early 1980s, with an escalating arms race and mutual ideological invective. Thirty-five years ago, a succession of aging, infirm Soviet leaders faced Ronald Reagan, a self-confident US president who denounced their country as an "evil empire." Today, the mutual mistrust, rhetorical invective, and steady military buildup are strongly reminiscent of the Cold War, as is the dissonance between the way America and Russia see each other.

But Cold War 2.0 is different. There is no universal ideological competition between the West and Russia. Russia's ideological appeal is to "compatriots" in the post-Soviet space, to left- and right-wing populists in the West, and to a diverse group of countries and people around the world who dislike the United States. The United States is much stronger militarily than is Russia, and it used to view Moscow more as a regional than as a global strategic competitor, although Russia believes it has recently indeed become a greater and global competitor to the United States, thanks to Putin's accomplishments. Moreover, Russia, unlike the USSR, is integrated into the global economy, and this gives it leverage the Soviets never had. It also gives it vulnerabilities.

This is no longer a bipolar world, for China has emerged as the key rising power that holds many big global cards. And there is another difference. During the Cold War, the USSR and the West engaged each other through established political and military government-to-government channels with rules of the game that they both accepted. In the system of personalized rule that Putin has created, these channels are moribund or largely gone, and there are fewer avenues for communication, and hence more opportunities for miscalculation and consequential mistakes. So the West has returned to the familiar dual-track Cold War prescriptions for dealing with an antagonistic Russia: deterrence and engagement.

Viewed from the Kremlin, however, Putin has achieved his major objectives. Russia has restored itself to its "rightful" place on the world stage. It has, once again, joined the global board of directors. The world can no longer ignore it. It is respected—and feared. Even as Russia's relations with the West deteriorate, the West has to deal with it. At a major defense and security conference in Moscow, the Chinese defense minister jolted his audience when he vowed that China would come to Russia's assistance were it to be attacked by the West. In 2018 China joined Russia in its massive Vostok military exercises. Western commentators may describe Russia as a "pariah state" or a "mafia state." But Beijing, as we have seen, aligns with Moscow in international fora, and much of the Middle East views Russia's role in the region as that of a pragmatic mediator and broker. In Central Asia, Russia is also recognized as a great power with which to be reckoned.

As the West wrestles over how to deal with Putin, it is important to remember that in many parts of the world Russia is viewed as a large authoritarian country ruled by a successful leader who is pursuing his country's legitimate national interests as he defines them. Moreover, much of the world's view of Russia is colored by how the world regards the United States. In the unpredictable age of Donald Trump, Russia's attractiveness has grown for some countries. As this book has shown, going back to 2014, China has upgraded Russia as a partner, taking advantage of the West's attempts to isolate Putin, and has sought to recruit Russia to its version of a post-West global order. Some of Russia's neighbors, especially Ukraine, view Russia as an antagonist. But Russia has managed to create several functioning multilateral institutions in the post-Soviet space, such as the Shanghai Cooperation Organization, the Collective Security Treaty Organization, and the Eurasian Economic Union. Key Middle Eastern countries—Iran, Syria, Saudi Arabia, Egypt, Israel—look to Russia to support their interests in the region, even though these countries are on opposite sides of ongoing conflicts and, in some cases, are deadly enemies. And the West itself is fragmented; it has no unified view of Russia as a hostile actor. For instance, after the poisoning of former Russian double agent Sergei Skripal and his daughter in Great Britain, the United States and more than two dozen other countries supported England in expelling Russian diplomats suspected of spying. But these were nearly all NATO or EU members, plus Australia and Ukraine, and even some EU members, such as Austria and Slovakia, refused to follow suit. Under Putin, some of Russia's former allies in the Warsaw Pact, notably Hungary, Slovakia, Bulgaria, and the Czech Republic, have moved closer to Moscow.

Vladimir Putin won his 2018 reelection by an unprecedented margin. True, no credible opponents challenged him, and there were many reported voting irregularities. But it is undeniable that he remains popular, particularly outside the major urban centers. The Kremlin controls virtually all electronic media and skillfully uses television to persuade the population of its narrative of world events. Many young people, who have known only Putin as their president, support him. They believe that Russia needs a strong leader and, like so many generations of Russians before them, are willing to delegate to him the authority to make decisions for them. During his election campaign, Putin appealed to the people both by warning them of the danger the United States and its allies posed to Russia and by reminding them that he had restored Russia to greatness. According to the respected Levada polling organization, many Russians believe the annexation of Crimea forced the West to respect Russia, and more than 70 percent say that Russia has achieved superpower status. Russia now has the ability to project power well beyond its neighborhood, and it is venturing back into Latin America, Africa, and other places from which it withdrew after the Soviet collapse. Its return to Latin America has been particularly striking, with a focus on Cuba, Colombia, Mexico, Brazil, and Venezuela, where it continues to prop up the failing Maduro regime both economically and militarily.[3] Despite its economic weakness, and an economy smaller than Italy's (Russia's $1.3 trillion GDP as opposed to the United States' $18.6 trillion, and per capita income in 2017 of $11,440 as compared to the US's $ 53,528), its global influence is spreading.[4]

The Seven Pillars of Putin's World

The core driver of Putin's world is the quest to get the West to treat Russia as if it were the Soviet Union. A review of both his words and his actions suggests his foreign policy has been shaped by seven key propositions—a sort of bill of rights in Moscow's view—for Russia on the international stage. These are all designed to reverse the consequences of the Soviet collapse and renegotiate the end of the Cold War:

Firstly, he believes, Russia has a right to a seat at the table on all major international decisions and will insist on inclusion. The West should recognize that Russia belongs to the global board of directors.

Second, Russia's interests are as legitimate as those of the West, and it will press for the US and Europe to acknowledge and accept this fact of life even if they disagree with Russia.

Third, Russia has a right to a sphere of privileged interests in the post-Soviet space. It defines its vital security perimeter not as the borders of the Russian Federation but as the borders of the post-Soviet space. Russia will work to ensure that its former Soviet neighbors not join any alliances deemed hostile to Russia. Hence, Moscow will seek to guarantee that no Euro-Atlantic structures—primarily NATO and the EU—move any closer to Russia than they already are because they threaten Russia's vital interests.

Fourth, some states are more sovereign than others. Great powers like Russia, China, India, and the United States enjoy absolute sovereignty, meaning they are free to choose which alliances they join. Smaller countries, like Ukraine or Georgia, are not fully sovereign and Russia will insist that they respect its wishes. Russia does not seek allies in the Western sense of the word but mutually beneficial instrumental partnerships with countries, such as China, that do not restrict Russia's freedom to act or pass judgment on its internal situation.

Fifth, Russia will continue to present itself as a supporter of the status quo, an advocate of conservative values, an international power that respects established leaders. The West, according to the Kremlin, promotes chaos and regime change, as happened during the Arab Spring—without thinking through the consequences of its actions. (Of course, in its own sphere of privileged interests, Russia can act as a revisionist power and upend the status quo when it considers its interests threatened, as the annexation of Crimea and the invasion of Georgia and Ukraine show.)

Sixth, Russia believes its interests are best served by a fractured Western alliance; hence it will continue to support anti-American and Euroskeptic groups in Europe and populist movements on both sides of the Atlantic.

Finally, Russia will push to jettison the post–Cold War, liberal, rules-based international order driven by the US and Europe in favor of a post-West order. For Russia, this order would resemble the nineteenth-century concert of powers, with China, Russia, and the United States dividing the world into spheres of influence.

Putin can take satisfaction that he has been quite successful in achieving his goals. After Ukraine, the West unsuccessfully sought to isolate Russia. But Russia has deepening partnerships in various multilateral fora, such as BRICS and the Shanghai Cooperation Organization, and it works in them with China, India, Pakistan, Brazil, South Africa, Turkey, and Iran. The list of fifty-eight countries that abstained in 2014 from condemning Russia for its annexation of Crimea in the UN General Assembly reveals that a variety of countries—both democratic and nondemocratic—do not want to antagonize Russia or impose sanctions on it.

Yet in reality Putin's foreign policy record is decidedly mixed. His clashes with the West—caused by Russia's aggression against Ukraine, its support of a military campaign in Syria that ignores the humanitarian catastrophe there, its ongoing election interference in the US and Europe, and the poisonings in the UK—came at a significant cost and have further alienated the US and Europe. Moreover, the Ukrainian intervention has created a situation where there is no obvious way out for Russia, short of a total withdrawal, which so far Putin has refused to contemplate. And despite formally leading two of Eurasia's major multilateral organizations—the CSTO and EEU—Russia does not have real allies as the concept is understood in the West. Partners from China to Belarus may support Russia in the United Nations and other fora, but, as this book has shown, these partnerships are wary and partial. There are no countries with which Russia is allied where the partnership involves a set of shared values and a commitment to a common strategy in the way NATO or the EU do. Russia's partnerships are ad hoc and largely instrumental with limited common interests. Perhaps this is what Putin prefers, but the result is a Russia that operates in its own orbit, largely depending on its own resources, while seeking to exploit and benefit from the existing divisions within the West. And despite talk of a post-West order and the current global turmoil, there are few signs that anything resembling a new order is emerging.

Moreover, it is important to distinguish between appearances and reality in Russian foreign policy. For instance, despite the impressive show of military might in the 2018 Vostok military exercises with China, observers questioned what these troops and tanks were actually doing. Putin wanted the world to see the 300,000 troops and 36,000 armored vehicles on display and to raise concerns in the West, but the results of their maneuvers may have been less consequential than initial appearances might suggest. Similarly, leaders from the Middle East and elsewhere may travel to Russia and sign memoranda of understanding for multibillion-dollar projects, but it is unclear how many of these MOUs will actually be implemented. Putin's world is designed to project an external image of military might, forward movement, and economic dynamism. But the reality may well be different. The extravagant rhetoric and external shows of strength in Putin's world mask serious domestic weaknesses.

Domestic Realities in Putin's World

Foreign policy successes may have helped him win reelection, but the domestic reality of Putin's world is rather different, given the state of the economy, demographic decline, and questions about succession. In nearly two decades in power, Putin has successfully crafted an economic system whose main accomplishment has been the preservation of state power and authority and its projection abroad. From 2000 to 2008, when oil prices rose from $25 to as high as $147 a barrel, GDP grew at an average of 7 percent per year, and individual household incomes also rose after the doldrums of the late 1990s. Putin was a beneficiary of rising oil prices. The 2008 financial crisis hit Russia hard, but GDP growth recovered—until 2014. Since the onset of the Ukraine crisis, GDP growth has been sluggish, below 2 percent.

Putin's economic system may, however, prove inadequate for a Russia seeking to strengthen its international role. Although its economy recovered from the combined blows of falling oil prices and Western financial sanctions in 2014, Russia remains largely dependent on its revenues from oil and gas, which constitute 50 percent of its national budget. Putin has yet to implement economic reforms—from raising the retirement age to diversifying the economy away from oil and gas, supporting small- and medium-sized businesses, and modernizing the economy. These reforms have been recommended to him by a succession of advisers since the early 2000s, most importantly by the former finance minister Alexei Kudrin. It is unclear whether he will introduce these reforms in his fourth term. In 2005, Putin abandoned pension reform when senior citizens took to the streets to protest. In 2018 he also modified his subsequent attempt to raise the retirement age after protests, but he did raise it to age 60 for women and age 65 for men—in a country where average male life expectancy is 66.5 years and female life expectancy 77.[5] Economic reform could adversely affect the vested interests of many of the people and groups who support Putin in the patrimonial rent-seeking system that prevails in Russia. If there is no far-reaching structural modernizing reform, then Russia will increasingly lag behind many of its neighbors, including China. The Russian economy can and will continue to muddle through, but without all of the effective institutions of a modern state, and given the pervasiveness of corruption from the top to the bottom of society, Putin's Russia will perpetuate the historical pattern of projecting military might as the major source of its power and influence while it remains economically far behind many of its competitors.

The United States' April 2018 sanctions against twenty-four businessmen and officials close to Putin and twelve businesses have adversely affected the billionaires' domestic and international holdings. But the sanctions will, if anything, make them more dependent on the Kremlin's largesse, and their companies are more likely to be bailed out by the Kremlin and de facto nationalized. Western sanctions may impose penalties, but they also strengthen Putin's ability to increase state control over the economy.

Demographics are another major challenge. Despite a mini baby boom in recent years, the Russian population is declining, and life expectancy lags behind that of most industrialized countries. The figures for mortality among young men aged eighteen to thirty are particularly striking: they resemble those of sub-Saharan Africa rather than those of advanced industrial countries. This has significant implications for the future workforce and for military recruitment. However, while the Slavic birthrate is falling, Russia's Muslim population continues to enjoy high birthrates and by 2020 Muslims will constitute one-fifth of the population of the Russian Federation, potentially challenging the tenuous ethnic peace that Putin has promoted.[6] Many of the best and brightest young people have emigrated, and the brain drain shows no signs of abating. Moreover, a combination of neglect and systemic corruption has left Russia with a decaying physical infrastructure that requires concerted attention. The question is whether Putin will continue to replicate the pattern of the late Brezhnev era: domestic stagnation because reform is considered too destabilizing politically, combined with foreign policy activism that appeals to the population's patriotism, and renewed nationalism that antagonizes the West.

A key question for the future is succession. According to the Russian constitution, this is Putin's last term in office, and he is obliged to step down in 2024, by which time he will have been in power for one year less than was Stalin. Historically, there are several models for succession in a millennium of Russian history. The most common succession mechanism in the tsarist and Soviet times was death by natural causes. There were also several instances of death by unnatural causes, when tsars were assassinated. Rulers have also been overthrown in palace coups, in both the tsarist and Soviet times, when Khrushchev was ousted by his erstwhile comrades. Rulers have been overthrown by popular revolutions too, as in 1917. In the post-Soviet era, there have been only two managed transitions: when Boris Yeltsin chose Putin to succeed him and when Putin picked Medvedev—in the latter case, only to switch places with him four years later and return to the Kremlin.

Will Putin choose his successor again? Some Russians question whether he will indeed step down, arguing that he may remain in the Kremlin for the rest of his life. Immediately after his 2018 election, Margarita Simonyan, editor-in-chief of the state-controlled television station RT, tweeted enthusiastically to the West: "Earlier he was simply our president and it was possible to replace him. And now he is our leader. We won't let you change him."[7] She used the word *Vozhd* (leader) to refer to Putin—echoing the term used to describe Stalin. Will Putin take his cue from Xi Jinping and Nursultan Nazarbayev and have the Duma declare him president for life? He could also change the constitution to permit himself another term, or he could leave the Kremlin and assume the position of elder statesman similar to that of China's Deng Xiaoping, wielding power as the "Father of the Nation."

As Putin continues in his fourth term, uncertainty about succession has already prompted maneuvering among the political class, trying to anticipate what might happen and seeking to position themselves advantageously while ensuring they are not adversely affected by what might come next. Putin has surrounded himself with a group of young technocrats who owe their careers and advancement to him. If he decides to pick a successor, the next president could well come from this group, many of whom are now running regional governments but lack an independent political base. A former Kremlin spin doctor has argued that the 2018 election "marks the arrival of post-Putin Russia regardless of whether Putin remains the head of state for the next six or sixteen years."[8] If Putin were to groom and pick a successor, he would have to avoid being viewed as a lame duck in the run-up to his retirement in 2024. All of this heightens the uncertainty about succession and introduces a simmering instability into the system—and provides a new dimension to Russia in the world.

The Putin system has produced a succession dilemma: Russian elites depend on Putin's patronage to continue to own their assets and maintain their power, so any managed succession must involve a candidate who will guarantee that Putin and his inner circle will keep their assets and their personal freedom after he leaves the Kremlin. When Putin took over from Yeltsin, he promised that the Yeltsin family would not be prosecuted and could keep their assets. He honored that part of the bargain. But within three years of taking office, Putin took aim at some of Yeltsin's oligarchs, forcing some into exile, seizing their businesses, and in the case of Mikhail Khodorkovsky, sending him to prison for a decade. The individual who succeeds Putin might well honor any agreement they made with the president himself, but would Putin's oligarchs be safe? The process of choosing a successor to Putin could be fraught and unpredictable.

The Challenge to the West

How should the West respond to Putin's Russia going forward? Since Putin has been in power, the major Western governments and Japan have pursued their own resets with Russia, but so far all of these have ended in disappointment.

The West should begin by reviewing its flawed assumptions about what Russians wanted after 1991 and how economic integration would affect political ties. It should ask what has not worked well over the past quarter century and seek to understand why relations with Russia have not turned out the way many had assumed and hoped they would. After the Soviet collapse, many in the West believed that what had prevented the USSR and the West from developing productive relations was the communist ideology that officially guided Soviet domestic and foreign policy. It was thought that with the communist system relegated to the dustbin of history, to paraphrase Trotsky, Russia would embark on its difficult transition to a market-based, democratic society and a post-imperial foreign policy. Transition theories flourished, and Western economic and political advisers enthusiastically flocked to Russia to embark on democracy-promotion programs and to advise Russians on how to implement economic reforms and create a market. Without revisiting a discussion of what are catalogued as Western and Russian mistakes during the

1990s, suffice it to say that by the time Putin took over in 2000, many Russians believed these Western policies and programs had led to chaos, the impoverishment of many, and the enrichment of a few, and that the West had not made good on its earlier promises of meaningful financial aid. Perhaps no one could understand how massive was the task of creating a capitalist economy out of the rubble of seventy years of a state-controlled, centrally planned economy.

Yet, as Putin consolidated his rule, it became clear to much of the world that a main reason for Russians' rejection of Western-style economic and political programs was because they are Russians, not because they were communists. Seventy years ago, George Kennan understood that communist ideology reinforced and exacerbated, but did not contradict, the characteristics of traditional tsarist rule. Communism had been superimposed on centuries of Russian autocracy and personalistic rule, and had, if anything, strengthened those traditions. The ideology was a means to consolidate the Bolsheviks' rule, mobilize society, and, with great pain, drag Russian peasants into modernity. But it became increasingly subordinate to traditional nationalism and an expansionist foreign policy so that, by the time the USSR collapsed, few party members still believed in the tenets of Marxism-Leninism, but many were Russian nationalists with an imperial mindset. The minority who supported Gorbachev and Yeltsin, and believed that Russia should become more like the West both politically and economically, were outnumbered from the outset. No wonder Putin likes to stand next to statues of Prince Vladimir and Tsar Peter the Great. Putin represents traditional, collectivist, authoritarian Russian political culture and appeals to a sense of Russian exceptionalism, which defines itself in opposition to the West. Russians' understanding of their own unique history and of the drivers of global politics is very different from that of the West. That does not mean America and Europe cannot work with Russia, but it does suggest the West has to recognize what Russia is—and not what it would like Russia to be.

Another misapprehension was the assumption that Russia's economic integration with the West would have a moderating effect on its political behavior. This was, after all, the basis of the West's détente policy in the 1970s, that closer economic ties would promote more productive political relations. During the 1970s, détente worked for some years until the Soviets invaded Afghanistan, because the USSR understood that it needed to import Western technology and it was prepared to offer political quid pro quos. Détente produced a landmark arms control treaty, significantly improved political ties, and partially opened a window on the world for some Russians. In the early 1990s, Yeltsin supported a Western agenda in the Balkans because he sought Western economic assistance and political support for his reforms. The rather Marxist belief that economics can influence politics persists, particularly in Europe. Germany led the EU in launching a "partnership for modernization" with Russia in 2010, believing this would result in a "strategic partnership."[9] But Putin has sought to decouple Russia's economic from its political ties to the West. Although the EU program still exists on paper, Russia's annexation of Crimea and the war in the Donbas have effectively put it on hold. Attempts to promote economic and judicial reform and support for civil society have been uneven, leading some to term this a "partnership without modernization."

The West initially hoped Russia would become a responsible stakeholder in a post–Cold War, rules-based liberal international order it had created. But the Kremlin viewed this as an attempt by the United States, supported by its allies, to impose an agenda on Russia in which it had no agency and which was inimical to Russia's real interests. Putin is more interested in power and scale than in rules. The West may see the 1990s as a time of promise in Russia, of greater pluralism and the move toward a market society. Most Russians today, led by Putin, see it very differently—as a time of poverty, upheaval, chaos, combined with rising economic inequality and humiliation by the West. Putin frequently repeats this historical catalogue of complaints to his Western interlocutors.

Viewed historically, cooperation with Russia has been the exception rather than the rule, at least in US-Russia relations. When people talk about "normalizing" US ties to Russia, they mean achieving an equilibrium between cooperation and competition. There have been a few high points in US-Russia ties: the Grand Alliance during World War Two, and coordination and intelligence sharing after the 9/11 attacks in the Afghanistan War. In both these instances, despite tensions in the relationship, Russia was an enthusiastic partner because Washington and Moscow had identified a common enemy they sought to defeat, and the Kremlin believed the United States was treating it as an equal. But when the common enemy was defeated, the alliance fell apart. More narrow cooperation on arms control has worked too. There were also other moments of cooperation during German unification, the First Gulf War, and the Bosnian War. Apart from these instances, US-Russia relations have been characterized largely by mutual mistrust and suspicion. This is, at the best of times, a limited partnership in which cooperation coexists with competition and conflict.

Europe's relationship with Russia has historically been more complicated. The Germany-Russia relationship has been the most significant. The two countries were on opposite sides in two world wars, a divided Germany was at the heart of the Cold War in Europe, and mutual suspicions prevailed during the Cold War and beyond. Since the Soviet collapse, the relationship has been generally cooperative—until 2014. France and Russia also have enjoyed periods of alliance and cooperation, while Poland's relations with Russia have largely been antagonistic and UK-Russian relations currently the worst of any European country. Europe's inclination, since the Soviet collapse, has been to promote economic and political dialogue and cooperation, but these expectations have been severely challenged since the start of the Ukrainian crisis and Russia's subsequent election interference. The reality is that Russia is partially integrated into the global economy and a major exporter of oil and gas to Europe and, increasingly, to Asia. Whenever Russia takes actions that are considered inimical to the United States or Europe, sanctions are the first resort. But these have a limited impact on Russian actions. The Trump administration and the US Congress have ramped up sanctions on Russia, but so far Russia has doubled down, refusing to cease its cyber activities and challenging every Western claim about its culpability, be it in election interference, the MH-17 crash, Russian soldiers in the Donbas, or the Skripal poisonings. This constant Russian pushback is likely to remain as long as Putin is in the Kremlin.

For the rest of Putin's term in office, Russia will assert its interests in its neighborhood, insisting both that Western encroachments there threaten its core interests and that the West should accept these concerns as entirely legitimate. It will project power abroad where it can, taking advantage of the disarray in US foreign policy. Putin will continue to use television and other media to play on the enemy image of the United States and Europe to ensure his popularity and power at home and among pro-Russia groups in the West. Under these circumstances, America and its allies have a limited number of difficult choices in dealing with Russia.

What is to be Done?

Russia's size and strategic location, its nuclear weapons arsenal, its veto in the United Nations Security Council, and its endowments of vast natural resources—as well as its ability to thwart Western interests—necessitate engagement. Russia cannot be isolated because it has partnerships with many countries that refuse either to criticize Russia or sign on to sanctions and do not see Russia's actions in Ukraine as threatening to their own interests.

Moreover, two decades of US and European democracy promotion have not succeeded in creating a more democratic society or institutionalizing the rule of law. Indeed, the Kremlin sees these efforts as a cloak for "regime change." Under Putin, the Kremlin has steadily closed the space for political competition and has ejected US and British organizations seeking to support Russian civil society. The Kremlin has worked hard to immunize Russian society from Western influence through its state-run media, particularly Russian television.

Given these constraints, Trump's ambassador to Russia, Jon Huntsman, has argued for the need to focus on those aspects of the relationship that demand pragmatic engagement:

> Where [Russia] has a national interest, they will engage. And you have to be smart enough to identify areas where we both have overlapping interests. Where we have interests and they don't, they're just not going to waste their time. And neither should we.[10]

For the United States, the issues on which Washington and Moscow can engage are Syria, terrorism, Ukraine, and strategic stability—arms control and nonproliferation. It is a constant challenge to coordinate, let alone cooperate, on these issues, but nonengagement with Russia could lead to an even greater escalation in tensions. For Europe, whose economic and energy interdependence with Moscow necessitates sustained engagement, the Ukraine crisis is the key issue, both because it has destabilized Europe's periphery and because EU sanctions and Russian counter-sanctions have adversely affected European economies.

The continuing Ukraine crisis has highlighted an enduring problem in Russia's relations with the West: disagreement on the shape of Euro-Atlantic security architecture and Russia's insistence that the West renegotiate the concept of European security with Moscow. So far, the West has rejected Russian proposals because they would essentially render NATO obsolete. But since the Crimean annexation, two realities have become clear: the West will not risk military confrontation with Russia over its actions in the post-Soviet space, and as a result of these actions, further NATO or EU enlargement to post-Soviet countries is highly unlikely. Russia has thus achieved one of Putin's major foreign policy goals.

The challenge for the US and Europe is to remain united in the era of Brexit and Trump, and rising populism on both sides of the Atlantic. The revival of trade disputes will inevitably weaken the commitment to the transatlantic relationship. The unity the US and Germany forged after Crimea is fraying, although the transatlantic sanctions regime remains. The US and Europe should prioritize maintaining a strong, effective alliance in the face of Russian attempts to divide NATO and prevent a coordinated response to its actions. Washington should refrain from actions that seek to undermine the alliance.

In the absence of a broader agreement between Moscow and the West, Russia will continue to nurse its growing list of grievances against the US and Europe. The West's task for the rest of Putin's tenure is to exercise strategic patience while containing Russia's ability to disrupt transatlantic ties as it strengthens its defenses against Russian incursions. It must consistently and robustly push back against Russian interference in Western elections. But it must also be prepared for new challenges as Putin focuses on building up Russia's artificial intelligence capabilities and deploying its considerable cyber prowess. Yet the US and Europe also should be prepared to reengage more actively with Russia should the Kremlin step back from its current confrontational policies and moderate its anti-Western stance. Off-ramps should always be available, and the West should take the long view, not expecting significant change to occur in the short term.

Putin's Russia during the president's fourth term could also likely bring new challenges. The Russian leader has been known to change course unexpectedly and take actions that few anticipated because they do not take his words seriously enough when he telegraphs his intentions. Russia is predictable until it is not, and the West may well confront unexpected developments during the next few years. Putin's world is one in which Russia has returned to the global arena on all cylinders in pursuit of influence and acceptance. Putin's strategy—if that is indeed the appropriate term for policies that often involve a rapid and shrewd response to opportunities created by Western disarray or inaction—has enabled Russia to reappear on the world stage in unanticipated ways that will continue to challenge the world.

In the two decades that have seen the rise of Putin's world, several lessons have become clear. Isolating Russia and refusing to deal with it, however appealing that may appear to some, is not an option. On the other hand, pursuing "resets" intended to achieve qualitative improvements in ties to Putin's Russia is, for the foreseeable future, a fruitless quest. Engagement must be realistic and flexible. Engage on issues of mutual interest and be prepared to be more forward-looking if Russia moderates its behavior. It is also important to remember that the Kremlin does not speak for all Russian citizens. The West should encourage a wider dialogue with Russians wherever possible. Above all, it should be prepared for surprises in dealing with Russia and agile enough to respond to them, just as Putin's judo mastery has taught him how to prevail over an indecisive opponent. In Putin's world, it is prudent to expect the unexpected.

EPILOGUE

THE JUDOIST'S NEXT MOVES

Once again Putin surprised the world with an unexpected move. In March 2020—amid global turmoil created by the COVID-19 virus, crashing stock markets, and an oil price war between Russia and Saudi Arabia—he appeared at a Duma session devoted to discussing changes to the 1993 constitution. He had earlier proposed revisions to the constitution during his State of the Nation speech. Russians speculated on what his next move would be as a hastily assembled working group debated a variety of amendments. Putin was greeted by Duma member Valentina Tereshkova, veteran Soviet cosmonaut, the first woman to go into space, and "Hero of the Soviet Union," who stood next to Nikita Khrushchev on the Kremlin Wall in 1963 to celebrate her pioneering mission. Tereshkova proposed a daring idea: Putin's presidential clock, set to run out in 2024, should be reset to zero. That would allow him to run for another two terms, enabling him to stay in power until 2036. By that time, he would be one of Russia's longest-ruling leaders, in power ten years longer than Josef Stalin and seven years less than Peter the Great.

Putin found this agreeable. With all the international uncertainty, he explained to the Duma, his role was clear: "the guarantor of the country's security, domestic stability and evolutionary development," especially because Russia's enemies, both domestic and foreign, were "waiting for us to make a mistake or to slip up."

This unexpected and pre-emptive move had all the hallmarks of an inspired judo play, throwing his audience off-kilter and eliciting constant speculation about what Putin would do when his term ended in 2024. He had dangled various options before the Russian public only to propose the most radical of them all: staying in power until he was at least 83 years old, quashing any talk of a succession struggle or lame-duck presidency.

He had answered the question "After Putin, who?" It was Putin, and his world could be with us for a long time.

Historical Revisionism

While Putin was contemplating his succession moves, Russia was stepping up in its role as a global player, venturing into farther-flung parts of the world from which it had retreated after the Soviet collapse. And the ideological divide with the West became clearer as Putin made plans for the May 9, 2020, celebration of Victory Day in Red Square—75 years after the end of World War Two, a celebration that was eventually upended by the Coronavirus pandemic. The Kremlin's increasing embrace of a revisionist view of the origins of World War Two—one that glossed over the August 1939 Molotov-Ribbentrop Pact—tried to shift blame for the outbreak of the war to Poland, minimized the US role in defeating Hitler, and highlighted the USSR's role as the main victor.

In response, Russia and Europe presented two distinctively different narratives about 1939. The European Parliament adopted a resolution blaming both the USSR and Germany for the outbreak of the war. It highlighted the Molotov-Ribbentrop Pact, whose secret protocols divided Poland into German and Soviet spheres of influence. Two weeks after Germany invaded Western Poland in September 1939, the Red Army marched into and occupied Eastern Poland—territory that became Western Ukraine in the postwar settlement. Russia reacted furiously to the European Parliament's resolution, denying altogether that the USSR had invaded Eastern Poland: "The Red Army entered 'Polish territories'—Belarus and Ukraine—occupied by Warsaw since 1920."

Putin went on to criticize Poland's role in the war, citing historical documents that he said showed that Warsaw was complicit in the Nazi invasion of Czechoslovakia and therefore bore responsibility for the outbreak of World War Two. At the Valdai meeting in 2019, he described Stalin's regime as "a black page in the history of our country," but denied Stalin started World War Two.

Russia's history wars continue unabated. Amendments to the Russian constitution stipulate that no one can question Russia's "victorious role" in World War Two, and Putin's narrative surrounding it has become one of the cornerstones of Russia's claim to be a great power whose interests must be respected.

The outbreak of the Coronavirus pandemic in the winter and spring of 2020 initially appeared to vindicate Putin's role as a decisive leader of a strong state. It was, from the Kremlin's viewpoint, a testimony to the importance of the nation-state and an indictment of globalization, which had both facilitated the virus's spread and exposed the impotence of international organizations in seeking to control its growth. So Putin presented himself to his population as the only leader who could save them in this dark time of the new plague while Europe and the United States dithered and were unprepared. In an interview with the *Financial Times* some months before, Putin declared that "the liberal idea has become obsolete." The West's inadequate response to COVID-19 seemed to prove his point. But as the pandemic spread to Russia, increasingly draconian measures had to be taken, and Russia itself faced the same challenges in containing the virus as the West.

Russia and the Fractured West

Russia's ties to the West are becoming more differentiated. In Europe, Poland, the Baltic states, and the United Kingdom, those in power remained staunchly critical of Russia and opposed to lifting EU sanctions in the absence of any progress on the war in Ukraine. But many other European countries have become skeptical about the wisdom of pursuing antagonistic ties to Russia at a time when there is doubt about the United States' commitment to its allies. Ukraine seems unable to deal with its fractious domestic politics, and internal corruption has stymied reform. The new president, comedian-turned-politician Volodymyr Zelensky, has so far found it very difficult to change the paradigm. Many EU countries are suffering "Ukraine fatigue," concerned about US policies and weary of perpetually confrontational ties to Russia, and are increasingly questioning the need for maintaining sanctions against Russia and arguing for an improvement in ties.

Foremost among those championing a reset with Russia is French president Emmanuel Macron, who seized the opportunity to take over the leadership in EU-Russia policy as Angela Merkel's departure from the Chancellery in 2021 loomed. Declaring NATO "brain-dead" and EU-Russia policy bankrupt, Macron insisted that Europe's Russia policy needed to be fundamentally rethought. Blaming Europe for not sufficiently taking Russia's interests into account in the 1990s as NATO enlarged, he called for a new engagement with Moscow. Despite Russia's ongoing war with Ukraine, he revived the two-plus-two meetings of the French and Russian Foreign and Defense Ministers, cut off after 2014. His call for improved ties with Russia has found receptive ears in many parts of Europe, including those Germans who believed that Merkel's policies were too harsh.

From the Kremlin's point of view, Putin's strategy appears to be paying off. Following the annexation of Crimea and the launch of the war in the Donbas, he calculated that there would be initial European outrage, including the imposition of sanctions. But, if history were any guide, Europeans eventually would tire of tension with Russia and, given the challenge of dealing with an American president who constantly attacks the EU and NATO, working with the more predictable—if aggressive—Putin appears to be an acceptable option.

US-Russian relations remained adversarial, despite Donald Trump's continuing commitment to improving them. Russia became an even more toxic subject domestically following the "Ukraine-gate" investigations and the impeachment of President Trump. A government Whistleblower claimed that Trump, in a call with President Zelensky, urged him to investigate Hunter Biden and Burisma, a Ukrainian gas company on whose board he had sat. Hunter Biden is the son of former vice president Joe Biden, Trump's Democratic opponent in the 2020 election. Trump, according to the Whistleblower, had linked the delivery of the next tranche of US weapons to assist Ukraine in its war with Russia, to Zelensky's willingness to pursue an investigation into whether Burisma—and Biden—had been engaged in corruption.

The claim that Trump and his lawyer Rudy Giuliani had been pursuing a back channel to Ukraine—as part of his re-election campaign—that was at odds with the official State Department policy and unknown to the rest of the administration led to hearings in the House of Representatives, which voted to impeach Trump. He was acquitted by the Republican-controlled Senate, but not before some of the most respected State Department officials—and Trump's former senior adviser on Russia, Fiona Hill—had testified to the inappropriateness of a parallel channel operating out of the White House in secret, conveying the very opposite message on corruption to the Ukrainians than that of the State Department and the top National Security Council officials. In fact, Hill testified that Russian disinformation about what was happening in Ukraine had contributed to the White House's critical view of Ukraine and its new president.

Meanwhile, Congress continued to impose sanctions on Russia. Most notably, it stopped the construction of the $11 billion Nord Stream II gas pipeline built to bring Russian natural gas under the Baltic Sea directly to Germany, bypassing Ukraine. It sanctioned a Swiss company, which was laying the final section of the pipeline. The Swiss company complied with the sanctions, forcing it to halt construction weeks before the pipeline was to be completed. This left Gazprom itself to complete the pipeline, but some time in the future. Sanctions were also imposed on two Rosneft trading arms because they were exporting Venezuelan oil. More sanctions were threatened were Russia to interfere in the 2020 US election. The end of arms control loomed ahead as the Trump administration made little effort to extend the New START treaty that limits strategic nuclear weapons, despite Russian willingness to do so.

Although both Trump and Putin continued to praise each other, the substance of the US-Russian relationship remained highly constrained. Pursuing productive ties with the United States ranks low in the priorities of Putin's world, nor will they rise in priority for the foreseeable future.

Russia and the Rest

While relations with the West remained brittle, Russia's ties to the Rest continued to expand—and nowhere more so than with China, which has become an even more indispensable partner. When asked why Russia was putting all its eggs in the Chinese basket, Putin replied succinctly: "We have many eggs but few baskets to put them in." So there were more joint military exercises on land and in the air. Putin also announced that Russia was helping China construct an anti-missile system. Cooperation in the cyber area and AI is increasing, and bilateral trade continues to grow. Faced with protests in Hong Kong and Moscow in the summer of 2019, China and Russia announced that they were cooperating to combat these expressions of popular unrest which, they claimed, were initiated and supported by the United States.

When the COVID-19 pandemic began, Russia took strong measures early on to close its long border with China and prevent Chinese citizens from entering the country. But, as the virus spread, the two countries agreed to cooperate in dealing with it.

As America's relationship with China became increasingly antagonistic, some argued that the United States should "peel" Russia away from China and get Washington and Moscow to work together to "contain" China. But these arguments ignore a fundamental reality: Those who believe that Russia would be willing to distance itself from China and align itself with Washington against Beijing underestimate the extent to which China's unequivocal support of Russia's domestic system is an existential issue for the Putin regime. Putin gives every sign that he continues to be convinced that some in the United States remain committed to regime change in Russia. Moreover, the steps that the US would have to take in order to improve ties substantially with Russia—such as lifting sanctions, recognizing Russia's sphere of influence in the post-Soviet space, agreeing that Ukraine will never join NATO, and accepting the annexation of Crimea—would be unacceptable domestically. And there remains the widespread conviction that Russia will continue to interfere in American elections. It's highly unlikely that Russia will rethink its partnership with China for the foreseeable future—one of the great successes of Putin's world.

With the partial US withdrawal from Syria, Russia's role both in Syria and more broadly in the Middle East has come under new scrutiny. Russian military personnel celebrated as they occupied a former US air base in Northern Syria after the US pulled out. Moscow's main focus continued to be supporting the Assad regime as it sought to end the civil war and take control of the rest of the country. This led to an intense battle around the province of Idlib which has produced many casualties and nearly a million new refugees. The Putin-Erdogan relationship was repeatedly put to the test as they supported different sides in this long and deadly conflict.

The Russian-Saudi relationship ran into new challenges. In March 2020, Russia concluded that it would agree to extend an existing OPEC/non-OPEC agreement limiting oil production. But the Saudis insisted on further sharp cuts in production in order to support higher prices; Russia did not agree. It appeared that Rosneft CEO Igor Sechin, who had never approved of the cooperation with OPEC to limit production, had won the day. In retaliation, the Saudis flooded the market, driving the price of oil further down and putting new stress on the Russian economy, as the ruble fell in value. This battle for market share was overwhelmed by the unprecedented drop in global oil demand and plummeting prices that came with the Coronavirus that hit all oil exporters, including Russia and Saudi Arabia. But Russia was better prepared to deal with this market challenge than many initially thought. Moreover, the political and security aspects of the Saudi-Russian relationship, which both Putin and Mohammad Bin-Salman have carefully cultivated, are likely to endure and give ballast to the volatile oil partnership.

Putin's world is still growing, as Russia returns to parts of the world from which it withdrew after the Soviet collapse. Russia held its first ever Africa summit in Sochi, attended by forty-three heads of state. Putin offered nuclear power plants, fighter jets, missile defense systems, and energy deals to African leaders, and many memoranda of understanding were signed—although it remains to be seen how many of these deals will actually be implemented. The Wagner Group has been operating for some time in the Central African Republic and Libya and continues to expand its presence in Africa and beyond. From the African point of view—and especially for those countries who remember how the Soviet Union supported them in their anti-colonial struggle—Russia's return was a welcome alternative to growing Chinese economic predominance in the continent and a waning US presence. For Putin, Africa offers another venue for Russia to project its political and economic clout.

Putin's project for a global Russia also extends to the United States' backyard. After all, in Putin's eyes, if the United States can interfere in Georgia and Ukraine, why shouldn't Russia become involved in the US sphere of influence? The most contentious area was Venezuela. Russia had supported the leftist strongman Hugo Chavez, and Rosneft had developed close energy ties with Venezuela's state oil company PDVSA. In 2008, Venezuela was one of a handful of countries to recognize the independence of Abkhazia and South Ossetia. After Chavez's death, his successor Nicolas Maduro presided over an increasingly dysfunctional and impoverished state. Following a disputed election, his opponent Juan Guaido was declared president by the National Assembly and recognized as such by the United States, most of the EU, and most of the countries in the Western Hemisphere. Maduro considered leaving for Cuba, but Russia persuaded him to remain in power. The Russian military and the

Wagner Group provide logistical support to the regime. A failed bid by Guaido and his followers to oust Maduro has increased Russian leverage in Venezuela.

2036 AND BEYOND

Russia's constitutional changes could mean that Putin will preside over this world until 2036. He will undoubtedly keep people guessing about his intentions until close to the end of his fourth presidential term in 2024. If he does indeed remain in power for another twelve years after that, will Russia continue to be against the West and with the Rest? That will largely depend not so much on what Russia does—because Putin is unlikely to radically change course—but whether Europe and the United States continue to improve their ties to Russia, making progress in resolving the Ukraine crisis and, of considerable importance, countering its cyber interference. As long as these issues remain on the table, relations are likely to remain difficult. But attitudes in the West may well change, particularly if, after contentious debates, some in Europe push to normalize or reset relations with Russia. It could well split over this issue and the sanctions be removed.

What happens in the United States will also affect how Europe interacts with Russia. If the next American president continues to criticize Europe and question the need for a transatlantic alliance, then European outreach to Russia may accelerate. But if the next president seeks to restore better relations with Europe, then the pace of EU outreach to Russia could slow. Europe's relationship with Russia will also be affected by how the next US president decides to deal with Russia and whether Russia's toxicity as a domestic American issue diminishes. An administration which returns to nuclear arms control and restores some channels of communication with Russia could join with Europe in engaging more systematically with Moscow on issues of mutual interest while continuing to push back against Russian malign activities.

The Coronavirus casts a shadow over all of these questions. The world will not be the same after the pandemic is over, but no one can say how different it will look. COVID has already provoked debate about the future of both Putin and his world as the virus continues its lethal spread through all of Russia's regions, raising questions about the Kremlin's handling of the outbreak in a country with an already weak public health system. Putin reluctantly had to postpone the Victory Day celebrations for the seventy-fifth anniversary of the end of World War Two, which would have brought world leaders to Moscow for the large military parade. Instead of presiding over a grand celebration in Red Square showcasing Russia's latest weapons, he appeared alone at the Tomb of the Unknown Soldier, placed a bouquet of red roses in front of the eternal flame, and knelt in front of the flame in silent meditation. He then gave a short, somber speech praising the Soviet people's heroism and sacrifices. He also had no choice but to postpone the April referendum that would have given him another two terms in office, injecting new uncertainty into the succession issue. For now, plans that could prolong his time in the Kremlin are on hold amid questions about the longer-term economic impact of the pandemic and the collapse of oil prices on Russia itself and on his continuing ambition to project Russia as a great power.

What if Putin decides against the 2036 option and leaves office in 2024? Will Vladimir Putin's world survive its creator? While Putin has certainly fashioned a world that bears his personal imprint, what he represents are centuries of Russian traditions—belief in a strong leader and a powerful state; conviction that Russia, as a great power, has a right to a sphere of influence in its backyard; suspicion of and antipathy toward the West and its individualistic and liberal values; and a belief in the individuality and superiority of Russian civilization. Another leader might pursue a less confrontational policy toward the West. But, if history is any guide, Russia will remain a global competitor with its unique values and worldview, one that will continue to challenge the West and find a positive reception in much of the Rest.

ACKNOWLEDGMENTS

This book represents the culmination of decades of thinking, writing, and teaching about Russian foreign policy and participating directly in the policy process—and traveling to Russia and its neighborhood frequently. When I began working in this field, the USSR was a superpower under geriatric leadership and soon destined to begin its decline. Mikhail Gorbachev ushered in an era of liberalization, reform—and hope. But the USSR was ultimately unreformable and collapsed because of its own internal weakness, leaving the new Russia to redefine its diminished role in the world. The Yeltsin decade was again one of reform and hope—but also one of disorder and poverty. When Vladimir Putin, the young, relatively unknown ex-KGB officer, entered the Kremlin in 2000, he promised to bring order to the country by restoring a strong state and reasserting Russia's role as a great power. This book is about how Putin has restored Russia on the global stage, the role Russia plays today, and what it means for the United States, Europe, China, the Middle East, and other countries—and for the future. At the same time, history also shapes Russia's relations, whether "against the West" or "with the rest," and I try to place this story in that larger context.

My work on Russian foreign policy has been informed both by my research as an academic and by two stints in the US government. I worked in the State Department's Office of Policy Planning just as Vladimir Putin was beginning to consolidate power. My second stint came as National Intelligence Officer for Russia and Eurasia at the National Intelligence Council when Putin was already asserting his ambitions for Russia as a great power. I thank my government colleagues for their insights into Russian foreign policy over the years and for our continuing dialogues.

Georgetown University has been my academic home for many years, providing a collegial and rigorous atmosphere for research and teaching. I would like to thank the leadership of Georgetown University—its president, John J. DeGioia, and Joel Hellman, dean of the School of Foreign Service, for providing a supportive environment for policy-relevant academic research. I thank my colleague Dr. Michael David-Fox for taking over the directorship of the Center for Eurasian, Russian and East European Studies while I was on sabbatical writing this book. I am grateful to the excellent and collegial staff of the Center for their commitment to our M.A. program and for organizing events and discussions around the theme of my book—Benjamin Loring, Sarah Radomsky, and Allie Vreeman. Special thanks to my Georgetown colleague Andrew Kuchins with whom I frequently discuss these issues. I also thank my colleague and Department Chair Charles King for his support of my work. And I am grateful to the many Georgetown students for our bracing discussions in and out of the classroom—many of whom, I take pride in noting, are now involved professionally with Russia in both public service and in the private sector.

I am grateful to those individuals and organizations who supported the research for this book. The German Marshall Fund's Transatlantic Academy and its director Steven Szabo provided a congenial and stimulating environment for me during my sabbatical when the six fellows there worked on a project on Russia and the West. Our debates were intense and sometimes contentious as we argued over Russia's intentions and the West's response. I would also like to thank Deana Arsenian and the Carnegie Corporation of New York for their support for the work of CERES, its faculty and students, and for their continued commitment to the importance of Russian-American relations and their support for that work.

I am grateful to the Brookings Institution and its former president Strobe Talbott, a distinguished "Russia Hand," for providing me with the opportunity to be a non-resident Senior Fellow and co-chair its monthly and informative Hewett Forum on Russian and Eurasian affairs, which brings together leading members of both the policy and academic communities. My thanks to Steven Pifer and Alina Poliakova for being my co-chairs.

I thank my colleagues with whom I have discussed these issues over the years: Horton Beebe-Center, John Beyrle, James Collins, Toby Gati, Fiona Hill, Jeffrey Mankoff, Eugene Rumer, Daniel Russell, and Steven Weisman.

Special thanks go to those who read all or part of this manuscript and gave me excellent comments: Thane Gustafson, Bobo Lo, Robert Nurick, Strobe Talbott, Nina Tumarkin, Daniel Yergin, and Rebecca Yergin.

I am grateful to Paula Ganga, Rianna Jansen, and Anna Bar for their excellent work as research assistants. Thanks also to Matt Sagers, head of the Russian and Caspian Energy Service at IHSMarkit, and to the staff at IHSMarkit in Moscow, led by Irina Zamarina, for their assistance on my frequent research trips to Moscow. The biannual RAND US-Russia Business Forum and its chair William Courtney also provided an instructive venue for discussing relations with Russia in Moscow, New York, and Washington.

Special appreciation goes to Sean Desmond, my outstanding editor at Twelve, for his encouragement and advice. He is indeed a gifted editor who has made this a better book. The idea for the book emerged after a dinner with Deborah Futter, formerly of Twelve books. I owe her a debt of gratitude for conspiring with my excellent agent Suzanne Gluck to sign me up to do the book. Thanks also to Rachel Kambury at Twelve and to Ruth Mandel for ingeniously finding the photographs.

I have benefited from conversations with senior officials from the United States, Russia, Europe, Asia, and Central Asia. I thank them all for their insights into the making of *Putin's World*.

I also want to acknowledge the enduring influence of my mentor and thesis adviser Adam Ulam, whose pioneering work on Soviet foreign policy inspired me to go into this field and whose judicious skepticism always provided a reality check.

My understanding of the views of the Russian leadership—and of Vladimir Putin himself—has been enhanced by my participation in the Valdai International Discussion Club, whose annual meetings I have attended for the past fifteen years. They have provided a unique opportunity to listen to the perspectives of Russian colleagues, policymakers, and opinion leaders—as those messages have changed over time. In these conferences, we have met with Putin for several hours each year, both in plenary sessions and in smaller, private settings, discussing Russian domestic and foreign policy.

Special thanks go to my family, which has encouraged me during the writing of the book. My children—Rebecca and Alexander, and Alex's wife, Jessica—always give me fresh insights and good-humoredly challenge my assumptions. My greatest debt goes to my husband, Daniel Yergin, my most enthusiastic supporter—and toughest critic. He read several drafts of the manuscript and brought his acute insights and formidable editing skills to improve the manuscript and encourage me to aim for the best. His love and support, and that of my children, have sustained me throughout the years.

NOTES

Introduction

1. "Putin Says World Cup Has Broken Stereotypes About Russia," Reuters, July 6, 2018, https://www.reuters.com/article/us-soccer-worldcup-putin-fifa/putin-says-world-cup-has-broken-stereotypes-about-russia-idUSKBN1JW1IO.
2. Gideon Rachman, "Russia 'Mood Swing' Points to Trouble for Putin," *Financial Times,* August 8, 2018, https://www.ft.com/content/15f4d8f2-9a32-11e8-9702-5946bae86e6d.
3. Julian Borger, "Barack Obama: Russia is a regional power showing weakness over Ukraine," *The Guardian*, March 24, 2015, https://www.theguardian.com/world/2014/mar/25/barack-obama-russia-regional-power-ukraine-weakness.
4. Jeffrey Taylor, "Russia Is Finished," *The Atlantic,* May 2001, https://www.theatlantic.com/magazine/archive/2001/05/russia-is-finished/302220/.
5. Steven Lee Myers, *The New Tsar* (New York: Alfred A. Knopf, 2015), 16; *Vechernyi Leningrad*, May 4, 1976.
6. George F. Kennan, *Russia and the West under Lenin and Stalin* (New York: Mentor Books, 1961), 367–68.

Chapter One: The Weight of the Past

1. "Full Text of Putin's Speech on Crimea," *Prague Post,* March 19, 2014, http://praguepost.com/eu-news/37854-full-text-of-putin-s-speech-on-crimea.
2. "Foreign Minister Sergey Lavrov's Remarks and Replies to Questions at the Russian Terra Scientia Educational Youth Forum on Klyazma Rover, Dvoriki, Vladimir Region, August 24, 2015," Ministry of Foreign Affairs of the Russian Federation, MID speech no. 1595-24-08-2015, http://www.mid.ru/en/foreign_policy/news/-/asset_publisher/cKNonkJE02Bw/content/id/1680936.
3. "Meeting of the Valdai International Discussion Club," President of Russia website, October 24, 2014, http://en.kremlin.ru/events/president/news/46860.
4. Many non-Russians living in Crimea—Ukrainians and Crimean Tatars—were effectively disenfranchised and unable to vote in the referendum.
5. Adam B. Ulam, *Expansion and Coexistence: Soviet Policy 1917–73,* 2nd ed. (New York: Praeger, 1974).

6. "It is extremely dangerous to encourage people to see themselves as exceptional, whatever the motivation" was Putin's advice to the United States in a *New York Times* op-ed. Vladimir Putin, "A Plea for Caution," op-ed, *New York Times,* September 11, 2013, http://www.nytimes.com/2013/09/12/opinion/putin-plea-for-caution-from-russia-on-syria.html?_r=0.
7. For the original announcement of the pact and its subsequent justification, see "Sovetsko-Germanskii Dogovor o Nenapadenie," *Pravda,* August 24, 1939, and "Sovetskaya Politika Mira I Druzhby Narodom," *Pravda,* September 30, 1939.
8. "Putin Polozhitel'no Otsenil Pakt Molotova-Ribbentropa," *Politika,* May 10, 2015.
9. There is no consensus among historians about how many Soviet citizens died in the purges, but two major figures, Robert Conquest and Alexander Yakovlev, agree on this figure.
10. Bill Keller, "Major Soviet Paper Says 20 Million Died as Victims of Stalin," *New York Times,* February 4, 1989, https://www.nytimes.com/1989/02/04/world/major-soviet-paper-says-20-million-died-as-victims-of-stalin.html.
11. "Putin Accuses Russia's Foes Of 'Excessive Demonization' Of Stalin," Radio Free Europe/Radio Liberty, https://www.rferl.org/a/russia-putin-decries-excessive-demonization-stalin/28559464.html.
12. Dominic Lieven, introduction to *Restless Empire: A Historical Atlas of Russia,* by Ian Barnes (Cambridge, MA: Harvard University Press, 2015), 1–5.
13. Fiona Hill and Clifford G. Gaddy, *The Siberian Curse: How Communist Planners Left Russia Out in the Cold* (Washington, DC: Brookings Institution Press, 2003).
14. Marshall Poe, *The Russian Moment in World History* (Princeton, NJ: Princeton University Press, 2003), xii.
15. "SSHA Postavili Zadachu Unichtozhit' Rossiiu," *Putin News,* https://putin-news.ru/3348-ssha-postavili-zadachu-unichtozhit-rossiyu.html.

Chapter Two: The Russian Idea

1. Kirk Bennett, "The Myth of Russia's Containment," *American Interest,* December 21, 2015, https://www.the-american-interest.com/2015/12/21/the-myth-of-russias-containment/.
2. "Interview, Mikhail Gorbachev: The Impetus for Change in the Soviet Union," transcript, *Commanding Heights,* PBS, April 23, 2001, http://www.pbs.org/wgbh/commandingheights/shared/minitext/int_mikhailgorbachev.html.
3. Neil Hauer, "Putin's Plan to Russify the Caucasus," *Foreign Affairs,* August 1, 2018, https://www.foreignaffairs.com/articles/russia-fsu/2018-08-01/putins-plan-russify-caucasus?cid=nlc-fa_fatoday-20180801.
4. Timothy J. Colton, *Yeltsin: A Life* (New York: Basic Books, 2008), 389–90.
5. Tim McDaniel, *The Agony of the Russian Idea* (Princeton, NJ: Princeton University Press, 1996), 11.
6. Edward L. Keenan, "Muscovite Political Folkways," *Russian Review* 45, no. 2 (1986): 115–81.

7. Cited in *Mr. Putin: Operative in the Kremlin,* by Fiona Hill and Clifford G. Gaddy (Washington, DC: Brookings Institution Press, 2015), 17.
8. Angela E. Stent, "Reluctant Europeans: Three Centuries of Russian Ambivalence Toward the West," in *Russian Foreign Policy in the Twenty-First Century and the Shadow of the Past,* ed. Robert Legvold (New York: Columbia University Press, 2007).
9. Astolphe de Custine, *Empire of the Czar: A Journey Through Eternal Russia,* translation of *La Russie en 1839* (New York: Doubleday, 1989), 619.
10. https://collections.dartmouth.edu/teitexts/arctica/diplomatic/EA15-39-diplomatic.htm.
11. Marshall Poe, *The Russian Moment in World History* (Princeton, NJ: Princeton University Press, 2003), 82.
12. The Communist Manifesto, https://www.marxists.org/archive/marx/works/1848/communist-manifesto/ch02.htm.
13. V. Orlov, "Evraziistvo: V Chem Sut'?" *Obchestvo I Eknomika,* September 1, 2001.
14. Marlene Laruelle, *Russian Eurasianism: An Ideology of Empire* (Washington, DC: Woodrow Wilson International Center for Scholars, 2008).
15. McDaniel, *The Agony of the Russian Idea,* 10.
16. Quoted in Angela E. Stent, *Russia and Germany Reborn: Unification, the Soviet Collapse, and the New Europe* (Princeton, NJ: Princeton University Press, 1999), 188.
17. "Interesi Rossii I Vneshnaia Politika. Andrei Kozyrev: K Slovu Patriotizm Prilagatel'nie ne Nuzhni," *Krasnaya Zvezda,* November 20, 1992.
18. "Evgenii Primakov o Vneshnei Politike Rossii v Novom Godu," *Krasnaia Zvezda,* October 1, 1997.
19. Fiona Hill, "In Search of Great Russia: Elites, Ideas, Power, the State, and the Pre-Revolutionary Past in the New Russia, 1991–1996" (unpublished PhD diss., Harvard University, 1998).
20. Mark MacKinnon, "Sergey Karaganov: The Man Behind Putin's Pugnacity," *Globe and Mail,* March 20, 2014, https://www.theglobeandmail.com/news/world/sergey-karaganov-the-man-behind-putins-pugnacity/article17734125/.
21. Bobo Lo, *Russian Foreign Policy in the Post-Soviet Era* (London: Palgrave Macmillan, 2002), 52.
22. "Meeting of the Valdai International Discussion Club," President of Russia website, September 19, 2013, http://en.kremlin.ru/events/president/news/19243.
23. "Vladimir Putin Prinial Uchastii v Plenarnom Zasedanii Iubilneinoi Sessii Generalnoi Assemblii OON v Niu Yorki," President of Russia website, September 28, 2015, http://kremlin.ru/events/president/news/50385.
24. Angela Stent, *Russia and Germany Reborn,* 21–26.
25. Mr. X [George F. Kennan], "The Sources of Soviet Conduct," *Foreign Affairs,* July 1947, https://www.foreignaffairs.com/articles/russian-federation/1947-07-01/sources-soviet-conduct.
26. Jonathan Steele, "Putin Warns of Security Backlash," *The Guardian,* September 5, 2004, https://www.theguardian.com/world/2004/sep/06/chechnya.russia2.

27. Peter Pomerantsev, "The Hidden Author of Putinism," *The Atlantic,* November 7, 2014, https://www.theatlantic.com/international/archive/2014/11/hidden-author-putinism-russia-vladislav-surkov/382489/.
28. Michael McFaul, *From Cold War to Hot Peace: An American Ambassador in Putin's Russia* (Boston: Houghton Mifflin, 2018).
29. "Transcript of the Inauguration of Vladimir Putin as President of Russia," President of Russia website, May 7, 2004, http://en.kremlin.ru/events/president/transcripts/48210.

Chapter Three: Ambivalent Europeans

1. *Pravda,* December 19, 1984.
2. "Vladimir Putin, interview to the Italian newspaper 'Il Corriere della Sera,'" *Corriere della Sera,* June 7, 2015, https://www.corriere.it/english/15_giugno_07/vladimir-putin-interview-to-the-italian-newspaper-corriere-sera-44c5a66c-0d12-11e5-8612-1eda5b996824.shtml?refresh_ce-cp.
3. Edward H. Carr, "Russia and Europe as a Theme of Russian History," in *Essays Presented to Sir Lewis Namier,* ed. Richard Pares and Alan John Percivale Taylor (London: St. Martin's Press, 1956), 385.
4. Angela E. Stent, "Reluctant Europeans: Three Centuries of Russian Ambivalence Toward the West," chap. 7 in *Russian Foreign Policy in the Twenty-First Century and the Shadow of the Past,* ed. Robert Legvold (New York: Columbia University Press, 2007).
5. Simon Sebag Montefiore, *The Romanovs 1613–1918* (New York: Alfred A. Knopf, 2016), 86.
6. "Vistuplenie M. S. Gorbacheva v Britanskom Parlamente," *Izvestiia,* December 18, 1984.
7. Address given by Mikhail Gorbachev to the Council of Europe, July 6, 1989, https://www.cvce.eu/content/publication/2002/9/20/4c021687-98f9-4727-9e8b-836e0bc1f6fb/publishable_en.pdf.
8. "U.S.: Rumsfeld's 'Old' And 'New' Europe Touches On Uneasy Divide," Radio Free Europe/Radio Liberty, January 24, 2003, https://www.rferl.org/a/1102012.html.
9. Susan Stewart, *Russland und der Europarat* (Berlin: Stiftung Wissenschaft und Politik, 2013), 7.
10. Council of Europe website, "Who We Are," https://www.coe.int/en/web/about-us/who-we-are.
11. William E. Pomeranz, "Uneasy Partners: Russia and the European Court of Human Rights," *Human Rights Brief* 19, no. 3 (2012): 17–21, http://digitalcommons.wcl.american.edu/hrbrief/vol19/iss3/3/.
12. "Russia Tests Council of Europe in Push to Regain Vote," *Financial Times,* November 26, 2017, https://www.ft.com/content/3cccaf92-d12c-11e7-b781-794ce08b24dc.

13. Adam Davy, "Pussy Riot Protesters Jailed for World Cup Final Pitch Invasion," *Moscow Times*, July 17, 2018, https://themoscowtimes.com/news/pussy-riot-protesters-jailed-world-cup-final-pitch-invasion-62267.
14. Michael Emerson, "EU-Russia: Four Common Spaces and the Proliferation of the Fuzzy," Opinions, EurActiv, May 24, 2005, https://www.euractiv.com/section/global-europe/opinion/eu-russia-four-common-spaces-and-the-proliferation-of-the-fuzzy/.
15. "Soglashenie ob Assotsiatsii Mezhdu Ukrainoi i ES," June 27, 2014, https://ria.ru/spravka/20140627/1013902739.html.
16. Press and Information Team of the Delegation to Russia, "The European Union and the Russian Federation," European External Access Service, November 21, 2017, https://eeas.europa.eu/headquarters/headquarters-homepage/35939/european-union-and-russian-federation_en.
17. European Parliamentary Research Service (EPRS), *EU-Russia Trade*, PE 557.023 (Brussels: May 2015); and EPRS, *Economic Impact on the EU of Sanctions over Ukraine Conflict*, PE 569.020 (Brussels: October 2015).
18. Péter Krekó, Marie Macaulay, Csaba Molnár, Lóránt Győri, "Europe's New Pro-Putin Coalition: The Parties of 'No,'" Institute of Modern Russia, August 3, 2105, https://imrussia.org/en/analysis/world/2368-europes-new-pro-putin-coalition-the-parties-of-no.
19. Luke Harding, "We Should Beware Russia's Links with Europe's Right," *The Guardian*, December 8, 2014, https://www.theguardian.com/commentisfree/2014/dec/08/russia-europe-right-putin-front-national-eu.
20. "Marine Le Pen's Party Asks Russia for €27 Million Loan," *Moscow Times*, February 19, 2016, https://themoscowtimes.com/news/marine-le-pens-party-asks-russia-for-27-million-loan-51896.
21. David D. Kirkpatrick and Matthew Rosenberg, "Russians Offered Business Deals to Brexit's Biggest Backer," *New York Times*, June 29, 2018, https://www.nytimes.com/2018/06/29/world/europe/russia-britain-brexit-arron-banks.html.
22. Nico Hines and Pierre Vaux, "Why Putin Is Meddling in Britain's Brexit Vote," *Daily Beast*, June 8, 2016, http://www.thedailybeast.com/articles/2016/06/08/why-putin-is-meddling-in-britain-s-brexit-vote.html; and T. Bordachev, J. A. Goldstone, A. Braun, and D. Elkin, "Russia and the Europe of the Future," in *Is Europe Unraveling?*, Russia Direct report no. 29 (July 2016), http://www.russia-direct.org/catalog/product/russia-direct-report-europe-unraveling.
23. Harriet Agerholm, "New UKIP Leader Diane James Names Thatcher, Churchill, and Putin as Her Political Heroes," *Independent*, September 18, 2016, http://www.independent.co.uk/news/uk/politics/ukip-leader-diane-james-names-thatcher-churchill-and-putin-political-heroes-a7314946.html.
24. "Russian, European Far-Right Parties Converge in St. Petersburg," *Moscow Times*, March 22, 2015, https://themoscowtimes.com/articles/russian-european-far-right-parties-converge-in-st-petersburg-45010.

25. "Front Soprotivleniia Vashingtonskim Upyriiam," *Gazeta,* September 20, 2015, https://www.gazeta.ru/politics/2015/09/20_a_7767635.shtml.
26. Alec Luhn, "Russia Funds Moscow Conference for US, EU, Ukraine Separatists," *The Guardian,* September 20, 2015, https://www.theguardian.com/world/2015/sep/20/russia-funds-moscow-conference-us-eu-ukraine-separatists.
27. Lukasz Adamski and Reinhard Krumm, *Russia and East Central Europe: A Fresh Start* (Berlin: Friedrich-Ebert-Stiftung and International Policy Analysis, 2013).
28. Slawomir Budziak, "Czech Echoes of the Kremlin's Information War," *New Eastern Europe,* March 30, 2015, http://neweasterneurope.eu/2015/03/30/czech-echoes-kremlins-information-war/.
29. Vaclav Klaus, "Valdai's Debate About Threats: The Threat Is Us," Valdai Discussion Club, October 27, 2015, http://valdaiclub.com/a/highlights/v-clav-klaus-valdai-s-debate-about-threats-the-threat-is-us/.
30. Ivan Krastev, "What Central Europe Really Thinks About Russia," op-ed, *New York Times,* April 27, 2015, http://www.nytimes.com/2015/04/28/opinion/what-central-europe-really-thinks-about-russia.html.
31. Dimitar Bechev, *Rival Power: Russia's Influence in Southeast Europe* (New Haven, CT: Yale University Press, 2017).
32. Ben Farmer, "Surveillance Photos 'Show Russian Intelligence Officers Plotting Montenegro Coup,'" *The Telegraph,* August 29, 2017, https://www.telegraph.co.uk/news/2017/08/28/surveillance-photos-show-russian-intelligence-officers-plotting/.
33. Jasmin Mujanovic, "Russia's Bosnia Gambit," *Foreign Affairs,* September 6, 2017, https://www.foreignaffairs.com/articles/bosnia-herzegovina/2017-09-06/russias-bosnia-gambit.
34. Angela Stent, "Franco-Soviet Relations from de Gaulle to Mitterrand," *French Politics and Society,* Winter 1989.
35. Tita Aver, "Russia-France Relations: The Fools of the Georgia War," *Nouvelle Europe,* January 18, 2011, http://www.nouvelle-europe.eu/en/russia-france-relations-fools-georgia-war.
36. Celestine Bohlen, "What Lies Behind French Conservatives' Love of Putin?" *New York Times,* October 4, 2016, https://www.nytimes.com/2016/10/04/world/europe/french-conservatives-sarkozy-putin-russia.html.
37. Marie Mendras, "Russia–France: A Strained Political Relationship," in *Russian Analytical Digest* 130 (July 1, 2013), http://www.css.ethz.ch/content/dam/ethz/special-interest/gess/cis/center-for-securities-studies/pdfs/RAD-130.pdf.
38. Begum Tunakan, "France to Make a Choice Between NATO and Russia," *Daily Sabah,* January 7, 2015, http://www.dailysabah.com/europe/2015/01/07/france-to-make-a-choice-between-nato-and-russia.
39. "Meeting with Marine Le Pen," President of Russia website, March 24, 2017, http://en.kremlin.ru/events/president/news/54102.
40. "Pravoslavnyi Tsentr v Parizhe: Simvol Very I Pamiatnik Sviazivaiiushchii Rossiiu I Frantsiiu," TASS, March 14, 2016, http://tass.ru/obschestvo/2736582.

41. Patrick Reevell, "Macron Tries to Woo Putin During State Visit," *ABC News,* May 25, 2018, https://abcnews.go.com/International/macron-woo-putin-state-visit/story?id=55433452.
42. "French Businessmen to Sign Around 20 Deals at SPIEF-2018—Embassy," TASS, May 24, 2018, http://tass.com/economy/1006144.
43. Mark Hollingsworth and Stewart Lansley, *Londongrad: From Russia with Cash: The Inside Story of the Oligarchs* (London: Fourth Estate, 2009).
44. "Eton Boys Given Private Audience with Vladimir Putin," *BBC News,* September 1, 2016, http://www.bbc.com/news/world-europe-37242146.
45. Owen Matthews, "Should Britain's Crackdown on Dirty Money Worry Russian Oligarchy?" *Newsweek,* February 27, 2018, http://www.newsweek.com/2018/03/09/britain-unexplained-wealth-orders-russian-oligarchs-821009.html.
46. Alan Cowell, "Putin 'Probably Approved' Litvinenko Poisoning, British Inquiry Says," *New York Times,* January 21, 2016, http://www.nytimes.com/2016/01/22/world/europe/alexander-litvinenko-poisoning-inquiry-britain.html?_r=0.
47. House of Lords, European Union Committee, *The EU and Russia: Before and Beyond the Crisis in Ukraine, 6th Report of Session 2014–15* (London: Stationery Office, 2015), https://www.publications.parliament.uk/pa/ld201415/ldselect/ldeucom/115/115.pdf.
48. Daniel Yergin, *The Quest: Energy, Security, and the Remaking of the Modern World* (New York: Penguin, 2012), 38.
49. BP, "Rosneft and BP Complete TNK-BP Sale and Purchase Transaction," news release, March 20, 2013, https://www.bp.com/en/global/corporate/media/press-releases/rosneft-and-bp-complete-tnk-bp-sale-and-purchase-transaction.html.
50. Elsa Vulliamy, "Vladimir Putin Says David Cameron's Claims About Russia's Pro-Brexit Stance 'Have No Basis and Never Did,'" *Independent,* June 26, 2016, http://www.independent.co.uk/news/world/europe/brexit-vladimir-putin-david-cameron-resigns-eu-referendum-russia-uk-a7104086.html.
51. James Landale, "Russian Spy: What Now for the UK/Russia Relationship?" *BBC News,* March 7, 2018, http://www.bbc.com/news/uk-43318103.
52. "Skripal? Pora Bainki, deti, a Zavtra my Rasskazhem vam Drugie Skazki," April 6, 2018, https://inosmi.ru/politic/20180406/241923955.html.
53. "Novichok: Amesbury Poisoning Couple 'Had High Dose,'" *BBC News*, July 9, 2018, https://www.bbc.com/news/uk-44768229.
54. Michael Schwirtz and Eric Schmitt, "Novichok Was in a Perfume Bottle, UK Victim Says," *New York Times,* July 24, 2018, https://www.nytimes.com/2018/07/24/world/europe/russia-uk-poison-charlie-rowley.html.
55. Richard Pérez-Peña and Ellen Barry, "U.K. Charges 2 Men in Novichok Poisoning, Saying They're Russian Agents," *New York Times,* September 5, 2018, https://www.nytimes.com/2018/09/05/world/europe/russia-uk-novichok-skripal.html.
56. "Skripal poisoning: suspects are civilians, not criminals, says Putin," *The Guardian*, https://www.theguardian.com/uk-news/2018/sep/12/skripal-poisoning-suspects-are-civilians-not-criminals-says-putin-novichok.

57. Heather Murphy, "Cheer Up, Berlusconi," *Slate,* November 9, 2011, http://www.slate.com/articles/news_and_politics/low_concept/2011/11/vladimir_putin_and_silvio_berlusconi_putin_s_sweet_attempt_to_cheer_up_his_italian_friend_.html.
58. *Financial Times,* https://www.ft.com/content/7bb8d0fa-34a7-11e6-ad39-3fee5ffe5b5b.
59. "Transcript of Meeting with Participants in the Third Meeting of the Valdai Discussion Club," President of Russia website, September 9, 2006, http://en.kremlin.ru/events/president/transcripts/23789.
60. See Angela E. Stent, *From Embargo to Ostpolitik: The Political Economy of West German–Soviet Relations, 1955–1980* (New York and Cambridge, UK: Cambridge University Press, 1981).
61. Jon Nordheimer, "Britain, Angry at US, Again Defies Sanctions," *New York Times,* September 11, 1982, http://www.nytimes.com/1982/09/11/business/britain-angry-at-us-again-defies-sanctions.html.
62. Yergin, *The Quest,* 341.
63. Jakub Godzimirski PISM Strategic file no. 27, http://www.pism.pl/Publications/PISM-Strategic-Files/PISM-Strategic-File-no-27-63.
64. "Lavrov Napomnil ob Ekonomicheskoi Vygode 'Severno Potoki 2,'" February 17, 2018, https://ria.ru/economy/20180217/1514835334.html.
65. "Vladimir Putin Arrived in Austria," President of Russia website, June 5, 2018, http://en.kremlin.ru/events/president/news/57677.
66. Justin Huggler, "Austria Rolls Out Red Carpet for Putin Despite Skripal Controversy," *The Telegraph,* June 5, 2018, https://www.telegraph.co.uk/news/2018/06/05/putin-denies-trying-divide-europe-ahead-visit-austria-accused/.

Chapter Four: Russia and Germany: The Fateful Relationship

1. Putin, Wladimir, "Rede im Deutschen Bundestag, Wortprotokoll vom 25 September 2001. Available online: www.bundestag.de/parlament/geschichte/gastredner/putin/putin/_wor.html.
2. Government statement by Angela Merkel, March 13, 2014.
3. www.aparchive.com/.../RUSSIA...SCHROEDER...VLADIMIR-PUTIN.
4. "Shreder-Pervyi, Aleksei-Vtoroi," *Komsomolskaia Pravda,* January 6, 2001.
5. "Leaders shun cosy diplomacy," *The Guardian*, https://www.theguardian.com/world/2000/jun/17/russia.johnhooper.
6. Stephen F. Szabo, *Germany, Russia, and the Rise of Geo-Economics* (London: Bloomsbury Academic, 2015), 76.
7. Guy Chazan and David Crawford, "A Friendship Forged in Spying Pays Dividends in Russia Today," *Wall Street Journal,* February 23, 2005, http://www.wsj.com/articles/SB110911748114361477.
8. "'Dekabr': Shreder," *Profil,* December 19, 2005.
9. "Schröder: 'Putin Ist Lupenreiner Demokrat,'" *Hamburger Abendblatt,* November 23, 2004, http://www.abendblatt.de/politik/deutschland/article106930893/Schroeder-Putin-ist-lupenreiner-Demokrat.html.

10. Patrick Wintour and Ben Doherty, "Vladimir Putin Leaves G20 After Leaders Line Up to Browbeat Him over Ukraine," *The Guardian,* November 16, 2014, https://www.theguardian.com/world/2014/nov/16/vladimir-putin-leaves-g20-after-leaders-line-up-to-browbeat-him-over-ukraine.
11. John Lough, *Germany's Russia Challenge,* Fellowship Monograph 11 (Rome: NATO Defense College, February 2018), 34, http://www.ndc.nato.int/news/news.php?icode=1139.
12. "The 2014 Lowy Lecture: Dr. Angela Merkel, Chancellor of Germany," speech transcript, Lowy Institute, November 21, 2014, https://www.lowyinstitute.org/publications/2014-lowy-lecture-dr-angela-merkel-chancellor-germany.
13. Bertelsmann Stiftung, Institute of Public Affairs, *Frayed Partnership: German Public Opinion on Russia* (Gütersloh, Germany: Bertelsmann Stiftung; Warsaw: Institute of Public Affairs, 2016), http://www.bertelsmann-stiftung.de/fileadmin/files/user_upload/EZ_Frayed_Partnership_2016_ENG.pdf.
14. Alexander Rahr, *Wladimir Putin: Der "Deutsche" im Kreml* (Munich: Universitas-Verlag, 2000).
15. Vladimir Putin, *First Person: An Astonishingly Frank Self-Portrait by Russia's President* (New York: PublicAffairs, 2000), 17.
16. Putin, *First Person,* 55.
17. Putin, *First Person.*
18. Putin, *First Person,* 69–70.
19. Fiona Hill and Clifford G. Gaddy, *Mr. Putin: Operative in the Kremlin* (Washington, DC: Brookings Institution Press, 2014), 167.
20. Rahr, *Wladimir Putin,* 55–56.
21. Rahr, *Wladimir Putin,* 55–56.
22. Hill and Gaddy, *Mr. Putin,* 111.
23. Karen Dawisha, *Putin's Kleptocracy: Who Owns Russia?* (New York: Simon and Schuster, 2014), 46–47.
24. Steven Lee Myers, *The New Tsar: The Rise and Reign of Vladimir Putin* (New York: Vintage, 2015), 52–54.
25. Stent, *Russia and Germany Reborn*, chap. 4.
26. Dawisha, *Putin's Kleptocracy,* 47.
27. Dawisha, *Putin's Kleptocracy,* 47.
28. Putin, *First Person,* 79.
29. Putin, *First Person,* 80.
30. Dirk Banse, Florian Flade, Uwe Müller, Eduard Steiner, and Daniel Wetzel, "Circles of Power: Putin's Secret Friendship with Ex-Stasi Officer," *The Guardian,* August 13, 2014, https://www.theguardian.com/world/2014/aug/13/russia-putin-german-right-hand-man-matthias-warnig.
31. Stefan Kornelius, *Angela Merkel: The Chancellor and Her World* (London: Alma Books, 2013), 18.
32. George Packer, "The Quiet German," *New Yorker,* December 1, 2014, http://www.newyorker.com/magazine/2014/12/01/quiet-german.

33. Simon Sebag Montefiore, *The Romanovs: 1613–1918* (New York: Alfred A. Knopf, 2016), 632.
34. Angela E. Stent, *From Embargo to Ostpolitik: The Political Economy of West German–Soviet Relations 1955–1980* (New York and Cambridge, UK: Cambridge University Press, 1981).
35. Stent, *Russia and Germany Reborn,* 164.
36. "Provody Proidut v Berline, a Otnosheniie Budut Razvivatsia," *Krasnaia Zvezda,* August 31, 1994.
37. U. Brandenburg, "The 'Friends' Are Leaving: Soviet and Post-Soviet Troops in Germany," *Aussenpolitik* (English edition) 44, no. 1 (1993): 76–88.
38. Quoted in *Germany, Russia, and the Rise of Geo-Economics,* by Stephen Szabo, 32.
39. Gregor Schoellgen, *Gerhard Schröder: Die Biographie* (Munich: Deutsche Verlags-Anstalt, 2015), 770.
40. Vladimir Putin, "Rossiia na Rubezhe Tysiacheletii" [Russia at the Turn of the Millennium], *Nezavisimaya Gazeta,* December 30, 1999.
41. Schoellgen, Gerhard Schröeder, op.cit.
42. Gerhard Schroeder, *Die Zeit,* December 15, 2001.
43. Angela E. Stent, *The Limits of Partnership: US-Russian Relations in the Twenty-First Century* (Princeton, NJ: Princeton University Press, 2015), 91.
44. Packer, "The Quiet German," http://www.newyorker.com/magazine/2014/12/01/quiet-german.
45. Stephen Szabo, *Germany, Russia, and the Rise of Geo-Economics,* 8.
46. "Vystuplenie na Vstreche s Predstaviteliami politicheskikh, Parlamentskikh i Obshchcestvenniykh Krugov Germanii, Speech at Meeting with German Political Parliamentary and Civic Leaders," President of Russia website, June 5, 2008, http://en.kremlin.ru/events/president/transcripts/320.
47. eeas.europa.eu/delegations/russia/eu_russia/tech_financial_cooperation/partnership_modernisation_facility/index_en.htm.
48. "Excerpts from the Joint News Conference with German Federal Chancellor Angela Merkel Following Russian-German Talk," European Parliament, June 5, 2010, http://www.europarl.europa.eu/meetdocs/2009_2014/documents/d-ru/dv/d_ru_20100916_23_/d_ru_20100916_23_en.pdf.
49. Kornelius, *Angela Merkel,* 185.
50. Packer, "The Quiet German," http://www.newyorker.com/magazine/2014/12/01/quiet-german.
51. Tuomas Forsberg, "From Ostpolitik to 'Frostpolitik'? Merkel, Putin, and German Foreign Policy Towards Russia," *International Affairs* 92, no. 1 (2016): 21–42, https://www.chathamhouse.org/sites/default/files/publications/ia/INTA92_1_02_Forsberg.pdf.
52. "German Industry Lobby Supports Tougher Sanction on Russia," Reuters, July 28, 2014, http://uk.reuters.com/article/uk-ukraine-crisis-sanctions-germany-idUKKBN0FX0I320140728.
53. Schoellgen, *Gerhard Schroder,* 771.

54. 2016, https://ru.tsn.ua/svit/shtaynmayer-zhestko-otvetil-lavrovu-po-iznasilovannoy-migrantami-russkoyazychnoy-devushki-568665.html.
55. Bertelsmann Stiftung, Institute of Public Affairs, *Frayed Partnership: German Public Opinion on Russia* (Gütersloh, Germany: Bertelsmann Stiftung; Warsaw: Institute of Public Affairs, 2016), http://www.bertelsmann-stiftung.de/fileadmin/files/user_upload/EZ_Frayed_Partnership_2016_ENG.pdf.
56. Katie Simmons, Bruce Stokes, and Jacob Poushter, "2. Russian Public Opinion: Putin Praised, West Panned," Pew Research Center, June 10, 2015, http://www.pewglobal.org/2015/06/10/2-russian-public-opinion-putin-praised-west-panned/.
57. Szabo, *Germany, Russia, and the Rise of Geo-Economics,* 106.
58. "Tramp Nazval Stroitel'stvo 'Severnogo Potoka-2' Bol'shoi Oshibkoi," https://tvzvezda.ru/news/vstrane_i_mire/content/201807131636-1m7c.htm.
59. "Germany's Heiko Maas Urges Russia to Change Its Ways," *Deutsche Welle,* April 15, 2018, http://www.dw.com/en/germanys-heiko-maas-urges-russia-to-change-its-ways/a-43397881.
60. "Germany's Angela Merkel Meets Russia's Vladimir Putin," *Deutsche Welle,* May 18, 2018, http://www.dw.com/en/germanys-angela-merkel-meets-russias-vladimir-putin/a-43838039.
61. "Joint News Conference with Federal Chancellor of Germany Angela Merkel," President of Russia website, May 18, 2018, http://en.kremlin.ru/events/president/transcripts/57497.
62. Alex Lockie, "Trumps Slams a Weakened Germany as 'Controlled by Russia' in Blistering Open to NATO Summit," *Business Insider,* July 11, 2018, http://www.businessinsider.com/trump-slams-germany-as-controlled-by-russia-in-open-to-nato-summit-2018-7.
63. Philip Kaleta and Emma Anderson, "Merkel Hits Back at Trump's Attack: I Remember Soviet Occupation," *Politico,* July 11, 2018, https://www.politico.eu/article/merkel-hits-back-at-trumps-attack-i-remember-soviet-occupation/.
64. Guy Chazan, "How Germany Became Trump's European Punchbag," *Financial Times,* August 3, 2018, https://www.ft.com/content/8f87c03c-93dc-11e8-b67b-b8205561c3fe.

Chapter Five: The "Main Opponent": Russia and NATO

1. Vladimir Putin, *First Person: An Astonishingly Frank Self-Portrait by Russia's President* (New York: PublicAffairs, 2000), 6.
2. Lord Hastings Ismay, NATO.org, https://www.nato.int/cps/us/natohq/declassified_137930.htm.
3. The Avalon Project, "Washington's Farewell Address 1796," Yale Law School website, http://avalon.law.yale.edu/18th_century/washing.asp.
4. Dean Acheson, *Present at the Creation* (New York: W. W. Norton, 1969), 283.
5. Acheson, *Present at the Creation,* 284.
6. Vojtech Mastny, *The Cold War and Soviet Insecurity: The Stalin Years* (New York: Oxford University Press, 1998), 74–75.

7. Frederick Kempe, "Colin Powell Looks Back—And Ahead," Atlantic Council blog, December 14, 2009, http://www.atlanticcouncil.org/blogs/new-atlanticist/colin-powell-looks-back-and-ahead.
8. Julij A. Kwizinskij, *Vor dem Sturm: Erinnerungen Eines Diplomaten* (Berlin: Siedler, 1993), 34.
9. http://static.kremlin.ru/media/acts/files/0001201612010045.pdf.
10. John J. Mearsheimer, "Why the Ukraine Crisis Is the West's Fault," *Foreign Affairs,* September/October 2014, https://www.foreignaffairs.com/articles/russia-fsu/2014-08-18/why-ukraine-crisis-west-s-fault.
11. Angela E. Stent, *Russia and Germany Reborn: Unification, the Soviet Collapse and the New Europe* (Princeton, NJ: Princeton University Press, 1999), chap. 5.
12. James Goldgeier, "Promises Made, Promises Broken? What Yeltsin Was Told About NATO in 1983 and Why It Matters," Commentary, *War on the Rocks,* July 12, 2016, https://warontherocks.com/2016/07/promises-made-promises-broken-what-yeltsin-was-told-about-nato-in-1993-and-why-it-matters/.
13. Mark Kramer, "The Myth of a No-NATO-Enlargement Pledge to Russia," *Washington Quarterly* 32, no. 2 (2009): 39–61.
14. Kramer, "Myth of a No-NATO-Enlargement Pledge," 39–61.
15. Michail S. Gorbatschow, *Erinnerungen* (Berlin: Siedler, 1995), 716.
16. *U.S. Policy Toward NATO Enlargement: Hearing Before the Committee on International Relations,* 104th Congress, 2nd Session (Washington, DC: US Government Printing Office, June 20, 1996), 31, https://archive.org/details/uspolicytowardna00unit.
17. Maxim Korshunov, "Mikhail Gorbachev: I Am Against All Walls," *Russia Beyond,* October 16, 2014, https://www.rbth.com/international/2014/10/16/mikhail_gorbachev_i_am_against_all_walls_40673.html.
18. "Razshirenie NATO: Obmanuli li Zapad Gorbacheva?Radio Free Europe/ e rest. thor name and date (in russian)nozine" *BBC News* (Russian edition), 2017, https://www.bbc.com/russian/features-42483896.
19. George F. Kennan, "A Fateful Error," op-ed, *New York Times,* February 5, 1997, https://www.nytimes.com/1997/02/05/opinion/a-fateful-error.html.
20. Steven Erlanger, "Russia Warns NATO on Expanding East," *New York Times,* November 26, 1993, https://www.nytimes.com/1993/11/26/world/russia-warns-nato-on-expanding-east.html.
21. James Goldgeier, "Promises Made, Promises Broken?" https://warontherocks.com/2016/07/promises-made-promises-broken-what-yeltsin-was-told-about-nato-in-1993-and-why-it-matters/.
22. Stent, *Russia and Germany Reborn,* 39.
23. "Pochemu Rasshirenie NATO Predstavliaet Ugrozu dlia Rossii: Memorandum," *Pravda,* March 15, 1999, https://www.pravda.ru/news/world/15-03-1999/903901-0/.
24. Boris N. Yeltsin, *Midnight Diaries* (New York: PublicAffairs, 2000), 131.
25. Strobe Talbott, *The Russia Hand: A Memoir of Presidential Diplomacy* (New York: Random House, 2000), 76.

26. Richard C. Holbrooke, *To End a War* (New York: Modern Library, 1999), 117.
27. Yeltsin, *Midnight Diaries,* 259.
28. Angela E. Stent, *The Limits of Partnership: US-Russian Relations in the Twenty-First Century* (Princeton, NJ: Princeton University Press, 2015), 161.
29. "Putin: Crimea Similar to Kosovo, West Is Rewriting Its Own Rule Book," RT, March 18, 2014, https://www.rt.com/news/putin-address-parliament-crimea-562/.
30. "Putin Rasskazal, chto on obsuzhdal s Klintonom vistuplenie Rossii v NATO," June 3, 2017, https://ria.ru/politics/20170603/1495759550.html.
31. Interview with Lord George Robertson in *Putin, Russia, and the West,* TV documentary, produced by Norma Percy, BBC, aired January–February 2012 on BBC Two.
32. Stent, *The Limits of Partnership,* 75.
33. Stent, *The Limits of Partnership,* 75.
34. James A. Baker III, "Russia in NATO?" *Washington Quarterly* 25, no. 1 (2010): 93–103.
35. "BBC Breakfast with Frost Interview: Vladimir Putin," transcript, *BBC News,* March 5, 2000, http://news.bbc.co.uk/hi/english/static/audio_video/programmes/breakfast_with_frost/transcripts/putin5.mar.txt.
36. "Speech by NATO Secretary General, Lord Robertson, and the Russian President Putin," transcript, NATO On-line Library, last modified October 4, 2001, http://nato.int/docu/speech/2001/s011003a.htm.
37. White House, Office of the Press Secretary, "Remarks by President Obama to the People of Estonia," news release, September 3, 2014, https://obamawhitehouse.archives.gov/the-press-office/2014/09/03/remarks-president-obama-people-estonia.
38. David A. Shlapak and Michael Johnson, *Reinforcing Deterrence on NATO's Eastern Flank,* research report, RR-1253-A (Santa Monica, CA: RAND Corporation, 2016), http://www.rand.org/pubs/research_reports/RR1253.html.
39. Richard Shirreff, *War with Russia: An Urgent Warning from Senior Military Command* (London: Coronet, 2016).
40. President of Russia, "Berlin: Speech at Meeting with German Political, Parliamentary, and Civic Leaders," transcript, June 5, 2008, http://www.europarl.europa.eu/meetdocs/2004_2009/documents/dv/d_ru_20080617_04_/D_RU_20080617_04_en.pdf.
41. "The Draft of the European Security Treaty," President of Russia website, November 29, 2009, http://en.kremlin.ru/events/president/news/6152.
42. Richard Weitz, "The Rise and Fall of Medvedev's European Security Treaty," policy brief, German Marshall Fund of the United States, May 29, 2012, http://www.gmfus.org/publications/rise-and-fall-medvedev%E2%80%99s-european-security-treaty.
43. *The Military Doctrine of the Russian Federation,* from Russian presidential website, February 5, 2010, CarnegieEndowment.org, http://carnegieendowment.org/files/2010russia_military_doctrine.pdf; and NATO, *The 2010 Strategic Concept: Active Engagement, Modern Defence* (Brussels: NATO Publications, 2010), http://www.nato.int/cps/en/natohq/topics_82705.htm.

44. Condoleezza Rice, *No Higher Honor: A Memoir of My Years in Washington* (New York: Random House, 2011), 672.
45. Quoted in Stent, *The Limits of Partnership*, 168.
46. *Kommersant*, "NATO Was Sold to a Blocking State," April 7, 2008, http://www.kommersant.ru/doc/877224.
47. Stent, *The Limits of Partnership*, 173–74.
48. "Lavrov Nazval Rasshirenie NATO Oshibkoi, ugrozaiushchei Bezopasnosti Evropa," https://www.kp.ru/online/news/3026757/.
49. Daniel Treisman, "Why Putin Took Crimea," *Foreign Affairs*, May/June 2016, https://www.foreignaffairs.com/articles/ukraine/2016-04-18/why-putin-took-crimea.
50. "Address by President of the Russian Federation," President of Russia website, March 18, 2014, http://en.kremlin.ru/events/president/news/20603.
51. Oksana Grytsenko and Veronika Melkozerova, "Ukrainians Fight and Die Among Russian Wagner Mercenaries," *Kyiv Post*, February 27, 2018, https://www.kyivpost.com/ukraine-politics/ukrainians-fight-die-among-russian-wagner-mercenaries.html.
52. Shaun Walker, "Vladimir Putin Admits Russian Military Presence in Ukraine for First Time," *The Guardian*, December 17, 2015, https://www.theguardian.com/world/2015/dec/17/vladimir-putin-admits-russian-military-presence-ukraine.
53. Agence-France Presse in Moscow, "Thousands of Russian Soldiers Sent to Ukraine, Say Rights Groups," *The Guardian*, September 1, 2014, https://www.theguardian.com/world/2014/sep/01/russian-soldiers-ukraine-rights-groups.
54. Interfax, "No Russian Troops in Ukraine—Pestov After Obama's Statement," *Russia Beyond*, September 4, 2014, https://rbth.com/news/2014/09/03/no_russian_troops_in_ukraine_-_peskov_after_obamas_statement_39528.html.
55. NATO, *Wales Summit Declaration* (Brussels: NATO e-Library, September 5, 2014), http://www.nato.int/cps/en/natohq/official_texts_112964.htm.
56. Cheryl Pellerin, "2018 Budget Request for European Reassurance Initiative Grows to $4.7 Billion," US Department of Defense News, June 1, 2017, https://www.defense.gov/News/Article/Article/1199828/2018-budget-request-for-european-reassurance-initiative-grows-to-47-billion/.
57. "Jens Stoltenberg: NATO Responds to 'Russia's Aggression Against Ukraine,'" interview, TASS, June 17, 2016, http://tass.com/world/883050.
58. Ewen MacAskill, "Russia Says US Troops Arriving in Poland Pose Threat to Its Security," *The Guardian*, January 12, 2017, https://www.theguardian.com/us-news/2017/jan/12/doubts-over-biggest-us-deployment-in-europe-since-cold-war-under-trump.
59. Steven Sestanovich, "Could It Have Been Otherwise?" *American Interest*, May/June 2015, http://www.the-american-interest.com/2015/04/14/could-it-have-been-otherwise/.
60. Cyra Master, "Trump Tells German Paper: NATO Is 'Obsolete,'" *The Hill*, January 15, 2017, http://thehill.com/homenews/administration/314432-trump-nato-is-obsolete.

61. "Russia Welcomes Trump Calling NATO 'Obsolete,'" Radio Free Europe/Radio Liberty, January 16, 2017, http://www.rferl.org/a/russia-welcomes-trump-nato-obsolete/28236452.html.
62. Lisa Ferdinando, "Mattis Stresses NATO Importance at Munich Security Conference," US Department of Defense News, February 17, 2017, https://www.defense.gov/News/Article/Article/1087792/mattis-stresses-nato-importance-at-munich-security-conference.
63. Jonathan Lemire and Jill Colvin, "Trump Claims Germany 'Controlled' by Russia, Merkel Differs," Associated Press, July 11, 2018.
64. David M. Herszenhorn and Lili Bayer, "Trump's Whiplash NATO Summit," *Politico,* July 12, 2018, https://www.politico.eu/article/trump-threatens-to-pull-out-of-nato/.
65. NATO, *Brussels Summit Declaration* (Brussels: NATO e-Library, July 11, 2018), https://www.nato.int/cps/en/natohq/official_texts_156624.htm.

Chapter Six: Russia and Its "Near Abroad": How Civilized a Divorce?

1. Tom Parfitt, "Spy Who Came in from the Cold," *The Guardian,* December 23, 2007, https://www.theguardian.com/world/2007/dec/23/russia.tomparfitt.
2. "Conference of Russian Ambassadors and Permanent Representatives," President of Russia website, July 1, 2014, http://en.kremlin.ru/events/president/news/46131.
3. "Moldova's President Dodon Lines Up with Putin at St. Petersburg Forum," *BNE IntelliNews,* June 2, 2017, http://www.intellinews.com/moldova-s-president-dodon-lines-up-with-putin-at-st-petersburg-forum-122814/.
4. Damien Sharkov, "Moldova's Prime Minister and President at Odds After Putin Trip," *Newsweek,* January 18, 2017, http://www.newsweek.com/moldovas-pm-president-odds-after-putin-trip-544008.
5. Alexander Cooley, *Great Games, Local Rules* (New York: Oxford University Press, 2012), 16–18.
6. Dmitri Trenin, *Post-Imperium: A Eurasian Story* (Washington, DC: Carnegie Endowment for International Peace, 2011), 27.
7. Bobo Lo, *Russia and the New World Disorder* (Washington, DC: Brookings Institution Press, 2014), 101.
8. Gerard Toal, *Near Abroad: Putin, the West, and the Contest over Ukraine and the Caucasus* (New York: Oxford University Press, 2016). On page 34, Toal describes that as "homeland nationalism—the nationalism of a successor state with spatial identity that extends beyond the borders inherited at the time of the collapse of the multi-national state."
9. The Baltic states fall into a different category from Russia's point of view. Although Russia was displeased when they joined NATO, the Kremlin has treated them differently from the other post-Soviet states because they only became part of the USSR in 1940.
10. Shaun Walker, "Russia's Rouble Crisis Poses Threat to Nine Countries Relying on Remittances," *The Guardian,* January 18, 2015, https://www.theguardian.com/world/2015/jan/18/russia-rouble-threat-nine-countries-remittances.

11. Sabine Fischer, *Not Frozen!* SWP research paper 09, German Institute for International and Security Affairs (Berlin: Stiftung Wissenschaft und Politik, 2016), 13–14.
12. "Viacheslav Nikonov: Russkii, Rossiiskii, Russkoiazichny Mir," February 28, 2011, http://ruskline.ru/news_rl/2011/02/28/net_nichego_rossijskogo_chto_ne_bylo_by_russkim/.
13. Mikhail Suslov, *"Russian World": Russian Policies Towards Its Diaspora,* report no. 103 (Paris: Ifri Russia/NIS Center, 2017), https://www.ifri.org/sites/default/files/atoms/files/suslov_russian_world_2017.pdf.
14. Vyacheslav Nikonov, "O Sozdanii Fonda 'Russkii Mir,'" *Russian Language Journal* 57 (2007): 222–28, http://rlj.americancouncils.org/issues/57/files/Nikonov_2007.pdf.
15. "About Russky Mir Foundation," Russky Mir website, http://russkiymir.ru/en/fund/.
16. Igor Zevelev, "The Russian World in Moscow's Strategy," Commentary, Center for Strategic and International Studies website, August 22, 2016, https://www.csis.org/analysis/russian-world-moscows-strategy.
17. Toal, *Near Abroad,* 89.
18. *The Basic Provisions of the Military Doctrine of the Russian Federation,* presented October 3 and 6, 1993, at the Russian Federation Security Council, adopted November 2, 1993, https://fas.org/nuke/guide/russia/doctrine/russia-mil-doc.html.
19. The CSTO treaty contains a general clause saying that an attack on one party will be considered an attack on all parties and speaks of "protection of independence on a collective basis," but there are no concrete provisions for implementing this clause.
20. Nikolai Bordiuzha, "Integratsiia: Organizatsiia Dogovora O Kollektivnoi Bezopasnosti," *Mezhdunarodnaia Zhizn',* February 28, 2005.
21. Cooley, *Great Games, Local Rules,* 57–58.
22. Joshua Kucera, "US Blocking NATO-CSTO Cooperation," Eurasianet, February 12, 2011, http://www.eurasianet.org/node/62882.
23. Trenin, *Post-Imperium,* 120.
24. Remi Camus, "'We'll Whack Them, Even in the Outhouse': On a Phrase by V. V. Putin," *Kultura,* October 10, 2006, https://www.academia.edu/489390/_We_ll_whack_them_even_in_the_outhouse_on_a_phrase_by_V.V._Putin.
25. Luke Harding, "WikiLeaks Cables: Chechnya's Ruler, a Three-Day Wedding, and a Golden Gun," *The Guardian,* December 1, 2010, https://www.theguardian.com/world/2010/dec/01/wikileaks-cables-ramzan-kadyrov-chechnya.
26. Shaun Walker, "'We Like Partisan Warfare.' Chechens Fighting in Ukraine—on Both Sides," *The Guardian,* July 24, 2015, https://www.theguardian.com/world/2015/jul/24/chechens-fighting-in-ukraine-on-both-sides.
27. Joshua Yaffa, "Chechnya's ISIS Problem," *New Yorker,* February 12, 2016, http://www.newyorker.com/news/news-desk/chechnyas-isis-problem.
28. Joshua Yaffa, "Putin's Dragon," *New Yorker,* February 8 and 15, 2016, http://www.newyorker.com/magazine/2016/02/08/putins-dragon.

29. Fiona Hill, Kemal Kirisci, and Andrew Moffatt, "Armenia and Turkey: From Normalization to Reconciliation," Brookings Institution, February 24, 2015, https://www.brookings.edu/articles/armenia-and-turkey-from-normalization-to-reconciliation/.
30. Thomas De Waal, "Nagorno-Karabakh: Crimea's Doppelganger," Open Democracy, June 13, 2014, https://www.opendemocracy.net/od-russia/thomas-de-waal/nagorno-karabakh-crimea-doppelganger-azerbaijan-armenia.
31. Anna Nemtsova, "A Bloodless Uprising in Armenia Just Forced the Leader to Resign: Will New Peaceful Revolutions Follow?" *Daily Beast*, April 23, 2018, https://www.thedailybeast.com/a-bloodless-uprising-in-armenia-just-forced-the-president-to-resign-will-new-peaceful-revolutions-follow.
32. Charles King, *The Moldovans: Romania, Russia, and the Politics of Culture* (Stanford, CA: Hoover Institution Press, 2000).
33. Charles King, "The Benefits of Ethnic War: Understanding Eurasia's Unrecognized States," *World Politics* 53, no. 4 (2001): 524–52.
34. Valentina Basiul, "2003: Proval 'Plana Kozaka,'" Radio Free Europe, August 20, 2016, https://www.europalibera.org/a/27935462.html.
35. William H. Hill, *Russia, the Near Abroad, and the West: Lessons from the Moldova-Transdniestria Conflict* (Washington, DC: Woodrow Wilson Center Press; Baltimore: Johns Hopkins University Press, 2012), chap. 10 and 11.
36. Luke Coffey, "A Tangled Web of Corruption Is Strangling Moldova," *National Interest*, August 29, 2016, http://nationalinterest.org/feature/tangled-web-corruption-strangling-moldova-17518.
37. Fischer, *Not Frozen!*, 46.
38. Ronald D. Asmus, *A Little War That Shook the World* (New York: Palgrave Macmillan, 2010), 56–57.
39. Clifford J. Levy, "The Georgian and Putin: A Hate Story," *New York Times*, April 18, 2009, http://www.nytimes.com/2009/04/19/weekinreview/19levy.html.
40. Independent International Fact-Finding Mission on the Conflict in Georgia, www.ceiig.ch/report.html.
41. "Rossiia Priznala Nezavisimost' Abkhazii I Iuzhnoi Osetii," *Lenta*, https://lenta.ru/news/2008/08/26/medvedev/.
42. Ellen Barry, "Abkhazia Is Recognized—by Nauru," *New York Times*, December 15, 2009, http://www.nytimes.com/2009/12/16/world/europe/16georgia.html?mcubz=1.
43. Oliver Stone, *The Putin Interviews: Oliver Stone Interviews Vladimir Putin* (New York: Hot Books, 2017), 186.
44. Lucy Pasha-Robinson, "Russia Quietly Moves Border Hundreds of Yards into Occupied Georgia," *Independent*, July 11, 2017, http://www.independent.co.uk/news/world/politics/russia-georgia-border-south-ossetia-move-hundreds-yards-occupied-nato-putin-west-ukraine-a7835756.html.
45. "Putin Visits Abkhazia on Anniversary of Russia-Georgia War," Radio Free Europe/Radio Liberty, August 8, 2017, https://www.rferl.org/a/putin-georgia-abkhazia/28665867.html.

46. Ivan Nechepurenko, "Russia-West Balancing Act Grows Ever More Wobbly in Belarus," *New York Times,* August 13, 2017, https://www.nytimes.com/2017/08/13/world/europe/belarus-russia-aleksandr-lukashenko.html.
47. Pravda.ru, February 19, 2004.
48. OSW 2017-01-04 Kamil Klysinski, https://www.osw.waw.pl/en/publikacje/analyses/2017-01-04/risk-escalating-tensions-minsk-moscow-relations
49. Lo, *Russia and the New World Disorder,* 115–16.
50. "Official Opening Ceremony of AIFC," Kazakh TV, July 5, 2018, http://kazakh-tv.kz/en/view/politics/page_195523_official-opening-ceremony-of-aifc.
51. "UN Nuclear Watchdog Opens Uranium Bank in Kazakhstan," Reuters, August 29, 2017, https://www.reuters.com/article/us-nuclear-kazakhstan-bank/u-n-nuclear-watchdog-opens-uranium-bank-in-kazakhstan-idUSKCN1B917V?il=0.
52. OSCE/ODIHR Election Observation Mission, *Republic of Kazakhstan: Early Presidential Election, 26 April 2015* (Warsaw: Office for Democratic Institutions and Human Rights, July 29, 2015), http://www.osce.org/odihr/elections/kazakhstan/174811?download=true.
53. Cooley, *Great Games, Local Rules,* 22.
54. Senior Kazakh official in conversation with the author.
55. David Trilling, "As Kazakhstan's Leader Asserts Independence, Did Putin Just Say, 'Not So Fast'?" Eurasianet, August 30, 2014, http://www.eurasianet.org/node/69771.
56. Casey Michel, "Take Note, Putin: Kazakhstan Celebrates 550 Years of Statehood," *The Diplomat,* September 14, 2015, http://thediplomat.com/2015/09/take-note-putin-kazakhstan-celebrates-550-years-of-statehood/.
57. Radio Free Europe/Radio Liberty, "Kazakhs Celebrate 550 Years of Statehood," posted September 11, 2015, YouTube video, 0:53, https://www.youtube.com/watch?v=j8eA7tX6BMU.
58. "Nazarbaev: Moe Mnogoletnee Sotrucnichestvo s Putinym: eto Fenomen," https://mir24.tv/news/16285556/nazarbaev-moe-mnogoletnee-sotrudnichestvo-s-putinym-eto-fenomen.
59. Gleb Bryanski, "Russia's Putin Says Wants to Build 'Eurasian Union,'" Reuters, October 3, 2011, http://www.reuters.com/article/us-russia-putin-eurasian-idUSTRE7926ZD20111003.
60. "Meeting of the Valdai International Discussion Club," President of Russia website, September 19, 2013, http://en.kremlin.ru/events/president/news/19243.
61. Jan Strzelecki, "The Eurasian Economic Union: A Time of Crisis," Commentary, Osrodek Studiow Wschodnich, February 1, 2016, https://www.osw.waw.pl/en/publikacje/osw-commentary/2016-02-01/eurasian-economic-union-a-time-crisis.
62. "Suverenitet ne Ikona," *Gazeta,* October 24, 2016, http://gazta.ru/business/2013/10/24/5722545.shtml.
63. Rilka Dragneva and Kataryna Wolczuk, Russia and Eurasia Programme, *The Eurasian Economic Union: Deals, Rules, and the Exercise of Power* (London: Chatham House, Royal Institute of International Affairs, May 2017), https://www.chathamhouse.org/sites

/default/files/publications/research/2017-05-02-eurasian-economic-union-dragneva-wolczuk.pdf.

64. " 'Nobody in Uzbekistan Knows Who Pushkin Is'?" *Meduza,* June 15, 2017, https://meduza.io/en/shapito/2017/06/15/nobody-in-uzbekistan-knows-who-pushkin-is.
65. Armenian official in conversation with the author, Moscow, May 2017.

Chapter Seven: "The Past Is Always Changing": Russia and Ukraine

1. Simon Sebag Montefiore, *The Romanovs: 1613–1918* (New York: Alfred A. Knopf, 2016), 232.
2. Serhii Plokhy, *The Gates of Europe: A History of Ukraine* (New York: Basic Books, 2015), 41–42.
3. Oliver Stone, *The Putin Interviews: Oliver Stone Interviews Vladimir Putin* (New York: Hot Books, 2017), 192–93.
4. Anatol Lieven, *Ukraine and Russia: A Fraternal Rivalry* (Washington, DC: United States Institute of Peace, 1999), 13.
5. Orest Subtelny, *Ukraine: A History* (Toronto: University of Toronto Press, 2009), 42.
6. Plokhy, *The Gates of Europe,* 50.
7. Paul Robert Magocsi, *A History of Ukraine: The Land and Its Peoples* (Toronto: University of Toronto Press, 2010), 194.
8. Plokhy, *The Gates of Europe,* 98–100.
9. "From 'Malorossiya' with Love?" Digital Forensic Research Lab, July 18, 2017, https://medium.com/dfrlab/from-malorossiya-with-love-8765ed30242d.
10. Marvin L. Kalb, *Imperial Gamble: Putin, Ukraine, and the New Cold War* (Washington, DC: Brookings Institution Press, 2015), 55.
11. Plokhy, *The Gates of Europe,* 226–27.
12. Plokhy, *The Gates of Europe,* 253.
13. Magocsi, *A History of Ukraine,* 574.
14. Mark Kramer, "Why Did Russia Give Away Crimea Sixty Years Ago?" Cold War International History Project, Wilson Center, March 19, 2014, https://www.wilsoncenter.org/publication/why-did-russia-give-away-crimea-sixty-years-ago.
15. Plokhy, *The Gates of Europe,* 298–99.
16. Roger Highfield, "25 Years After Chernobyl, We Don't Know How Many Died," *New Scientist,* April 21, 2011, https://www.newscientist.com/article/dn20403-25-years-after-chernobyl-we-dont-know-how-many-died/.
17. Reuters, "After the Summit; Excerpts from Bush's Ukraine Speech: Working 'for the Good of Both of Us,'" *New York Times,* August 2, 1991, http://www.nytimes.com/1991/08/02/world/after-summit-excerpts-bush-s-ukraine-speech-working-for-good-both-us.html?pagewanted=all.
18. Serhii Plokhy, *The Last Empire: The Final Days of the Soviet Union* (New York: Basic Books, 2014), 306–15.
19. "Annual Address to the Federal Assembly of the Russian Federation," President of Russia website, April 25, 2005, http://en.kremlin.ru/events/president/transcripts/22931.

20. Samuel Charap and Timothy Colton, *Everyone Loses: The Ukraine Crisis and the Ruinous Contest for Post-Soviet Eurasia* (London: International Institute for Strategic Studies, 2016), 56.
21. Global Witness, *It's a Gas: Funny Business in the Turkmen-Ukraine Gas Trade,* https://www.globalwitness.org/en/reports/its-gas/.
22. Steven Pifer, *The Eagle and the Trident: US-Ukraine Relations in Turbulent Times* (Washington, DC: Brookings Institution Press, 2017).
23. "Rossisko-Amerikanskii Dialog v Kremle," *Krasnaia Zvezda,* January 14, 1994.
24. Strobe Talbott, *The Russia Hand: A Memoir of Presidential Diplomacy* (New York: Random House, 2002), 114. See "Tri Prezidenta Stavit v Kremle Posledniuiu Tochku v Kholodnoi Voini," *Izvestiia,* January 15, 1994.
25. Pifer, *The Eagle and the Trident,* 70.
26. Celestine Bohlen, "Ukraine Agrees to Allow Russians to Buy Fleet and Destroy Arsenal," *New York Times,* September 4, 1993, http://www.nytimes.com/1993/09/04/world/ukraine-agrees-to-allow-russians-to-buy-fleet-and-destroy-arsenal.html.
27. Pifer, *The Eagle and the Trident,* 31.
28. Angela E. Stent, "Ukraine's Fate," *World Policy Journal* 11, no. 3 (Fall 1994): 83–87.
29. Michael Specter, "Setting Past Aside, Russia and Ukraine Sign Friendship Treaty," *New York Times,* June 1, 1997, http://www.nytimes.com/1997/06/01/world/setting-past-aside-russia-and-ukraine-sign-friendship-treaty.html.
30. Pifer, *The Eagle and the Trident,* 197–98.
31. Margareta M. Balmaceda, *Energy Dependency, Politics, and Corruption in the Former Soviet Union* (New York: Routledge, 2008).
32. Andrew Fedynsky, "Perspectives," *Ukraine Weekly,* September 21, 2003, http://www.ukrweekly.com/old/archive/2003/380316.shtml.
33. Condoleezza Rice, *No Higher Honor: A Memoir of My Years in Washington* (New York: Random House, 2011), 358.
34. Andrei Litvinov, "Vybory. Vladimir Putin Ukazal Viktoru Ianukovychu Na Mesto," *Gazeta* 188, October 11, 2004.
35. Oleksandr Sushko and Olena Prystayko, "Western Influence" in Anders Aslund and Michael McFaul, ed., *Revolution in Orange: The Origins of Ukraine's Democratic Breakthrough* (Washington, DC: Carnegie Endowment for International Peace, 2006).
36. Kenzi Abou-Sabe, Tom Winter, and Max Tucker, "What Did Ex-Trump Aide Paul Manafort Really Do in Ukraine?" *NBC News,* June 27, 2017, http://www.nbcnews.com/news/us-news/what-did-ex-trump-aide-paul-manafort-really-do-ukraine-n775431.
37. Steven R. Weisman, "Powell Says Ukraine Vote Was Full of Fraud," *New York Times,* November 25, 2004, http://www.nytimes.com/2004/11/25/politics/powell-says-ukraine-vote-was-full-of-fraud.html.
38. Angela E. Stent, *The Limits of Partnership: US-Russian Relations in the Twenty-First Century* (Princeton, NJ: Princeton University Press, 2015), 115.
39. Stone, *The Putin Interviews,* 175.

40. Rajan Menon and Eugene Rumer, *Conflict in Ukraine: The Unwinding of the Post-Cold War Order* (Cambridge, MA and London, UK: MIT Press, 2016), 38.
41. "Ukraine Ditches Plans for EU Deal, Turns to Russia," Sputnik, November 21, 2013, http://en.ria.ru/russia/20131121/184845623/Ukraine-Rejects-Laws-to-Free-Tymoshenko-Jeopardises-EU-Deal.html.
42. "Joint Declaration of the Eastern Partnership Summit, Vilnius, 28–29 November 2013," Lithuanian Presidency of the Council of the European Union, archives, December 2, 2013, http://www.eu2013.lt/en/news/statements/-joint-declaration-of-the-eastern-partnership-summit-vilnius-28-29-november-2013.
43. "In Pictures: Inside the Palace Yanukovych Didn't Want Ukraine to See," *The Telegraph,* 2014, http://www.telegraph.co.uk/news/worldnews/europe/ukraine/10656023/In-pictures-Inside-the-palace-Yanukovych-didnt-want-Ukraine-to-see.html?frame=2834873.
44. "Demokraticheskii Gosperevorot v Ukraine," http://ru-an.info/новости/государственный-переворот-в-украине-подготовлен-сионистской-мафией/.(/novosti/gosudarstvennyi-perevorot-v-ukraine-podgotovlen-sionistskoi-mafiei).
45. "Kerry's Statement on Ukraine," *New York Times,* December 10, 2013, http://www.nytimes.com/2013/12/11/world/europe/kerrys-statement-on-ukraine.html.
46. Marci Shore, *The Ukrainian Night: An Intimate History of Revolution* (New Haven, CT: Yale University Press, 2017), 69.
47. Senior German diplomat, who was present at the talks, in conversation with the author. The European side believed that Yanukovych had signed the agreement in good faith.
48. Mikhail Zygar, *All the Kremlin's Men* (New York: PublicAffairs, 2016), 275.
49. Many Ukrainians and Crimean Tatars were prevented from voting, so these official Russian figures should be treated with caution.
50. "Address by President of the Russian Federation," President of Russia website, March 18, 2014, http://en.kremlin.ru/events/president/news/20603.
51. Sergey Lavrov, "Speech by Sergey Lavrov at the 51st Munich Security Conference," Voltaire Network, February 7, 2015, http://www.voltairenet.org/article186844.html.
52. Sabrina Tavernise and Noah Sneider, "Bodies from Malaysia Airlines Flight Are Stuck in Ukraine, Held Hostage over Distrust," *New York Times,* July 20, 2014, http://www.nytimes.com/2014/07/21/world/europe/malaysia-airlines-jet-ukraine.html?_r=0.
53. "Intercepted Audio of Ukraine Separatists," *New York Times,* July 17, 2014, video, 2:13, http://www.nytimes.com/video/world/europe/100000003007434/intercepted-audio-of-ukraine-separatists.html.
54. Will Stewart, Jill Reilly, and Gordon Darroch, "How Do You Solve a Problem Like Maria?[...]," *Daily Mail,* July 25, 2014, http://www.dailymail.co.uk/news/article-2705308/How-solve-problem-like-Maria-Putin-s-daughter-said-fled-Holland-boyfriend-Dutch-fury-Russia-s-response-MH17-disaster.html.
55. "Full Text of the Minsk Agreement," *Financial Times,* https://www.ft.com/content/21b8f98e-b2a5-11e4-b234-00144feab7de.

56. Natalia Zinets and Matthias Williams, "Russia to Blame for 'Hot War' in Ukraine: US Special Envoy," Reuters, July 23, 2017, https://www.reuters.com/article/us-ukraine-crisis-volker-idUSKBN1A80M4.
57. Alexander J. Motyl, "Kiev Should Give Up on the Donbass," *Foreign Policy,* February 2, 2017, http://foreignpolicy.com/2017/02/02/ukraine-will-lose-its-war-by-winning-it/.
58. Terence McCoy, "What Does Russia Tell the Mothers of Soldiers Killed in Ukraine? Not Much." *Washington Post,* August 29, 2014, https://www.washingtonpost.com/news/morning-mix/wp/2014/08/29/what-does-russia-tell-the-mothers-of-soldiers-killed-in-ukraine-not-much/?utm_term=.d78235ee6a87.
59. "MH17: The Netherlands and Australia Hold Russia Responsible," Ministry of General Affairs, Government of the Netherlands, May 25, 2018, https://www.government.nl/topics/mh17-incident/news/2018/05/25/mh17-the-netherlands-and-australia-hold-russia-responsible.
60. Michael Birnbaum, "Dutch-Led Investigators Say Russian Missile Shot Down Malaysia Airlines Flight 17 over Ukraine in 2014," *Washington Post,* May 24, 2018, https://www.washingtonpost.com/world/dutch-led-investigators-say-russian-military-missile-shot-down-flight-mh17-over-ukraine-in-2014/2018/05/24/1e2ff92e-5f3c-11e8-8c93-8cf33c21da8d_story.html?utm_term=.80db8e0fcacf.
61. Kevin G. Hall, "Russian GRU Officer Tied to 2014 Downing of Passenger Plane in Ukraine," McClatchy DC Bureau, May 25, 2018, http://www.mcclatchydc.com/news/nation-world/world/article211836174.html.
62. "Rossii Prizvali Dokazat' chto Obvinenia Protiv Moskvy po Delu MH 17 Lozhnye," https://ria.ru/mh17/20180610/1522491823.html.
63. Joost Akkermans and Henry Meyer, "Putin Rejects Dutch, Australian Claim of Russia Role in MH17," Bloomberg, May 25, 2018, https://www.bloomberg.com/news/articles/2018-05-25/netherlands-australia-hold-russia-liable-for-its-part-in-mh17-jhlqz5ti Bloomberg news.
64. Patricia Zengerle, Reuters, "U.S. doesn't want to be 'handcuffed' to Ukraine agreement," https://www.reuters.com/article/us-usa-diplomacy-tillerson-idUSKBN19528J.
65. Henry A. Kissinger, "To Settle the Ukraine Crisis, Start at the End," *Washington Post,* March 5, 2014, https://www.washingtonpost.com/opinions/henry-kissinger-to-settle-the-ukraine-crisis-start-at-the-end/2014/03/05/46dad868-a496-11e3-8466-d34c451760b9_story.html?utm_term=.e5f9f68a043a.
66. Victor Pinchuk, "Ukraine Must Make Painful Compromises for Peace with Russia," *Wall Street Journal,* December 29, 2016, https://www.wsj.com/articles/ukraine-must-make-painful-compromises-for-peace-with-russia-1483053902.

Chapter Eight: Russia and China: Duo of the Willing?

1. "Interview to TASS and Xinhua News Agencies," President of Russia website, September 1, 2015, http://en.kremlin.ru/events/president/news/50207.
2. Associated Press, "In Putin Meeting, China's Xi Praises Russia Ties," February 7, 2014, https://english.alarabiya.net/en/News/world/2014/02/07/In-Putin-meeting-China-s-Xi-praises-Russia-ties.html.

3. "Former Russian Embassy—Beiguan, Short Introduction and Directions," DrBn.net, last updated June 28, 2017, http://www.drben.net/ChinaReport/Beijing/Landmarks-Hotspots/DongCheng/Frmr_Russian_Embassy/Russian_Embassy-Bei_Guan-Introduction-Directions1.html.
4. Henry Kissinger, *On China* (New York: Penguin, 2012), 57.
5. Harrison E. Salisbury, *War Between Russia and China* (New York: Alfred A. Knopf, 1969), 136.
6. Bobo Lo, *Axis of Convenience: Moscow, Beijing, and the New Geopolitics* (London: Chatham House; Washington, DC: Brookings Institution Press, 2008).
7. Salisbury, *War Between Russia and China,* 20.
8. Jonathan D. Spence, *The Search for Modern China* (New York: W. W. Norton, 1990), 119.
9. Ian Barnes, *Restless Empire: A Historical Atlas of Russia* (Cambridge, MA: Harvard University Press, 2015), 76–77.
10. Fu Ying, "How China Sees Russia," *Foreign Affairs,* January/February 2016, p. 99, https://www.foreignaffairs.com/articles/china/2015-12-14/how-china-sees-russia.
11. John K. Fairbank, ed., *The Cambridge History of China,* vol. 12, pt. 1 (Cambridge, UK: Cambridge University Press, 1983), 656–57.
12. Philip Short, *Mao: A Life* (New York: Henry Holt, 1999), 422.
13. Adam B. Ulam, *Expansion and Coexistence: Soviet Policy 1917–73,* 2nd ed. (New York: Praeger, 1974), 492–93.
14. Kissinger, *On China,* 115.
15. Kissinger, *On China,* 166.
16. Daniel Wolf, Eugene B. Shirley Jr., and E. G. Marshall, producers, *Messengers from Moscow: The East Is Red,* episode 2 of 4, TV documentary, aired 1995, 59:44 (London and New York: Barraclough Carey Productions, WNET, Pacem Productions, BBC Bristol, 1994).
17. Spence, *The Search for Modern China,* 589.
18. William E. Griffith, *The Sino-Soviet Rift* (Cambridge, MA: MIT Press, 1964).
19. When the author arrived in Moscow to begin a period of graduate study at Moscow State University in 1974, she was waiting at the metro station when a group of Chinese made their way onto the platform. Russians waiting for a train cursed them and told her that Chinese were "fanatics."
20. Ezra Vogel, *Deng Xiaoping and the Transformation of China* (Cambridge, MA: Harvard University Press, 2011), 610; and "Sovetsko-Kitaiskii Otnosheniia Normalizirovany," *Izvestiia,* May 16, 1989.
21. "Novyi Etap v Sovetsko-Kitaiskikh Otnosheniiakh," *Pravda,* May 20, 1989.
22. "Inter'viu M.S. Gorbacheva Kitaiskomu Televidenii," *Pravda,* May 18, 1989.
23. A diplomat who accompanied Mr. Shevardnadze, in conversation with the author.
24. Vogel, *Deng Xiaoping,* 626.
25. Kissinger, *On China,* 458.
26. Valdai Discussion Club meeting, October 2014.

27. Cited in John Lewis Gaddis, *We Now Know: Rethinking Cold War History* (Oxford, UK: Clarendon Press, 1997), 67. According to Liu's interpreter, the Chinese were so offended that they refused to drink to Stalin's toast, thereby angering their host.
28. "Granitsa S Kitaem Stanovitsia Zona Sotrudnichestvo," *Krasnaia Zvezda,* November 11, 1993.
29. *Washington Post,* December 19, 1992.
30. For the text, see *Rossiskiie Vesti,* April 25, 1997.
31. Daniel Williams, "Missiles Hit Chinese Embassy," *Washington Post,* May 8, 1999, http://www.washingtonpost.com/wp-srv/inatl/longterm/balkans/stories/belgrade050899.htm.
32. *Kommersant,* December 10, 1999.
33. "Pervy Vizit Putin—V Kitae?" *Nezavisimaia Gazeta,* March 2, 2000.
34. "Putin Provedet v Kitae Dva Dnia," *Ekonomicheskie Novosti,* June 5, 2012.
35. "I am just too busy for summit in America, Putin tells Obama," *The Times UK,* https://www.thetimes.co.uk/article/i-am-just-too-busy-for-summit-in-america-putin-tells-obama-d7ncdknhghc.
36. Joshua Kucera, "China's Russian Invasion," *The Diplomat,* February 19, 2010, https://thediplomat.com/2010/02/chinas-russian-invasion/.
37. P. Ukhutubuzhsky [a pseudonym for Nikolai Dmitrievich Obleukhov], quoted in "Chinese Migrants and Anti-Chinese Sentiments in Russian Society," by Viktor Dyatlov, chap. 5 in *Frontier Encounters,* ed. Franck Billé, Gregory Delaplace, and Caroline Humphrey (Open Book Publishers, 2012), 71–87, https://books.openedition.org/obp/1531.
38. Dragos Tirnoveanu, "Russia, China, and the Far East Question," *The Diplomat,* January 20, 2016, http://thediplomat.com/2016/01/russia-china-and-the-far-east-question/.
39. Mikhail Alekseev, "'They Take a Long View': Russian Perceptions of Border Disputes with China" (PowerPoint presentation, Kennan Institute, Washington, DC, February 24, 2016).
40. *Financial Times,* http://www.ft.com/intl/cms/s/0/700a9450-1b26-11e5-8201-cbdb03d71480.html#axzz473m2bPvL.
41. *Financial Times,* February 6–7, 2016.
42. Tatiana Sidorenko, "The Scope of Economic Cooperation Between Russia and China and Future Prospects," *Problemas del Desarrollo* 45, no. 176 (2014), http://www.probdes.iiec.unam.mx/en/revistas/v45n176/body/v45n176a2_1.php.
43. "S-500 in 2016?" *Russian Defense Policy* (blog), posted April 18, 2016, https://russiandefpolicy.wordpress.com/2016/04/18/s-500-in-2016/.
44. http://www.minergo.gov.ru/china/oil.
45. "Putin Otpravil Gaz v Kitai," *Izvestiia,* October 14, 2009.
46. Elena Mazneva and Stepan Kravchenko, "Russia, China Sign $400B Gas Deal After Decade of Talks," *Bloomberg,* May 21, 2014, http://www.bloomberg.com/news/articles/2014-05-21/russia-signs-china-gas-deal-after-decade-of-talks.
47. Gazprom, "Linear Part of Power of Siberia Gas Pipeline Completed by 75.5 Per Cent," news release, March 21, 2018, http://www.gazprom.com/press/news/2018/march/article413496/.

48. "The Evolution of the Shanghai Cooperation Organization," *IISS Strategic Comments,* vol. 24, June 2018, https://mail.google.com/mail/u/0/#search/Strategic.comments%40iiss.org/164463b26184ad88.
49. Richard Weitz, "The Shanghai Cooperation Organization's Growing Pains," *The Diplomat,* September 18, 2015, http://thediplomat.com/2015/09/the-shanghai-cooperation-organizations-growing-pains/.
50. http://www.thenewage.co.za/164578-1020-53-.
51. Lo, *Axis of Convenience,* 95–96.
52. Stent, *The Limits of Partnership,* chap. 4.
53. Alexander Gabuev, "China's Silk Road Challenge," Carnegie Moscow Center, December 11, 2015, https://carnegie.ru/commentary/61949.
54. Nathan Hutson, "Proekt 'Odin Poias, Odin Put': Kto v Vyigryshe I Naskol'ko?," Eurasianet, December 22, 2017, https://inosmi.ru/economic/20171222/241057172.html.
55. "V Pekine Sostaialsia Forum 'Odin Poias, Odin Put' s Uchastiem Glav 29 Gosudarstv,'" March 14, 2017, https://www.rbc.ru/newspaper/2017/05/15/59159e0d9a7947318586f81f.
56. "Belt and Road International Forum," President of Russia website, May 14, 2017, http://en.kremlin.ru/events/president/news/54491/.
57. *Kommersant,* March 6, 2017, https://www.kommersant.ru/doc/3235889.
58. http://russiancouncil.ru/rucn2016; http://russiancouncil.ru/en/rucn2017.
59. Alexander Gabuev, "Belt and Road to Where?" op-ed, Carnegie Moscow Center, December 8, 2017, http://carnegie.ru/2017/12/08/belt-and-road-to-where-pub-74957.
60. Alexander Gabuev, "Did Western Sanctions Affect Sino-Russian Economic Ties?" *Asia Dialogue,* April 26, 2016, https://blogs.nottingham.ac.uk/chinapolicyinstitute/2016/04/26/did-western-sanctions-affect-sino-russian-economic-ties/.
61. Alexander Gabuev, "A Pivot to Nowhere: The Realities of Russia's Asia Policy," Carnegie Moscow Center, April 22, 2016, http://carnegie.ru/commentary/2016/04/22/pivot-to-nowhere-realities-of-russia-s-asia-policy/ixfv.
62. Bobo Lo, *A Wary Embrace: What the Russia-China Relationship Means for the World* (Docklands, Victoria: Penguin Random House, 2017), 138.
63. Stephen Blank, "New Momentum in the Russia-China Partnership," *Eurasia Daily Monitor,* March 30, 2016, https://jamestown.org/program/new-momentum-in-the-russia-china-partnership/#.VwEtsBIrLdQ.
64. Lo, *A Wary Embrace,* xiv.
65. Franz-Stefan Gady, "Russian, Chinese Troops Kick off Russia's Largest Military Exercise Since 1981," September 12, 2018, *The Diplomat*, https://thediplomat.com/2018/09/russian-chinese-troops-kick-off-russias-largest-military-exercise-since-1981/.
66. *The Economist,* September 8, 2018, p. 43.
67. *Financial Times*, February 6/7, 2016.
68. Anna Dolgov, "Russia and China Boost Student Exchange Programs," *Moscow Times,* October 13, 2014, http://www.themoscowtimes.com/article.php?id=509353.

69. Fu Ying, "How China Sees Russia," 104–5, https://www.foreignaffairs.com/articles/china/2015-12-14/how-china-sees-russia.

Chapter Nine: Wary Neighbors: Russia and Japan in the Shadow of World War Two

1. Daniel Sneider, "Japan," *Christian Science Monitor,* April 10, 1991, http://www.csmonitor.com/1991/0410/otrip.html.
2. "Interview by Vladimir Putin to Nippon TV and Yomiuri Newspaper," President of Russia website, December 13, 2013, http://en.kremlin.ru/events/president/news/53455.
3. Senior Japanese official in conversation with the author, 2017.
4. Geoffrey Jukes, *The Russo-Japanese War 1904–1905* (Oxford, UK: Osprey, 2002), 21.
5. Joseph P. Ferguson, *Japanese-Russian Relations 1907–2007* (New York: Routledge, 2008), 1–2.
6. Jukes, *Russo-Japanese War 1904–1905,* 21–23.
7. Ferguson, *Japanese-Russian Relations 1907–2007,* 12.
8. Simon Sebag Montefiore, *The Romanovs: 1613–1918* (New York: Alfred A. Knopf, 2016), 523.
9. Ian Barnes, *Restless Empire: A Historical Atlas of Russia* (Cambridge, MA: Harvard University Press, 2015), 78.
10. Jukes, *Russo-Japanese War 1904–1905,* 86.
11. Adam B. Ulam, *Expansion and Coexistence: Soviet Policy 1917–73,* 2nd ed. (New York: Praeger, 1974), 308.
12. Hiroshi Kimura, *The Kurillian Knot: A History of Japanese-Russian Border Negotiations* (Palo Alto, CA: Stanford University Press, 2008), 41.
13. Ulam, *Expansion and Coexistence,* 308.
14. Kimura, *The Kurillian Knot,* 1.
15. John H. Miller, "Russia-Japan Relations: Prisoners of History?" in *Asia's Bilateral Relations Special Assessment Series,* ed. Satu P. Limaye (Honolulu, HI: Asia-Pacific Center for Security Studies, October 2004), 6, https://apcss.org/wp-content/uploads/2010/PDFs/SAS/AsiaBilateralRelations/AsiasBilateralRelationsComplete.pdf.
16. Miller, "Russia-Japan Relations: Prisoners of History?" 44, 46, https://apcss.org/wp-content/uploads/2010/PDFs/SAS/AsiaBilateralRelations/AsiasBilateralRelationsComplete.pdf.
17. Office of the Historian, "Agreement Regarding Entry of the Soviet Union into the War Against Japan," US Department of State, February 11, 1945, https://history.state.gov/historicaldocuments/frus1945Malta/d503.
18. "Stalin's Address to the People, September 2, 1945," transcript, Marxist Internet Archive, 2009, originally published as *Works,* vol. 16, by Red Star Press, London, 1986, https://www.marxists.org/reference/archive/stalin/works/1945/09/02.htm.

19. A. Y. Song, "A Half-Step Forward: An Assessment of the April 1991 Soviet-Japanese Summit," *Asian Perspective* 16, no. 1 (1992): 103–28.
20. "Normalizatsiia Sovetsko-Japonskikh Otnoshenii," *Izvestiia,* August 4, 1956.
21. "Sovmest'niaia Deklaratsiia Soiuza Sovetskikh Sotsialisticheskikh Respublik I Iaponia," *Pravda,* October 20, 1956.
22. Michail S. Gorbatschow *Erinnerungen* (Berlin: Siedler, 1995), 791.
23. "Territoria'lnyi Spor Mezhdu SSSR I Iaponiei Kasaetsia Ostrov: Iturup, Kunashir, Shikotan, I Ostrovnoi Griady. Khabomia, Mirnyi Dogovoer 'Severnye Territorii,'" *Argumenty I Fakty,* no. 15, April 11, 1991.
24. "Sovmestnoe Sovesko-Iaponskoe Zaiavlenie," *Pravda,* May 19, 1991.
25. Nobuo Shimotomai, "Japan's Russia Policy and the October 1993 Summit," in *"Northern Territories" and Beyond: Russian, Japanese, and American Perspectives,* ed. James Goodby, Vladimir Ivanov, and Nobuo Shimotomai (Westport, CT: Praeger, 1995), 121.
26. John-Thor Dahlburg and Teresa Watanabe, "Yeltsin Shocks Japanese by Calling Off Sensitive Visit [. . .]," *Los Angeles Times,* September 10, 1992, http://articles.latimes.com/1992-09-10/news/mn-329_1_disputed-islands.
27. Peggy Falkenheim Meyer, "Moscow's Relations with Tokyo: Domestic Obstacles to a Territorial Agreement," Asian Survey, Vol. 33, no. 10 (October 1993), 953-67.
28. Thomas Easton, "Yeltsin Visits Japan Under Heavy Guard," *Baltimore Sun,* October 12, 1993, http://articles.baltimoresun.com/1993-10-12/news/1993285082_1_trip-to-japan-ministry-of-foreign-yeltsin.
29. Richard Boudreaux and Teresa Watanabe, "Yeltsin Apologizes to Japan for Abuse of WWII Prisoners [. . .]," *Los Angeles Times,* October 13, 1993, http://articles.latimes.com/1993-10-13/news/mn-45338_1_russian-president.
30. Hiroshi Kimura, *Japanese-Russian Relations Under Gorbachev and Yeltsin* (Armonk, NY: M. E. Sharpe, 2000), 211–13.
31. "Eltsin I Khashimoto Izluchaiut Optimizm," *Komsomol'skaiai Pravda,* November 4, 1997.
32. Boris N. Yeltsin, *Midnight Diaries* (New York: PublicAffairs, 2000), 153–56.
33. Vladimir Putin, *First Person: An Astonishingly Frank Self-Portrait by Russia's President* (New York: PublicAffairs, 2000), 19.
34. Hisane Masaki, "Putin's Diplomatic Victory in Tokyo: Regional Perspectives on Russia-Japan Relations," *Asia-Pacific Journal* 3, no. 11 (2005): 8, https://apjjf.org/-Hisane-MASAKI/2081/article.html.
35. Ferguson, *Japanese-Russian Relations 1907–2007,* 103.
36. Kimura, *The Kurillian Knot,* 117–18.
37. Leszek Buszynski, "Oil and Territory in Putin's Relations with China and Japan," *Pacific Review* 19, no. 3 (2006): 297.
38. Kimura, *The Kurillian Knot,* 122.
39. Natasha Kuhrt, *Russian Policy toward China and Japan* (Abingdon, UK: Routledge, 2011), 145.
40. Ferguson, *Japanese-Russian Relations 1907–2007,* 109–10.

41. "Dmitrii Medvedev Posetil Iuzhnye Kurily," President of Russia website, http://kremlin.ru/events/presidint/news9388.
42. "Russian PM Medvedev's Visit to Disputed Islands Irks Japan," *BBC News,* July 3, 2012, http://www.bbc.com/news/world-asia-18688388.
43. David Nowak, Associated Press, "Russia Flexes Muscles over Island Spat with Japan," *Washington Post,* November 3, 2010, http://www.washingtonpost.com/wp-dyn/content/article/2010/11/03/AR2010110304682.html.
44. Abrahm Lustgarten, "Shell Shakedown," *Fortune* (archive), February 1, 2007, http://archive.fortune.com/magazines/fortune/fortune_archive/2007/02/05/8399125/index.htm.
45. Buszynski, "Oil and Territory in Putin's Relations with China and Japan," 290.
46. *Financial Times,* https://www.ft.com/content/bb70550a-47c3-11e5-b3b2-1672f710807b?mhq5j=e1.
47. Businessman in conversation with the author, Tokyo, 2017.
48. Ankit Panda, "Japan Sanctions Russia over Ukraine," *The Diplomat,* July 29, 2014, http://thediplomat.com/2014/07/japan-sanctions-russia-over-ukraine/.
49. A foreign ministry official complained to the author about US assistant secretary of state Victoria Nuland: "She lectured us on Russia. She doesn't understand Asia and why it is so important to improve relations with Russia."
50. "Japanese PM Wants to Invite Putin to G7 Summit," Joinfo.com, January 1, 2016, https://joinfo.com/world/1013579_japanese-pm-wants-to-invite-putin-to-g7-summit.html.
51. Samuel Osborne, "Japanese Prime Minister Shinzo Abe Says Donald Trump Encouraged Him to Improve Relations with Vladimir Putin," *Independent,* February 14, 2017, http://www.independent.co.uk/news/world/americas/us-politics/japan-prime-minister-shinzo-abe-donald-trum-p-improve-russia-relations-valdimir-putin-us-president-a7579166.html.
52. "Ahead of His Official Trip to Japan, Putin On The Kuril Islands Dispute: 'We Have No Territorial Problems At All; It Is Only Japan That Believes It Has Territorial Problems With Russia,'" MEMRI, December 15, 2016, https://www.memri.org/reports/ahead-his-official-trip-japan-putin-kuril-islands-dispute-we-have-no-territorial-problems.
53. John Micklethwait, "Putin Discusses Trump, OPEC, Rosneft, Brexit, Japan (Transcript)," *Bloomberg,* September 5, 2016, https://www.bloomberg.com/news/articles/2016-09-05/putin-discusses-trump-opec-rosneft-brexit-japan-transcript.
54. Atsuhito Isozaki, "Time for a Japanese Rethink on North Korea?" *The Diplomat,* June 7, 2017, http://thediplomat.com/2017/06/time-for-a-japanese-rethink-on-north-korea/.
55. Franz-Stefan Gady, "Putin: Russian Force Buildup in Kuril Islands a Response to US Military Actions," *The Diplomat,* June 5, 2017, http://thediplomat.com/2017/06/putin-russian-force-buildup-in-kuril-islands-a-response-to-us-military-actions/.
56. "Ushakov Rasskazal o Printsipakh Budushchego Mirnogo Dogovor c Iaponiei," *RIA Novosti, Rossiia Segogniia,* May 23, 2018.

57. "Abe Nadeetsia, Chto Kuril'skie Ostrova Stanut Symvolom Sotrudnichestva," *RIA Novosti,* May 25, 2018.
58. National Institute for Defense Studies (Japan), *East Asian Strategic Review: 2016* (Tokyo: Japan Times, 2016), 223–24.
59. Hiroko Maeda, "Japan-China Relations at a Crossroads," *The Diplomat,* July 22, 2016, https://thediplomat.com/2016/07/japan-china-relations-at-a-crossroads/.
60. Zachary Keck, "Most Chinese Expect War with Japan," *The Diplomat,* September 11, 2014, https://thediplomat.com/2014/09/poll-majority-of-chinese-expect-war-with-japan/.
61. http://en.kremlin.tu/events/president/transcripts/58848.

Chapter Ten: The New Power Broker: Russia and the Middle East

1. Senior Israeli official in conversation with the author, January 2018.
2. Owen Matthews, Jack Moore, and Damien Sharkov, "How Russia Became the Middle East's New Power Broker," *Newsweek,* February 9, 2017, http://www.newsweek.com/how-russia-became-middle-easts-new-power-broker-554227.
3. Andrew Roth, "On Visit to Syria, Putin Lauds Victory over ISIS and Announces Withdrawals," *Washington Post,* December 11, 2017, https://www.washingtonpost.com/world/putin-makes-first-visit-to-syria-lauds-victory-over-isis-and-announces-withdrawals/2017/12/11/f75389de-de61-11e7-8679-a9728984779c_story.html?utm_term=.5ef20ab69336.
4. Yonetim, "Jerusalem, Missile Defense Dominate Putin's Quick Turkey Visit," *Kafkassam,* December 14, 2017, https://kafkassam.com/jerusalem-missile-defense-dominate-putins-quick-turkey-visit.html.
5. Adam B. Ulam, *Expansion and Coexistence: Soviet Foreign Policy 1917–73,* 2nd ed. (New York: Praeger, 1974), 584.
6. Yevgeny Primakov, *Russia and the Arabs: Behind the Scenes in the Middle East from the Cold War to the Present* (New York: Basic Books, 2009), 101.
7. Quoted in *Russia, Iran, and the Nuclear Question: The Putin Record,* by Robert O. Freedman (Carlisle, PA: Strategic Studies Institute, US Army War College, 2006), 81.
8. "Iran Shchastlivo, Chto Eltsin I Klinton ne Dogovorilis' I Predlagaet Soiuz I Druzhby," *Izvestiia,* May 30, 1995.
9. "Vladimir Putin delivered a speech at the Organization of Islamic Conference Summit," October 16, 2003, The Kremlin, http://en.kremlin.ru/events/president/news/29550.
10. Quoted in Nikolas Gvosdev and Christopher Marsh, *Russian Foreign Policy: Interests, Vectors, Sectors* (Sage Publishers 2013), 297.
11. Primakov, *Russia and the Arabs,* 320–21.
12. Voloshin quoted in Angela E. Stent, *The Limits of Partnership,* 91.
13. Alex Rodriguez, "Putin calls war on Iraq a 'mistake,'" *The Chicago Tribune,* March 21, 2003, http://www.chicagotribune.com/news/ct-xpm-2003-03-21-0303210260-story.html.

14. "Medvedev: RF Soznatel'no ne Nalozhil Veto na Rezolutsiu SBOON Po Livii," March 21, 2011, https://ria.ru/arab_ly/20110321/356344423.html.
15. RBC.ru, March 21, 2011, http://www.rbc.ru/fnews.open/20110321190605.shtml.
16. Clifford J. Levy and Thom Shanker, "In Rare Split, Two Leaders in Russia Differ on Libya," *New York Times,* March 21, 2011, https://www.nytimes.com/2011/03/22/world/europe/22russia.html.
17. "Putin: Nevozmozhno Bez Otvrashcheniia Smotret' Na Kadry Ubiistva Kadaffi," https://ria.ru/arab_ly/20111026/471693000.html.
18. Dmitri Trenin, *What Is Russia Up to in the Middle East?* (Cambridge, UK: Polity, 2017), 47.
19. "Za Siriu Za Asada: Kogda and Zachem Moskva Reshila Voevat," https://www.rbc.ru/politics/30/09/2015/560bffdd9a794744eb92da3b.
20. Quoted in *The Silk Roads: A New History of the World,* by Peter Frankopan (New York: Vintage, 2017), 443.
21. David M. Herszenhorn, "For Syria, Reliant on Russia for Weapons and Food, Old Bonds Run Deep," *New York Times,* February 18, 2012, http://www.nytimes.com/2012/02/19/world/middleeast/for-russia-and-syria-bonds-are-old-and-deep.html.
22. David M. Herszenhorn, "Russia Rejects U.S. Evidence on Syrian Chemical Attack," *New York Times,* Sept. 2, 2013, https://www.nytimes.com/2013/09/03/world/middleeast/russia-syria.html.
23. Vladimir V. Putin, "A Plea for Caution from Russia," op-ed, *New York Times,* September 11, 2013, http://www.nytimes.com/2013/09/12/opinion/putin-plea-for-caution-from-russia-on-syria.html.
24. Trenin, *What Is Russia Up to in the Middle East?,* 54.
25. Quoted in "Putin's Power Play in Syria," by Angela E. Stent, *Foreign Affairs,* January–February, 2106, https://www.foreignaffairs.com/articles/united-states/2015-12-14/putins-power-play-syria.
26. Oliver Stone, *The Putin Interviews: Oliver Stone Interviews Vladimir Putin* (New York: Hot Books, 2017), 132.
27. Erik de Castro, Reuters, "Russia Named Top Source of Foreign Fighters in Syria and Iraq," *Moscow Times,* October 26, 2017, https://themoscowtimes.com/news/russia-named-top-source-of-foreign-fighters-in-syria-and-iraq-59380.
28. "John Kerry Says Assad 'Has to Go'—But Only Through Negotiation," Vice.com, September 19, 2015, https://news.vice.com/article/john-kerry-says-assad-has-to-go-but-only-through-negotiation.
29. Michael R. Gordon, Helene Cooper, and Michael D. Shear, "Dozens of US Missiles Hit Air Base in Syria," *New York Times,* April 6, 2017, https://www.nytimes.com/2017/04/06/world/middleeast/us-said-to-weigh-military-responses-to-syrian-chemical-attack.html.
30. Shaun Walker, "Moscow: Syria Airstrikes 'Significant Blow to Russian-US Relations,'" *The Guardian,* April 7, 2017, https://www.theguardian.com/world/2017/apr/07/us-airstrikes-syria-russian-american-relations-vladimir-putin.

31. Katya Golubkova and Tom Perry, "Russia's Putin Hosts Assad in Fresh Drive for Syria Peace Deal," Reuters, November 20, 2017, https://www.reuters.com/article/us-mideast-crisis-putin-assad/russias-putin-hosts-assad-in-fresh-drive-for-syria-peace-deal-idUSKBN1DL0D5.
32. Justin Worland, "President Trump's Pick for Secretary of State Just Confirmed 'Hundreds' of Russians Were Killed in a US Attack in Syria," *Time,* April 12, 2018, http://time.com/5237922/mike-pompeo-russia-confirmation/. See also "American-Russian Relations in Syria? Less Rosy Than Trump and Putin Claim," by Eric Schmitt and Thomas Gibbons-Neff, *New York Times*, July 17, 2018, https://www.nytimes.com/2018/07/17/world/middleeast/american-russian-military-syria.html.
33. Sergey Sukhankin, *"Continuing War By Other Means": The Case of Wagner, Russia's Premier Private Military Company on the Middle East* (Washington, DC: Jamestown Foundation, July 13, 2018), https://jamestown.org/program/continuing-war-by-other-means-the-case-of-wagner-russias-premier-private-military-company-in-the-middle-east/?mc_cid=efdddbeac9&mc_eid=2598204a29.
34. Julie Hirschfeld Davis, "Pompeo Defends Trump with 'Proof' of Administration's Actions vs. Russia," *New York Times,* July 25, 2018, https://www.nytimes.com/2018/07/25/us/politics/senate-pompeo-trump-putin-north-korea.html.
35. Fiona Hill and Omer Taspinar, "Turkey and Russia: Axis of the Excluded?" Brookings Institution, March 1, 2006, https://www.brookings.edu/articles/turkey-and-russia-axis-of-the-excluded/.
36. "Turtsia Sbila Rossiiskii SU-24," https://www/kp.ru/daily/26461/3332082/.
37. Associated Press, "Turkey Slapped with Russian Sanctions over Jet Downing," *Al Jazeera,* November 28, 2015, http://www.aljazeera.com/news/2015/11/erdogan-expresses-sadness-russian-jet-shot-151128112138694.html.
38. "Turtsia Sbila SU-24 Chtob Obezopasit' Perevozku Nefti Boekov: Putin," https://tvzvezda.ru/news/vstrane_i_mire/content/201511302145-g2kb.htm.
39. Neil MacFarquhar, "Russia and Turkey Hurl Insults as Feud Deepens," *New York Times,* December 3, 2015, https://www.nytimes.com/2015/12/04/world/europe/putin-russia-turkey.html.
40. "Turtsia Izvinilas' Za Sbityi Samolot," http://www.interfax.ru/russia/515570.
41. Neil MacFarquhar, "Russia and Turkey Vow to Repair Ties as West Watches Nervously," *New York Times,* August 9, 2016, https://www.nytimes.com/2016/08/10/world/europe/putin-erdogan-russia-turkey.html.
42. Reuters, "NATO-Member Turkey Finalizes Deal to Buy Advanced Russian S-400 Missile Systems," *Haaretz,* December 31, 2017, https://www.haaretz.com/middle-east-news/turkey/1.832142.
43. Nolan D. McCaskill, "Trump Says Turkish President Gets 'Very High Marks,'" *Politico,* September 21, 2017, https://www.politico.com/story/2017/09/21/trump-erdogan-turkey-praise-242986.
44. Sevil Erkus, "Eurasian Economic Union 'Would Welcome' Turkey's Membership," *Hürriyet Daily News,* January 23, 2015, http://www.hurriyetdailynews.com/eurasian-economic-union-would-welcome-turkeys-membership-77316.

45. Kemal Kirisci, "The Implications of a Turkish-Russian Rapprochement," Brookings Institution,August10,2016,https://www.brookings.edu/blog/order-from-chaos/2016/08/10/the-implications-of-a-turkish-russian-rapprochement/.
46. Reuters, "US 'Surprised' Israel Did Not Support UN Vote on Ukraine's Territorial Integrity," *Jerusalem Post,* April 15, 2014, http://www.jpost.com/International/US-surprised-Israel-did-support-UN-vote-on-Ukraines-territorial-integrity-348564.
47. Vladimir Putin, *First Person: An Astonishingly Frank Self-Portrait by Russia's President* (New York: PublicAffairs, 2000), 11.
48. Michal Margalit and Polina Garaev, "I Was Vladimir Putin's Teacher," YNetNews.com, March 29, 2014, https://www.ynetnews.com/articles/0,7340,L-4504539,00.html.
49. Cnaan Lipshiz, "Why Russian Chief Rabbi Stands by Vladimir Putin," *Forward,* June 5, 2015, http://forward.com/news/breaking-news/309514/russian-chief-rabbi-berel-lazar-stands-by-vladimir-putin/.
50. Olga Gershenson, "How Russia Created a Jewish Museum and Tolerance Center Even Vladimir Putin Can Tolerate," *Forward,* January 8, 2016, http://forward.com/culture/art/328682/how-russia-created-a-jewish-museum-and-tolerance-center-even-vladimir-putin/.
51. From the author's notes, Valdai Discussion Club meeting, Sochi, September 2010.
52. Yaakov Katz and Amir Bohbot, "How Israel Sold Russia Drones to Stop Missiles from Reaching Iran," excerpt from *The Weapon Wizards, Jerusalem Post,* June 15, 2017, http://www.jpost.com/Magazine/Books-Israel-and-the-saleof-advanced-drones-to-Russia-480326.
53. Dmitri Trenin, *What Is Russia Up to in the Middle East?* (Cambridge, UK: Polity, 2017), 89–90.
54. JPost.com Staff, "Watch: Russian Ambassador to Israel—Hamas, Hezbollah Not Terrorists at All," *Jerusalem Post,* June 15, 2017, http://www.jpost.com/Arab-Israeli-Conflict/WATCH-Russian-Ambassador-to-Israel-Hamas-Hezbollah-not-terrorists-at-all-496829.
55. Raoul Wootliff, "Netanyahu to Putin: Israel Will Act If Needed Against Iran in Syria," *Times of Israel,* August 23, 2017, https://www.timesofisrael.com/netanyahu-to-putin-israel-willing-to-act-against-iran-in-syria/.
56. "Putin Poblagodaril Netaniakhu za Vizit v Moskvu na 9 Maia," https://life.ru/t/novosti/1115161.
57. This was a gesture of respect to Russia. The Nazis' surrender to the US and UK came into force on May 8, but they did not surrender to the Soviets until May 9.
58. Maxim A. Suchkov, "As Tensions Flare with Iran, Israel Embraces Russia," *AL Monitor,* May 10, 2018, https://www.al-monitor.com/pulse/originals/2018/05/tensions-flare-israel-iran-russia-netanyahu-putin.html.
59. "Peregovory Budut Tiazhelymi" Chto Planiruiut Obsuzhdit Lideri Rossii I Izraeilia v Den' Pobedy," RT, 2018, https://russian.rt.com/world/article/510647-putin-netanyahu-vizit-den-pobedy.

60. Nikita Vladimirov, "Russia Recognizes Jerusalem as Israel's Capital," *The Hill,* April 6, 2017, http://thehill.com/policy/international/327673-russia-recognizes-jerusalem-as-israeli-capital.
61. "Putin Obsuzhdet s Salmanom Situatsiu Na Neftianom Rynke," *Gazeta,* https://www.gazeta.ru/politics/2017/10/04_a_10917716.shtml?updated.
62. "Saudovskii Korol' Potratit Chetvert' Millairda Na Moskovskie Oteli," https://mir24.tv/news/16270892/saudovskii-korol-potratit-chetvert-milliarda-na-moskovskie-oteli.
63. Donna Abu-Nasr, Associated Press, "Putin 1st Russian Leader to Visit Saudis," *Washington Post,* February 11, 2007, http://www.washingtonpost.com/wp-dyn/content/article/2007/02/11/AR2007021100048.html.
64. Stephen Letts, "Oil Supply Deal Between Saudi Arabia and Russia an Unlikely Alliance," *ABC News* (Australia), September 8, 2016, http://www.abc.net.au/news/2016-09-09/saudi-arabia-russia-oil-deal/7831902.
65. Richard Mably and Yara Bayoumy, "Exclusive: OPEC, Russia Consider 10- to 20-Year Oil Alliance—Saudi Crown Prince," Reuters, March 27, 2018, https://www.reuters.com/article/us-saudi-oil-exclusive/exclusive-opec-russia-consider-10-to-20-year-oil-alliance-saudi-crown-prince-idUSKBN1H31SK.
66. Javier Blas and Jack Farchy, "Riyadh Dances with Trump but Goes Home with Putin to Prop Up Oil," *Bloomberg,* May 20, 2017, https://www.bloomberg.com/news/articles/2017-05-21/setting-differences-aside-saudi-russian-courtship-underpins-oil.
67. Mark N. Katz, "Russia Sees New Saudi 'Realism' on Display at Moscow Summit," Arab Gulf States Institute in Washington, October 10, 2017, http://www.agsiw.org/russia-sees-new-saudi-realism-display-moscow-summit/.
68. Henry Meyer and Glen Carey, "Even the Saudis Are Turning to Russia as Assad's Foes Lose Heart," *Bloomberg,* September 8, 2017, https://www.bloomberg.com/news/articles/2017-09-08/even-the-saudis-are-turning-to-russia-as-assad-s-foes-lose-heart.
69. Karoun Demirjian, "Russia-Iran Relationship Is a Marriage of Opportunity," *Washington Post,* April 18, 2015, https://www.washingtonpost.com/world/russia-iran-relationship-is-a-marriage-of-opportunity/2015/04/18/5de80852-e390-11e4-ae0f-f8c46aa8c3a4_story.html?utm_term=.4f490e094f03.
70. "Acting Foreign Minister Sergey Lavrov's Remarks and Answers to Media Questions at a Joint News Conference Following Talks with German Federal Minister for Foreign Affairs Heiko Maas, Moscow, May 10, 2018," Ministry of Foreign Affairs of the Russian Federation, http://www.mid.ru/en/web/guest/meropriyatiya_s_uchastiem_ministra/-/asset_publisher/xK1BhB2bUjd3/content/id/3213546.
71. Stiftung Wissenschaft und Politik, Deutsches Institut für Internationale Politik und Sicherheit; and Azadeh Zamirirad, *Iran und Russland: Perspektiven der Bilateralen Beziehungen aus Sicht der Islamischen Republik* (Berlin: SWP Studien, 2017).
72. Ellie Geranmayeh and Kadrii Liik, "The New Power Couple: Russia and Iran in the Middle East," European Council on Foreign Relations, September 13, 2016, http://www

.ecfr.eu/publications/summary/iran_and_russia_middle_east_power_couple_7113.

73. Dmitri Trenin, *Post-Imperium: A Eurasian Story* (Washington, DC: Carnegie Endowment for International Peace, 2011), 73.
74. Stepan Kravchenko, Henry Meyer, and Golnar Motevalli, "Putin in Iran Rallies Opposition to Trump Threat on Nuclear Deal," *Bloomberg,* November 1, 2017, https://www.bloomberg.com/news/articles/2017-11-01/putin-to-visit-iranian-leaders-as-moscow-defends-nuclear-accord.
75. Olzhas Auyezov, "Russia, Iran, and three others agree Caspian status, but not borders," Reuters, https://www.reuters.com/article/us-kazakhstan-caspian-borders/russia-iran-and-three-others-agree-caspian-status-but-not-borders-idUSKBN1KX0CI.
76. See Liik and Zamirirad.
77. Reuters, Associated Press, "Israel Rejects Russian Offer to Keep Iranian Forces 100km from Golan," July 23, 2018, YNetNews.com, https://www.ynetnews.com/articles/0,7340,L-5315360,00.html.

Chapter Eleven: Three Failed Resets: Russia and America Before the Trump Era

1. "Speech and the Following Discussion at the Munich Conference on Security Policy," President of Russia website, February 10, 2007, http://en.kremlin.ru/events/president/transcripts/24034.
2. "Transcript: Obama's End-of-Year News Conference on Syria, Russian Hacking, and More," *Washington Post,* December 16, 2016, https://www.washingtonpost.com/news/post-politics/wp/2016/12/16/transcript-obamas-end-of-year-news-conference-on-syria-russian-hacking-and-more/?utm_term=.5a42c8a154f1.
3. "Cheney's Speech in Lithuania," transcript, *New York Times,* May 4, 2006, https://www.nytimes.com/2006/05/04/world/europe/04cnd-cheney-text.html.
4. "Speech and the Following Discussion at the Munich Conference," http://en.kremlin.ru/events/president/transcripts/24034.
5. "Speech and the Following Discussion at the Munich Conference," http://en.kremlin.ru/events/president/transcripts/24034.
6. "Gates' Prepared Remarks at 43rd Munich Security Conference," transcript, *Washington Post,* February 12, 2007, http://www.washingtonpost.com/wp-dyn/content/article/2007/02/12/AR2007021200572.html.
7. Quoted in *George F. Kennan: An American Life,* by John Lewis Gaddis (New York: Penguin, 2011), 51.
8. Mr. X [George F. Kennan], "The Sources of Soviet Conduct," *Foreign Affairs,* July 1947, https://www.foreignaffairs.com/articles/russian-federation/1947-07-01/sources-soviet-conduct.
9. William Taubman, *Khrushchev: The Man and His Era* (New York: W. W. Norton, 2003), 420–31.
10. Daniel Yergin, *Shattered Peace: The Origins of the Cold War and the National Security State* (London: Penguin Books, 1990), 66.

11. Raymond L. Garthoff, *Détente and Confrontation: American-Soviet Relations from Nixon to Reagan* (Washington, DC: Brookings Institution Press, 1985), 26, 30, 36, 43.
12. Abraham Rabinovich, "The Little-Known US-Soviet Confrontation During Yom Kippur War," PRI, October 26, 2012, https://www.pri.org/stories/2012-10-26/little-known-us-soviet-confrontation-during-yom-kippur-war.
13. Ronald Reagan, "Evil Empire Speech, Voices of Democracy," March 8, 1983, http://voicesofdemocracy.umd.edu/reagan-evil-empire-speech-text/.
14. William Taubman, *Gorbachev: His Life and Times* (New York: W. W. Norton, 2017), 286.
15. Angela Stent, "Gorbachev's Reagan," *Weekly Standard*, October 27, 1996, http://www.weeklystandard.com/gorbachevs-reagan/article/9118.
16. Cited in *The Russia Hand*, by Strobe Talbott (New York: Random House, 2003), 42.
17. Angela E. Stent, *The Limits of Partnership: US-Russian Relations in the Twenty-First Century* (Princeton, NJ: Princeton University Press, 2015).
18. Bill Clinton, *My Life* (New York: Vintage, 2005), 508.
19. Boris N. Yeltsin, *Midnight Diaries* (New York: PublicAffairs, 2000), 134.
20. Angela E. Stent, *The Limits of Partnership: US-Russian Relations in the Twenty-First Century* (Princeton, NJ: Princeton University Press, 2015), 52.
21. Fiona Hill and Clifford G. Gaddy, *Mr. Putin: Operative in the Kremlin* (Washington, DC: Brookings Institution Press, 2015), chap.12.
22. Stent, *The Limits of Partnership*, 53.
23. Stent, *The Limits of Partnership*, 61–62.
24. Donald Rumsfeld, *Known and Unknown* (New York: Penguin, 2011), 167.
25. Joseph Biden, "Remarks by the Vice President at the 45th Munich Conference on Security Policy," American Presidency Project, February 7, 2009, http://www.presidency.ucsb.edu/ws/index.php?pid=123108.
26. "Medvedev v SShA: iPhone v Podarok I Gamburger c Obamoi," Postimees, https://rus.postimees.ee/280187/medvedev-v-ssha-iphone-v-podarok-i-gamburger-s-obamoy.
27. Stent, *The Limits of Partnership*, 219–20, 241–42. The popular US TV series *The Americans* was loosely based on the lives of these spies.
28. Elise Labott, "Clinton Cites 'Serious Concerns' About Russian Election," *CNN*, December 6, 2011, https://www.cnn.com/2011/12/06/world/europe/russia-elections-clinton/index.html.
29. David M. Herszenhorn and Ellen Barry, "Putin Contends Clinton Incited Unrest over Vote," *New York Times*, December 8, 2011, http://www.nytimes.com/2011/12/09/world/europe/putin-accuses-clinton-of-instigating-russian-protests.html.
30. Andrew Roth and Ellen Barry, "Snowden Seeks Asylum in Russia, Putting Kremlin on the Spot," *New York Times*, July 1, 2013, https://www.nytimes.com/2013/07/02/world/europe/snowden-applies-for-asylum-in-russia.html.
31. Steve Holland and Margaret Chadbourn, "Obama Describes Putin as 'Like a Bored Kid,'" Reuters, August 9, 2013, https://www.reuters.com/article/us-usa-russia-obama/obama-describes-putin-as-like-a-bored-kid-idUSBRE9780XS20130809.

32. Scott Wilson, "Obama dismisses Russia as 'regional power' acting out of weakness," *New York Times*, March 25, 2014, https://www.washingtonpost.com/world/national-security/obama-dismisses-russia-as-regional-power-acting-out-of-weakness/2014/03/25/1e5a678e-b439-11e3-b899-20667de76985_story.html?utm_term=.be73e35362e6.
33. Vladimir V. Putin, "A Plea for Caution from Russia," op-ed, *New York Times,* September 11, 2013, http://www.nytimes.com/2013/09/12/opinion/putin-plea-for-caution-from-russia-on-syria.html.

Chapter Twelve: The Rivals: Russia and America in the Age of Trump

1. "Presidential Address to the Federal Assembly," President of Russia website, March 1, 2018, http://en.kremlin.ru/events/president/news/56957.
2. Reuters, "Russia Names Putin's New 'Super Weapons' After a Quirky Public Vote," *Moscow Times,* March 23, 2018, https://themoscowtimes.com/news/russia-names-putins-new-super-weapons-after-a-quirky-public-vote-60924.
3. US Department of Defense, *Summary of the 2018 National Defense Strategy of the United States of America,* https://www.defense.gov/Portals/1/Documents/pubs/2018-National-Defense-Strategy-Summary.pdf.
4. US Department of Defense, *Nuclear Posture Review,* February 2018, https://media.defense.gov/2018/Feb/02/2001872877/-1/-1/1/EXECUTIVE-SUMMARY.PDF.
5. "Text: Mueller Indictment on Russian Election Case," *Politico,* February 16, 2018, https://www.politico.com/story/2018/02/16/text-full-mueller-indictment-on-russian-election-case-415670.
6. Office of the Director of National Intelligence, *Background to "Assessing Russian Activities and Intentions in Recent US Elections: The Analytic Process and Cyber Incident Attribution,"* Intelligence Community Assessment, January 6, 2017, https://www.dni.gov/files/documents/ICA_2017_01.pdf.
7. Oliver Stone, *The Putin Interviews: Oliver Stone Interviews Vladimir Putin* (New York: Hot Books, 2017), 219.
8. Philip Rucker, "Hillary Clinton Says Putin's Actions Are Like 'What Hitler Did Back in the 1930s,'" *Washington Post,* March 5, 2014, https://www.washingtonpost.com/news/post-politics/wp/2014/03/05/hillary-clinton-says-putins-action-are-like-what-hitler-did-back-in-the-30s/?utm_term=.561aee30b05a.
9. "Putin o Trampe: On Iarkii Chelovek, Drugikh Kharakteristik Ia Ne Daval," June 17, 2016, https://ria.ru/politics/20160617/1448985748.html.
10. Luke Harding, *Collusion* (New York: Vintage, 2017), 226.
11. Russian member of Gorbachev's delegation in conversation with the author.
12. "Moskva Primet u Sebia Konkurs 'Miss Vselennaia,'" June 17, 2013, https://rg.ru/2013/06/17/miss-vselennaya-site-anons.html.
13. Harding, *Collusion,* 240.
14. "Donald Tramp Nazval Vladimira Putina Zhestkim Chelovekom, s Kotorym Mozhno Poladit," *Kommersant,* July 15, 2018, https://www.kommersant.ru/doc/3687698.

15. " 'Putin Is Corrupt' Says US Treasury," *BBC News,* January 25, 2016, http://www.bbc.com/news/world-europe-35385445.
16. Andrew Kaczynski, Chris Massie, and Nathan McDermott, "80 Times Trump Talked About Putin," *CNN,* March 2017, http://www.cnn.com/interactive/2017/03/politics/trump-putin-russia-timeline/.
17. "Donald Trump's Foreign Policy Speech," transcript, *New York Times,* April 28, 2016, https://www.nytimes.com/2016/04/28/us/politics/transcript-trump-foreign-policy.html.
18. Harding, *Collusion,* 244.
19. Miles Parks and Tamara Keith, "Timeline of Trump and Russia in Mid-2016: A Series of Coincidences or Something More?" *Morning Edition,* National Public Radio, July 17, 2017, https://www.npr.org/2017/07/17/537323120/timeline-of-trump-and-russia-in-mid-2016-a-series-of-coincidences-or-something-m.
20. Harding, *Collusion,* 118.
21. Dana Priest, "Trump Adviser Michael T. Flynn on His Dinner with Putin and Why Russia Today Is Just Like CNN," *Washington Post,* August 15, 2016, https://www.washingtonpost.com/news/checkpoint/wp/2016/08/15/trump-adviser-michael-t-flynn-on-his-dinner-with-putin-and-why-russia-today-is-just-like-cnn/?utm_term=.ce89b012e887.
22. David E. Sanger, "Obama Strikes Back at Russia for Election Hacking," *New York Times,* December 29, 2016, https://www.nytimes.com/2016/12/29/us/politics/russia-election-hacking-sanctions.html.
23. Patrick Reevell, "Timeline of the US and Russia Trading Diplomatic Blows," *ABC News,* September 1, 2017, http://abcnews.go.com/International/timeline-us-russia-trading-diplomatic-blows/story?id=49564623.
24. John Kruzel, "Flynn's Guilty Plea Confirms He Talked Russian Sanctions, Misled FBI," Politifact, December 1, 2017, http://www.politifact.com/truth-o-meter/article/2017/dec/01/flynns-guilty-plea-confirms-he-talked-russian-sanc/.
25. The July 13, 2018, indictments by Robert Mueller describe how the GRU-connected hackers gave the e-mail to "Organization One," which is WikiLeaks. US Department of Justice, "Grand Jury Indicts 12 Russian Intelligence Officers for Hacking Offenses Related to the 2016 Election," news release, July 13, 2018, https://www.justice.gov/opa/pr/grand-jury-indicts-12-russian-intelligence-officers-hacking-offenses-related-2016-election.
26. Robert D. Blackwill and Philip H. Gordon, *Containing Russia,* Council Special Report no. 80 (New York: Council on Foreign Relations, January 2018), 7, https://www.cfr.org/sites/default/files/report_pdf/CSR80_BlackwillGordon_ContainingRussia.pdf.
27. "Interview with Austrian ORF Television Channel," President of Russia website, June 4, 2018, http://en.kremlin.ru/events/president/news/57675.
28. Blackwill and Gordon, *Containing Russia,* 8, https://www.cfr.org/sites/default/files/report_pdf/CSR80_BlackwillGordon_ContainingRussia.pdf.
29. Andrei Soldatov and Irina Borogan, *The Red Web: The Kremlin's War on the Internet* (New York: PublicAffairs, 2017), chap. 16.

30. Huib Modderkolk, "Dutch Agencies Provide Crucial Intel About Russia's Interference in US Elections," *De Volkskrant,* January 25, 2018, https://www.volkskrant.nl/tech/dutch-agencies-provide-crucial-intel-about-russia-s-interference-in-us-elections~a4561913/.
31. Greg Miller, Ellen Nakashima, and Adam Entous, "Obama's Secret Struggle to Punish Russia for Putin's Election Assault," *Washington Post,* June 23, 2017, https://www.washingtonpost.com/graphics/2017/world/national-security/obama-putin-election-hacking/?utm_term=.fa240cf45dc6.
32. Senior intelligence official in conversation with the author.
33. Louis Nelson, "Obama Says He Told Putin to 'Cut It Out' on Russia Hacking," *Politico,* December 16, 2016, https://www.politico.com/story/2016/12/obama-putin-232754.
34. Senior State Department official in conversation with the author.
35. David Corn, "A Veteran Spy Has Given the FBI Information Alleging a Russian Operation to Cultivate Donald Trump," *Mother Jones,* October 31, 2016, https://www.motherjones.com/politics/2016/10/veteran-spy-gave-fbi-info-alleging-russian-operation-cultivate-donald-trump/.
36. John Sipher, "A Second Look at the Steele Dossier," Just Security, September 6, 2017, https://www.justsecurity.org/44697/steele-dossier-knowing/.
37. Harding, *Collusion,* 32.
38. Spencer S. Hsu, Devlin Barrett, and Justin Jouvenal, *Washington Post,* September 14, "Manafort will cooperate with Mueller as part of guilty plea, prosecutor says," https://www.washingtonpost.com/world/national-security/manafort-plans-to-plead-guilty-to-second-set-of-charges/2018/09/14/a1541068-b5c9-11e8-a7b5-adaaa5b2a57f_story.html?utm_term=.3f5ec64c6c3d&wpisrc=nl_headlines&wpmm=1.
39. Pew Research Center, *Stark Partisan Divisions over Russia Probe, Including Its Importance to the Nation,* December 7, 2017, http://www.people-press.org/2017/12/07/stark-partisan-divisions-over-russia-probe-including-its-importance-to-the-nation/.
40. "Meeting of the Valdai International Discussion Club," President of Russia website, October 19, 2017, http://en.kremlin.ru/events/president/transcripts/53151.
41. Andrew S. Weiss, "What Was Trump's Russia Plan?" *Wall Street Journal,* December 8, 2017, https://www.wsj.com/articles/what-was-trumps-russia-plan-1512752496.
42. Neil MacFarquhar, "Putin and Trump Talk on Phone and Agree to Improve Ties, Kremlin Says," *New York Times,* November 14, 2016, https://www.nytimes.com/2016/11/15/world/europe/putin-calls-trump.html?mtrref=query.nytimes.com.
43. Craig Timberg, Rosalind S. Helderman, Andrew Roth, and Carol D. Leonnig, "In a Crowd at Trump's Inauguration, Members of Russia's Elite Anticipated a Thaw Between Moscow and Washington," *Washington Post,* January 20, 2018, https://www.washingtonpost.com/politics/amid-trumps-inaugural-festivities-members-of-russias-elite-anticipated-a-thaw-between-moscow-and-washington/2018/01/20/0d767f46-fb9f-11e7-ad8c-ecbb62019393_story.html?utm_term=.e5d3bd913d3b.

44. Greg Miller and Greg Jaffe, "Trump Revealed Highly Classified Information to Russian Foreign Minister and Ambassador," *Washington Post,* May 15, 2017, https://www.washingtonpost.com/world/national-security/trump-revealed-highly-classified-information-to-russian-foreign-minister-and-ambassador/2017/05/15/530c172a-3960-11e7-9e48-c4f199710b69_story.html?utm_term=.e446a9bb3fe7.
45. Roberta Rampton and Jeff Mason, Reuters, July 7, 2017, "Trump and Putin find chemistry, draw criticism in first meeting," https://www.reuters.com/article/us-g20-germany-trump-putin-talks-idUSKBN19S24E.
46. Roberta Rampton and Jeff Mason, "Trump and Putin Find Chemistry, Draw Criticism in First Meeting," Reuters, July 17, 2017, https://www.reuters.com/article/us-g20-germany-trump-putin-talks/trump-and-putin-find-chemistry-draw-criticism-in-first-meeting-idUSKBN19S24E.
47. "News Conference Following the G20 Summit," President of Russia website, July 8, 2017, http://www.en.kremlin.ru/events/president/news/55017.
48. David A. Graham, "The Other Putin-Trump Meeting," *The Atlantic,* July 18, 2017, https://www.theatlantic.com/politics/archive/2017/07/trump-putin-second-meeting/534099/.
49. Office of the Spokesperson, "Joint Statement by the President of the United States and the President of the Russian Federation," news release, US Department of State, November 11, 2017, https://www.state.gov/r/pa/prs/ps/2017/11/275459.htm.
50. "Meeting of the Valdai International Discussion Club," President of Russia website, October 19, 2017, http://en.kremlin.ru/events/president/news/55882.
51. John Hudson, "Russia Sought a Broad Reset with Trump, Secret Document Shows," BuzzFeed, September 12, 2017, https://www.buzzfeed.com/johnhudson/russia-sought-a-broad-reset-with-trump-secret-document-shows?utm_term=.ikqEoR1wZ0#.ov3WyZqaAN.
52. John Hudson, "Putin Spokesman Confirms Russia Offered a Reset with Trump," BuzzFeed, September 13, 2017, https://www.buzzfeed.com/johnhudson/putin-spokesman-confirms-russia-reached-out-to-trump?utm_term=.hxVa8KdlqZ#.dnO6Pe3YOk.
53. Henry Foy, "'We Need to Talk About Igor': The Rise of Russia's Most Powerful Oligarch," *Financial Times,* March 1, 2018, https://www.ft.com/content/dc7d48f8-1c13-11e8-aaca-4574d7dabfb6.
54. John Hudson, "The Trump Administration Has a New Plan for Dealing with Russia," BuzzFeed, June 19, 2017, https://www.buzzfeed.com/johnhudson/this-is-the-trump-administrations-plan-for-dealing-with?utm_term=.digvxJ512z#.ys2ZV3Ny7b.
55. Amie Ferris-Rotman, Emily Tamkin, and Robbie Gramer, "Trump's Man in Moscow," *Foreign Policy,* March 14, 2018, http://foreignpolicy.com/2018/03/14/trumps-man-in-moscow-ambassador-jon-huntsman-russia-trump-investigation/.
56. "Statement by President Donald J. Trump on the Signing of H.R. 3364," Whitehouse.gov, August 2, 2017, https://www.whitehouse.gov/briefings-statements/statement-president-donald-j-trump-signing-h-r-3364/.

57. US Department of the Treasury, "Treasury Sanctions Russian Cyber Actors for Interference with the 2016 US Elections and Malicious Cyber-Attacks," news release, March 15, 2018, https://home.treasury.gov/news/press-releases/sm0312.
58. Peter Baker, "Trump Praises Putin Instead of Critiquing Cuts to US Embassy Staff," *New York Times,* August 10, 2017, https://www.nytimes.com/2017/08/10/world/europe/putin-trump-embassy-russia.html.
59. Zach Dorfman, "The Secret History of the Russian Consulate in San Francisco," *Foreign Policy,* December 14, 2017, http://foreignpolicy.com/2017/12/14/the-secret-history-of-the-russian-consulate-in-san-francisco-putin-trump-spies-moscow/.
60. Nahal Toosi, "Tillerson Blasts Russia over Alleged Nerve Agent Attack in UK," *Politico,* March 12, 2018, https://www.politico.com/story/2018/03/12/tillerson-russia-nerve-gas-attack-457845.
61. Mark Landler, "Trump Congratulates Putin, but Doesn't Mention Meddling in US," *New York Times,* March 20, 2018, https://www.nytimes.com/2018/03/20/us/politics/trump-putin-russia.html.
62. "Telephone Conversation with US President Donald Trump," President of Russia website, March 20, 2018, http://en.kremlin.ru/events/president/news/57100.
63. Alan Rappaport, "Treasury Dept. Hits Russia with New Sanctions," *New York Times,* June 11, 2018, https://www.nytimes.com/2018/06/11/us/politics/russia-sanctions-treasury-department.html.
64. United States of America v. Viktor Borisovich Netyksho et al., 18 USC 2, 371, 1030, 1028A, 1956, and 3551 et seq., https://d3i6fh83elv35t.cloudfront.net/static/2018/07/Muellerindictment.pdf.
65. Philip Rucker, "After Being Told of Russian Indictments, Trump Still Aspired to Be Friends with Putin," *Washington Post,* July 13, 2018, https://www.washingtonpost.com/politics/after-being-told-of-russia-indictments-trump-still-aspired-to-be-friends-with-putin/2018/07/13/c24f5420-86b8-11e8-8553-a3ce89036c78_story.html?utm_term=.6165027e2776.
66. "Trump Believes Putin That the Russian Federation Did Not Interfere in the Elections" [in Russian], July 17, 2018, https://korrespondent.net/world/3990660-tramp-veryt-putynu-chto-rf-ne-vmeshyvalas-v-vybory.
67. "Putin-Trump Talks Were Better than Super, Says Russian Top Diplomat," TASS, July 16, 2018, http://tass.com/politics/1013439.
68. Alex Ward, "John Bolton's Complete Reversal on Russia, in One Tweet," *Vox,* July 26, 2018, https://www.vox.com/2018/7/26/17617096/bolton-russia-trump-mueller-witch-hunt.
69. Nick Schifrin, Dan Sagalyn, and Larisa Epatko, "John Bolton: North Korea Has Not 'Taken Effective Steps' to Denuclearize," *PBS News Hour,* August 6, 2018, https://www.pbs.org/newshour/show/john-bolton-north-korea-has-not-taken-effective-steps-to-denuclearize.
70. Tatyana Stanovaya, "Two Trumps in Helsinki: Russia's Approach to the US President," Carnegie Moscow Center, August 2, 2018, https://carnegie.ru/commentary/76962.

71. "Vladimir Putin I Donal'd Tramp: Press Konferentsiia," Echo, July 16, 2018, https://echo.msk.ru/blog/day_video/2241360-echo/.
72. " 'Konkretniki Bylo Mnogo': A Chem Govorili Vladimir Putin I Donal'd Tramp na Sammite v Khelsinki," RT, July 16, 2018, https://russian.rt.com/world/article/537125-putin-tramp-sammit-helsinki-itogi.
73. Maegan Vazquez, "Former Intel Chiefs Condemn Trump's News Conference with Putin," *CNN*, July 17, 2018, https://www.cnn.com/2018/07/16/politics/john-brennan-donald-trump-treasonous-vladimir-putin/index.html.
74. David J. Kramer, "I'm on Putin's Hit List but I'm Not the Real Victim," *Politico,* July 22, 2018, https://www.politico.eu/article/vladimir-putin-william-browder-the-real-victims-of-putins-enemies-list/.
75. Dmitri Trenin, "Russia Must Show Caution Now That It Has Publicly Sided with Trump," Carnegie Moscow Center, July 23, 2018, https://carnegie.ru/commentary/76883.
76. Andrew Higgins, "North Koreans in Russia Work 'Basically in the Situation of Slaves,' " *New York Times,* July 11, 2017, https://www.nytimes.com/2017/07/11/world/europe/north-korea-russia-migrants.html.
77. Heather Nauert, "New START Treaty Central Limits Take Effect," news release, US Department of State, February 5, 2018, https://www.state.gov/r/pa/prs/ps/2018/02/277888.htm.
78. Steven Pifer, "Arms Control, Security Cooperation, and US-Russian Relations," Brookings Institution, November 17, 2017, https://www.brookings.edu/research/arms-control-security-cooperation-and-u-s-russian-relations/.
79. Rebecca Kheel, "Trump: We Must 'Modernize and Rebuild' Nuclear Arsenal," *The Hill,* January 30, 2018, http://thehill.com/policy/defense/371537-trump-we-must-modernize-and-rebuild-nuclear-arsenal.
80. Steven Pifer, "The Future of the INF Treaty," Brookings Institution, January 25, 2018, https://www.brookings.edu/testimonies/the-future-of-the-inf-treaty/.
81. Staff, "Russian Oil Industry Pipe Maker TMK Prepares for US Spin-Off," Reuters, November 30, 2017, https://www.reuters.com/article/us-trubnaya-metal-ipo/russian-oil-industry-pipe-maker-tmk-prepares-for-u-s-spin-off-idUSKBN1DU10G.
82. Simon Saradzhyan and William Tobey, "US-Russian Space Cooperation: A Model for Nuclear Security," *Bulletin of the Atomic Scientists,* March 7, 2017, https://thebulletin.org/us-russian-space-cooperation-model-nuclear-security10600.
83. Gary Brown and Christopher D. Yung, "Evaluating the US-China Cybersecurity Agreement, Part 1: The US Approach to Cyberspace," *The Diplomat,* January 19, 2017, https://thediplomat.com/2017/01/evaluating-the-us-china-cybersecurity-agreement-part-1-the-us-approach-to-cyberspace/.
84. Anne Gearan and Felicia Sonmez, "Trump issues new order authorizing additional sanctions for interfering in upcoming U.S. elections," *Washington Post*, September 12, https://www.washingtonpost.com/politics/trump-issues-new-order-authorizing-additional-sanctions-for-interfering-in-upcoming-us-elections/2018/09/12

/a90898a0-b6b0-11e8-a7b5-adaaa5b2a57f_story.html?noredirect=on&utm_term=.26fb07ab8bac.

85. "CNBC Transcript: President Donald Trump Sits Down with CNBC's Joe Kernen," news release, CNBC, July 20, 2018, https://www.cnbc.com/2018/07/20/cnbc-transcript-president-donald-trump-sits-down-with-cnbcs-joe-kern.html?__source=sharebar|email&par=sharebar.

Chapter Thirteen: What Kind of Engagement with Russia?

1. Vladislav Surkov, "Odinochestvo Polukrovki (14+)," *Rossiia v Global'noi Politike,* April 9, 2018, https://www.globalaffairs.ru/global-processes/Odinochestvo-polukrovki-14-19477.
2. For videos of these events, see www.kremlin.ru.
3. Julia Guganus, "Russia is Playing a Geopolitical Game in Latin America," https://carnegieendowment.org/2018/05/03/russia-playing-geopolitical-game-in-latin-america-pub-76228.
4. https://tradingeconomics.com/russia/gdp-per-capita.
5. "Pension Reform in Russia in 2018 and Putin in 2005. What changed?" Polygraph.info, June 12, 2018, https://www.polygraph.info/a/pension-reform-in-russia-in-2018-and-putin-in-2005/29311267.html; Sasha Trubetskoy, "Life expectancy in Russia," Sashat.me, https://sashat.me/2018/03/27/life-expectancy-in-russia/.
6. "Islam in Russia," Al Jazeera, March 7, 2018, https://www.aljazeera.com/indepth/features/islam-russia-180307094248743.html.
7. Radio Free Europe/Radio Liberty editors, "RT's Top Editor Toasts Putin: 'He Used to Be Our President; Now He Is Our Leader,'" *Transmission* (blog), March 19, 2018, https://www.rferl.org/a/rt-top-editor-simonyan-toasts-putin-he-is-now-our-leader/29109679.html.
8. Ivan Krastev and Gleb Pavlovsky, "The Arrival of Post-Putin Russia," policy brief, European Council on Foreign Relations, March 1, 2018, http://www.ecfr.eu/publications/summary/the_arrival_of_post_putin_russia.
9. "The German-Russian Modernization Partnership—Federal Foreign Minister Westerwelle and Russian Foreign Minister Sergey Lavrov in the FAZ," Federal Foreign Office, May 31, 2010, https://www.auswaertiges-amt.de/en/newsroom/news/100531-bm-faz/232468.
10. Amie Ferris-Rotman, Emily Tamkin, and Robbie Gramer, "Trump's Man in Moscow," *Foreign Policy,* March 14, 2018, http://foreignpolicy.com/2018/03/14/trumps-man-in-moscow-ambassador-jon-huntsman-russia-trump-investigation/.

BIBLIOGRAPHY

Acheson, Dean. *Present at the Creation.* New York: W. W. Norton, 1969.

Adamski, Lukasz and Reinhard Krumm. *Russia and East Central Europe: A Fresh Start.* Berlin: Friedrich-Ebert-Stiftung and International Policy Analysis, 2013.

Aslund, Anders and Michael McFaul, eds. *Revolution in Orange: The Origins of Ukraine's Democratic Breakthrough.* Washington, DC: Carnegie Endowment for International Peace, 2006.

Asmus, Ronald D. *A Little War That Shook the World.* New York: Palgrave Macmillan, 2010.

Barnes, Ian. *Restless Empire: A Historical Atlas of Russia.* Cambridge, MA: Harvard University Press, 2015.

Bechev, Dimitar. *Rival Power: Russia's Influence in Southeast Europe.* New Haven, CT: Yale University Press, 2017.

Charap, Samuel and Timothy Colton. *Everyone Loses: The Ukraine Crisis and the Ruinous Contest for Post-Soviet Eurasia.* London: International Institute for Strategic Studies, 2016.

Clinton, Bill. *My Life.* New York: Vintage, 2005.

Colton, Timothy J. *Yeltsin: A Life.* New York: Basic Books, 2008.

Cooley, Alexander. *Great Games, Local Rules.* New York: Oxford University Press, 2012.

Dawisha, Karen. *Putin's Kleptocracy: Who Owns Russia?* New York, Simon and Schuster, 2014.

De Custine, Astolphe. *Empire of the Czar: A Journey Through Eternal Russia,* translation of *La Russie en 1839.* New York: Doubleday, 1989.

Fairbank, John K., ed. *The Cambridge History of China.* Vol. 12, pt. 1. Cambridge, UK: Cambridge University Press, 1983.

Ferguson, Joseph P. *Japanese-Russian Relations 1907–2007.* New York: Routledge, 2008.

Frankopan, Peter. *The Silk Roads: A New History of the World.* New York: Vintage, 2017.

Freedman, Robert O. *Russia, Iran, and the Nuclear Question: The Putin Record.* Carlisle, PA: Strategic Studies Institute, US Army War College, 2006.

Gaddis, John Lewis. *George F. Kennan: An American Life.* New York: Penguin, 2011.

Gaddis, John Lewis. *We Now Know: Rethinking Cold War History.* Oxford, UK: Clarendon Press, 1997.

Garthoff, Raymond L. *Détente and Confrontation: American-Soviet Relations from Nixon to Reagan.* Washington, DC: Brookings Institution Press, 1985.

Goodby, James, Vladimir Ivanov, and Nobuo Shimotomai, eds. *"Northern Territories" and Beyond: Russian, Japanese, and American Perspectives.* Westport, CT: Praeger, 1995.

Gorbatschow, Michail S. *Erinnerungen.* Berlin: Siedler, 1995.

Griffith, William F. *The Sino-Soviet Rift.* Cambridge, MA: MIT Press, 1964.

Gvosdev, Nikolas and Christopher Marsh. *Russian Foreign Policy: Interests, Vectors, Sectors.* Los Angeles: Sage Publishers, 2013.

Harding, Luke. *Collusion.* New York: Vintage, 2017.

Hill, Fiona and Clifford G. Gaddy. *Mr. Putin: Operative in the Kremlin.* Washington, DC: Brookings Institution Press, 2015.

Hill, Fiona and Clifford G. Gaddy. *The Siberian Curse: How Communist Planners Left Russia Out in the Cold.* Washington, DC: Brookings Institution Press, 2003.

Hill, William H. *Russia, the New Abroad, and the West: Lessons from the Moldova-Transdniestria Conflict.* Washington, DC: Woodrow Wilson Center Press; Baltimore: Johns Hopkins University Press, 2012.

Holbrooke, Richard C. *To End a War.* New York: Modern Library, 1999.

Hollingsworth, Mark and Stewart Lansley. *Londongrad: From Russia with Cash: The Inside Story of the Oligarchs.* London: Fourth Estate, 2009.

Jukes, Geoffrey. *The Russo-Japanese War 1904–1905.* Oxford, UK: Osprey, 2002.

Kalb, Marvin L. *Imperial Gamble: Putin, Ukraine, and the New Cold War.* Washington, DC: Brookings Institution Press, 2015.

Kennan, George F. *Russia and the West under Lenin and Stalin.* New York: Mentor Books, 1961.

Kimura, Hiroshi. *The Kurillian Knot: A History of Japanese-Russian Border Negotiations.* Palo Alto, CA: Stanford University Press, 2008.

King, Charles. *The Moldovans: Romania, Russia, and the Politics of Culture.* Stanford, CA: Hoover Institution Press, 2000.

Kissinger, Henry. *On China.* New York: Penguin, 2012.

Kornelius, Stefan. *Angela Merkel: The Chancellor and Her World.* London: Alma Books, 2013.

Kuhrt, Natasha. *Russian Policy toward China and Japan.* Abingdon, UK: Routledge, 2011.

Kwizinskij, Julij A. *Vor dem Sturm: Erinnerungen Eines Diplomaten.* Berlin: Siedler, 1993.

Laruelle, Marlene. *Russian Eurasianism: An Ideology of Empire.* Washington, DC: Woodrow Wilson International Center for Scholars, 2008.

Legvold, Robert. *Russian Foreign Policy in the Twenty-First Century and the Shadow of the Past.* New York: Columbia University Press, 2007.

Lieven, Anatol. *Ukraine and Russia: A Fraternal Rivalry.* Washington, DC: United States Institute of Peace, 1999.

Lo, Bobo. *Axis of Convenience: Moscow, Beijing, and the New Geopolitics.* London: Chatham House; Washington, DC: Brookings Institution Press, 2008.

Lo, Bobo. *Russia and the New World Disorder.* Washington, DC: Brookings Institution Press, 2014.

Lo, Bobo. *Russian Foreign Policy in the Post-Soviet Era.* London: Palgrave Macmillan, 2002.

Lo, Bobo. *A Wary Embrace: What the Russia-China Relationship Means for the World.* Docklands, Victoria: Penguin Random House, 2017.

Magocsi, Paul Robert. *A history of Ukraine: The Land and Its Peoples.* Toronto: University of Toronto Press, 2010.

Mastny, Vojtech. *The Cold War and Soviet Insecurity: The Stalin Years.* New York: Oxford University Press, 1998.

McDaniel, Tim. *The Agony of the Russian Idea.* Princeton, NJ: Princeton University Press, 1996.

McFaul, Michael. *From Cold War to Hot Peace: An American Ambassador in Putin's Russia.* Boston: Houghton Mifflin, 2018.

Menon, Rajan and Eugene Rumer. *Conflict in Ukraine: The Unwinding of the Post-Cold War Order.* Cambridge, MA and London, UK: MIT Press, 2016.

Myers, Steven Lee. *The New Tsar: The Rise and Reign of Vladimir Putin.* New York: Vintage, 2015.

Pares, Richard and Alan John Percival Taylor, eds. *Essays Presented to Sir Lewis Namier.* London: St. Martin's Press, 1956.

Pifer, Steven. *The Eagle and the Trident: US-Ukraine Relations in Turbulent Times.* Washington, DC: Brookings Institution Press, 2017.

Plokhy, Serhii. *The Gates of Europe: A History of Ukraine.* New York: Basic Books, 2015.

Plokhy, Serhii. *The Last Empire: The Final Days of the Soviet Union.* New York: Basic Books, 2014.

Poe, Marshall. *The Russian Moment in World History.* Princeton, NJ: Princeton University Press, 2003.

Primakov, Yevgeny. *Russia and the Arabs: Behind the Scenes in the Middle East from the Cold War to the Present.* New York: Basic Books, 2009.

Putin, Vladimir. *First Person: An Astonishingly Frank Self-Portrait by Russia's President.* New York: Public Affairs, 2000.

Rahr, Alexander. *Wladimir Putin: Der "Deutsche" im Kreml.* Munich: Universitas-Verlag, 2000.

Rice, Condoleezza. *No Higher Honor: A Memoir of My Years in Washington.* New York: Random House, 2011.

Rumsfeld, Donald. *Known and Unknown.* New York: Penguin, 2011.

Salisbury, Harrison E. *War Between Russia and China.* New York: Alfred A. Knopf, 1969.

Sebag Montefiore, Simon. *The Romanovs 1613–1918.* New York: Alfred A. Knopf, 2016.

Shirreff, Richard. *War with Russia: An Urgent Warning from Senior Military Command.* London: Coronet, 2016.

Shore, Marci. *The Ukrainian Night: An Intimate History of Revolution.* New Haven, CT: Yale University Press, 2017.

Short, Philip. *Mao: A Life.* New York: Henry Holt, 1999.

Soldatov, Andrei and Irina Borogan. *The Red Web: The Kremlin's War on the Internet.* New York: PublicAffairs, 2017.

Spence, Jonathan D. *The Search for Modern China.* New York: W. W. Norton, 1990.

Stent, Angela E. *Franco-Soviet Relations from De Gaulle to Mitterrand.* Washington, DC: National Council for Soviet and East European Research, 1989.

Stent, Angela E. *From Embargo to Ostpolitik: The Political Economy of West German-Soviet Relations, 1955–1980.* New York and Cambridge, UK: Cambridge University Press, 1981.

Stent, Angela E. *The Limits of Partnership: US-Russian Relations in the Twenty-First Century.* Princeton, NJ: Princeton University Press, 2015.

Stent, Angela E. *Russia and Germany Reborn: Unification, the Soviet Collapse, and the New Europe.* Princeton, NJ: Princeton University Press, 1999.

Stewart, Susan. *Russland und der Europarat.* Berlin: Stiftung Wissenschaft und Politik, 2013.

Stone, Oliver. *The Putin Interviews: Oliver Stone Interviews Vladimir Putin.* New York: Hot Books, 2017.

Subtelny, Orest. *Ukraine: A History.* Toronto: University of Toronto Press, 2009.

Szabo, Stephen F. *Germany, Russia, and the Rise of Geo-Economics.* London: Bloomsbury Academic, 2015.

Talbott, Strobe. *The Russia Hand: A Memoir of Presidential Diplomacy.* New York: Random House, 2000.

Taubman, William. *Gorbachev: His Life and Times.* New York: W. W. Norton, 2017.

Taubman, William. *Khrushchev: The Man and His Era.* New York: W. W. Norton, 2003.

Toal, Gerard. *Near Abroad: Putin, the West, and the Contest over Ukraine and the Caucasus.* New York: Oxford University Press, 2016.

Trenin, Dmitri. *Post-Imperium: A Eurasian Story.* Washington, DC: Carnegie Endowment for International Peace, 2011.

Trenin, Dmitri. *What is Russia Up to in the Middle East?* Cambridge, UK: Polity, 2017.

Ulam, Adam B. *Expansion and Coexistence: Soviet Foreign Policy 1917–73,* 2nd ed. New York: Praeger, 1974.

Vladislav Surkov, "Odinochestvo Polukrovki" (14+) *Rossiia v Global'noi Politike* April 9, 2018

Voennaia Doktrina Rossiiskoi Federatsii, 5 February 2010, kremin.ru/supplement/461

Vogel, Ezra. *Deng Xiaoping and the Transformation of China.* Cambridge, MA: Harvard University Press, 2011.

Yeltsin, Boris N. *Midnight Diaries.* New York: PublicAffairs, 2000.

Yergin, Daniel. *The Quest: Energy, Security, and the Remaking of the Modern World.* New York: Penguin, 2012.

Yergin, Daniel. *Shattered Peace: The Origins of the Cold War and the National Security State.* London: Penguin Books, 1990.

Zygar, Mikhail. *All the Kremlin's Men.* New York: Public Affairs, 2016.

PHOTO CREDITS

1. WikiCommons
2. The State Hermitage, Museum, St. Petersburg; Photograph © The State Hermitage Museum/photo by Vladimir Terebenin
3. Courtesy of the author
4. Russian Archives/ZUMA Wire
5. www.kremlin.ru
6. Alexander Demianchuk/Reuters Pictures
7. Dmitry Astakhov/AFP/Getty Images
8. Mikhael Klimentyev/Sputnik via AP
9. Christian Hartmann/Reuters Pictures
10. REX/Shutterstock
11. Photo by Mao Jianjun/China News Service/VCG via Getty Images
12. Ukrainian two-hryvna image: © Andriy Nekrasov/123RF; Russian thousand-ruble image: Центробанк РФ/Wikimedia.org
13. Dmitry Serebryakov/AFP/Getty Images
14. POOL New/Reuters Pictures
15. AP Photo/Sergei Grits
16. RIA Novosti/Reuters Pictures
17. ITAR-TASS/Sergei Velichkin, Vladimir Rodionov/Getty Images
18. Sputnik Photo Agency / Reuters Pictures
19. Alexei Druzhinin, Sputnik, Kremlin Pool Photo via AP
20. Mikhail Klimentyev, Sputnik, Kremlin Pool Photo via AP
21. POOL New/Reuters Pictures
22. Omar Sanadiki/Reuters Pictures

23. Grigory Sysoev/Sputnik via AP
24. AP Photo/Alexander Zemlianichenko
25. Pool New / Reuters Pictures
26. Mikhail Klimentyev, Sputnik, Kremlin Pool Photo via AP
27. Michael Klimentyev/Sputnik via AP

INDEX